SOCIAL WORK PRACTICE

Bridges to Change

KAY S. HOFFMAN
Wayne State University

ALVIN L. SALLEE
New Mexico State University

Allyn and Bacon

BOSTON   LONDON   TORONTO   SYDNEY   TOKYO   SINGAPORE

Senior Editor: Karen Hanson
Editor-in-Chief, Social Sciences: Susan Badger
Series Editorial Assistant: Sarah Dunbar
Cover Administrator: Linda K. Dickinson
Cover Designer: Design Ad Cetera
Manufacturing Buyer: Louise Richardson

This book is printed on
recycled, acid-free paper.

Library of Congress Cataloging-in-Publication Data

Hoffman, Kay Seeley
    Social work practice : bridges to change / Kay S. Hoffman, Alvin
L. Sallee.
        p.   cm.
    Includes bibliographical references and index.
    ISBN 0-205-13959-0
    1. Social work education.   I. Sallee, Alvin L.   II. Title.
HV11.H55   1994
361.3′2—dc20   93-9217
                                                                          CIP

Printed in the United States of America

10 9 8 7 6 5 4 3 2   98 97 96 95 94

Photo Credits: p. 4: Tony Freeman/PhotoEdit; p. 12: Gale Zucker/Stock, Boston;
pp. 21, 127: UPI/THE BETTMANN ARCHIVE; pp. 29, 82, 332: Robert Harbison;
p. 50: Yves de Braine/Black Star; p. 58: Peter Menzel/Stock, Boston; p. 67: Alan
Carey/The Image Works; p. 71: Peter Main—©1988 *The Christian Science Monitor;*
p. 73: Bob Daemmrich/The Image Works; p. 95: Christopher McLeod; p. 107:
Elizabeth Crews/Stock, Boston; p. 112: Richard Wood/THE PICTURE CUBE; pp. 137,
289: © Joel Gordon 1992; p. 155: Donna Jernigan/Monkmeyer Press Photo Service;
p. 174: Tom McKitterick/Impact Visuals; p. 178: Jean-Claude Lejeune/Stock, Boston;
p. 198: Dorothy Littell Greco/The Image Works; p. 209: Martha Tabor/Impact Visuals;

(Continued on page 367, which constitutes a continuation of the copyright page)

To Doris Seeley Pettengill
K.S.H.

To Carol W. Sallee and my grandmothers
for their love and guidance
A.L.S.

Contents

Chapter 2

Choosing Social Work as a Profession   19

Chapter 3

Linking Theory to Practice   48

Chapter 4

Generalist Roles, Skills, and Process   76

Part II

Overview of Planned Change

Chapter 5

Identifying Areas of Concern
and Engagement   104

Chapter 6

Information Gathering   **134**

Chapter 7

Assessment 166

Chapter 8

Assessment of Small, Medium, and Large Systems 190

Chapter 9

Designing, Planning, and Contracting for Change   224

Chapter 10

Implementing Change   246

Chapter 11

Evaluation and Transition   283

Part III

Putting It All Together: The Bridge Model of Social Work Generalist Practice

Foreword

The most difficult area of the curriculum to conceptualize and teach in social work education programs has traditionally been social work practice. The reason for this is the complexity of the social work profession: the range of problems that it addresses, the vast spectrum of people it serves individually and in groups, as well as the scope of the agencies in which social workers function, the multiform stress that many social workers experience, and the sheer range of specific generalist practice skills a social worker must possess.

No one had figured out how to address these issues in a comprehensive way until this book. The authors have done a masterful job of conceptualizing all these pieces so that students will have a clear idea of their learning goals. In addition to helping students understand where they are going, the book provides detailed content on how to get there—specific practice skills.

This book has been blessed with a long gestation period and has been refined and even rethought many times. In the process, it has been exposed to extensive peer review at professional meetings, which was always welcomed.

I have been involved in the refining process and can only express my respect for the energy and determination that the authors brought to the refining and reconceptualizing task. It must have been painful to discard ideas laboriously developed and to start thinking in a new direction. But the final result richly reflects their mature understanding of interconnections and new possibilities.

The book begins with the major organizing device—the Bridge Model. Students are introduced to social work as a linking profession. Just as a bridge links two shores, so generalist social work practice links people with the resources they need to thrive. This simple yet powerful idea leads to a number of important professional issues: for example, who has access to the bridge and how (concern with human diversity); what holds the bridge up (knowledge and skill); and how the social worker helps someone move across the bridge (practice skills based on a thorough, professional analysis of the situation).

Once the student has a context for knowledge and skill, the authors provide a brief but cogent overview of significant social work knowledge. Values are emphasized as being of critical importance, especially in the analytic process and as a route to self-awareness.

Finally, students learn specific practice skills with individuals, small groups, and organizations. They learn interviewing skills and how to participate productively in various group activities. This reinforces their view of social work as a profession that serves many different kinds of people experiencing a wide range of problems.

Social Work Practice: Bridges to Change is fresh and creative in its approach. It is richly detailed in its content, and I think students will relate to it very easily. The instructor will want to pick and choose among the many themes for specific assignments.

Ronald C. Federico

Preface

Social work students, educators, and practitioners meet and develop relationships with one another throughout the course of the student's professional education. They share the classroom and the field experience while exchanging ideas and concerns. Students try to listen and learn, while professors and field instructors give a great deal of themselves in furthering the student's understanding and expertise in social work. Despite their interactions, we believe that professors speak one language and students speak another. Social work practitioners, busy in their own agency work, look askance at both—the student and professor—and wonder if either understands. This book's purpose is to enhance the educational process and to pave a way for students, educators, and field instructors to speak a common language about the "doing" of social work.

When we began to discuss the concept of this book, we agreed that finding words to convey generalist practice is difficult. We completed two studies that confirm this view and lead us to believe there is a critical need to clearly conceptualize generalist social work practice. Based on our findings, we developed two pictures of social work generalist practice that provide the heart of this book: the Bridge and Crystal models.

The Bridge Model of generalist practice and the Crystal Model: Process of Planned Change are teaching/learning models. The Bridge Model is meant to illustrate the many components of generalist practice. In a nonlinear manner, the Crystal Model conceptualizes the complexity of the change process. Neither model is the definitive answer for students and professors in social work, but we hope that both help us bridge the gap between theory and practice.

There are many people to thank for inspiring us through these years of writing this book. First, Ron Federico, who wrote the Foreword, gave us strong encouragement while we were generating our concepts. His many contributions to social work education continue to be felt, even in his absence. Irv Rockwood guided us through the early stages of developing our ideas and presenting them to reviewers. Karen Hanson of Allyn and Bacon provided a calm presence coupled with enthusiasm and support.

This book could never have been written without the wonderful support from the people who make up the Association of Baccalaureate Program Directors. They listened to our endless presentations and made helpful and critical comments. Students, faculty, and administrators at Marygrove College, Wayne State University, and New Mexico State University helped through their critical analysis of each stage of the development of the models in the book and through their support by teaching classes when we were out of town or by reading the rough manuscript. At Wayne State University, Ted Goldberg gave of himself, sharing his vision of social work education and practice. At New Mexico State University, Christine Marlow and Pat Sandau-Beckler and the other faculty asked the right questions and helped keep the creative juices flowing. We are especially grateful to Mary Ann Suppes from Mount St. Mary College in Milwaukee, whose comments and critiques enhanced the text. We are indebted to Roberta Yarbrough, the Administrative Secretary for the Department of Social Work at New Mexico State University, for, as a miracle worker, she typed, edited, and tracked down details to produce the text. We also wish to acknowledge the generous help of Kenneth Walters, Chair of the Greek and Latin Department, Wayne State University, who loaned us his original software package to assist in the development of a complete index.

We wish to acknowledge the reviewers of the manuscript: Rosalie Ambrosino, University of Texas; Janet Black, California State University, Long Beach; Richard Blake, Seton Hall University; Geraldine Faria, The University of Akron; Gary Lowe, Indiana University; Dorris Perry, Grand Valley State University; Patricia Sandau-Beckler, New Mexico State University; Brad Sheafor, Colorado State University; Mary Ann Suppes, Mount St. Mary College; and Mary Urban, Boston University.

We are, of course, also indebted to our families. Eric and Abigail Hoffman read the manuscript and offered helpful comments from college students' points of view. To D.A., thank you for everything.

Charles, Shawn, and Joan Sallee, without complaint, gave up evenings and parts of weekends to Dad's "working on the book," focusing on the good times we have together. Kathy Sallee, as wife and friend, always supported the investment of time and energy.

Finally, we extend our deepest gratitude to our students, whose keen interest in our work inspired and gave us the desire and drive to complete this book. Our wish is that their knowledge and skills help individuals, groups, families, and communities whose needs seem so apparent in our society.

K.S.H.
A.L.S.

Chapter 1

Building Bridges
The Theme of Generalist Practice

SOCIAL WORK GENERALISTS AT WORK

Charles

Afternoon light filters through the fine dust of the dirt road and disappears into a bright yellow ball. The scene could be any rural area: the San Joaquin Valley of California, eastern Washington State, the Rio Grande Valley of Texas, rural Mississippi, upstate New York, or the Bread Basket of Iowa—just about anywhere.

Shadows draw long lines from the homes; the church and the silo line the dirt road. Charles, a generalist social worker, leans on the hood of his 1956 Chevy, one boot hooked over the bumper, his baseball hat pulled low across his eyes. Squinting into the brightness, Charles sees a young woman, Maria, slowly coming toward him. She holds a baby to her breast; with her other hand, she leads a three-year-old boy. As they walk, small clouds of dust rise around their feet. Coming closer, Charles notices Maria's eyes appear much older than her nineteen years; she looks tired, but resolved.

Charles reviews what he knows about Maria. She is a Hispanic mother of two children; the baby was born prematurely and weighed only $3^{1}/_{2}$ pounds. Her husband had abused her and then walked out. Her extended family, including her husband's family, is supportive and helps with babysitting and basic needs. Maria dropped out of high school in the eleventh grade when she became pregnant with her first child.

As Maria approaches, Charles warmly greets her. She apologizes for arriving late, and they walk toward her small, neat home, while she explains she had been visiting her grandmother who lives down the road. Maria puts the baby down and fixes a snack for three-year-old José, and Charles considers the many facets of Maria's situation he must take into account to help Maria work out some solutions to her dilemmas. He keeps in mind the social-work values and tries to be sensitive to her Mexican-American background.

From this illustration and background information, what aspects of Maria's life do you think are important for Charles to consider with her in assessing her situation? What special needs might her children have? What strengths can she build on from her Mexican-American heritage?

Juanita

Horns honk; brakes squeak; Juanita's car radio blares to keep the other sounds away. Although Juanita is accustomed to the big-city confusion, she knows it contributes to her exhaustion each evening. Hurrying along, she thinks about the meeting she is leading tonight with a group of parents who have children with developmental disabilities. The group came together after the school mailed letters with offers of a free course to parents. Juanita knows the parents, too, are battling the rush-hour traffic, trying to make the meeting.

The parents in the group, mostly mothers, represent a number of ethnic groups, ages, income levels, and different levels of experience as parents. Juanita conducted individual interviews with the parents and is pleased with how the group has progressed since that first awkward session. Now, parents in the group telephone each other during the week, offering support and building a network of mutual aid. Juanita is confident that she can understand the roles the different parents assume during group meetings, the dynamics of the group, and the overall group process.

As a generalist social worker, what skills would you use in a group situation? What impact does the context of urban pressure have on these parents? Their children? How can the group give power to each individual?

Carol

It is a clear, cold morning as Carol drives through the post gate. The M.P. on duty snaps a crisp salute, and she weakly waves back. She has not grown entirely comfortable with working as a civilian social worker on a military base. Although she is ambivalent about the military and still feels some value conflict, she is glad she accepted the job, because she understands that military families need help in much the same way as do civilian families.

As an Army Community Services social worker, Carol is responsible for social services for families relocating to this base. The programs range from the provision of household items such as pots and pans, to child care, family and marriage counseling, and even working with victims of incest. She is glad she has been prepared as a generalist.

Glancing at her desk calendar, she sees that her first appointment is with a Sergeant Williams, referred by his commanding officer for suspected child abuse. The Williams family has just returned "stateside" after a two-year tour in Germany. Their youngest child was born in Bonn, and the other two children, ages seven and four, have known little stability, moving every two years.

For Carol, the military setting is very different from her first two years working for the public child-welfare agency in town. There, she went out to families' homes to investigate child neglect and abuse and had worked with a number of women who did not really want any help. Here, military personnel are ordered to attend counseling, and it is never easy learning just how open they are to the process, as their discipline and rigidity sometimes stand in the way.

How does Carol's agency setting affect her methods of working? What is the connection between her values, her professional ethics, and where she works? What are some of the unique problems facing her clients, and what generalist skills can she use?

INTRODUCTION TO GENERALIST PRACTICE

Charles's, Juanita's, and Carol's vignettes illustrate the knowledge, skill, and value base of generalist social work practice. Charles, in working with Maria, a Mexican-American woman, must tap into knowledge of human behavior and the social environment to help him understand Maria's situation, paying special attention to her ethnic background. Juanita, an established practitioner, reflects on the helping skills she uses in serving a group of parents who need support in raising their children with developmental disabilities. Carol, new to her job on a military base, works through her value conflict about taking the job she holds. She settled her own dilemma, knowing that her services are important to her clients even though she feels out of place.

Charles, Juanita, and Carol, all generalist social workers, combine their knowledge, skills, and value base to help people — whether they are individuals or members of families, groups, communities, and organizations — obtain the resources they need to live with dignity. The social workers' work is complex because they must understand people as they interact with their environments, as they are affected by their environments, and as they seek to have an impact upon their environments. In so doing, social work generalists are likely to connect people with what they need, span gaps that exist in services, and try to create necessary services that do not exist (Boehm, 1958). We think of generalist social workers as "bridge builders."

Developing the Theme

Bridges represent the process and the purpose of generalist social work. At first glance, thinking of bridges in relationship to social work may seem far-fetched. Yet, the idea of a bridge, its uses, and purpose are all found in the aims of generalist social work.

Generalist social work practitioners act as "bridge builders." Bridges connect people with goals. They bring communities together, and they make passage from one area to another possible. Building bridges of all kinds is a human endeavor. Bridges bring ideas together, and they bring people together. Building bridges

Generalist social work is practiced in varied situations with client systems of different sizes.

exercises our creative ability to solve problems—to make something new out of disparate sections, linking the old and the new and reaching a goal. Generalist social work fits the Bridge Model, and we present the model to you to help you understand social work practice in all its components.

Establishing a Primary Goal

Generalists help people use the personal and social bridges they have available to them to achieve a primary goal and thereby enhance their lives, interpersonally, intrapersonally, and socially. What this means is that social workers work with people as they face life's challenges, as they attempt to cope with their environments, as they grow and accomplish life tasks (Germain and Gitterman, 1980).

Generalists rely on the problem-solving method to meet the primary goal, all the while recognizing how complex, intricate, and sturdy must be the change process that guides our work with people. Again, think of the generalist as a "bridge builder" and social work as a bridge. We use planned change just as we use a bridge to "get to where we're going."

Building Bridges between People

When human relationships are under stress and people are experiencing difficult life transitions—for example, the arrival of an infant in a family, children acting out and growing up, parents aging, families losing loved ones—social workers may provide services. Social workers serve individuals, families, groups, communities, and organizations, and they are often involved in the most compelling and urgent issues that people face. Social workers are employed in social service agencies, hospitals, schools, mental health clinics, and even in corporations and factories. They are the helping professionals who work with families in which children are abused and neglected; they work with substance abusers, prisoners, and parolees. They work with the elderly and with people who are very ill and dying. Social workers are found in social agencies, schools, hospitals, clinics, and factories across this country. Social workers help build bridges when they are needed the most—when relationships are broken, when pain and losses are acute, and when stress is intense (Shulman, 1991).

Generalists also bridge differences and conflicts within and among people. They bring people together, whether they are parts of families, groups, communities, or organizations, to identify their needs and to assist them in solving their problems. By helping people recognize and build upon their own strengths and resources, social workers help people find their own strength to deal with the many changes, stresses, and strains that must be faced in life.

Connecting People to Resources

Social work generalists help people obtain resources that may seem far away and unattainable. Living in an abundant society that appears to offer unlimited resources is confusing and disappointing to many, often simply because our social service resources are difficult to locate. Social workers can provide connections to these resources. For example, a hospitalized elderly woman who must have a safe environment in which to live, as well as an environment that allows her the greatest freedom and choice possible is referred by her physician to a hospital social worker, who advises her of appropriate options. A generalist social worker employed in a shelter for battered women helps the residents find housing and schooling for their children, and, in turn, helps them find employment or educational programs for themselves.

People need resources, whether those resources are other people or more money or a better education. It is our job as generalist social workers to help those who are most in need gain access to resources that may already exist—decent, affordable housing, education, health care, transportation—to name just a few. Nothing separates people more than unequal access to resources. Social workers can help widen access to critical resources among those who need them most.

Building Bridges to Create Resources

In rural and urban areas, dangerous gaps exist between people. If we think of bridges in a social way—that is, as a symbol for connecting people with resources—we realize that we also need new social bridges. We need inventive ways to help people care for and educate their families; we need fresh career paths for young people; we need better ways to maintain the dignity of the elderly; and we need creative, nonviolent means to help all of us get along in a world in which people from a variety of cultures and ethnic groups share social institutions (Sa-leeby, 1990).

Creating resources may involve influencing public policy. Other possibilities include working with a group of homeless families and the Board of Education to provide school programs for homeless children. Or, it may mean lobbying a large hospital corporation to place a satellite clinic in a rural community. It may mean cultivating relationships with legislators in order to encourage them to support policies that create new jobs and job training for thousands of unemployed people (Mahaffey and Hanks, 1982).

At the other extreme, a generalist social worker may be working with an individual family to help the parents create new resources within themselves in order to provide a stable environment for their children. These two pictures of the generalist social worker may seem worlds apart, but, nonetheless, they are both concerned with creating resources.

Building Bridges Empowers People

Empowerment means changing society to give those with the least power and fewest resources and skills an opportunity to advance in our world. Empowerment occurs in one of three ways: (1) we help increase options, (2) we help people use a new perspective on the problem, or (3) we help increase life skills. A social worker can help a client take advantage of more options in life: more money, and better education, transportation, health care, and living conditions and equal access. Increasing a client's life skills may include attending parenting classes or learning how to access a complex bureaucracy to obtain food stamps. A new perspective on problems may involve the social worker helping a client "talk through" a troublesome situation so that the client gains a deeper and better understanding of his or her situation.

While reaching the fully realized "good" society is not possible, striving to create a better society, in which individuals and groups, regardless of their ethnicity, sex, sexual orientation, place of birth, language, disability, or economic condition are treated with dignity and respect, benefits us all. This is empowerment in its broadest sense. Enhancing human relationships, connecting people to vital resources, and creating new resources—all part of the generalist's job—are all directed toward supporting and empowering people to create what they need for themselves and to create the kind of society that strives toward equality for all its members (Solomon, 1976).

Believing in Change

Social work generalists believe that people can change and improve their lives and that societal institutions can also change, becoming more humane and caring. But as any social worker can attest, change does not come easily. To effect change, the social worker must be competent and trustworthy. When we meet competent professionals, we trust them because we know they can help us (Clark and Arkava, 1979). Otherwise, we look elsewhere for help. Let us look at the areas of competency generalist social workers must develop.

SOCIAL WORK GENERALISTS: ARCHITECTS OF CHANGE

As we have said, social work generalists are in the "bridging" business; and, like architects, we plan, design, and carry out our work. Like architects, we work collaboratively and in teams. It may be helpful to think of generalist social workers as architects of social bridges. Social work architects are change agents. As such, generalists take on a variety of social work functions that allow the purposes of social work to be achieved. The functions are, in fact, a compilation of the values, skills, and knowledge of the generalist social worker. Social work generalists broker resources, counsel clients, manage conflict, collaborate with other workers, teach, mobilize people and resources, and advocate for clients. Each function differs from the others, but they all utilize basic social work generalist skills. In Chapter 4 of this book, we discuss social work functions, roles, and skills and their relationship to the planned-change process that social work generalists employ. Mastery of the generalist roles and skills enables us to be competent social work professionals.

COMPETENCIES OF THE GENERALIST

In 1978, Baer and Federico published an important study distinguishing in just what areas entry-level generalist social workers should be competent. Through their exhaustive work, they demarcated ten competencies expected of the entry-level generalist social worker (pp. 86–89). In general, we think of social work competency as the ability to use theory and practice skills to bridge differences among and between people, to connect people to resources, and to build bridges that will help create new resources. While this general description of social work competency is useful, it is important to understand the ten competencies in detail, for this will help the social worker gain exactness.

Although a broad education is quite appropriate to generalist practice, social work programs often agree upon minimum competencies, and the profession expects the B.S.W. graduate and the generalist practitioner to possess these competencies. Throughout this text, we refer to the ten competencies to illustrate the process and skills of doing generalist social work. These ten competencies are as follows:

1. *Identify and assess situations in which the relationship between people and social institutions needs to be initiated, enhanced, restored, protected, or terminated.* The first competency describes the social worker's ability to point out and analyze exactly where dysfunctions, problems, and uneasiness between people and the social environments they create are found. Competent generalists are skilled observers and communicators. They are adept at gathering appropriate information from many sources and then analyzing it to discern just where the areas of concern or problems lie. Competent generalists are expected to (1) review and assess agency policies and procedures, (2) assess client systems (those individuals, families, groups, and committees who are helped by the social worker), regardless of their background or how they found out about the agency, (3) work

openly with other social workers and agencies, and (4) when called upon, be a part of a team to participate in all the activities mentioned.

2. *Develop and implement a plan for improving the well-being of people, based on problem assessment and the exploration of obtainable goals and available options.* After a situation is understood, it is up to the social worker, working closely with the persons in need (clients), to figure out just what can be done to solve the problem or to ease the situation. We cannot overemphasize the need to engage clients themselves in this process. In fact, part of the competency itself is the social worker's ability to involve the client in the activities which must happen in order for the problem to be solved.

3. *Enhance the problem-solving, coping, and developmental capacities of people.* Competency three is a natural outgrowth of the preceding competency. Engaging clients in the solution of their own problems inevitably enhances their overall coping and problem-solving capabilities. Social workers are there to assist clients to develop their own strengths to be called upon long after the social worker is removed from the clients' lives. An example of this important competency would be a social worker teaching people to make better use of their own environments, the people they already are in contact with, and the communities in which they already live. Often social workers give emotional support to clients to assist them in moving toward a more fulfilling life in which their own capabilities are more fully used.

4. *Link people with systems that provide them with resources, services, and opportunities.* Linking people with other people who can help with services and with new opportunities for growth are simply instances of helping people develop their own unique capabilities. In order to link people with necessary resources, the social worker ought to have extensive knowledge of the community. Using information and referral services — that is, computer banks in which services are categorized so that exact information about all aspects of the service and the agency can be given to the client — is a logical step in linkage. Social workers assist clients to become aware of their own resources, internal and external, and help clients understand their use.

5. *Intervene effectively on behalf of populations most vulnerable and discriminated against.* Social workers competent in this area work effectively with people of color, low-income populations, women, children, the elderly, gay and lesbian people, and other discriminated against groups. These are at-risk populations. At-risk populations live in oppressive conditions. Therefore, help that, in general, leads toward empowerment (the presentation of options) is preferred. This is *effective* intervention. In addition, the social worker should be able to facilitate change in policies and legislation that impede the provision of resources or services to vulnerable populations. Once the lack of resources is identified, the social worker must be effective in developing resources as well as in making maximum use of existing services and resources. Professional standards and ethics are utilized when evaluating services and, again, the social worker must be aware of his or her own values regarding human diversity.

6. *Promote the effective and humane operation of the systems that provide people with services, resources, and opportunities.* This competency includes the ability to maximize agency policies and structures to help client systems through the provision of services, resources, and opportunities. In order to do this, the social worker must have the skills to analyze agency planning and policy-making processes and the ability to participate effectively in activities to improve or initiate agency services or procedures. Social workers develop collegial support networks and use interpersonal skills and relationships within the organization. The social worker has the ability, in a timely and efficient manner, to implement agency procedures. The social worker has the ability to participate in the agency decision-making process as deemed appropriate, using professional standards and ethics as a guide. In making policy, it is necessary to have special sensitivity to the needs of involuntary clients.

7. *Actively participate with others in creating new, modified, or improved service, resource, opportunity systems that are more equitable, just, and responsive to consumers of services, and work with others to eliminate those systems that are unjust.* In order to accomplish this tall order, the social worker must have the skills to do evaluative research, planning, and policy making. This includes the ability to include, as much as possible, clients in planning. The social worker creates support networks and resources, sensitive to the needs of clients who may not be able to express themselves or use the service-delivery system. The social worker should develop options and have the ability to influence organizations and communities. The ability to work with colleagues and facilitate change within the agency is also important.

8. *Evaluate the extent to which the objectives of the intervention plan were achieved.* This competency includes evaluation of the processes and skills used to bring about change. Clients should be involved in the evaluation process, letting us know what helped and why. In addition to evaluation, the ability to use what we learned in order to make policy changes within the agency is critical.

9. *Continually evaluate one's own professional growth and development through assessment of practice behaviors and skills.* The process the generalist social worker uses to assess his or her own practice and activities involves obtaining feedback from client systems, conferring with colleagues, and learning from professional continuing education. In addition, the ability to read and draw upon current professional literature helps to increase the social worker's self-awareness and may improve his or her skills. The generalist should be committed to lifelong learning.

10. *Contribute to the improvement of service delivery by adding to the knowledge base of the profession as appropriate and by supporting and upholding the standards and ethics of the profession.* This competency includes personal involvement in the activities of professional associations, such as the National Association of Social Workers, the National Association of Black Social Workers, the Council on Social Work Education, or other professional social work organizations. The social worker should have a thorough knowledge of professional standards and ethics and an ongoing involvement in professional continuing education and licensure. The social worker should be able to collaborate with colleagues in activities to advocate for support of professional standards, new legislation, and opportunities of employment. One should contribute from one's own experience and research to the knowledge base of the social work profession.

Study these competencies and try to put them into your own words. Understanding them in a very personal way will help you assess just where you are as you venture forward in this field. The expectations held for the generalist practitioner are great, but the need for competent practitioners is also great. We hope you will be inspired as you gain awareness of the major work you will be accomplishing as a generalist practitioner.

EMPLOYING SKILLS, FUNCTION, AND ROLES

Social workers develop an array of skills, founded on professional knowledge and values. These skills are effectively and humanely applied through roles to effect change. Skills are informed by extensive knowledge of the human condition. One focus of generalist practice is at the point where the person and social environment interact. A brief example of a generalist practitioner at work is presented in Case Example 1.1 and illustrates her activities as she works toward attaining some social work objectives.

Basic Skills of Social Work

Interactional Skills

Communicating with others, developing relationships, conducting interviews, writing letters, addressing groups, and even talking on the telephone are all interactional activities. Developing skills in these areas is essential for the generalist practitioner.

Social workers who possess sound interactional skills are able to:

1. verbally communicate in a clear, concise manner;
2. astutely observe others' behavior;
3. understand the nature of nonverbal behaviors;
4. accept and understand behaviors of persons from different backgrounds;
5. listen to both the overt content of what others are saying as well as to the underlying or hidden content;
6. respond to persons' messages in a helpful, appropriate way;
7. express ideas clearly using the written word; and
8. make use of technology such as computers that can be helpful in storing and retrieving information.

It is helpful to read about skills in this text, but practicing them in class simulations and role plays is even better preparation for a field internship and for professional social work situations (Shulman, 1979). The process of adopting sound interactional skills endures throughout one's education and career in social work.

CASE EXAMPLE 1.1

Linda Dennis

Linda Dennis is a social worker in a shelter for the homeless in a large midwestern city. There are three social workers on the staff; one who administers and supervises, one who interviews and enrolls clients, and Linda Dennis, who works intensively with client families.

In the past few months, there has been an increase in the number of women with small children who are seeking refuge in the shelter. Generally, these are minority women who have left abusive spouses and who have preschool children, but there are also women who have recently been released from a large state mental health hospital. Adequate community facilities were not available and these patients found themselves on the street. For the most part, Linda has worked with clients individually, but now she is beginning to see the possibility and opportunity of working with these women in a group.

Case Discussion

Linda will utilize a number of skills, which we will present in Chapter 4, as she works collaboratively with her client group. Undoubtedly, when working directly with them in a group setting, she will listen to their concerns, help them to develop their own capacities within their cultural context, and attempt to link them to existing resources through referrals. She will also need to advocate the needs of her clients in an attempt to get needed services from other agencies' workers. To do this, Linda must understand the organizational structure of her agency and its funding sources. At the same time, she must consider the context of the community in which her agency is maintained. Her perspective must be broad yet concentrated, and her skills must be multiple. She must take into account social work values, particularly the client's self-determination and the dignity and worth of each of these women, their children, and their abusive spouses.

There are two major skills areas in social work which Linda Dennis uses. These are interactional and analytic skills, as discussed in the text.

Indeed, effective social work simply cannot be accomplished if one does not acquire excellent interactional skills.

Analytic Skills

To analyze is to be able to think critically. Our ability to help clients makes sense of conflicting and competing situations, whether they are within an individual or found in the interactions people have with others in their social environments, is based upon clear and logical analysis.

Becoming skilled in critical thinking is not just the property of social work education. Your entire undergraduate and graduate education is designed to improve your analytic skills. In fact, if you look back over all of your education, including grade school and high school, becoming an analytic thinker is a basic goal. In order to understand the world in which we live, to identify social problems, to understand the political process and to make choices as citizens of a country, we need to be analytic thinkers.

It is absolutely essential for the effective generalist practitioner to acquire analytic skills. The social worker deals with a great amount of information either directly received or observed. The social worker must put relevant information together in a clear way in order to assist clients in solving problems, living through difficult situations, or dealing with crises and losses in their lives. The social worker must understand how the social institutions affect the persons with whom he or she is working. Understanding individuals, families, groups, and communities entails the use of analytic skills (Gambrill, 1990).

Assessment, a key step in meaningful problem solution, is based upon sound analytic skills. In fact, in this text, we sometimes refer to assessment as analysis. All the steps in the change process that follows assessment are based upon correct analyses of situations. We will describe steps in effective assessment and provide examples of quality written assessments.

Combining Interactional and Analytic Skills

Social work is, above all, an action-oriented profession (Morales and Sheafor, 1989). Social workers believe that through their actions they can improve both institutions and people's lives.

Analytic skills and interactional skills complement each other, and the combination results in actions. Taking this a step further, effective action is a result of a well-conceived plan in which critical thinking had to be applied. Concurrently, solid interactional skills are the basis for the professional social work relationship, which is an essential ingredient of action that is directed toward problem solving.

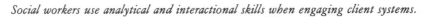

Social workers use analytical and interactional skills when engaging client systems.

The synthesis of analysis and interactional skills is demonstrated when social workers develop assessment plans with their clients. In Case Example 1.2, the social worker, Della Lynn, is working with her client, a 47-year-old man who was diagnosed as a paranoid schizophrenic, on a community placement in an adult foster care home.

Appropriate Roles in Social Work

Closely allied to the skills of social worker are the roles that social workers play as they carry out their work. For example, at work, a generalist may take on the role of supervisor. While at her church, she may serve in the role of volunteer, and at home she may be in the roles of mother and wife. Depending on the setting, she takes on a different role incorporating different expectations, demands, and skills.

It is the same for generalist social workers as they move from setting to setting. For example, a social worker may take on the role of a social broker when functioning as someone who connects people with resources. If a family is asking for services that the social worker's agency cannot meet, the social worker refers them to another agency or helps them identify other resources. We will explore the social work roles in more depth in Chapter 4.

CASE EXAMPLE 1.2

Andrew Carson

Andrew Carson has been readmitted to the state hospital several times. Each time he has been released, few plans were made for his care in the community. Adrift and alone, Andrew wound up back in the hospital after shaky plans did not work out, and Andrew had virtually no support in the community.

This time, the community mental health worker, Della Lynn, was determined to work toward a more positive outcome. Della visited Andrew at the hospital three times, planning with him for his release. She talked at great length with him about his illness, his problems in taking his medication, his interest in work, and his ideas regarding what sort of foster care he would imagine for himself.

Della also pored over his medical records and spoke with the psychiatrist and the nurses who saw him every day. She asked questions about his behavior, about his strengths, and about his limitations.

Della shared the information she had gathered with Andrew. He had a remarkably clear idea of his limitations, but had much less understanding of his own strengths. Della knew this was a typical response for many persistently mentally ill people.

Della and Andrew visited a foster care home she thought would be appropriate and then the two of them visited the community mental health center where Andrew would be in a day treatment program for job training. The entire day was a wonderful experience for Andrew and proved to be the positive beginning he so desperately needed.

Della had asked the right questions and she had probed Andrew's medical records and interviewed others who provided services to him. All the while, she framed her work in solid analytic skills so that his placement in the community rested on a solid assessment.

OVERVIEW OF THE BOOK

Following Chapter 1, the book is divided into three parts:

Part I

- Social work values
- Professionalism and social work
- Human diversity
- Social work knowledge, skills, and values
- Systems approach to understanding practice

Part II

- Overview of planned change process
- Each step and phase in the planned change process
- Skills and techniques of practice

Part III

- Putting It All Together: The Bridge Model of social work generalist practice
- Illustrations of practice
- The future of social work and you

In Part I, Chapters 1 through 4, we provide the foundation and frameworks necessary for generalist social work practice. In Chapter 1, we have presented the theme of generalist practice as building bridges to people, families, groups, organizations, and communities.

Chapter 2 addresses choosing social work as a profession by examining the history of the generalist, special groups social workers work with, and the values of the generalist. The chapter concludes with a professional self-awareness inventory.

How we use knowledge in working with people is the topic of Chapter 3, Linking Theory to Practice. A framework for change drawn from systems theory is introduced. What roles and skills social workers use in generalist practice is a major component of Chapter 4. Also in this chapter, we present a new approach to the traditional problem-solving process, the Crystal Model: Process of Planned Change.

Part II, Chapters 5 through 11, constitutes the "doing" of generalist social work practice, following the stages of the Crystal Model.

Chapter 5 is stage one, the identification of the area of concern and the development of relationships. Once we have identified the area of concern and established the beginning relationships with the various individuals and groups with whom we will be working, we need to collect more information. Raw data includes objective, observable information as well as feelings and intuition about a situation. In Chapter 6, we examine how to collect information from various sized systems after establishing a strategy for data collection.

In Chapters 7 and 8, the assessment phase is explored. Practitioners must make sense of the information collected by ordering data collected with existing theories and empirical findings about human behavior. The assessment process in social work focuses first upon strengths of client, focal, and action systems. The at-risk conditions are taken into account in the context of the continuum from opportunity to at-risk.

Chapter 9 delineates the design and planning steps necessary to implement action. Through an analysis of the problem, we are able to design possible options for change. This helps us identify specific steps and actions necessary to implement the solution. In order that all parties understand the plan, we develop contracts with systems.

In Chapter 10, we explain the important step of implementation. How we put the plan into action with various sized systems, and once we have introduced the change, how that change is maintained by the client system after the transition phase has occurred constitute the remainder of the chapter.

Chapter 11 addresses evaluation and transition. Through evaluation, we determine the effectiveness of our change efforts in meeting the client system's goals over a time-limited period. We introduce the processes used to evaluate overall problems, and then we discuss the importance of social workers' contributions to professional practice through research and its dissemination. The remainder of this chapter addresses the transition systems undergo as the change process ends.

Part III, Chapters 12 and 13, concludes the text by presenting the Bridge Model as an overview of all of the pieces of generalist practice. An extended case illustration, the community of Dupree, through example ties generalist practice together in an everyday case. Chapter 12 enables the student to integrate theory, skills, roles, and values presented in previous chapters, into generalist practice. Chapter 13 helps the student to look to the future by building upon strengths and examining new challenges. Some tips on working in social services are provided at the conclusion of the chapter.

Developing a Framework for Planned Change

You will find the first part of the book a restatement of some of the knowledge you may have gained from your Introduction to Social Work and your Human Behavior and Social Environment courses. We recap for you so that you are able to make direct applications of knowledge and values to social work practice.

The social work values of affirming the worth and dignity of all persons, enhancing social justice, and supporting self-determination are all discussed in relation to your own values and to conflicting values found in society. In Chapter 2, we present a section on those populations social workers are, by way of their own values, committed to serve. You need to understand special populations not only to enhance your knowledge base, but also to discover any value conflicts you might have in working with people who may be quite different from yourself. In Part I, we provide an opportunity to assess your own values in relation to social work values. It is important that you critically assess your feelings toward social work at this point in your education.

We review the knowledge base, particularly in sociology and psychology, and how that knowledge base fits into a social work practice framework. The social work framework called Framework for Planned Change uses a systems perspective and helps us put our knowledge to work. In addition, we show how a general systems understanding enhances your ability to consider systems of most concern to social work practice (Nearn, 1969; Compton and Galaway, 1989).

Of course, knowledge acquisition alone does not produce a social worker. You must have learned a variety of skills that are used within the context of social work functions—that is, the behavior of social workers in terms of the tasks with which they are involved. You will be introduced to the generalist functions, and we will discuss the skills that are basic to all of social work generalist practice. We describe interactional skills in detail that are applicable to various phases of the problem-solving process. For example, you will learn some steps in developing good listening skills when we discuss how you begin to develop relationships during the early phases of the change process. Further, you will be given suggestions regarding class activities and role plays that might help develop your own personal interactional skills (Hepworth and Larson, 1986).

Learning the Skills and the Process of Planned Change

Part II of the book describes in detail the planned change process used in social work generalist practice. Most of this discussion follows along the tried and tested problem-solving process derived from science—that is, the scientific method. We identify a problem or situation to study; we gather information regarding it; we assess its significance; we decide how we will solve it; we attempt to solve or improve the problem; and then we evaluate whether or not the methods used to solve the problems worked or did not work. Perlman (1957) is known as the "grandmother of the problem-solving process" in social work, and we refer to her important work as we adapt her problem solving process to generalist social work (Compton and Galaway, 1989). In Chapters 6 through 11, when you are learning the planned change process, we will give you examples of analytic skills.

Crystal Model Process of Planned Change

Our adaptation of the problem solving process in this text is called the Crystal Model of Planned Change. While it is similar to Perlman's work (1957) in problem solving, it more closely fits the purposes of generalist practice, and we believe it reflects the actual practice of social work which includes not only problem solving, but planned change (Pincus and Minahan, 1973), where concerns as well as problem areas are addressed. Social work generalists work in situations in which problems alone are not what brings about the need for social work intervention. Social work generalists are concerned about prevention of problems; they are cognizant of the many ways people define what has happened to them that brings them to social work intervention. In other words, problems, alone, are not the focus of our practice. You will be introduced to many situations in which clients do not think they are in problem situations. They may be deeply involved in life transitions or uncomfortable interactions with others, but such situations are not always problem-focused.

The Crystal Model shows how we adapt to work with interconnected systems of different sizes. Work with small systems is not the only arena for the generalist. In other words, generalists work not only with individuals, but also with groups, families, communities, and organizations. The Crystal Model guides us to understand situations and solve problems from a variety of perspectives. In addition, the Crystal Model reflects the complex situations in which we work. Although planned change is a step-by-step process, it also is a process that seems chaotic when it is applied to the ongoing lives of people when no event or variable is consistent for very long.

Like the planned change process, crystals consist of multiple facets. Each side of a crystal is different and seems to grow into another, reflecting similar characteristics. The Crystal Model Process of Planned Change helps us see that change may be taking place with different sized systems simultaneously, and that steps in planned change follow at various paces. When we work with people, we must begin where they are and try to pace our work in accordance with their movement. Sometimes we begin to work on a situation or problem and find that something new emerges in our work with people and that we must retrace our steps and move back in the change process. Working with people is not as orderly as following the scientific method in a laboratory setting.

Each step of the Crystal Model is introduced in detailed discussions. We explain the phases of the process and describe the functions, roles, and skills that are part of each phase.

Pulling It All Together: Bridge Model of Generalist Social Work Practice

Part III begins with a presentation of a model for practice: The Bridge Model of social work practice. How knowledge, values, and skills fit into practice and into each phase of the planned change process is concretely illustrated. The Bridge Model fits the generalist notion of social work practice. Like a bridge, generalist social work connects people with what they need and want in life. Generalists work with their clients to decide how to solve concerns and problems that are barriers in their lives. You will get a feel for the actual practice of social work. You may want to discuss the material in class or compare the work presented in the chapters to work you engage in during your field placement. Part III ends with a discussion of the future of social work and you.

References

Baer, Betty L., and Federico, Ronald (1978). *Educating the Baccalaureate Social Worker: Report of the Undergraduate Social Work Curriculum Development Project*. Cambridge, MA: Ballinger, pp. 86–89.

Boehm, Werner, W. (1958). The Nature of Social Work, *Social Work*, 3(2), 10–18.

Clark, Frank W., and Arkava, Morton L. and Associates. (1979). *The Pursuit of Competence in Social Work*. San Francisco: Jossey-Bass.

Compton, Beulah Roberts, and Galaway, Burt. (1989). *Social Work Process*, 4th ed. Belmont, CA: Wadsworth, p. 507.

Gambrill, Eileen. (1990). *Critical Thinking in Clinical Practice: Improving the Accuracy of Judgments and Decisions About Clients*. San Francisco: Jossey-Bass.

Germain, Carol B., and Gitterman, Alexander. (1980). *The Life Model of Social Work Practice*. New York: Columbia University Press, p. 2.

Hearn, Gordon (ed.). (1969). *The General Systems Approach: Contributions Toward An Holistic Conception of Social Work*. New York: Council on Social Work Education.

Hepworth, Dean H., and Larson, JoAnn. (1986). *Direct Social Work Practice: Theory and Skills*. Chicago: Dorsey Press.

Mahaffey, Maryann, and Hanks, John. (1982). *Practical Politics: Social Work and Political Responsibility*, Silver Spring, MD: National Association of Social Workers.

Morales, Armando, and Sheafor, Bradford. (1989). *Social Work: A Profession of Many Faces*, 5th ed. Boston: Allyn and Bacon, p. 5.

Perlman, Helen Harris. (1957). *Social Casework: A Problem Solving Process*. Chicago: University of Chicago Press.

Pincus, Allen, and Minahan, Anne. (1973). *Social Work Practice: Model & Method*. Itasca, IL: F.E. Peacock.

Saleeby, Dennis. (1990). Philosophical Disputes in Social Work: Social Justice Denied, *Journal of Sociology and Social Welfare*, 17(2), 29–40.

Shulman, Lawrence. (1979). *The Skills of Helping*. Itasca, IL: F.E. Peacock, p. 11.

Shulman, Lawrence. (1991). *Interactional Social Work Practice: Toward an Empirical Theory*. Itasca, IL: F.E. Peacock.

Solomon, Barbara. (1976). *Black Empowerment: Social Work in Oppressed Communities*. New York: Columbia University Press.

Choosing Social Work as a Profession

OVERVIEW

During one's education, one must assess one's capacity and interest in the profession one hopes to enter. A career as a professional defines a major part of one's adult life by offering an identity that goes beyond the work day. Indeed, a professional career can become a major organizing factor of a person's life. Self-assessment involves a thorough look at how one's own values, goals, personal history, and career expectations interface with the values, goals, and traditions of the chosen profession. Values are an important element of social work and, therefore, greatly help to define it. The purpose of this chapter is to assist you, the social work student, to assess how your values fit with the profession of social work.

Self-Assessment

To begin the process of self-assessment, one must become acquainted with how generalist social work evolved from its roots to the present. Familiarity with how the practice orientation of social work came about helps one gain an understanding of the core values of the social work profession (Boehm, 1958).

Social workers frequently find themselves in "value dilemmas" in which difficult choices must be made. But a knowledge of how the social work profession has put its values into ethical standards helps these practitioners make appropriate judgments and find answers to these dilemmas. Self-assessment is an ongoing, continuous process in which social work students as well as seasoned practitioners engage. It is also the basis for practice evaluation, another process used by the novice social worker.

Social work values can be understood only in the context of the world in which we live. Placing values in a context does not mean values are capricious. We mean that values are only known when applied to living situations. Therefore, the

19

basic, core social work values are best understood when discussed with applications. We concentrate on how our values become actualized, especially in relation to some of the most pressing issues of our times.

Populations at Risk

Social work, since its beginning, has been concerned with people whose opportunities are most limited. Social workers understand their commitment to groups who are discriminated against and who are oppressed. The social work student, therefore, needs to become acquainted with the special populations social work serves and to determine his or her interest in and commitment to working with them (Schorr, 1988).

Along with addressing issues of oppressed and discriminated-against populations, one needs to have an understanding of human diversity (Cheetam, 1982; Devore and Schlesinger, 1981). Differences alone create unease, and learning to approach differences, to become comfortable with differences, and, finally, to affirm and celebrate differences are all components of generalist social work education. Not only are we different as individual human beings, but how we live and conditions under which we live also present us with issues of diversity which we, as social workers, must understand and address. We call these differences *contextual diversity*. Putting human diversity and contextual diversity together furthers one's understanding of generalist social work.

Taken all together, this chapter will provide you with the information you will need to begin your own self-assessment. To assist you, we have provided a paper-and-pencil inventory for you to use as a guide in your thinking and exploration. It is found at the end of the chapter and may be used in discussion with your instructor and fellow students, or privately, on your own.

THE EVOLUTION OF GENERALIST SOCIAL WORK

The Seeds of Generalist Social Work

For over one hundred years, there has been a debate in social work practice over whether social workers should be educated for specialist positions such as hospital social work or psychiatric social work, or whether they should be educated as generalists, able to function in a variety of settings. Although generalist social work has been practiced for many years, a clear, conceptual knowledge base continues to emerge.

The roots of generalist social work can be traced to the Charity Organization Society movement, which began in New York; the Settlement House movement, associated with Jane Addams; and Hull House in Chicago in the late 1800s. These movements required the social worker to be able to work with the community as well as with groups and with individuals.

The Settlement House and Charity Organization Society movements and other social work efforts in recreation and group work led to a landmark book, *Social Diagnosis*, written by Mary Richmond in 1917. This was the first scholarly attempt to identify common elements of social work practice. In the Preface, she writes,

> Fifteen years ago, I began to take notes, gather illustrations, and even draft a few chapters for a book on social work and families. I hoped to pass on to the younger people coming into the Charity Organization field an explanation of the methods that their seniors have found useful. It soon became apparent, however, that no methods or aims are particularly and solely adapted to the treatment of families that found their way into the Charity Organization Society; that, in essentials, the methods and aims of social work casework were or should be in the same type of service, whether the subject was homeless, paraplegic, the neglected boy of drunken parents, or the widowed mother of small children. Some procedures, of course, were particular to one group of cases and some to another according to the special social disability under treatment. But the things that most needed to be said about casework were things that were common to all. The division of casework into departments and specialties was both a convenience and a necessity; fundamental resemblances remain, however. (Richmond, 1917, p. 5)

In 1919, Edith Abbott, commenting on Mary Richmond's generalist orientation, stated, "The good social worker, says Miss Richmond, does not go on helping people out of a ditch. Pretty soon she begins to find out what ought to be done to get rid of the ditch" (Abbott, 1919, p. 313). Social work professionals and agency

Mary Richmond, author of Social Diagnosis.

administrators during this time were also searching for common ground, a search which led to the Milford conference in 1929, hosted by the American Association of Social Workers. During the conference, commonalities were recognized as constituting generalist practice, but generalist practice was not conceptualized. The eight elements identified were:

1. Knowledge of typical deviation from acceptable standards of social life
2. The use of normals of human life and human relationship
3. The significance of social history as a basis of particularizing the human in need
4. Established methods of study and treatment of humans in need
5. The use of established community resources in human treatment
6. The adaptation of scientific and formulations of experienced to the requirements of social casework
7. The consciousness of the philosophy that determines the purposes, ethics, and obligations of social work
8. The blending of the foregoing into social treatment (Schatz, Jenkins, and Sheafor, 1990, pp. 218–219).

Multimethods Debate

After the Milford conference, social work professionals attempted to broaden the base of practice. In 1950, Ernest Hollis and Alice Taylor (1951) (Schatz, Jenkins, and Sheafor, 1990) decided that social work students should be prepared in the multimethods approach. During the 1950s, there were seven professional organizations, representing different specializations in social work. In 1958, the National Association of Social Workers was formed through a merger of these seven organizations, creating the need for a common method and definitions of what it was that made a person a social worker.

The search for common ground continued with the 1959 curriculum study conducted by Werner Boehm, an attempt by social work educators to broaden the view of social work practice. This study had an impact on social work education through the 1960s and 1970s. Instead of relying on the multimethod concept, educators tried to supply social workers with a single set of flexible tools to work in various settings with a variety of client groups. These social workers were to represent what Ripple in 1974 referred to as the "utility worker" who could provide an initial response to almost any problem experienced by clients (*Encyclopedia of Social Work*, 1986).

Conceptualizing Practice

Exploration of the generalist was very active in the 1970s as a number of textbooks emerged that addressed the generic foundation and the composition of generalist social work practice. The major texts include one by Pincus and Minahan, published in 1973, which presented a systems approach as a way to understand the common ground of generalist practice. Some of Pincus and Minahan's concepts can be found in this textbook. In 1975, through a more prescriptive method, Max Siporin presented lengthy outlines encompassing the person in the environment perspective, that is, people are to be understood only in relationship to their social environments. In the 1980s, Morales and Sheafor (1983), Joseph Anderson (1981), and Maria O'Neil (1984) all contributed textbooks that offered a conceptualization of social work practice.

In 1978, the major study by Baer and Federico produced, through an extensive research project, the ten basic competencies for generalist social work practice. These have been used through the years by many social work programs as outcomes for generalist practice. These competencies were discussed in Chapter 1 of this book.

In 1992, the Council on Social Work Education, in their curriculum policy statement, further institutionalized generalist social work, particularly at the undergraduate level, by stating,

> At the baccalaurate level, professional social work education prepares students for generalist practice with systems of all sizes. Practice content emphasizes professional relationships that are characterized by mutuality, collaboration, and respect for the client system. Content on practice assessment focuses on the examining of client strengths and problems in the interactions among individuals and between people and their environments. (*Curriculum Policy Statement for Baccalaureate Degree Programs in Social Work Education*, 1992, p. 8)

Studies of Generalist Practice

In 1987, Schatz, Jenkins, and Sheafor completed a Delphi study which drew upon an expert panel of forty-two generalist practitioners who identified eleven features critical to the generic foundation of social work practice and several initial competencies. The features included, for example, the proviso that generalist social workers must be able to skillfully select and use multilevel intervention modes and to intervene in different-sized systems to achieve the client's goals and social change. They also found that the generalist should be able to perform varied practice roles, as was discussed in Chapter 1 in the section "Choosing an Appropriate Role" (Schatz, Jenkins, and Sheafor, 1990, p. 225).

In a 1990 study, Hoffman and Sallee surveyed 246 alumni from nine universities on what generalist social work skills they use in day-to-day practice. This study revealed that B.S.W.'s use their generalist skills primarily with individuals and families and less so with larger systems, although the study represented practitioners from all types of agencies. The B.S.W.'s had the most difficulty in identifying a theory base for practice or a way of conceptualizing generalist practice. Thus, students in B.S.W. programs may simply reflect the confusion found in social work education regarding how to conceptualize generalist practice. Through the years, social workers have done an excellent job of identifying the key elements and competencies that are necessary for generalist social work practice, but they have had difficulty conceptualizing a generalist theory.

ADDRESSING HUMAN DIVERSITY

Human beings differ in age, physical ability, gender, height, color, sexual preference, emotional development, and personality. According to Berger and Federico, "The sources of human diversity are biological, psychological, socio-structural and cultural" (Berger and Federico, 1985, p. 89). Social workers affirm human diversity, but similar affirmation is seldom found in society at large. In fact, as individuals, we often see our own differences not fitting into society, or at least not accepted by society.

Dual Perspective

In social work, we use the term *dual perspective* to further understand human diversity (Norton, 1978). One part of the dual perspective is the manner in which individuals see their own behavior. How we see ourselves, how we accept ourselves, and the values we place upon ourselves are shaped largely by our nurturing environment—that is, the intimate land of our family life. But we do not live alone, nor even alone with our families. Outsiders play a part in our development as well as in the ongoing quality of our lives. The values that the larger society places on us as individuals form the other piece of the dual perspective. For example, minority group members experience prejudice and discrimination in the outside world, even though in the safety of their own homes, they may be loved and accepted. When there are great differences between the two environments, people live in precarious balance. The consequences of living with the dual perspective differ among individuals as well as groups. Certainly some individual people seem to balance differences more easily, while others do not. Accordingly, some groups experience greater harshness from the outside world than do others. In fact, the oppression that is experienced in the outside world cannot help but influence even the intimate environment of families. Low-income people with few resources who are discriminated against because of color live even more precariously. Human diversity must be understood if we are to affirm individuals and if we are to help people in the best way possible (Lum, 1986).

Contextual Diversity

Human beings live in a variety of places—rural, suburban, or urban; wealthy and low-income. The places we live all have their own character and style. Our communities differ according to not only their size and per-capita income, but also according to their histories, their regions, the weather, the political climate and structure, and availability of resources. In social work, we are concerned with how the person and the environment interact and with the problems and concerns people experience at the point of that interaction. The environment is the *context* in which people live, and the variety of individual environments provides contextual diversity.

Rural-Suburban-Urban

The rural-urban continuum is a way of distinguishing one community from another. Communities differ from one another, and two major differences are population size and economic base (Redfield, 1962). The rural community, of course, is small in population, and often its economy is dependent upon farming. People may live in small villages or on farms, separated by miles. Suburban communities, on the other hand, are often high-growth areas, their business and shopping centers are difficult to distinguish one from another, and there are many more single-family homes than multiple dwellings. Suburban areas are changing. Business and industry are increasingly located there, and land development is lucrative because of the need for apartments, condominiums, and attached homes (townhouses) in which to house workers and families. Urban areas are, of course, the cities of our nation, and are highly populated areas. Some cities are economically diverse, while others are not. Cities in the industrial belt of the country are experiencing many changes, especially with regard to availability of decent jobs and the provision of adequate resources for their populations.

Poverty is endemic to urban areas, especially inner cities. While housing starts increase in suburbia, the number of homeless in our cities multiplies. Population size of the community or area in which we live is a determining factor in resource allocation.

Social Stratification

Income level, education level, and occupation are the ingredients of social class. Some economists believe social class is more significant than race or color in determining opportunities, quality of life, and access to needed resources from the environment. Social stratification refers to the way in which social class differences are layered, thus creating a way to understand how income level, education level, and occupations influence the quality of life.

The social work profession has been particularly concerned with the life chances of people who are most at-risk from economic and educational reference points. Although the *underclass* is a debated term, this demographic description cuts through to the core of what social workers must face in their work. William Wilson (1987) says, "The communities of the underclass are plagued by massive joblessness, flagrant and open lawlessness, and low-achieving schools. . . ." (p. 58).

Put together the two concepts of community population size and social stratification, and you begin to see the importance of contextual diversity. A low-income family living in a rural area has a different life experience than a low-income family living in an inner city or in a suburb. Making use of contextual diversity implies layering of contextual issues, examining how the layers fit together, and what the configuration of layers means for a group, family, individual, organization, or even a community.

Regional Economies and Diversities

Although the nation is more heterogeneous than ever before — that is, there is an ever-increasing number of immigrants from countries whose cultures are far different from that of the U.S., there are regional characteristics that identify one part of the country from another in a general way. For instance, life in a rural area of the deep South or even in an urban area of the deep South is quite different from life in New England. The landscape differs, the weather differs, history divides us, and values brought from various immigrant groups seem to influence local regions. Understanding how those differences influence people's lives is a task of the social work generalist.

Economies seem to differ according to regions. In some rural areas, the open "farmer's market," where people bring their vegetables and knick-knacks to sell without city interference, differs mightily from the "farmer's market" in a large urban area that is controlled by licensing procedures and regulations. The economy of New England is characterized by high-tech industry, while the economy of the Midwest features heavier industry. How people earn their livings, the stability and versatility of the region, and the economic forecasts for various occupations are determining factors in quality of life.

Basic Resources

Access to resources is a key element in the quality of life. Those with unencumbered access, who have the money to purchase services and goods, are advantaged, while those whose access is less than adequate are disadvantaged. Some environments have better resources and better access to them than others. Housing, transportation, education, and child care are resources of great significance, and, outside of decent employment and income, determine quality of life. Social workers must consider how communities and regions provide these resources in working with client systems. For example, some communities have alarming rates of homelessness. In such communities, there is not enough decent public housing for individuals and families to meet the demand for it. Sections of some cities are undergoing gentrification, while homelessness is a major problem in those same cities. Homes and apartments formerly occupied by low-income people are purchased by developers, renovated, and are sold or rented to middle- and high-income people, thus squeezing out the low-income residents. At the same time, public housing waiting lists are long, and the possibilities for decent housing wane for too many urban dwellers.

America is in love with the private automobile, but not everyone can afford one. Public transportation is a basic service lacking in countless communities, both rural and urban, throughout the country. Therefore, even if health or education services are available in such a community, accessing them, for some people, is next to impossible. Consider an elderly couple living on their family farm. Each is in need of medical attention, and there is a fine facility 30 miles away. The couple owns a car, but it is not reliable, and neither feels safe with the other driving it. Their trips to the facility are limited, and preventive medical care is nonexistent. In addition, lingering health problems are simply pushed aside. The couple could certainly use medical care, but accessing it is not possible.

The quality of education in a community is another basic resource that is important. Although education is valued highly in this society, its structure and services are in jeopardy. Funding education is problematic no matter where one lives. Tax bases erode, people leave central cities, and the division between those with decent incomes and housing and those without becomes even more pronounced. Along with education is the related issue of child care. The social worker must take into account how the benefits of enlightened child care are distributed in a community, where child care facilities are located, and the quality of child care programs in understanding the context of individuals' and families' lives.

POPULATIONS AT RISK

In social work, there is a strong emphasis on serving at-risk populations. We mentioned earlier in this chapter your need to become familiar with these groups and then to decide, given your own value system, whether or not you want to work with those traditionally served by social work. Thus, a preliminary understanding of these population groups is necessary as you proceed.

Social Work and Women

Social work has been traditionally identified as a "woman's profession," similar to nursing and teaching (Morell, 1987). The majority of professional social workers are women, and the majority of clients who are served by social workers are also women. Further, the problems identified as those which fall within the boundaries of social work intervention are often associated with family functioning. The family is where the traditional role of women is most clearly defined. Women and children experience poverty at a higher rate than men and, in fact, the feminization of poverty is an overarching concern of social work (Goldberg and Kreman, 1990). A close examination of the social work profession reveals that supervisory and administrative positions in social work are often occupied by men. There are salary inequities between men and women similar to those found in society on a whole. In short, social work has not escaped the sexism which pervades society (Bernard, 1981).

Sexism has as its foundation a strict division of sex roles. Sexism is followed by devaluing of women's sex roles and a subjugation to male roles. This subjugation is manifest in a number of discriminatory actions, including unequal pay for work, the overburdening of women in the home, and barriers to women in education and certain occupations and professions. In addition, there are limitations placed upon women regarding their reproductive rights.

As social workers, it is important not only to be knowledgeable about the unique needs and problems of women, but also to be sensitive in one's own practice to women's issues. It is necessary to listen closely to the voices of individual women and relate them to the social problems of women as a group. Knowledge

and sensitivity must be funneled into a commitment to undoing the damage
done to women. The way to undo the damage is to work toward changing the
existing institutions and policies that perpetuate sexism (Whitehead and Reid,
1992).

At the end of this chapter, you will be given the opportunity to assess yourself
in the area of gender relationships. Female students may wish to examine their
histories for the roles they have played as daughters, wives, and sisters, and to
assess how their gender experiences affected their commitment to social work.
Male students may wish to consider the view of their relationships with women in
their own families, in the workforce, and among women with whom they relate in
friendship and intimacy. "Macho" values and unresolved hostility brought on by
oppressive conditions must both be attended to if the values of social work are to
be upheld. Social work can only be practiced fully if both men and women are
served humanely. Self-assessment regarding attitudes about gender relationships
and a commitment to redressing the lack of equity perpetuated by sexism are basic
elements in contemporary practice of social work.

Ethnic Minorities of Color

When we investigate and recount social problems in society, we find that the burden falls most heavily on people of color—ethnic minorities such as African
Americans, Hispanics, Native Americans, Asians, and other groups (Dodd,
Foerch, and Anderson, 1988). Minorities are overrepresented among the disenfranchised, the economically oppressed, the homeless, and the severely and persistently mentally ill. Further, ethnic minorities experience the most formidable
barriers when it comes to obtaining society's resources (Loo and Rolison, 1986).
The needs, problems, and lack of access to resources of ethnic minorities is of special concern to social workers.

Racism

Racism is the key factor in the continued oppression of people of color. There
are different types of racism. Their complexity as well as interrelatedness makes
racism an extremely strong and prevalent force in American society. The three
types of racism are (1) institutional racism, (2) individual racism, and (3) respectable racism (Piliawsky, 1982).

Institutional Racism   We define *institutional racism* as "institutional behavior which treats members of different ethnic and racial groups inequitably and
differently from the majority" (Morales and Sheafor, 1986, p. 334). Institutional
behavior consists of laws and policies and other forces in society that are difficult
to pin down and are often accepted as correct and useful. Sometimes institutional
racism is blatant, as it was during the latter part of the nineteenth century when,
for example, the Mississippi constitution was rewritten and stated directly: "The
policy of crushing out the manhood of Negro citizens is to be carried on to success" (Silberman, 1964, p. 23). More recently and more subtly, the Supreme

Ethnic minority children are of special concern to social workers.

Court ruled in *McCleskey* v. *State of Georgia* (1987) that the death penalty, although disproportionately experienced by Black men and seldom experienced by the convicted killers of Black persons, was fair and equitable. Other examples of institutional racism include many of the social policies propagated in the 1980s in which social programs most likely to benefit minorities of color were deeply cut.

Individual Racism   *Individual racism,* which is defined as discriminatory and/or violent acts by individuals against members of minority groups simply based upon their minority status and color, continues to be present in our society. The civil rights movement of the 1960s resulted in the extension of certain rights to minorities. Affirmative action policies designed to promote racial and gender equity in the work place and educational institutions that followed the Civil Rights Act have not achieved the results anticipated by reformers. In fact, a backlash has recently developed in reaction to perceived gains of minorities and affirmative action. Individual racism is on the rise. There are reports of increases in Ku Klux Klan activities, and some college campuses report cases of blatant individual racism among their student bodies.

Respectable Racism   *"Respectable" racism,* according to Piliawsky (1982), is an outgrowth of institutional and individual racism and is more subtle than either. In our society, it is no longer as permissible as it once was to express any form of individual racism. The laws that have been passed to protect the rights of minorities have not resulted in equality, and racism that continues, although more covert, is nonetheless present and is called respectable racism. It is found today in such terms as "tuition tax credits," used instead of "school segregation," or in "reverse discrimination," used in place of "affirmative action." Respectable racism is particularly dangerous because it attempts to deprive minorities of the validity of their grievances. It makes the demands of minorities appear outrageous (Piliawsky, 1982). Respectable racism tends to result in the popular belief that there have been enormous economic and social gains by minorities. When the facts are known that many minorities continue to exist in poverty or are overrepresented in prisons, these problems, even then, are not viewed as social problems created by injustices, but rather as evidence of individual failures. This perception appears to lower the worth of minority persons and minority cultures. Indeed, respectable racism allows the majority population to speak against racial injustice even while supporting policies that do great harm to those who are most vulnerable.

Other At-Risk Populations

In addition to ethnic minorities and women, there are other at-risk populations to which social workers are committed. Gay men and lesbian women, the elderly, the physically and mentally handicapped, and the persistently and severely mentally ill are all groups that claim minority status. These groups continue to experience the effects of discrimination in ways similar to minorities of color and women.

Gay Men and Lesbian Women

Gay men, particularly in the age of AIDS, experience deep prejudice by the majority population (Cadwell, 1991). Once based on their sexual orientation, the prejudice has developed into an irrational fear of homosexual men (Paradis, 1991). This has served to further alienate the gay community from the rest of society. A more detailed discussion of working with persons with AIDS and their families is found later in this text in Chapter 10.

Lesbian women encounter discrimination in a number of settings, including child custody cases and work situations. Lesbian women are stereotyped as masculine. The prejudice is so strong that heterosexual women who demonstrate masculine characteristics in society are labeled lesbians. Either way, the lesbian tag discredits their capabilities as parents, professionals, and working persons. Many child welfare cases, including adoptions, make sexual orientation an unnecessary issue (Falk, 1989). For example, two women in a stable relationship have a difficult time convincing agencies they would make adequate parents.

The Elderly

In a society that emphasizes physical attractiveness, productivity, and youthful activities, the elderly are often left along the wayside. Discrimination against people because of their age is called *ageism*. Ageism is observable in society in many forms. In social work practice, there is sometimes a reluctance to work with elderly clients, and there are studies that show distinct differences in referrals for treatment based upon the age of clients (Morales and Sheafor, 1983).

Ageism is a process of systematic stereotyping and discrimination against people because of age (Beauvoir, 1972). Its dynamics are similar to those we have examined that are associated with racism and sexism. Older people are characterized as old-fashioned in their lifestyles and rigid in thought and behavior. Ageism allows younger people to see the elderly as different from themselves, and even permits the young a subtle lack of identification with the elderly as human beings. Ageism is also a way of denying the aging process. History has taught us that this is not a new phenomenon. Ponce de Leon's search for the Fountain of Youth in Florida and other accounts demonstrate society's inability to cope with the aging process.

A number of schools of social work now teach courses in gerontology, the study of the elderly. There is an increased understanding of the policies adverse to the elderly, including work disincentives, low Social Security benefits, mandatory retirement, and the increase in the institutionalization of the elderly in nursing homes and other forms of segregation from society (Pfeiffer, McClelland, and Lawson, 1989).

Changes in the American family as well as greater geographical mobility have altered the manner in which the elderly are cared for. Medical advances and the slowing of the processes of aging prolong life, but the quality of living for the frail elderly will be of even greater concern in the future.

The Physically and Mentally Challenged

The physically and mentally challenged are discriminated against. Their individuality is discounted, and, as a group, they are feared. As with the other "isms," treating people differently because they are disabled physically, mentally retarded, or have learning disabilities limits the potential of that individual (Lieberman, 1989). Physically and mentally handicapped persons were often incarcerated in schools for the mentally retarded or in other ways hidden from society, thus completing their isolation.

Again, in a society that values attractiveness, intelligence, and being normal, these persons are treated differently. But unlike people of color, who, as a population group, experience not only social and personal discrimination but also economic injustice, the mentally retarded and those with physical disabilities have obtained increased resources because such disabilities know no economic nor social boundaries. Wealthy, influential families experience these problems as often as do the poor. Special Olympics for the mentally retarded came about precisely because their physical limitations have no social boundaries. Our attitudes toward these people, however, are too often condescending. Mentally retarded adults, for example, may be treated as children, supporting an assumption that they are also emotionally retarded. Issues concerning sexuality and work among these populations are often avoided by social workers even though they are crucial to full adult development.

Culturally Competent Practice

As social workers, we need to become aware of our biases and prejudices in the whole area of intergroup relations. Racism touches upon all persons in our society regardless of who they are or where they live. Minority students must become aware of their own experiences in the society and how oppression has influenced their lives and perspectives on a range of issues. Majority students must be cognizant of how their behavior contributes to racism's continuation or to its retraction. In either case, it is a powerful force that needs to be understood and addressed in social work practice (Hopps, 1988).

Social work students must learn the history and cultural references of various ethnic groups with which they may work in order to:

1. Understand the nature of client populations;
2. Develop interventive modes or helping skills which are appropriate for each group, and
3. Understand the values and cultural norms of particular groups. (Cultural Competence Continuum, 1988)

To be culturally competent is no small undertaking, and is most likely a life-long process for social work practitioners. Its importance cannot be overstated.

What complicates the process of understanding diverse populations is that there are two processes occurring at the same time. First, one must understand the intervening variables of racism and oppression while at the same time taking into account one's own biases. All of this occurs while one is attempting to understand the client's problems and appropriate interventions. If the social work student does not begin to understand these complex processes, success will be greatly limited.

VALUES AND ETHICS: PROMOTING HUMAN WORTH AND DIGNITY

What Is a Value?

Some social workers have stated that the easiest way to define social work is as a group of people who share a common value base. Social work has, at its roots and within its core, a value base undergirding the profession. A *value* is a belief or notion about what ought to be and about what is preferred (Levy, 1976). Organizing social work values as preferences can be stated in three areas:

1. Values as preferred understandings of people
2. Values as preferred outcomes for people
3. Values guiding the manner in which relationships, secondary or primary, are conducted.

For clarity regarding these three concepts, one must understand just what is meant by "preferred." To the best of our abilities, we attempt to understand people based upon the best knowledge we have available about the human condition. Knowledge is gained from multiple sources, including experience, common sense, observation, and tested and untested theories. All of the knowledge gained from these sources, however, is sifted through one's values. Therefore, when knowledge areas are chosen for use by social workers, they must be congruent with social work values. One knowledge area about human beings is drawn from ego psychology, which asserts that people are capable of growth throughout life. Seeing people in a perpetual state of growth is certainly more congruent with social work values than regarding people as victims of their own destructive drives, which is a major component of a competing theory, also drawn from psychology.

Likewise, when outcomes are conceived for people, the values that inform outcomes must fit with social work values. They must fit with the ways the relationships are conducted and the types of skills used with people (Albers and McConnell, 1984). The social work relationship is central to the process of working with and on behalf of people and can, to a large extent, determine the outcomes of work with clients. The relationship is a nonexploitive, positive one that is conducted for the ultimate good of the client system. It is neither personal nor distant (Albers and Morris, 1990). Rather, it is professional because it takes place in defined limits and is always aimed at client growth, problem solving, and the desired change. Skills used must also be congruent with social work values. The skill of coercion can be a powerful force and can bring about significant changes in a person's behavior. But coercing people to change is not consistent with our beliefs and values about how people ought to be treated. Coercion may be efficient, but it is not a part of social work (Katz, 1984). Relationship and skill values need to be in concert with social work values.

Indeed, values are inherent in every activity in which we participate. In social work practice, it is important to evaluate the possible conflicts between personal and professional values (Egan, 1975). One method of identifying values is by taking the Professional Self-Awareness Inventory provided at the end of this chapter and comparing your values to the following professional values.

Professional Social Work Values

Tradition of Values

The profession of social work adopted elements of the Judeo-Christian tradition regarding the person in its value base. According to social work values, persons are worthwhile in and of themselves (Boehm, 1958). Worth is not linked to who one is or what one produces. We believe people are inherently worthwhile, and social work values insist upon supporting ways in which human dignity can be maintained. Dignity is a state or status which implies certain rights, boundaries and types of treatment. This status reinforces worth and esteem of the individual person. The dignity and worth of the individual is the single most important social work value, and other values grow from it (Biestek, 1957).

Social Justice

Closely related to the worth and dignity of persons is the value of creating structures—organizations, families, and communities—in which a person's dignity and worth can be supported (Reeser and Leighninger, 1990). Values about building communities based upon respect and equality grow out of the Judeo-Christian tradition and have been further identified through the democratic philosophy of American society. This philosophy promotes equality and justice in an environment that supports human growth and fulfillment (Saleeby, 1990). It is manifested through equal participation in the governance of one's community. How individuals conduct their daily lives and how they obtain resources are every bit as important as the products they produce or the financial success they experience. This is important to understand in our capitalistic society and, particularly, within society's values in the latter part of the twentieth century, when attaining material wealth, often without examining the means by which it is secured, is a goal so many aspire to (Bellah, et al., 1991).

Self-Determination

Client self-determination has been an underlying social work value since the profession's beginning (Biestek, 1957). Self-determination is a way of further explaining human worth and dignity. It takes notice of a person's need to control his or her own life and to make one's own decisions. Self-determination certainly supports human dignity. It is important enough to be explored, based upon its own merits, and to understand why it is so fundamental to social work values.

Social work clients are often the most vulnerable of all persons in society and, as such, may have less control over their own lives. For example, Ms. J. is a low-income woman who is the sole support of three children and is also responsible for an aged mother. She has very little time to consider her own needs and personhood. In fact, her time is spent working, caring for her children and mother, and maintaining the household. She feels as though she has few personal choices and no opportunity to make changes. Affirming her right to self-determination, to the extent that it is possible and within the parameters of her life, is a way of putting social work values into action. This may mean assisting her to obtain day care, linking her with a home health aide for her mother, or just listening to her plans to obtain a better future for herself.

Social workers also work with persons who do not seek help and are involuntary clients by way of their societal status. Involuntary clients are working with a social worker not because they want to, but because they have been ordered to by some authority of the state. These clients have little say concerning self-determination. For example, a social worker may be working with a group of youthful offenders in a residential treatment program. The youths have limited control over their own lives and were assigned to the program partly because of their lack of impulse control. While the social workers are well aware of their limitations, they also attempt to create situations in which the youth can practice self-determination. By creating situations in which the youths take responsibilities for themselves, the social worker is assisting them to broaden their lives and create new opportunities.

Although the right to self-determination is a fundamental value, some social worker positions require elements of social control. In other words, there are real limits on a client's self-determination. Parents who abuse and/or neglect their children are seen in a public social work agency, not because they choose to, but because they are forced to by law. Abusive parents, batterers, and convicts under social controls may be forced to receive help from social workers. Their self-determination can be considered only within boundaries usually set down by law. A value dilemma in social work may be created if self-determination is carried to its logical conclusion. For example, if suicidal persons exercise total self-determination, they kill themselves. As social workers who value self-determination, we must understand its limits and realize how we can support self-determination to the extent possible (Clouser, 1991).

VALUE CONFLICTS AND DILEMMAS

It is important for social workers to be aware of their own values, as well as those of clients. To take this one step further, social workers should be conscious of the possible conflicts that can exist between different sets of values, and the dilemmas that often arise from these conflicts.

Societal Values

Individualism is an enduring societal value that influences all manner of public policy and services, and it affects what people believe and what they aspire to. Individualism is a value that has a strong tradition, having been an important part of the culture of the founding mothers and fathers and the framers of the American Constitution. De Tocqueville described this phenomenon in *Democracy in America*, published in 1835 and 1840. "Individualism is a calm and considered feeling which disposes each citizen to isolate himself from the mass of his fellows and withdraw into the circle of family and friends; with this little society formed to his taste, he gladly leaves the greater society to look after itself" (de Tocqueville in Bellah, et al., p. 37). Individualism has been both a positive and a negative force in the society (Bellah, et al., 1985). For example, the social work value supporting the worth and dignity of each person is clearly an outgrowth of individualism. We believe our value to be both important and good—a value strong enough to guide a profession. However, in a society in which individual achievement is the yardstick of success, individualism shows another side. In this society, our propensity to blame the victim and to explain social problems by focusing on individual weaknesses are also related to individualism and do not reflect social work values. The societal value of individualism places us in conflicts, and, as social workers, we must sort through experiences to clarify what parts of individualism fit with social work values.

Themes that appear contradictory to individualism are also part of the texture of American society. Civic responsibility and community involvement engaged our early settlers and were the foundation of our democracy (Bellah, et al., 1985). Being a good citizen means participation in the political process in many different ways, from voting, to membership on the school board, to participation in a block club. All are manifestations of the self-governing citizen. Americans value good citizenship, but contemporary life finds more of us busy with paid work or school, thus reducing our time commitments to our communities.

Many of you who are our returning students in social work are women who have given a great deal in time and energy to your citizenship. You have been the room mothers, the block club chairs, the precinct volunteers. Now you are social work students and your other roles in the community are, perhaps, taking a back seat to your education. Dilemmas arise out of your situations because everyone with whom you associate does not understand your new responsibilities. They may be fearful of your new commitments. But you are taking on new challenges which will allow your own contributions to change and perhaps even to widen. You may move from neighborhood concerns to city-wide concerns, from precinct work to state capitol work. It helps to recognize your conflicts and to understand that you will be even better equipped to contribute to the social welfare of your community in the years to come.

Group Values

American society consists of many ethnic, religious, and cultural groups. All groups hold values which are important to them and with which other groups may be in conflict. You may be a member of a religious or cultural group that holds values that are somewhat different than "mainstream" American values. You may find yourself experiencing value conflicts because of your group affiliation, or you as a social worker may find your own group values in conflict with the values of persons with whom you are working. At this point in our social history, certain religious groups are particularly potent in terms of their influence on current issues with which social workers need to deal.

Current religious movements mirror the two values previously discussed in the section on societal values—individualism and democracy. Americans cherish their privacy regarding their religion and accept the separation of church and state, while at the same time they support the notion that religion ought to be concerned with the whole of life, including politics and public policy (Bellah, et al., 1985). Some social work students come into the profession with profound religious beliefs, while others bring more pragmatic philosophies with them. Regardless of background, however, social work students must look at the values stemming from different religious backgrounds and how they influence the practice of social work. The most controversial issue with religious connotations is abortion. There is little doubt that somewhere in your educational experience or in your practice as a social worker you will be faced with a dilemma regarding the question of abortion. However, reproductive rights is not the only confusing issue. The role of women in church and society is seen differently from different religious groups. The rights of gays and lesbians can also conflict with the values of major religions.

Groups often have contradictory values and this, in itself, is confusing. In working with members of groups, social work students need to be aware of how the prevailing forces—the social and political climates—actually influence social work, clients, and social workers.

Personal Values

Our values help define us as persons—our uniqueness, our differences, our simi-larities. What we do is influenced by our own values as well as what we believe and what we care about. We live in a complex world with huge amounts of confusing and contradictory information at our disposal. At the same time, all of us grew up in families in which the personal values taught or learned through example were, by necessity, limited. Making sense of our values, experimenting with new values, and choosing the values to which we should adhere to are all part of the process of growth and development. In fact, the process of establishing our purpose in life is based upon recognition of our unique values and how they fit in with the larger picture in society (Moustakes, 1959).

Choosing a career like social work involves a deep exploration of values. Soci-etal values influence social workers, and social workers must understand how their values conflict or rest comfortably with them. For example, are you aware of the extent to which you are guided by the value of individualism? Can you see your way beyond it when necessary? Do you understand how it fits into your own value system? Concomitantly, social workers must look at their own group values and assess their differences and similarities to the values of their groups and to the values of groups with whom they work. Value conflicts that grow out of group differences are common experiences for all of us.

For the social worker, clarifying personal values is a process that begins during student years and continues throughout a professional career. It is a never-ending experience. Social workers need to be in touch with their own values precisely be-cause they work so closely with people who may hold different values. You have learned the source of values for people, and it is important to know that you can-not inflict your values upon others. We are often placed in the position of having to examine our previously comfortable certainties when we are faced with conflict-ing values and behaviors. Because groups and individuals hold different values does not imply rightness or wrongness of values. As social workers, we understand our own values, we clarify them and we use them, not to judge others, but to open our appreciation of the differences among us. Respect for other persons and reinforcing their worth and dignity comes when we know ourselves and accept others for who they are.

EXAMINING ETHICAL STANDARDS

You are now familiar with the values upon which social workers base their prac-tice. You know they are beliefs about what ought to be, about what we believe is good in ourselves and in our world, and about what we would like to see live on, even after we are gone. They are intrinsic parts of ourselves, and because of their very nature—beliefs, ideas, nudges, feelings, and so on—sometimes they seem vague, and we do not always know how we can actually use them. You also know some of the major value conflicts we experience in our daily lives and are aware of their inevitability. One study of social workers in health care settings showed that 98 percent participated in ethical decisions in some way, and 43 percent were involved often to very often (Joseph, 1988, p. 8). It is time to move logically beyond values as beliefs to the instrumentation of values. In other words, you need to know how we, as social workers, use values. A 1987 study of a random sample of 105 social workers found that few understood how to frame ethical concerns. Rather, they relied on the decision of others or personal experiences (Joseph and Conrad, 1989, p. 22; Thomasma and Pisaneschi, 1977, pp. 15–20). For example, one question addressed an adoptive girl's need to know about her biological mother. Few social workers framed this as the girl's right to know versus the right of the adoptive parents to confidentiality (Joseph, 1988).

Values to Ethics

Values are translated into ethics, which are practical rules or principles to assist us in making difficult choices. Most decisions in social work are not clear-cut. They involve "gray areas," and simplistic solutions are hardly sufficient. In social work, we have set down a code of ethics based upon our agreed-upon values to guide our professional behavior. It is important to remember that most codes of ethics (and the social work code of ethics is not exempt) are minimal standards of behavior and conduct. They are similar to laws based upon state and federal constitutions. State and federal constitutions are the standards upon which law is based, just as values are the bases for the code of ethics. We know that obeying the law is valued, but we also know that some situations are so important and so complex that, as such, they must be thought out individually, and we must use our professional consciences to guide us. "Ethical standards cannot tell helpers what to do or why they should behave in a certain way. Final authority must rest with the helper in determining what is right in a particular situation" (Corey, Corey, and Callahan, 1988). The code of ethics guides us but does not solve our dilemmas. Our own human judgment does that.

Joseph (1988) has suggested a model for ethical decision making that:

1. Makes the ethical dilemma explicit,
2. Brings value biases to the surface, and
3. Provides a guide for ethical choices.

The model consists of steps which include:

1. Gaining a clear understanding of the dilemma,
2. Gathering background information,
3. Prioritizing values,
4. Formulating alternatives with a justification for each, and
5. Selecting an ethical position. (Joseph, 1988, p.12)

Try to select a position which can protect all parties, understanding that not all ethics are equal. For example, if you have to break a confidence to keep a child from being abused, what would you do? As generalist practitioners face more complex issues, value dilemmas become even more critical. Social work is a profession with a strong commitment to both values and justice.

Substantive differences exist between the social work code of ethics and the codes of ethics of other helping professions. All codes of ethics guide behavior between the helper and the person who is being helped. Therefore, they emphasize concern for the individual person's well-being and protection. The social work code, naturally, also guides conduct between the social worker and the client, but it goes beyond the individual to guide the conduct of the social worker in regard to the general welfare of society. As such, our ethical standards contain guidelines for behavior when it comes to social change, combating racism, sexism, and discrimination, and expanding opportunities for those who have been most disadvantaged by society. Naturally, our concern for the general welfare of society includes respect for the separate cultural traditions of ethnic and religious groups. Therefore, regard for society as a whole does not negate affirmation of differences.

With this said, let us look at the National Association of Social Workers' Code of Ethics, the code most often relied upon by social workers and then look at two case examples to illustrate the complexities of ethical decision making and strengths and limitations of the NASW Code of Ethics.

Social Work Code of Ethics

The Code of Ethics of the National Association of Social Workers (NASW), as it now stands, was adopted in 1979. Of course, the profession has had a code in effect for many years. This particular code was reapproved in 1980 by the NASW Delegate Assembly. In its preamble, it states that the code is based upon the "fundamental values of the social work profession that include the worth, dignity and uniqueness of all persons as well as their rights and responsibilities" (Code of Ethics, Preamble, National Association of Social Workers, 1980). The code is used to guide ethical behavior among social workers and to serve as a "basis for the adjudication of issues in ethics when the conduct of social workers is alleged to deviate from the standards expressed or implied in this code." When complaints of unethical behavior are made against individual social workers or against the practices of an agency or organization, the NASW Code of Ethics is the ground on which actions are judged.

The code contains six separate areas guiding social workers in the many roles in which they are professionally involved. The summary version of the code is contained below.

NASW Code of Ethics
Summary of Major Principles

I. The Social Worker's Conduct and Comportment As a Social Worker

A. Propriety. The social worker should maintain high standards of personal conduct in the capacity or identity as social worker.

B. Competence and Professional Development. The social worker should strive to become and remain proficient in professional practice and the performance of professional functions.

C. Service. The social worker should regard as primary the service obligation of the social work profession.

D. Integrity. The social worker should act in accordance with the highest standards of professional integrity.

E. Scholarship and Research. The social worker should act in accordance with the highest standards of professional integrity.

II. *The Social Worker's Ethical Responsibility to Clients*

F. Primacy of Clients' Interests. The social worker's primary responsibility is to clients.

G. Rights and Prerogatives of Clients. The social worker should make every effort to foster maximum self-determination on the part of clients.

H. Confidentiality and Privacy. The social worker should respect the privacy of clients and hold in confidence all information obtained in the course of professional service.

I. Fees. When setting fees, the social worker should ensure that they are fair, reasonable, considerate, and commensurate with the service performed and with due regard for the clients' ability to pay.

III. *The Social Worker's Ethical Responsibility to Colleagues*

J. Respect, Fairness, and Courtesy. The social worker should treat colleagues with respect, courtesy, fairness, and good faith.

K. Dealing with Colleagues' Clients. The social worker has the responsibility to relate to the clients of colleagues with full professional consideration.

IV. *The Social Worker's Ethical Responsibility to Employers and Employing Organizations*

L. Commitments to Employing Organizations. The social worker should adhere to commitments made to the employing organizations.

V. *The Social Worker's Ethical Responsibility to the Social Work Profession*

M. Maintaining the Integrity of the Profession. The social worker should uphold and advance the values, ethics, knowledge, and mission of the profession.

N. Community Service. The social worker should assist the profession in making social services available to the general public.

O. Development of Knowledge. The social worker should take responsibility for identifying, developing, and fully utilizing knowledge for professional practice.

VI. *The Social Worker's Ethical Responsibility to Society*

P. Promoting the General Welfare. The social worker should promote the general welfare of society.

The above constitutes a summary of the Code effective July 1, 1980, as adopted by the 1979 NASW Delegate Assembly.

Using the Code of Ethics

Now that you are familiar with the code, think about its breadth and depth. It guides you in your behavior as a social worker and in your relationships with clients, colleagues, agencies where you work and with your profession. It also includes guides for your responsibilities to the society. The code, however, cannot address every issue. Throughout your education, you will be asked, first in classroom situations and then in the field, to test yourself in the area of ethical decisions. Read the following case examples and then try to answer the questions designed to clarify your values and assist you to make an ethical decision. Notice the differences between the two cases—one deals with personal conflict, and the other with a legal conflict. Each is a valid representation of the dilemmas social workers face.

These two cases and the discussion questions are designed to illustrate how social workers use the Code of Ethics. The code gives direction to our values: it helps social workers make difficult decisions and it unifies the social work profession.

Ethical Guides

Loewenberg and Dolgoff (1985) developed a priority list of consequences which might develop after the social worker has taken action to solve an ethical dilemma. The priority list would be used in making the best decision. For example, Loewenberg and Dolgoff list "survival of the client, other people or society" (p. 114) as the highest priority when weighing consequences of your actions on the client. In the following cases, you might ask yourself if anyone's survival is an issue in the Julie McNeal and Sam Thornton cases. Others include: (1) the effect of the social worker's action on the autonomy, independence, or freedom of the client; (2) whether or not "equality of opportunity" or "equality of access" for the client would be limited; (3) the extent to which the quality of life of the client might be compromised; (4) whether or not confidentiality would be breached; (5) the possibility that you, the social worker, may need to withhold the truth or not fully disclose information; or (6) whether the action you choose might be in conflict with any rules or regulations you have accepted as personal or agency standards (p. 114). Try to use these consequences as yardsticks to assist you in your ethical choices.

You will refer to the Code of Ethics throughout your professional career. It is helpful to know it thoroughly to think through possible conflicts. We cannot operate without a code of ethics. Nonetheless, its presence can only guide us. It is a document which is evolving and will change as society changes and as new issues emerge. We will also improve and clarify it. What undoubtedly will remain a constant is the value base informing it.

CASE EXAMPLE 2.1

Julie McNeal's Ethical Dilemma

Julie McNeal is a senior at the local university where she is a social work major. This year she is completing her field placement at Family and Children's Services of Kenmore County. She feels fortunate because she is one of three social work students at the agency who are working on their BSW degrees, and she has enjoyed the camaraderie experienced through her close contact with the other students. The three students share an office and in their free time have a chance not only to discuss supervisors and field liaisons, but they also critique each other's work and are beginning to actually practice some peer supervision.

One of the other students, Marge Stewart, struggles to keep up with her work. She is a divorced mother of two children who are ten and twelve years old. School, the field placement, a part-time job, and the children and housework keep her just at the breaking point. One evening when Julie and Marge were leaving the office, Julie notices Marge carrying out five or six confidential records belonging to the agency. They are records on Marge's clients, and Marge explains that the only way she can finish her work at the agency and complete all her other work is to take the records home with her to complete her recordings and social histories there. Julie reminds her that taking confidential records out of the agency is not acceptable, and both women talk about it. Marge sees no other way to deal with her many demands.

The next day Julie approaches Marge, wondering if she has thought further about the problem of taking the records home with her. Julie reminds her that clients' right to confi-

dentiality could be compromised. What if her car were robbed or stolen? What if someone saw the records lying on the kitchen table at home? Marge is familiar with the nature of confidentiality and understands its relationship to the need to affirm the worth and dignity of people. Yet, she wants to complete her work. She feels she needs high grades in order to get a good job, and she just cannot get everything done at the agency. She asks Julie to please drop the discussion; she has work to do.

Julie McNeal has been placed in a difficult spot. On the one hand, she values Marge Stewart's friendship, and she admires her. After all, going to school is relatively easy for Julie. She lives in an apartment with four friends; her parents pay her expenses, and Julie only works during the summer. Evenings and weekends in the apartment are quiet because everyone living there studies hard. Julie has her own room and no responsibilities to speak of. She has no idea how Marge manages. On the other hand, Julie wonders if her responsibility to her profession outweighs her personal feelings for Marge. Julie is in the midst of an ethical dilemma.

Discussion Questions

1. Is Marge violating the Code of Ethics or is Julie being supersensitive?
2. How are Julie's values in conflict with the agency, the profession, society?
3. How can Julie maintain a working relationship with Marge after this incident?

SELF-ASSESSMENT INVENTORY

Throughout this chapter, we have talked about the importance of knowing one's own values, of clarifying them, and of assessing how they fit or do not fit with the overall purposes of social work and with the values underlying our profession. To assist you in the task of value assessment, we have developed a Self-Assessment

CASE EXAMPLE 2.2

Sam Thornton's Ethical Dilemma

Sam Thornton, a new Adult Protective Services worker in the State Human Services Department, is called to District Court to testify on behalf of an abused elderly woman, Mary M. Her husband, Mr. M., is the suspected abuser. Sam must rely heavily on the previous social worker's process notes and conclusions in his presentation to the court. Yet, he has other information regarding this case which he learned from his previous job in the local Mental Health Center. As part of his work at the Mental Health Center, he had read Mary M.'s medical reports which had been released to the center with Mary M.'s permission. The doctor stated that, at times, Mary M. had psychotic paranoid breaks which resulted in violent behavior and could result in injury.

Sam's dilemma is complex. He has information which he obtained on his other job in confidence which could be useful to the court.

Now he works for an agency to protect victims. Furthermore, the previous worker had reason to believe from her work that Mr. M. was the abuser.

The judge asks Sam, as a sworn expert witness, if he has any other knowledge that would be helpful to the court on this case. What should Sam do?

The Code of Ethics protects a client's confidentiality. Not telling violates Sam's oath to tell the truth and the whole truth to the court. Taking issue with the previous worker's conclusions without discussing it with the worker or at least the supervisor may violate his ethical responsibility to his colleague. Sam has a responsibility to his agency, and finally, his primary responsibility is to the client, Mary M. In what ways can Sam resolve these questions?

Inventory. The inventory will guide you as you look at your own values, how they have emerged, and which are most important to you. After completing it, you may have a better idea of how you fit with social work or with what direction in social work your career will lead you. Sometimes students use inventories to stimulate discussion in class. Other times, they are used privately and not shared. Either way is fine. What is essential is *your* assessment, your knowledge gained about yourself.

Professional Self-Awareness Inventory

Understanding one's self is critical if you are to be an effective change agent in society. The following inventory adapted from Vest (1991) examines your self-awareness with regard to a number of variables that are critical in understanding where you have been, what you are now, what you hope to become, and an objective assessment of your strengths and weaknesses. Be as honest as possible and use this inventory as an aid in your own professional growth and self-development.

1. *Social background*. What is your family background; your ethnicity; who are your parents; what do they do; what was your family upbringing like; what was your extended family like; who are your brothers and sisters?

2. *Gender*. What is your general orientation toward gender roles? Who are you as a sexual person?

3. *Social roles*. What roles do you play in your life? Which roles are most important to you, and which roles do you identify most with? Who do you relate to in which roles, such as friend, lover, colleague, parent, sibling, and so on?

4. *Mind, body, and spirit*. What are your abilities and critical thinking? Who are you and how do you make decisions or solve problems? What do you think and feel about your body's image? How do you treat your body? What substances do you abuse? Do you allow your body to become objectified, or do you objectify the bodies of others? What message does your body convey to others?

5. *Creative freedom*. How much freedom do you allow yourself to be creative, to let go? How do you test your search for your limits? Are you dependent, independent or interdependent? Can you ask for help? What is your potential, and what are your talents?

6. *Values*. What things or issues are the most important to you? What themes do you tend to follow in your life? Who or for what are you willing to put yourself out?

7. *Professional self*. Who are you as a professional? How do you feel about the kind of work you do or are about to do? What place does your professional work have in your life and how is it related to your personal identity? How much time do you spend preparing for or working on your job?

8. *Strengths*. Based upon the comments that you made above regarding your self-assessment, what do you identify as the strengths that are helping you to become an effective professional social worker? Be specific as to how these strengths help you prepare for being a professional social worker.

9. *Weaknesses*. Again, based upon the above self-assessment, what weaknesses did you identify that you feel may be hindering you from becoming an effective professional social worker? Be specific as to how they hinder you, and also propose some solution to overcome them.

CONCLUSION

Social work is a profession marked by its strong value base. Generalist practice, with its goals of (1) empowering persons, (2) linking people to needed resources, and (3) creating new resources, is guided by our values, and our values are the most important inheritance we maintain from our rich and varied history as a profession. The social work values most deeply entrenched in our profession are: (1) the belief in the worth and dignity of each human person; (2) the belief that people can best live and grow in social systems that are just and humane, and (3) the belief that people have a right to self-determination to the greatest extent possible. Other values add to these basic beliefs regarding the human condition. Social work has concerned itself with working with and on behalf of special populations who are the most vulnerable in society. They are women, ethnic minorities of color, gay and lesbian persons, the severely and persistently mentally ill, the elderly, and the physically challenged. These are also groups which have been most discriminated against and which society has defined in prejudicial ways. It is important for social workers to understand the populations with whom they work and to separate myths about them from reality.

Understanding your values, social work values, and possible conflicts between them is an essential task of the social work student. We provided an inventory to assist you in this important work.

References

Abbott, Edith. (1919). "The Social Caseworker and the Enforcement of Industrial Legislation." In *Proceedings of the National Conference on Social Work, 1918*. Chicago: Rogers & Hall, p. 313.

Albers, Dale, and McConnell, Susan. (1984). "Redefining Social Work Practice." Paper presented at the International Association of Schools of Social Work, Montreal, Quebec, Canada.

Albers, Dale, and Morris, Richard. (1990). "Conceptual Problems in Social Workers' Management of Confidentiality." *Social Work, 35*(4), 361–362.

Anderson, Joseph. (1981). *Social Work Methods and Processes*. Belmont, CA: Wadsworth.

Baer, Betty, and Federico, Ronald. (1978). *Educating the Baccalaureate Social Worker: Report of the Undergraduate Social Work Curriculum Development Project*. Cambridge, MA: Ballinger.

Beauvoir, Simone de (1972). *The Coming of Age*. New York: Putnam.

Bellah, Robert, et al. (1985). *Habits of the Heart: Individualism and Commitment in American Life*. New York: Knopf, p. 37.

Bellah, Robert, et al. (1991). *The Good Society*. New York: Knopf.

Berger, Robert L., and Federico, Ronald C. (1985). *Human Behavior: A Social Work Perspective*, 2nd ed. New York: Longman Press, p. 89.

Bernard, Jessie. (1981). *The Female World*. New York: Free Press.

Biestek, Felix. (1957). *The Casework Relationship*. Chicago: Loyola University Press.

Boehm, Werner. (1958). "The Nature of Social Work." *Social Work, 3*(2), 10–18.

Brenden, Mary Ann, and Van Soest, Dorothy. (1987). "An Integrative Model for Social Work Practice." Paper presented at the Council on Social Work Education Annual Program Meeting, St. Louis, MO.

Cadwell, Steve. (1991). "The Stigma Suffered by Gay Men with AIDS." *Smith College Studies in Social Work*, June *61*(3), 236–246.

"Campus Racism: Seeking the Real Victim." *Newsweek, 115*(21), (1990), p. 33.

Cheetham, J. (1982). *Social Work and Ethnicity*. Winchester, MA: Allen and Unwin.

Clouser, K. Danner. (1991). "The Challenge for Future Debate on Suicide." *Journal of Pain and Symptom Management*, 6(5), 306–311.

Code of Ethics, Preamble, National Association of Social Workers, 1980.

Corey, G., Corey, M. Schneider, and Callahan, P. (1988). *Professional and Ethical Issues in Counseling and Psychotherapy*, 3rd. ed. Pacific Grove, CA: Brooks/Cole.

Cultural Competence Continuum (1988). *Focal Point, 3*(1). Portland, OR: Portland State University Research and Training Center, Regional Research Institute for Human Services.

Curriculum Policy Statement for Baccalaureate Degree Programs in Social Work Education, Council on Social Work Education, July 19, 1992, p. 8.

de Tocqueville, Alexis. (1835 and 1840). *Democracy in America*. (2 vols.).

de Tocqueville, Alexis. (1969). *Democracy in America*. (George Lawrence, trans.; J. O. Mayer, ed.) New York: Doubleday (Anchor Books).

Devore, W., and Scheslinger, E. G. (1981). *Ethnic-Sensitive Social Work Practice*. St. Louis: C. V. Mosby.

Dodd, David, Foerch, Barbara, and Anderson, Heather. (1988). "Content Analysis of Women and Racial Minorities as News Magazine Cover Persons." *Journal of Social, Behavior and Personality*, 3(3), 231–236.

Egan, Gerald. (1975). *The Skilled Helper: A Model for Systematic Helping and Interpersonal Relating*. Monterey, CA: Brooks/Cole.

Encyclopedia of Social Work. (1986). 18th ed., vol 1.

Falk, Patricia. (1989). "Lesbian Mothers: Psychosocial Assumptions in Family Law." *American Psychologist*, June 44(6), 941–947.

Finkelstein, Michael O. (1987). "A Shared Fate." *The Nation, 244*, May 9, 1987, p. 599.

Goldberg, Gertrude, and Kreman, Eleanor (eds.). (1990). *The Feminization of Poverty*. New York: Greenwood Press.

Hoffman, Kay, and Sallee, Alvin (1990). "Follow-up Study of BSW Social Workers: Implications for Education and Generalist Practice." Paper presented at the Council on Social Work Education Annual Program Meeting, Reno, Nevada.

Hopps, June. (1988). "Deja Vu or New View?" *Social Work*, July–August 33(4), 291–292.

Joseph, M. V. (1988). *Developing and Teaching of Ethical Decision Making*. Chicago: School of Social Work, Loyola University, p. 8.

Joseph, M. V., and Conrad, Ann P. (1989). "Social Work Influences Interdisciplinary Decision Making in the Health Care Setting." *Health and Social Work*, 14, (1/1–80), 22.

Katz, Jay. (1984). *The Silent World of Doctor and Patient*. New York: Free Press.

Levy, Charles S. (1976). *Social Work Ethics/Charles S. Levy*. New York: Human Science Press.

Lieberman, Florence. (1989). Clients or Patients: Families of Children with Developmental Disabilities. *Child and Adolescent Social Work Journal*, Winter 6(4), 253–257.

Loewenberg, Frank, and Dolgoff, Ralph. (1985). *Ethical Decisions for Social Work Practice*. Itasca, IL: F. E. Peacock, p. 114.

Loo, Chalsa, and Rolison, Garry. (1986). Alienation of Ethnic Minority Students at a Predominantly White University. *Journal of Higher Education*, 57(1), 58–77.

Lopreato, Joseph, and Lewis, Lionel. (1974). *Social Stratification: A Reader*. New York: Harper & Row.

Lum, Doman. (1986). *Social Work Practice and People of Color: A Process Stage Approach*. Monterey, CA: Brooks/Cole.

Morales, Armondo, and Sheafor, Bradford. (1983). *Social Work: A Profession of Many Faces*, 3rd ed. Boston: Allyn & Bacon.

Morales, Armondo, and Sheafor, Bradford. (1986). *Social Work: A Profession of Many Faces*, 4th ed. Boston: Allyn & Bacon, p. 334.

Morell, Carol. (1987). "Cause is Function: Toward A More Feminist Model of Integration for Social Work." *Social Service Review*, 61(1), 144–145.

Moustakes, Clark E. (1959). *Psychotherapy with Children: The Living Relationship*. New York: Harper & Row.

Norton, Dolores. (1978). "Incorporating Content on Minority Groups into Social Work Practice Courses." *The Dual Perspective*. New York: Council on Social Work Education.

O'Neil, Maria. (1984). *The General Method of Social Work Practice*. Englewood Cliffs, NJ: Prentice Hall.

Paradis, Bruce. (1991). "Seeking Intimacy and Integration: Gay Men in the Era of AIDS." *Smith College Studies in Social Work*, June 61(3), 260–274.

Pfeiffer, Barbara, McClelland, Tina, and Lawson, Joan. (1989). "Use of Functional Assessment Inventory to Distinguish Among the Rural Elderly in Five Service Settings." *Journal of the American Geriatric Society*, March 37(3), 243–248.

Piliawsky, Monty. (1982). *Exit Thirteen: Oppression & Racism in Academia*. Boston: South End Press.

Pincus, Allen, and Minahan, Anne. (1973). *Social Work Practice: Model and Method*. Itasca, IL: F. E. Peacock.

Redfield, Robert. (1962). *The Little Community and Peasant Society and Culture*. Chicago: University of Chicago Press.

Reeser, Linda, and Leighninger, Leslie. (1990). "Back to our Roots: Toward a Specialization in Social Justice." *Journal of Sociology and Social Welfare*, 17(2), 69–87.

Richard, Austin. (1990) "Bigots in the Ivory Tower." *Time*, 135(7), p. 104–106.

Richmond, Mary. (1917). *Social Diagnosis*. New York: Russell Sage Foundation, p. 5.

Ripple, L. (1974). *Report to the Task Force on Structure and Quality in Social Work Education*. New York: Council on Social Work Education.

Roach, Jack, Gross, Llewellyn, and Gursslin, Orville. (1969). *Social Stratification in the United States*. Englewood Cliffs, NJ: Prentice Hall.

Saleeby, Dennis. (1990). "Philosophical Disputes in Social Work: Social Justice Denied." *Journal of Sociology and Social Welfare*, 17(2), 29–40.

Schatz, Mona S., Jenkins, Lowell E., and Sheafor, Bradford W.(1990). "Milford Redefined: A Model of Initial and Advanced Generalist Social Work." *Council on Social Work Education Journal*, 26(3) 218–219, 225.

Schorr, Lisbeth. (1988). *Within Our Reach*. New York: Doubleday.

Silberman, Charles E. (1964). *Crisis in Black and White*. New York: Random House.

Siporin, Max. (1975). *Introduction to Social Work Practice*. New York: Macmillan.

Stallard, K., Ehrenrich, B., and Sklar, H. (1983). *Poverty in the American Dream: Women and Children First*. Boston, MA: South End Press, Institute for New Communications.

"Thinking About the Death Penalty." *America, 156*, May 16, 1987, p. 393.

Thomasma, D. C., and Pisaneschi, J. I. (1977). "Allied Health Professionals and Ethical Issues." *Journal of Allied Health, 6*, 15–20.

Vest, Gerald (1991). "Holistic Analysis of 30-Hour Orientation-Learning Experience." *New Mexico State University Department of Social Work 1990–1991 Field Practicum Resource Guide*, pp. 13–14.

Warren, Roland. (1978). *The Community in America*. Chicago: Rand McNally.

Whitehead, Tony, and Reid, Barbara V. (eds.). (1992). *Gender Constructs and Social Issues*. Urbana, IL: University of Illinois Press.

Wilson, William J. (1987). *The Truly Disadvantaged, The Inner City, The Underclass, and Public Policy*. Chicago: University of Chicago Press, p. 58.

Chapter 3

Linking Theory to Practice

THE ROLE OF KNOWLEDGE IN PRACTICE

Having become familiar with social work values and the ethical principles that guide practice, we turn our attention to the knowledge base. Like values and ethics, knowledge clearly informs and guides what we do. However, the task of linking knowledge to practice can be as difficult as expressing our values through ethical principles. In actualizing both, we must build bridges between what we know and what we are able to do.

The knowledge base in social work is interdisciplinary and based largely upon the social and behavioral sciences. Sociology, psychology, and anthropology are particularly relevant to social work practice, but information from economics, history, biology, and even the vast array of material from the humanities instructs the practice of social work.

Given such a broad foundation of knowledge, coupled with the multiplicity of situations we work within, finding a usable knowledge-practice framework is mandatory. In this chapter, we present a framework that should help you organize your knowledge base into a "framework for planned change" that makes use of (1) principles derived from the major knowledge sources informing practice, (2) the systems approach to organizing phenomena, and (3) the ecological perspective. The framework further organizes psychology and sociology principles, systems, and the ecological perspective into a way of understanding the individuals, families, groups, communities, and organizations social workers help. Our focus in social work is on the strengths we see in people and society, rather than the deficits. At the same time, we need to be aware of what causes people to be in jeopardy or in stressful situations so that we will know how to help. Knowledge of the resources people bring and the resources in society further our understanding of ways to effect the changes people want and need.

This chapter summarizes knowledge you have gained in human behavior and social environment courses and focuses that knowledge upon generalist social work practice. We discuss each component of the "framework for planned change," giving a number of examples to explain our points. The framework we present ought to help you become a generalist social worker who is not only undergirded by a strong value system, but also one who uses knowledge from many sources to guide practice.

THE UNDERPINNINGS OF SOCIAL WORK KNOWLEDGE

Beginning with core knowledge derived from psychology and sociology, we attempt to help you sift through the material that has been presented to you in your social and behavioral sciences coursework. Our focus on psychology, sociology, and anthropology does not connote that knowledge from the other arenas is irrelevant. However, the core of practice knowledge is derived from both what we know and can predict about human behavior and the social environment that surrounds all of us. We include a discussion of culture and diversity in the section on anthropology. These distinct social sciences contain instructions and implications for practice that go far beyond our introductory remarks. You may want to refer to your human behavior in the social environment courses for depth of knowledge in these areas.

Principles Derived from Psychology

Social workers employ material from a number of theories in psychology. The social work profession has strong roots in psychoanalytic theory, developmental ego psychology, studies of cognition and learning, and behaviorism. Individuals are understood as complex beings with both an inner and an outer life. We feel; we think; we remember; we plan for the future. Individuals have a great many needs that psychology has helped us understand. We know that children must feel wanted and loved in the world, at least by one or two people. We know children need to feel secure, especially early in life, and we know that the quality of early relationships with caregivers sets the stage for much of how persons interpret and experience their individual lives.

Developmental ego psychology points to the passages through which we proceed in the stages of our lives. The manner in which each stage is experienced, with its inherent developmental tasks, has bearing upon how later stages are encountered. Most social work students are well versed in Erikson's eight stages of psychosocial development (Erikson, 1963) and his regard for the full breadth of life's tasks, from infancy to old age.

The foundation of the social work profession includes behaviorism or learning theory. Pavlov and B. F. Skinner, although miles apart in their explanations regarding behavior, embrace individuals' ability to learn and to change or modify behavior based upon responses they receive in the environment (LeVine and Sallee, 1992).

Jean Piaget wrote of the importance of a stimulating environment.

Cognitive development is taken into consideration and included in the social work foundation knowledge. Intellectual growth depends not only upon one's brain chemistry, but also upon a stimulating environment (Piaget, 1970). Just as children need love, empathy, and acceptance, they also need an environment in which mental capacities are encouraged.

This brief summary is meant to turn your attention to what you already have been exposed to in other courses. Psychology is one facet of the whole that makes up your knowledge base, which must be fused into a practice model.

The pivotal contributions from psychology we consolidate into the framework for planned change are:

1. The recognition of the complexity of individual persons who are biological, cognitive, mental and emotional beings;

2. The necessity for human beings to experience a nurturing world in which to grow and the consequences when such a world is absent;

3. Human beings' capacity to grow emotionally, mentally, and cognitively over a lifetime, despite challenges and barriers to their growth;

4. The unique experience of each individual life, not duplicable regardless of the environment.

What we cull from psychology, most of all, is an appreciation of the individual human person. Each of us has strengths, needs, wants, and challenges—all a part of a total life.

Too often, social workers have relied exclusively on psychology sources, probably because inherent in the study of psychology is the study of treatment modalities for which social workers constantly search. Yet psychology alone falls short as a knowledge base when one examines the complex interactions human beings have with their environment and the power of the environment to further shape us.

Principles Derived from Sociology

Sociology is the study of human beings in groups. It is the study and analysis of society. It is a discipline that delves into the components of our social order, attempting to make sense of how human beings interact with each other in relation to what is happening in the larger world. Unlike psychology, sociology offers no treatment modalities or suggestions regarding how to improve upon society. Instead, its purpose is to focus our attention on society and the interrelationships existing therein.

C. Wright Mills, the noted American sociologist, speaks of the "sociological imagination as the necessary ingredient to ascertain some semblance of what is happening in the complex, dynamic world of which we are a part. This imagination is the capacity to leap from one perspective to another—from the political to the psychological; from the examination of a single family to comparative assessment of national budgets of the world; from the theological school to the military establishment; from consideration of an oil industry to studies of contemporary poetry. It is the capacity to range from the most impersonal and remote transformations to the most intimate features of the human self—and to see the relationship between the two" (Mills, 1959, p. 7).

The use of sociological material calls upon us to develop a world view that takes into account a host of variables in the environment and their relationship to each other. The approach is necessary in order to understand the "big picture"—not just that of the individual, but the individual interacting with the social environment and the interaction of groups and communities within the environment. Out of the vast assortment of areas of interest and units of analysis in sociology, there are key, indispensable findings that need consideration within a social work practice model.

Essential Principles

Those essential principles (derived from theory and empirical observations) are:

1. *Individual Self.* The individual self (the combination of personality and mind) develops as an outgrowth of social experiences. "The self has a character which is different from that of the physiological organisms proper. The self is something which has a development . . . that is, develops in the given individual as a result of their relations to that process as a whole and to other individuals

within that process" (Mead, 1982, p. 135). Socialization, itself, is the ongoing process whereby individual selves acquire group norms, which, in turn become internalized, adding to the social nature of the self.

2. *Groups.* Human beings live in groups, and group interaction has long-term effects on the sense of self acquired by individuals, but also contributes to the quality of everyday experiences (Cartwright and Zander, 1968). Luft describes the group as "a living system, self-regulating through shared perception and interaction, sensing, and feedback, and through interchange with its environment" (Luft, 1984, p. 2). Group interactions contribute to individual and group behaviors, and the analysis of groups augments our knowledge base. Group work, a social work method, grew out of this particular element of sociological inquiry.

3. *Roles.* Role theory helps us understand people in relationship to their status as well as to other persons (Merton, 1968). Roles are sets of behaviors that are based upon shared expectations. The student role includes expectations that class is attended, textbooks and assignments are read and completed, and tests are taken. Role conflict and role overload characterize many students today who not only carry out the student role, but carry on roles at home as parents, spouses, siblings, even while they are in a worker role, full- or part-time.

Role theory helps us see the reciprocity in relationships among people. Roles can only be carried out when there are other roles present to help define them. In other words, differentiation of expected behaviors related to a particular status actually defines a role. One cannot have a role without complementary roles also in existence. Again, this area of sociology points out the importance of the social experience on human behavior (Biddle, 1966).

4. *Organization.* Organizations and communities spring up from social interaction among human beings. We organize ourselves so that we can survive, not only in our complex world, but also in the most traditional societies on earth (Hall, 1972). Bureaucratic organizations characterize complex societies, and are pervasive in our lives (Etzioni, 1961). Social work practice, most often, takes place within a bureaucratic organizational framework that sometimes impedes services to clients, while at other times it makes service efficient and effective.

Communities are geographic groupings, but are also considered psychological and social groupings (Holland, 1950). Although their definition is still somewhat illusive, especially given their rather broad interpretation, for the most part, communities are understood as networks of relationships and social structures that are usually defined as locality-relevant (Warren, 1978). In other words, we think of communities as places where people live and/or work and where resources, to a greater or lesser extent, are found.

5. *Social Stratification.* Social stratification appears to be a condition of most groups, communities, and organizations. "Social stratification is the layering and ranking of people in a vertical arrangement (hierarchy) that differentiates them as superior or inferior" (Zinn and Eitzen, 1987, p. 139). Capitalism breeds stratification resulting in great differences among groups in wealth and power. Wealth and power differences are further associated with class, race, and gender. For example, as groups, the poverty rate of African-Americans and Hispanics far exceeds the poverty rate of whites (Wilson, 1987). Social class is clearly associated with income, and minorities tend to be lower on the socioeconomic scale. In addition, while women make up more than half the population, their incomes, especially when they are single or divorced and heads of families, are low in comparison to men.

Social class is a stratified system based upon income, occupation, and education. Although there is some movement among social classes, those who are born in very poor families rarely make great leaps in social class, simply because educational and occupational doors are closed—not by law, but de facto.

Principles Derived from Anthropology

Culture and Diversity

Social workers learn about and appreciate differences based upon culture and ethnicity, drawing from anthropology. The practices of honoring traditions within cultures and acknowledging the varied habits, tools, and belief systems of cultural and ethnic groupings are part of social work. Individuals and families from minority cultures are diverse when compared to the majority culture. However, when we note how many persons from minority groups of color are at the lower end of the economic and educational scale, we need to know how cultural differences are related to structural inequality (Zinn and Eitzen, 1987).

Cultural differences do not account for the social problems with which many minority groups struggle. If it were a question of cultural diversity alone, Blacks would not be at the bottom of the scale in family income and at the top of the scale in infant mortality rates. There would be differences without inequality because culture itself does not cause such economic and social conditions.

Even if overt racism were eliminated today, institutional structures would still create inequality for Blacks. For example, there are few African-American professors in universities because the majority of Blacks live in poverty and attend substandard schools. Thus, Black students have many more barriers to overcome in reaching the high level of education necessary to become a college professor.

Class and Culture

Other minority groups have been brought or came to the United States under force created by economic conditions. Minorities of color have not gained access on an equal basis to such resources as education, employment, housing, and health services. Therefore, all of those resources which must be obtained for a quality standard of living are not available on an equal basis to minorities of color. Class distinctions emerge, and minorities find themselves, preponderantly, in lower socioeconomic groupings, unable to move upward because they do not have access to resources, prerequisites to membership in higher levels of society (Cherry, 1989). We find an unequal balance of minority groups assigned to the lower class. Understanding how ethnicity or race and social class converge in social stratification is an additional step we need to make as generalist social workers.

THE SYSTEMS APPROACH

Studies in the social sciences, taken together with the preceding discussion of the fundamentals of the knowledge base in social work, point to the need to organize the ever-growing knowledge base, with its origins in so many disciplines, to ensure its applicability to professional social work.

When we work with people, we may be struck by the chaos of their lives, especially when we try to understand people not only as individuals, but as actors in their social environments. For several decades, social work literature has referred to systems theory or the systems approach to help practitioners understand the complex situations in which they work (Garvin and Seabury, 1984). The systems approach helps us make sense of seemingly chaotic experiences by unravelling them.

Social work has borrowed the systems approach from the biological sciences and has adapted it for use in our profession. Some systems principles are applicable in understanding individuals, families, groups, and communities.

Applying Systems Principles

There are countless applications using systems. Mathematical models are systems-based; biologists look at their findings in a systems approach; and economists, sociologists, psychologists, and political scientists all rely on systems thinking to understand data. Systems, themselves, are atheoretical. They merely represent a way of thinking and a way of understanding observations and the data that are elicited from observations (Garvin and Seabury, p. 38). The five systems principles we believe are most applicable to social work situations are:

1. *All systems seek goal attainment and balance*. Systems move forward, but they do so while trying to maintain balance. In other words, forward pushes can throw systems off balance temporarily; so there is, in effect, a movement backward to recapture an old balance. A certain paradox lies within this dual activity of systems.

2. *All systems have boundaries*. Systems are identified from one another through their boundaries. "A system is an entity that has a boundary or properties that distinguish it from other entities in the universe" (Garvin and Seabury, 1984, p. 38). Boundaries of living systems increase and decrease, and withstanding destruction or extinction, boundaries remain. No matter how changeable the boundaries, the boundaries, themselves, exist.

3. *All systems are made up of subsystems*. Every system has many parts, and each of those parts is also a system, or more specifically, a subsystem. Subsystems have the same general characteristics as systems. Your class may break up into work groups. The work groups are subsystems, while the entire class is a system.

4. *The whole is greater than the sum of its parts*. Understanding that systems are made up of subsystems, we might expect, in reference to Case Example 3.1, that if we put all the subsystems in the class together, we would have a definition of the whole system. On the contrary, the very existence of interacting subsystems where

movement and changing boundaries are present creates new conditions and variables. The whole turns out to be an entity that is more than even all its parts.

5. *All systems create feedback.* The system itself creates conditions in which change and alteration of direction can take place through its own interaction. A system is never static; and movement, itself, is the precondition forcing the system to change direction. Switch on a heating system in a house in which the furnace is thermostat-controlled. When the house temperature decreases, the mercury in the thermostat also drops. Automatically, that change causes an electrical circuit to the heater to switch on the heat from the furnace. Then, when the air in the room is heated to the point where the thermostat had been set, the mercury in the thermostat rises, and the circuit clicks off.

The Systems Approach Applied to Families

The systems approach is applicable to families, and we can call a family a system, just as we refer to individuals, groups, and communities as systems. Systems understanding is simply applied to families. However, theories based upon systems' understanding have developed in relation to families that are used in treating families in family therapy (Hartman and Laird, 1983, p. 76). Social work generalists do not engage in family therapy per se. Perhaps with future training and specialization, they may choose to do that. However, generalists do make use of family systems theory. In fact, family-centered practice, whether for generalists or specialists, is a legitimate focus in social work (Hartman and Laird, p. 8.) With this in mind, and as a way of further explaining how the systems approach is actually used in social work, we reiterate principles of the systems approach and apply them in Case Examples to two families: the Lewis family and the Palazola family.

Systems Principles Illustrated

1. *All systems seek both balance and goal attainment.* Families achieve balance or homeostasis at various points in their development. There is a comfort in balance that we reach for, even if that balance is based upon miscommunication; individuals losing their own identity with needs going unmet or simply a rigidity of roles and role functions in a family which may even be passed intergenerationally, from one generation to the next. This is not to say that balance is inherently dysfunctional as Case Examples 3.1 and 3.2 may seem to reinforce. Balance in a family may be dysfunctional, even for some members while quite functional for others. On the other hand, balance may be a positive period in the life of a family and its members allowing the family to obtain its goals. Goal attainment is most likely to occur when the system reaches homeostasis (balance). The struggle inherent in attaining what a system strives for is implicit in the state in which the system finds itself preceding homeostasis. Our example of the Lewis family helps to illustrate this principle.

Case Example 3.1 illustrates goal attainment and homeostasis in a family system. The Lewis family is not a perfect family. As a group and individually, they will experience more problems and turmoil. It is likely the family will find itself

CASE EXAMPLE 3.1

The Lewis Family

Bonnie Lewis is eighteen. She graduated from high school and, in the fall, plans to attend community college. Her parents, John and Ann, are grateful she finished school and chooses to further her education. During her sophomore and junior years in high school, Bonnie was heavily involved in the drug scene. She drank regularly, smoked pot, and frequently used LSD. Her life was organized almost exclusively around drugs. Her friends used drugs; the parties they attended were events where substances could easily be obtained and ingested. Some of her friends used cocaine, and crack had been introduced to her crowd.

The family was in turmoil. John and Ann did not know how to handle the problems with Bonnie. Ann blamed herself because she, herself, drank too much, and John blamed himself because he was seldom home to help with the tasks of raising a teenager. John and Ann were both angry with Bonnie and with each other. Bonnie was sure her parents did not understand her pressures, why she used substances, and how she felt about herself. The family was out of balance.

John, Ann, and Bonnie all had goals for their family. All wanted a more peaceful and less tumultuous life, and all three wanted Bonnie to become a productive adult member of society. No one knew how to get on with things. It was Bonnie who finally made a decision. Although she had experimented with nearly every substance with which she came in contact, she did not consider herself addicted. She knew she wanted more out of life than an inexorable reliance on drugs and alcohol. She

was sure she did not want a life resembling her parents'. She had friends and teachers who seemed to believe in her, and she knew her parents, despite their shortcomings, loved her. Bonnie sought help from the school social worker. She joined a group at school of former substance abusers. She spent many hours talking with the school social worker and with a new group of friends from the group who were no longer users. Bonnie even tried to explain to her parents, especially her mother, the dangers of alcohol abuse. To put it simply, Bonnie wanted more out of life.

Her poor grades during the years of substance abuse precluded her from attending a four-year college. Besides, she was not sure she was ready to leave home, and her parents were not sure they wanted to invest money into her education. She chose the community college. She now works part-time and experiences some independence. She keeps in touch with some of the friends from the group. She misses the school social worker a great deal and has not forgotten what the social worker meant to her. The family now functions under much less stress. Ann, her mother, still drinks, but Bonnie is not participating in assisting her or enabling her. John does not spend much more time at home, but when he is there he makes a real effort to communicate with Bonnie. An important family goal was reached: Bonnie finished high school and is involved in constructive activity that will help her to become an independent adult. The family is in balance, albeit temporarily. Everyone grew emotionally—Bonnie most of all.

out of balance at a later date. But the relative success of this sequence in their lives serves to strengthen the family system so that the next time a crisis occurs, the family will likely be more equipped to deal with it.

2. *All systems have boundaries.* Boundary is a term used often when referring to the family system and indicates the separation of one entity or subsystem from another. Boundaries are the limits of systems. "In the case of a family," according to Hartman and Laird, "the boundary consists of an invisible set of loyalties, rules and emotional connections" (p. 81). Thus, boundaries are difficult to define and specify because in their applications to social work situations, they are known only through interpretations by those who are involved in the systems or by those who are observing the system; and interpretations, themselves, are, by definition, imprecise (Garvin and Seabury, 1984, p. 42).

Nonetheless, systems' boundaries is an important concept that helps us see how systems maintain their integrity or wholeness. In families, boundaries keep out certain behaviors, people, values, and beliefs. For example, some families do not tolerate drinking or lying to one another. Boundaries also keep certain "things" in. Intimate knowledge about a family member or about a past event may be shared only within the family system. To share such information with outsiders would be intolerable to the system. Boundaries allow some things to leave the system. If there were no family boundaries, when children grow up and leave home, no one would notice. We need boundaries so that people can leave the family. Conversely, boundaries allow other people and behaviors and attitudes to enter the system. Again, with no boundaries, we would not notice the adoption of an additional child in the family or the welcoming of an extended family member for a visit. Boundaries keep the system maintained and intact (*Minnesota Home-Based Family Parent-Provider Training Manual*, 1988).

Sometimes systems have boundaries that are too loose. Anyone can come and go; almost any behavior is tolerated. Secrets are never kept, and there are no restrictions. Such families are sometimes called *disengaged* (Minuchin, 1974). In disengaged families, the bonds that keep families together are loose. People do not identify with their families; there is limited interaction among family members. Energy is focused outside the family, and anyone or anything can be brought in. Children in such families are emotionally starved, and trust among family members is low.

Contraposed to the disengaged family is the *enmeshed* family (Minuchin, 1974). Boundaries in enmeshed families are too rigid. The exchange of ideas, people, and attitudes among outside systems is minimal. Children are kept close to home in every way. They may have few friends and little interaction at school. Leisure time is spent exclusively together. In enmeshed families, the notion of children leaving home is not tolerated. Sometimes children stay in enmeshed families until their aging parents die. Intimate relationships beyond the family are impossible. If young adults do marry, rarely are the relationships satisfactory. Family loyalty is intense, even to the extent of protecting someone who defies the family or social value system. Problems in enmeshed families are hidden. Allowing a third person, even a helping person, into the system may be unbearable. While external boundaries are rigid, internal boundaries are meshed with one another. A father may play the role of husband to a child and vice versa. Incest can occur in enmeshed families when boundaries are unclear within the family and are too structured outside the family.

In most families, boundaries hover between being too rigid and too loose. Boundaries are most likely on a continuum. Families with fairly flexible bounda-

Families are critical systems for social workers to understand.

ries can endure change, adapt to altering circumstances and are likely to ensure the health and well-being of family members. For example, parents with young children may spend more time with children, have more rules for behaviors, set limits, decide upon rudimentary, everyday decisions. However, as families grow and develop, the old limits, rules, and behaviors are no longer adaptive. Parents with adolescent children must allow more freedom for young people or they will not become autonomous adults. Space has to be given for adolescents' decision making, even if mistakes result. Values are tested during the adolescent years, and sometimes testing places stress on a family system. Families which flourish hold to flexible boundaries while they continue to maintain their integrity as whole systems.

3. *All systems are made up of subsystems.* Applying this aspect of systems thinking to the family helps us see the many parts of families. Naturally, families consist of individuals. We define individuals as systems, or, in this case, as subsystems because the family is the system (whole unit) under consideration. Each individual contributes to the wholeness of the family. Each individual takes on various roles, behaviors, and characteristics which add to the understanding of the whole family. The subsystems make up the system (Chess and Norlin, 1988). However, subsystems in families can also be groups of more than one person. For example, the father and youngest daughter are components of a subsystem, as are the siblings, the parents, combinations of parents and children, and subsystems within the sibling group. The number of subsystems within families is staggering, even in small families. What does all this mean? In trying to unravel the complex-

ities of a family, we need to look at all the subgroupings within the family. What part do particular subsystems have in the definition of a problem that a family brings to an agency? What subsystems in the family are particularly at risk? Which are particularly strong? By seeing the family with its subsystem components, we are able to see beyond the individual without losing the special characteristics, nuances, and idiosyncrasies of individuals and small groups. The subsystem concept is infinitely helpful in our attempt to understand families. See Case Example 3.2 for a view of a subsystem within a family.

4. *All systems create feedback.* Feedback denotes movement within and through a system created by its own interaction. Systems interact with other systems; systems interact with subsystems. The interaction produces inevitable change. Change may be positive or negative or somewhere in between. There is no such entity as a static family. Even the most seemingly stable family is constantly undergoing change in direction simply by virtue of the fact of its inevitable interaction with other systems and with its own subsystems (Chess and Norlin, 1988, p. 105).

Family members age, new family members are added, others leave. The needs of the family as a whole as well as the subsystems of the family change through time and according to circumstance. Again, we refer to the Palazola family in Case Example 3.2. A very different picture of a family emerges at this juncture in time,

---

CASE EXAMPLE 3.2

The Palazola Family

Libro Palazola is the patriarch of his family. He is sixty years old and the father of five sons and one daughter. His wife, Consuela, is fifty years old. Their sons are all grown and have left home but live in surrounding neighborhoods and communities. The daughter, Nina, the youngest at fifteen, is still living at home. There is a powerful bond between Nina and her mother. Libro talks almost daily with his sons, and not a week goes by that some of them do not visit. Consuela misses the boys, but because Nina is home, she throws all her attention toward her. The subsystem of Nina and her mother seems to overshadow, at least at this time, all other relationships and systems in the household. Libro is increasingly jealous of the time Consuela spends with Nina and derides Nina regarding her performance in school. Nina is constantly compared to her older, successful brothers and told she

will never amount to anything. Consuela consoles her daughter, but resentment mounts toward Libro for his inattention to Nina as well as his lack of concern for her manifested by his almost total focus on his sons. Consuela considers leaving the family home with Nina, but cannot imagine where she would go. For over thirty years, she has been financially and emotionally dependent upon Libro. She decides to talk to someone in a mental health clinic about her worries.

The Palazola family is large. There are many relationships and subsystems. Nina and Consuela have a strong bond, and their subsystem is both a strength of the family as well as the focus of the problems in the family. Understanding subsystems helps us understand the whole, and working with various subsystems is quite appropriate in social work practice.

compared to what the family must have been when all the sons, the parents and daughter lived under one roof. One can imagine a large, boisterous, male-dominated family, instead of the snapshot of the Palazola family today. In the future, yet another picture of the family will exist, most likely when Nina leaves home, and Libro and Consuela are left with the empty nest. The interaction of all members of the family create energy and movement that pushes the family toward new beginnings. All movement may not be experienced in a happy and positive way; but, nonetheless, movement is inevitable.

5. *The whole is greater than the sum of its parts.* Systems are made up of subsystems, yet the whole of the system is more than all of the subsystems combined. Two plus two do not equal four in the case of systems. Translated into a family application, let us look again at the Palazola family. We know that Consuela and Nina are a subsystem, just as are Nina and Libro and Consuela and Libro. In addition, the older brothers are all parts of subsystems connected to each other, their parents, and their sister. The flavor, experience, and the identity of the Palazola family are all much more than a sum of all of the subsystems. The behaviors, the beliefs, the countless other qualities of the family are more than the individuals, more even than the dyads and the triads. The whole of the family is unique, in and of itself.

There are numerous examples of the systems approach in relation to families. We presented the most basic concepts. Interventive techniques in family therapy are based upon systems thinking. However, generalists also use implementation techniques that take advantage of the systems approach in working with all client groups. Developing an understanding of how families are systems is basic to our work as generalists, because, inevitably, families come up in our practice.

You will see in the next section that the systems approach may need some alteration for a full use by social workers. It is still uncomfortable for us to use the mechanistic vocabulary of systems and to apply the wording to human beings (Germain, 1979, p. 6). Language from the biological sciences (that is, ecology) seems to fit better with social workers' vocabulary.

The Ecological Perspective

Social workers typically use the terms "ecological perspective" and the "systems approach" interchangeably. According to Germain, "ecology is a form of systems theory" (p. 7). Understanding the relationship of living organisms to each other and to their environments (ecology) certainly entails some of the systems principles we described. An ecological understanding suggests sensitivity to the person-in-environment configuration to which many social work scholars refer in describing their theoretical position.

According to Germain and Gitterman, the "person-in-environment" combines a growing appreciation of the blending of Eastern religious thought and scientific notions that refute dualistic thinking and "shift away from certainties to probabilities, from dichotomies to complementarities, and from the dualism of subject-object to interactional fields" (Germain and Gitterman, 1980, p. 4). How people interact with their environments, the impact persons have on environment, and, likewise, the impact the environment, with all of its systems and sub-systems, has upon persons reflect consonant holistic attitude understood in Eastern religions, as well as the ecological perspective noted in social work litera-ture and, concurrently, in the systems approach, also utilized in social work. What is particularly appealing to social workers in using the ecological vocabulary is its move away from the rather perfunctory language of systems.

NEUTRALITY, VALUES, AND PLANNED CHANGE

Employing your knowledge for practical use in social work presupposes you have organized that knowledge base. The systems approach and the ecological perspec-tive are both ways of organizing knowledge for use. Inherent in these organizing structures is their neutral viewpoint about human beings and the conditions in which they exist. In fact, their greatest strength is their movement away from value-based, narrowly conceived perceptions of human beings toward more inclu-sive, holistic ways of understanding.

Understanding human behavior and the social environment from a neutral or value-free stance is important, at least in a first step of analysis. But it is neither realistic nor desired for when we actually attempt to put our knowledge to work in everyday situations.

When working with people in social work situations, a concern or a problem exists suggesting a need for social work change. That problem or concern suggests some sort of poor fit with the environment, a risk to human growth and develop-ment coming from the environmental adjustment or a life change that causes dif-ficulties for people (Germain and Gitterman, 1980). Therefore, we need to take our knowledge base and put it into a neutral way of analyzing persons' conditions and situations so that in working with people we can be open to them, so that we can have clarification regarding our beliefs and their beliefs, and so that we can use the most effective means of helping available. Implicit in our discussion is our own conviction that planned change is best achieved when tested change instru-ments are used.

FRAMEWORK FOR PLANNED CHANGE

Garbarino (1982, p. 21) built upon the work of Urie Bronfenbrenner when he analyzed systems affecting children along a continuum of risk to opportunity. We adapt Garbarino's framework to help you apply systems thinking to the practice of social work, which is really the process of planned change.

Our knowledge base relies upon our analytic skills in order for planned change to occur. There is no point in accumulating knowledge in social work un-less it can be applied in some way to helping. Therefore, included in our frame-work for planned change is a focus on systems of most concern to social workers. In other words, even though we may know how to organize our knowledge, we must be able to direct our knowledge in a systematic way congruent with social work values. Again, we have adapted previous work into our framework. We turn to

Pincus and Minahan's (1973) "systems of concern to social workers" to further define our framework. Taken all together, the framework for planned change helps social workers analyze the persons and situations they encounter in social work practice, giving deeper meaning to the ecological perspective and helping to focus the performance component of social work.

Framework Elements

1. *All systems have general issues with which they must contend* (Garbarino, p. 28). All people, notwithstanding context, have needs that must be met in order for their lives to continue. Of course, some needs are more immediate and imperative than others, and, therefore, having them continue unmet is likely life-threatening. The attempt to have needs met is an ongoing, life-sustaining process with which groups, families, and even organizations and communities struggle. The issues are usually in the following areas: (1) In the needs of the system which must be met; (2) in the transitions the systems pass through; and (3) in the interactions with other systems which are in touch with the original system (Germain and Gitterman, 1980; Pincus and Minahan, 1973, p. 14).

All systems also pass through inevitable life transitions. For example, children are born; the elderly die; children in families are raised and leave the nest; support groups become cohesive only to disintegrate at a later date; communities gain and lose their economic bases and organizations accomplish goals that lead them to new purposes and directions. Transitions are simply another example of the ongoing nature of living systems and their certainty is indisputable.

Systems, regardless of their size, also interact with other systems and the interactions are noteworthy because new conditions are created based upon the interaction. No system is able to live without interaction with other systems. People cannot exist alone, nor can groups live without the interaction of their members. Interaction is the "stuff" of living systems. Needs, transitions, and interactions all suggest activity in systems—new situations, new conditions, and even new problems.

The Palazola family illustration offers an example of this first component of the framework. The family is under stress brought on by ordinary and inevitable changes in the family system. The issues the Palazola family deals with—children growing up, the mother examining her role, the father reaching back to more comfortable times—are living, breathing issues from which no family is immune.

We can use our knowledge about general issues families and other systems face to help us understand the Palazolas. We must not forget that this family is unique to all others with a personal history apart from other families. While we apply understanding of general issues, we cannot overlook how unique systems experience their needs, their transitions, and their interactions.

2. *All systems are at risk.* A system may not get its needs met, it may not pass adequately through transitions, and it may have unsuccessful, unsatisfactory, or dysfunctional interactions with other systems. In other words, "things" happen. No human being, no family or group avoids pitfalls, problems, or barriers as long

as one is alive or as long as a family or group exists. Seeing systems as potential at risk is not a cloaked attempt to find a reason for failure or a way to blame. The view allows the social worker to analyze a system in order to assist its forward motion or to become nonexistent. "Risk factors have been used for centuries to predict the probability of damage—first by shop owners and insurers figuring the chances of losing precious cargo in unexplored waters" (Schorr, 1988, p. 24). The presence of risk factors in individuals or even in families does not necessarily result in damage. Their occurrence does point to an increased probability of damage and keys the social worker to weigh risk factors—not only in assessments upon which direct service interventions are based, but also on setting the groundwork for necessary changes in policies and programs (Schorr, 1988).

It is well to remember that systems are at risk not only because of internal threats, but also because of circumstances outside the system. Barriers to family functioning often come from societal conditions such as unemployment, racial and ethnic discrimination, and even natural disasters—earthquakes, droughts, tornadoes, and hurricanes. Alleviating all risk conditions in order to enhance the well-being of individual families is a broad and complex process.

3. *All systems have opportunity.* Just as there are inherent risks in systems, there are also inherent areas of growth and opportunity. All persons, their families, and groups have strengths. They may lie in the physical prowess of an individual or in the enduring traditions of family life. Newly formed groups may have opportunities because of able leadership or because of a clearly defined sense of purpose shared by all its members. There are countless opportunities for growth in systems, even in systems in which stress is cumulative and resources are limited. Both risk factors and opportunity factors represent bases for predictions. Risk factors predict damage while opportunity factors predict growth and development. Both need to be considered in order to build an effective framework for the analysis of systems.

4. *All systems are on a continuum of risk to opportunity.* A continuum represents both extremes as well as all places between the extremes. Theoretically, there are total risk conditions and total opportunity conditions. In the real, living world, neither of these two extremes exists. If only risk factors emerged, the system becomes inert and ceases to exist. On the other hand, if only opportunity factors are present, a perfect human being in a perfect world would dawn. Common sense warns of that impossibility. Therefore, what remains are the multitude of places between the two extremes. Our framework for analysis helps you position systems on a continuum, not to pigeonhole them, but to help you visualize them in their complexity and variety with potential for both growth and destruction.

5. *Social work focuses upon essential systems.* Pincus and Minahan (1973, p. 54) helped conceptualize the work of social work generalists by defining the systems with which social workers come in contact as they deliver services to people. "Each social worker must decide what his purposes and relationships should be in working with all the various people he encounters. He needs to be clear about who will benefit from his change efforts, who has given him sanction to work for change, who will need to be changed or influenced, and whom he will need to work with in order to achieve different goals in his change efforts." The systems of concern to the generalist are conceptualized as: (1) the change system, (2) the client system, (3) the focal system, and (4) the action system.

Systems of Concern to the Generalist

1. *Change System.* The *change system* is the agency or organization with which the social worker practitioner (change agent) is affiliated. *Change agents* are those persons employed by the change system to help clients meet their goals. A change agent may be the social worker or a counselor, psychologist, or other helping professional. For our discussion, however, we will be writing of social workers as change agents. As agents of change in organizations and agencies, social workers are professionals first, and, as such, are bound by professional values and ethics and educated in a common core. Change agents carry with them their professional status into the organizations in which they are employed. The settings in which social workers engage in practice are of immense variety, but as a general rule, these organizations and agencies are governed by boards, funding sources, laws, policies, by-laws, and so on. In other words, social workers, unless they are lone practitioners, practicing privately as entrepreneurs, work within the boundaries of a given agency or organization. As such, the work in which a social worker engages is influenced by the organization because the organization may pay the worker's salary and always maintains some sort of contract with the worker. Even in the face of this, social workers often engage in changing the very organizations in which they practice.

Pincus and Minahan (1973) point out how important the relationships are that social workers have within their agencies and organizations. Work relationships can have significant impact upon those employed there. If people are demoralized in an organization, that negative influence, inevitably, is felt by the people who need and qualify for services. Likewise, an organization in which people experience positive regard, good working conditions, decent salaries, and good supports pass on their good fortune through better services to recipients.

The change system is more than the social work generalist. The system represents the relationships the practitioner has within the agency, the policies and procedures of the agency, the climate and ambiance of an agency, and many other factors that influence how work is actually carried out in social service and social work agencies and organizations.

2. *Client System.* The *client system* is defined as the person or persons who will be helped or service rendered by the change system. Client systems are individuals, groups, families, communities, and organizations. Sometimes the client system requests help. A family makes an appointment at a family service agency because of a problem with an adolescent. The family begins contact with an agency and a social worker on a completely noncoercive and open basis. We call such client systems *voluntary*. At other times, persons with whom we work are strongly encouraged to see a social worker, much in the way a family practitioner

may refer a patient to a cardiologist. The patient does not have to go, but is under a very real pressure to see the cardiologist.

Social workers can be employed in agencies and organizations that have a social-control function in society. In other words, social workers work in courts, in jails, or with persons who have committed crimes or are suspected of committing crimes. We call clients who are ordered to work with us *involuntary* clients. *Involuntary* clients are: (1) parents of abused and neglected children; (2) adolescent status offenders; (3) criminal offenders; (4) agencies that are regulated (nursing homes and group homes), and (5) communities mandated to provide certain services.

Pincus and Minahan (1973) call such clients "potential" clients. More recently, others use the client definition, but acknowledge that service delivery differs significantly from service delivery to voluntary clients (Rooney, 1988, pp. 131–140). Throughout the book, we refer to both *voluntary* and *involuntary* clients, and as we discuss the steps in the change process, we describe differences between the two types of client systems.

3. *Focal System.* The *focal system* is defined as the person or persons who must change in order to meet the client system's goals. The focal system is referred to as the target system by Pincus and Minahan. We prefer the term "focal" to avoid stereotyping the people who must change. Our change efforts are directed toward persons or groups influencing client systems in such a way that change for the client is meaningless unless change in other arenas takes place as well. A clear example of a *focal* system is the teacher in whose classroom a child who is having problems in school is placed. The child tells the school social worker that her teacher does not call on her; she sits in the back of the room shy and fearful of saying something wrong, and the teacher's disregard of the child further solidifies the child's view that she is not a good student. The teacher must change her attitude in order for the child to see some progress. In this case, the teacher is a part of the focal system.

Another example involves a group of homeless people who are part of the Homeless Union advocating for decent housing and accessible social services. In order for the needs of the homeless to be met, the city will have to provide more shelters on a temporary basis and must work toward long term solutions in the development of safe, clean, decent and affordable housing for low-income people. In this case, the head of the Housing Authority or Department of Housing in the city is the focal system.

It may appear that the focal systems and client systems can be identical (Pincus and Minahan, 1973). Yet, as social workers we must take into account other systems outside of the client. The contextual issues for the client system will help guide you in identifying other systems that may make up the focal system. Therefore, the focal system and the client system cannot be one in the same. Who must change? This helps us avoid blaming the victim.

The focal system must be a person or persons. The focal system cannot be an "it"—the policy, the legislature, the economic picture. Who writes the policy? Who in the legislature can pass this bill? Who can find a job for this client? By naming a person, we focus our attention on who must change to help meet the client system's goal.

4. *Action system.* Although change efforts are focused toward the focal system, the social work generalist does not work in isolation separated from other people (Pincus and Minahan, 1973, p. 63). In fact, there are many others who may need to be involved when working with client systems. After all, the lives of the people with whom one is working are interrelated with others. Like the client system, the social worker is not isolated.

In order to produce effective change, other people and groups sometimes are involved in the work. They are called the *action system*. They may influence the client system to become engaged in the work; they may be the persons or group with whom the social worker gains sanction or permission in order to work with the client. For example, a social worker in a school district may want to begin a series of substance prevention groups. In order to do so, she works with support from the school superintendent in the district, and, on the other end of the spectrum, she may have the support and cooperation of student leaders who can influence other students to participate. The social worker's preparatory work may include a number of persons who will not be recipients of service, but certainly are central in the effort to help the groups to form and to continue.

The four systems—client system, change system, focal system, and action system—are all utilized when the generalist social worker is working with and on behalf of others. It is important for the social worker to understand the extent of involvement as well as the functions of both the clients and of those who influence and in some way impinge upon the social work process.

Through this systems approach, we are able to gain a clearer understanding of just who the people are who are a part of our clients' world and who, of those people, need to be worked with directly or indirectly in order for the change to happen. Naming systems and specific persons in them with whom we must interact helps us delineate the tasks we need to accomplish. If we know who people are and what their positions and roles are in relation to our client systems, then we are better able to understand what needs to be done to effect change.

RESOURCES AS RISKS AND OPPORTUNITIES

No person, family, group, or organization can function separately and autonomously without the interaction and cooperation of other systems. Understanding resource systems helps the generalist to identify persons, places, and means to help our client systems meet their goals and accomplish their tasks. While organizing our generalist tasks around an ecological or systems perspective gives us a better understanding of what we need to do and with whom we need to interact, there is yet another consideration that informs our work. Looking back to the framework for planned change, consider the first point: *All systems have general issues, situations, and so on with which they must contend.* Contending with problems and issues implies interaction with outside systems—that is, systems other than the identified system. In other words, a family relies on many systems in its social world in order to meet its needs, accomplish life tasks, and interact with other individuals, families, groups, and organizations.

Resource Systems

Some of the systems with which families and individuals interact serve as *resources*—that is, they can be seen as *opportunities*—while other systems seem to drain or impede a person's accomplishing life tasks. These systems are *barriers* which may make the resource system inadequate, placing the client system *at risk*. We rely on resource systems to help us meet our life tasks in our complex, postindustrial world. We turn to Pincus and Minahan (1973) for their discussion of *resource systems*. Pincus and Minahan name three different resource systems: *informal resources, formal resources,* and *societal resources.* A discussion of each follows.

Informal resource systems consist of our family, friends, acquaintances, and sometimes bartenders or hairdressers, natural helpers. These are persons with whom we come into contract on a fairly regular basis who can help with many of the day-to-day life tasks that all persons face. Informal resources provide advice, emotional support, information, concrete services, such as money and furnishings, and babysitting as well as access to other systems. Informal resources may include traditions, rituals, and cultural aspects of a person's life.

Consider the type of support that a woman may receive after the death of her husband. Depending upon the cultural context, she may receive support from the

Family, friends, and neighbors are informal resource systems.

clergy, extended family, and acquaintances. Church members may prepare meals for her and her family after the funeral. Telephone calls, letters, cards and flowers offer sympathy and support from other acquaintances. The custom in our society of allowing a funeral procession to have the right of way on a highway or street is a community response to the death of a community member. These actions and goods may be limited, but they offer the bereaved woman the knowledge that others care and that her loss is recognized not only by loved ones but also by strangers in the community. These supports are types of activities that are derived from the informal resource system.

Not everyone has an extensive informal resource system. In fact, in working with many clients, we find that it is important to understand the breadth of informal resource systems. Persons who try to function in our complex society without the informal resources do so at a great disadvantage. For example, single parents are at a great disadvantage in the work place if they must take days off from work or make child-care arrangements to replace the informal resources. The absence or scantiness of an informal resource system requires clients to rely more upon themselves. What if the woman whose husband died had few informal resources? Consider—if the clergy who was called did not know the woman and had never met her husband, there would have been no church group to provide comfort at the time of the funeral. Perhaps the woman's friends and acquaintances were far away in another city where she and her husband had previously lived, and therefore, she received little personal condolence. She faces her loss completely on her own. Without adequate informal resources, her healing from her loss is slower and fraught with more problems and setbacks in general. It is common for social work generalists to assist people to activate, strengthen, and sometimes replace their informal resources.

At-Risk Conditions or Barriers to Informal Resources

Let us move from the previous example into a new scenario. A family moves from out of state to a new community where the husband begins a new job as a middle-management employee in a major corporation. The family is financially secure. However, they lack informal resources that cannot be purchased. As part of the stress of the move and change of climate, the husband becomes ill and is hospitalized for a period of two weeks. The wife has extra duties—learning a new community, enrolling the children in school—while at the same time agonizing about her husband. Clearly, this is a time when informal resources, family, and friends would be very critical. Yet, because this family is new to the community, the family and friends are not accessible.

In some communities, fear of crime, coupled with high mobility, results in anonymity even in neighborhoods. People are afraid to ask for help or show any weakness. In such cases, the informal resource system has potential, but it is not in a usable form. Low-income, high-mobility neighborhoods are vulnerable to such conditions.

Informal resources may prove to be inadequate because people experiencing problems may be ashamed or unable to turn to friends. Consider a teenage girl who becomes pregnant and, in her opinion, loses the resource of her parents because she is ashamed and afraid of what they may say or do. The resource is not really lost, but it certainly becomes inaccessible.

An additional barrier exists when the informal resource systems are not equipped or trained to meet people's needs in a crisis situation. Easy answers bordering on "pop psychology" do not work in the complex situations in which people find themselves. A neighbor hanging over the backyard fence advising Mrs. Jones on her marriage does not replace marriage counseling. Perhaps the neighbor has only her life experience and her relationship with her husband as the sole source of her information. Her advice may, in fact, create more stress and difficulties with Mrs. Jones's marriage. At other times when there is a crisis, family, friends, and neighbors may be drawn into the crisis and be unable to provide an objective, helpful response. Therefore, the informal resource system cannot meet the client system's needs.

In general, informal resources provide us with the basic day-to-day help we need to complete life tasks in the normal ebb and flow of life. Yet there are times informal resources prove inadequate simply because they do not exist, or the situation may be beyond what the person in crisis wants to share with a family. Finally, the problems facing the client may be beyond the means of the informal resource system.

Case Example 3.3 illustrates how greatly informal resource systems are needed, even in families that seem to be financially secure.

Formal Resource Systems

The *formal resource system* consists of organizations or groups that provide an individual person power through membership. For example, persons in industrial societies have memberships in groups that assist them in accomplishing their life tasks. Labor unions are good examples of membership groups that ideally represent the needs of the workers for better pay, health insurance, and protection within the work place.

Clients use formal resources such as parent-teacher organizations, block clubs, and governing boards with agencies and institutions. An interesting example of a client's use of a formal resource involves adolescents placed in residential treatment programs who are encouraged to participate in formal self-governing boards. A residential treatment agency may afford a young person the opportunity to hold an office, to participate in planning trips and excursions, and to organize work duties. Such participation helps the individual as well as the group the individual represents to build self-confidence and to develop skills necessary for successful living.

Professional social workers also use formal resource systems. The National Association of Social Workers is the key formal, professional resource. Membership in NASW affords an individual social worker more influence on social legislation and improving programs and services to clients, as well as helps the social worker maintain professional standards of practice. Individual social workers can also purchase liability insurance, life insurance, and other benefits by belonging to a larger

CASE EXAMPLE 3.3

Donna Hansen

Donna Hansen is forty-five years old. Her parents, who are seventy-eight and eighty years old, live down the street. Their health is deteriorating; in fact, her father is now hearing-impaired. Donna is married to a successful insurance executive who travels a great deal and spends many hours at his office and in board meetings. He provides a good income for the family. Donna, herself, is a third-grade teacher. She loves her work and has been employed for most of the last twenty years except when she was pregnant with her two children and when they were infants. Her children, eighteen and nineteen years old, are now in college. Her daughter attends a prestigious Ivy League school. She is a brilliant scholar and plans to continue her education for years to come. Her son is an engineering student at a large midwestern university. Annual college tuition runs in the thousands of dollars. Although the family is well off, their expenses are very high. Donna needs to work. Besides, she is a teacher and wants to work. However, she is also a mother, daughter, and wife. All of her roles are demanding.

Donna worked hard to help her children through some stormy adolescent years. Although her son is doing very well, there were a few years when both she and her husband were not sure whether they had failed or succeeded as parents. Raising their son was an onerous task. Donna was happy to see the children leave for college, but at the same time found herself missing her daughter, who had acted as an important support for her. Her mother also was a support, but in recent years had major health problems and was not available as she once had been when the children were younger. Donna was a resource system for all members of her family and some of her family members were support systems for her.

At this point in her life, Donna feels she has nothing left to give and no support coming in to help her. She feels depleted. Her parents need her, yet she wants to continue working; in fact, her dream had been to go on for a higher degree once the children left home. Her children's college costs, however, are so astronomical that she has put that dream away, much to her own discomfort and unhappiness. She and her husband have an adequate relationship, but his support has always been mostly in the area of financial provision. A once rich and complex informal resource system seems to be at risk as more and more pressures impinge upon it.

group. The professional journal, newsletter, and the *NASW News* help keep social workers informed of trends in practice as well as potential employment opportunities.

Even the most articulate and knowledgeable individual social worker appearing before a congressional committee presenting his or her own ideas does not have the influence one does when representing an organization with a huge membership. While the legislators might listen to an "expert," the fact that the person may be speaking for 125,000 professional social workers exercises considerable clout.

At-Risk Conditions and Barriers to Formal Resources

Unfortunately, formal resources are not often available to those who need them the most. Service workers in low-paying jobs without benefits may not have

Caring for aging parents may raise resource system questions for their children.

labor unions to represent them. They are left on their own without health insurance and virtually little or no job security. Domestic workers, working in private homes, have no organization to represent them. Child-care center workers are women who spent years raising other people's children and keeping other people's houses and do not have the opportunity for collective bargaining. Past overt sexual and racial discrimination has kept many groups and individuals from obtaining membership in labor unions and other professional organizations because they do not have the "sheepskin." In addition, people may fail to join formal resource systems because they feel unwelcome and because they do not recognize the need for the potential benefits that membership might provide them.

Discrimination, racism, and sexism all contribute to the creation of barriers in formal resources. Membership groups, although they serve to meet people's needs, also can be designed to keep people out so that needs do not get met. Not so long ago, labor unions discriminated against African-Americans, and, by so doing, protected the jobs of the white majority. A gay man who wishes to join the ROTC in his college or university will have a very difficult time participating because of overt discrimination based on sexual orientation. Women have been kept from joining many organizations and labor unions that would have benefited them, but sexist policies kept them out.

We are now more aware of sexism, racism, and discrimination, but they continue to persist and affect the formal organizations of society. We need to be aware of the masked, subtle forms of discrimination and racism. Case Example 3.4 helps to define this barrier.

Societal Resources

Societal resources are the agencies and services which help us manage in our daily lives. A complex society with a large population calls for societal resources that benefit everyone. These resources are usually delivered through large bureaucracies and are designed to meet the needs of specific groups with specific needs or problems.

Given our capitalistic society, a person's place of employment is a major societal resource. Societal resources also range from services provided by police and fire departments to education systems, hospitals, and social welfare organizations and agencies.

All societal resources have eligibility criteria whether they are general or highly specific. For example, in order to use the fire department's firefighters, one needs to have an identified need (a fire). Using the education system requires one to fit into one's particular program or age category. Places of employment require special skills or the ability to learn such skills. Working persons are also expected to follow general rules of the organization, factory, school, or wherever they are employed.

At-Risk Conditions or Barriers to Societal Resources

Societal resources require persons wishing to use them to meet eligibility criteria. Not all persons who need societal resources are able to meet criteria. For example, a family with large expenses may need the special free-lunch program offered in a school district. However, the family income is too high and the children do not qualify. Free lunches might greatly assist the family, but it is not able to use them.

Societal resources are not as readily available to various ethnic or cultural groups because of barriers in service delivery. For example, an agency that does not

---

CASE EXAMPLE 3.4

Juan Ortega

Juan Ortega, a carpenter, joins a carpenter union. Some years back, Juan's father was not permitted to join because he was Hispanic. Now Juan can join, but he is low on the seniority list. When the union calls carpenters out on jobs, the most experienced are called first. Juan misses out on many jobs because he is still reaping the results of past discrimination. Although Juan is a highly skilled carpenter, having learned his trade, in part, from his father, no consideration is given to the many years of discrimination that his father faced and, in a round-about way, but very real way, Juan also faces.

provide in home services to families may exclude many families who, because of their cultural habits and beliefs, are unable to come to an office and voluntarily make an appointment for help. Services need to be organized free of cultural bias in which language and the affirmation of traditions are recognizable components of the delivery system.

Societal resources may not be accessible to those who need them. Transportation is a major problem in getting to agencies and services, not only in rural areas but also in urban settings. The hours an agency is open and its location in relation to those to whom it is supposed to deliver services further influence accessibility.

Those who are the most vulnerable with the least influence and political power have fewer societal resources. Homeless people fight to be counted in the census, while the incarcerated have almost no voice in even their own living conditions. Agencies that serve vulnerable populations have a difficult road to follow because their resources are so limited and their services are the first to be severed.

Societal resources may exist but are not known to those in need and the absence of this information is a further barrier to their use. Prevention programs for substance abuse, child abuse, and spouse abuse may be available in a community, but unless potential users know about the programs, they are largely ineffective.

Accessing existing services to clients is an enormous challenge in social work. An entire field of service information and referral has grown up to meet this need.

Using societal resources may cause further problems and barriers in a person's life just by virtue of the fact of having used the service (Pincus and Minahan, p. 7). A societal resource may, in fact, add to the problems, such as creating a dependency or confusing the client system. For example, the Smith family has multiple problems, including substance abuse, teen pregnancy, truancy, and marriage problems. They are being served by four different agencies, each putting different demands and expectations on them. The family becomes even more con-

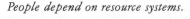

People depend on resource systems.

fused and frustrated, not knowing what or whom to believe, whose advice to take, or what path to follow. Even our own professional expertise can get in the way of effectively using societal resources.

CONCLUSION

In this chapter we have reviewed material from psychology, sociology, anthropology, the systems approach, and the ecological perspective to help you organize what you know into a plan for generalist social work practice. The framework for planned change is a step in preparing you for actual involvement in the change process with client systems, focal systems, and action systems. The overall purpose of this chapter is to help you use your knowledge base so that you can become an effective helping person.

Learning to become a generalist social worker is a building-block process. First, you must understand the purposes of social work, followed by the values and ethics that guide our work. Next, the knowledge base must be understood, accompanied with ways of organizing that knowledge for helping. The framework for planned change is your blueprint for using knowledge. We ended this chapter with a brief discussion of the resources that you call upon as you begin the process of change.

References

Biddle, Bruce J., and Thomas, Edwin. (1966). *Role Theory*. New York: Wiley.

Cartwright, Dorwin, and Zander, Alvin. (1968). *Group Dynamics; Research and Theory*. New York: Harper & Row.

Cherry, R. (1989). *Discrimination: Its Impact on Blacks, Women, and Jews*. Lexington, MA: Lexington Books.

Chess, Wayne, and Norlin, Julia. (1988). *Human Behavior and the Social Environment*. Boston: Allyn & Bacon. p. 105.

Erikson, Erik H. (1963). *Childhood and Society*, 2nd ed. New York: Norton.

Etzioni, Amitai. (1961). *A Sociological Reader on Complex Organizations*. New York: Holt, Rinehart and Winston.

Garbarino, James. (1982). *Children and Families in the Social Environment*. New York: Aldine, pp. 21 and 28.

Garvin, Charles, and Seabury, Brett. (1984). *Interpersonal Practice in Social Work: Processes and Procedures*. Englewood Cliffs, NJ: Prentice Hall, pp. 38 and 42.

Germain, Carol B. (ed.). (1979). *Social Work Practice, People and Environments, An Ecological Perspective*. New York: Columbia University Press, pp. 6–7.

Germain, Carol B., and Gitterman, Alex. (1980). *The Life Model of Social Work Practice*. New York: Columbia University Press, p. 4.

Hall, Richard. (1972). *Organizations: Structure and Process*. Englewood Cliffs, NJ: Prentice Hall.

Hartman, Ann, and Laird, Joan. (1983). *Family-Centered Social Work Practice*. New York: Free Press, pp. 8, 76, and 81.

Holland, John. (1950). "Contrasting Types of Group Relationships." In Leo Haak (ed.), *Source Book for Effective Living*. East Lansing, MI: Michigan State University Press.

LeVine, Elaine, and Sallee, Alvin. (1992). *Listen to Our Children: Clinical Theory and Practice,* rev. ed. Dubuque, IA: Kendall/Hunt.

Luft, Joseph. (1984). *Group Processes, An Introduction to Group Dynamics,* 3rd ed. Palo Alto, CA: Mayfield, p. 2.

Mead, George Herbert. (1982). *Mind, Self, and the Society: Unpublished work of George Herbert Mead.* Chicago: University of Chicago Press.

Merton, Robet King. (1968). *Social Theory and Social Structure.* New York: Free Press.

Mills, C. Wright. (1959). *The Sociological Imagination.* London and New York: Oxford University Press, p. 7.

Minnesota Home-Based Family Parent-Provider Training Manual. (1988). St. Paul, MN: Author.

Minuchin, Salvador. (1974). *Families and Family Therapy.* Cambridge, MA: Harvard University Press.

Pavlov, I. P. (1927). *Conditioned Reflexes.* London: Oxford University Press. (Reprinted by Dover, New York, 1960).

Piaget, Jean. (1970). *The Origins of Intelligence in Children.* New York: International Universities Press.

Pincus, Allen, and Minahan, Ann. (1973). *Social Work Practice: Model and Method.* Itasca, IL: F. E. Peacock, pp. 7, 14, 54, and 63.

Rooney, Ronald. (1988). "Socialization Strategies for Involuntary Clients." *Social Work.* March 1988, pp. 131–140.

Schorr, Lisbeth. (1988). *Within Our Reach.* New York: Doubleday, p. 24.

Skinner, B. F. (1974). *About Behaviorism.* New York: Knopf.

Warren, Roland. (1978). *The Community in America.* Chicago: Rand McNally.

Wilson, William J. (1987). *The Truly Disadvantaged, the Inner City, the Underclass, and Public Policy.* Chicago: University of Chicago Press.

Zinn, Maxine, and Eitzen, D. Stanley. (1987). *Diversity in American Families.* New York: Harper & Row, p. 139.

Generalist Roles, Skills, and Process

OVERVIEW

In this chapter, we identify the primary social work roles and the skills related to each system. In addition, we explain the "Crystal Model: Process of Planned Change," a systems approach to change.

Social work roles indicate what social workers do. *Role* is a term drawn from sociology and is used widely in all the social sciences. And, of course, it is also a term used in the theater. Behavior, dress, and physical appearance are linked to roles. For example, when we see a surgeon dressed in a surgical top and pants, we have expectations of his or her behavior. The behavior becomes the predominant definition of the surgeon's role.

A role also implies the concept of *reciprocity.* Roles are enacted in relationship to other roles and are dependent on others' roles. An actor plays a role, but that role is meaningless without other characters and an audience. Likewise, the surgeon depends on the patient for the fulfillment of his or her role.

An additional way to understand the concept of role is to consider roles in relationship to the systems social workers use in their work. For example, social workers use a variety of roles within the change system. Social workers switch roles according to client needs. In other words, social workers' roles are dependent on client needs. In addition to the roles social workers assume when working with clients, social work roles include work with other social workers and helpers in the change system who, directly or indirectly, affect the client system.

Skill is the ability to do something well. Social workers act within roles, and this, in itself, demands particular behaviors (talking to people, answering questions, giving information, and so on), and implicit in the actualization of a social work role is the prospect that the social worker will be competent and able to use interactional and analytic skills. A competent social worker is able to perform well in countless situations with a whole variety of client systems. Becoming a competent social worker means acting within social work roles and using social work skills. Defined in Chapter 1, interactional and analytic skills are the base from which more specific skills related to social work roles spring. The first part of this chapter is about social work roles and their associated skills.

The chapter ends with a description of the "Crystal Model: Process of Planned Change," introduced in Chapter 1. We expand on its definition, contrasting it to traditional problem solving and setting the stage for our presentation of each step in the Crystal Model, with its related roles and skills.

SOCIAL WORK ROLES AND SKILLS

In this section, we present the major generalist roles with the accompanying related skills for each. The main roles are social broker, advocate/activist, collaborator/networker, enabler, and conflict manager. We begin with the role of broker.

The Social Broker Role

Brokers act as agents between client systems and the resources in a community. They represent clients by discerning client needs. Utilizing their knowledge of what exists in the community, they link people to needed resources. The social broker role and its related skills are closely associated with a social service known as Information and Referral Services. Communities throughout the country provide services to clients and change agents related to available resources. Community Information and Referral Services are listed and described in a computerized data base. The United Way of America has developed the United Way of America Services Identification System I (UWASIS I) (United Way of America, 1972). The social work generalist can access information in most cities in this huge information base to find appropriate resources for the client system.

The familiar stock broker and real estate broker roles shed light on the social broker role. Real estate agents find out the buyers' needs, wants, and financial resources, and then they scout for an available house that seems right for the buyer. Stock brokers attempt to help buyers find the investments that fit their pocketbooks as well as their plans for the market.

Social brokers deal in broader issues than stock portfolios. They are concerned with many needs, transitions, and interactions of client systems. Sometimes client systems are large groups, or even communities, that seek major institutional responses and resources. Brokering at an organizational level is often accomplished by the social worker. Case Example 4.1 is offered as an example to illustrate brokering at an organizational level.

At other times, a client system may be a family with a premature infant who needs ongoing social and medical services. The hospital social worker identifies community resources for the family and informs the family of the continuing medical services in the health care system.

Social brokering may appear to be a cut-and-dried sort of activity. On the contrary, helping people find what they need requires definite expertise and is a major activity of social work generalists, calling forth our best social work skills.

CASE EXAMPLE 4.1
Pine River Treatment Center

The Pine River Treatment Center is a small, private residential care agency for adolescents that is in serious financial trouble. The center's bookkeeper made many errors, and Internal Revenue Service forms and reports were not completed in a timely and accurate fashion. The agency director was forced to fire the bookkeeper, but, unfortunately, the agency books were in such shambles, they could not afford the expensive financial services required to help the agency out of this difficult spot.

The case manager on staff, educated as a generalist, advised the agency director about Retired Senior Volunteer Program (RSVP). RSVP has a cadre of retired persons who volunteer their services and skills. At this point, several retired accountants and bookkeepers are eager to help put the agency back on the right track. The generalist social worker, who was well aware of social brokering at the organizational level, helped the agency find a solution to its difficult financial problems.

Social Brokering Skills

There are three primary skills associated with the social broker role. They are: (1) accessing resource systems, (2) linking between systems or agencies, and (3) follow-up skills. It is important to keep in mind that these skills are first found in our general framework of interactional and analytic social work skills. Social broker skills are more specifically defined in the context of each social work role.

Accessing Resource Systems

The ability to access resources is a significant skill employed by social work generalists. It is directed primarily toward individual and family client systems. Accessing skills require the generalist to have obtained considerable information about societal resources, particularly data about services' eligibility criteria.

After acquiring the knowledge of resources, the generalist must be able to help the client system use the appropriate resources. Interactional skills such as listening, responding, asking appropriate questions, and clearly informing client systems of what the community has to offer are components of the accessing skill.

Social work generalists prepare clients to receive services. Some services require clients to provide identification and documentation (birth records, death records, marriage licenses, and so on) to prove eligibility. The accessing skill includes helping clients understand why particular documentation is called for and helping them become prepared for questions generated from another resource in the community. Preparing the agency for the client system is another aspect of accessing skills. Clients may have special needs and unique characteristics, and if the agency understands the client system, the client's utilization of the resources will be enhanced.

Linkage Skills

Linkage skills are similar to accessing skills, but are directed toward linking larger systems or agencies to each other. Change systems must be linked in order to provide adequate services for client systems. The agency that has a contract with a state social services department to provide a particular service must stay linked in order to meet accountability and service criteria. For example, if an agency is unaware of procedural changes at the state level, and discovers too late that it must change part of its service delivery system in order to continue receiving state funds, the agency may be forced to close, thus eliminating a societal resource.

Analytic skills are important components in linkage. Understanding changes in procedures, budgets, and service delivery and how such changes influence services in other agencies, as well as direct service to clients make up the analytic elements in linkage skills. Likewise, the social worker needs interactional skills in order to interpret possible changes to the board and staff of the agency being effected by changes at the staff level. This means using excellent verbal and written communication skills to convey the changes.

Follow-Up Skills

Accessing resources for people and linking agencies to needed information and resources require follow-up on these activities. Follow-up is a skill associated with evaluation, a step in the Crystal Model. In fact, following up on whether a client system used a service, discerning its value and applicability to the client situation, and keeping track of such data characterizes evaluative work.

Requisite to follow-up skills are the two primary skills in social work practice: analytic and interactional skills. Three activities comprise follow-up skills: (1) collecting information from client systems regarding their use of the accessed or linked resource, (2) analyzing its fit with client system's needs, and (3) keeping track of the client system's further needs as well as the resource to which the client system was referred. The third activity demands that the social worker keep accurate records of his or her work so that another client system can benefit from past transactions between client systems and resource systems.

The Advocate/Activist Role

The advocate represents the interests of client systems and speaks and acts on behalf of others, while the activist organizes people to change laws, procedures, and institutions. Activists also work directly toward the removal of someone from public office or, conversely, work toward a particular person's election. The advocate and activist roles are complementary, and sometimes the terms are used simultaneously (Compton and Galaway, 1989).

Inherent in the advocate role is the fact that social workers are professionals who hold positions in the community often more favorable and powerful than the client systems whom they are representing. The social worker uses his or her position to advance the cause of the client system. Testifying in social service budget hearings at the state level is an activity taken on by the advocate. The advocate's purpose is to reduce the distance between those who have power and those who do not.

Activists are also advocates, but may use more direct strategies toward change. They understand the distance between those who have power and those who do not, and they engage in activities directly related to changing that balance (Corrigan and Leonard, 1978). Electing an ethnic minority person to public office who will more fairly represent constituents may be a goal for the activist.

Advocates work with all system sizes: individuals, families, groups, communities, and organizations. Advocacy on behalf of individuals and families is called *case advocacy.* Consider a family inadequately served by a health care facility. The case advocate speaks to the health care professionals to insist that the client system receive the care entitled to the family and, through her discussion, infers that this family represents many others who need more adequate care. In other words, *case advocacy* may lead to *cause advocacy.*

Cause advocacy refers to work on behalf of a whole group or community of unempowered people — for example, welfare mothers. Their needs as a group are spoken for at a state social services budget hearing in an effort to more fairly distribute societal resources.

Advocacy and Activist Skills

Skills in the advocacy and activist arena are not well developed in most social workers. O'Neil (1984) says, "Although social workers engage in some political activities, they are found generally to be ineffective in the political arena" (p. 325). While this may be true in general, at the time of this writing, one U.S. senator is a social worker, along with a number of congresspersons, mayors, and local elected officials. Although all social workers are not comfortable in the political arena, the National Association of Social Workers Code of Ethics guides us to create a more just society. One such way to work toward social justice is through the political process. Advocacy and activism involve redistributing resources in the community, and the roles that are manifested as a result of those activities are political roles. Politics concerns itself with how resources are developed, and social workers need political skills to bring about a more equitable redistribution of resources (Mahaffey and Hanks, 1982).

Advocacy and activist skills grow out of the analytic/interactional skill framework. What follows are the major advocate/activist skills.

Testifying

The advocate/activist is called upon to offer testimony in a number of arenas: state legislatures, court rooms, city councils, newspapers, television and radio stations, university classes, funding sources, and professional organizations.

Testimony must be well-researched, clearly and succinctly written, and presented orally in a manner that fits a particular audience. One must be able to analyze adequately the problem addressed. For example, if there is movement at the state level to cut Aid to Families with Dependent Children grants, it is important in giving testimony to include data on current expenditures, buying power, and the short- and long-term effects of budget reductions.

Good writing skills cannot be overemphasized in developing the skill of testifying. You may be asked to submit written testimony, and you must present your arguments for your position in a convincing manner. However, developing an argument on paper alone is usually not sufficient.

Giving testimony calls upon the advocate/activist to use all his or her persuasive powers. The testifier must convince the audience of the worthiness and justice of the testifier's point of view. As such, one's personal presence and speaking ability, similar to the litigator's oral skills, are of great importance in effective testifying.

Campaigning

Campaigning is primarily an interactional skill. The advocate/activist needs to convince a number of audiences that his or her cause is worthwhile. Therefore, what the advocate says must be persuasive. Presenting facts, opinions, values, and beliefs is part of political inducement. Political campaigns involve intensive organizational work as well as the ability to convey a message that can be understood by the public. Campaigning may also include convincing people to contribute financially to a candidate or a cause (Mahaffey and Hanks, 1982).

Not all social workers feel comfortable in the political domain, but there is little question that more of us need to be involved in redistributing resources to those most in need.

Boycotting/Demonstrating

At various times in a democracy, citizens must put pressure on systems in order to change them. Without civil rights activists in the 1960s, major civil rights legislation would not have become the law of the land. Holding on to these civil rights continues to be a struggle that social workers need to join.

Certain situations demand boycotts on the part of consumers, and social work generalists ought to be skilled in organizing such boycotts. Social workers in California and throughout the country joined with the United Farm Workers to boycott California grapes. The boycott brought recognition of the union and better working conditions for some farm laborers. Boycotting is a powerful activity in a consumer-oriented, capitalistic economy. Too often, social workers shy away from such system-changing behavior.

Organizing groups of people for marches, sit-ins, and public gatherings is a legitimate activity of the social work generalist. Letting the state legislature know the conditions of a constituency can have long-term and powerful effects. Older people join forces to let politicians know that they have needs they think the government ought to be involved in, and when they come out in huge numbers at demonstrations, the elected officials recall their demand to meet the needs of the voters. Remarkable legislation supporting medical services for the elderly has come about not because the elderly were unorganized, sitting at home; but be-

Organizing demonstrations is a powerful skill.

cause they were present in a large numbers at demonstrations all over the country and in Washington, D.C.

Negotiating

Within the advocacy role, social workers use their negotiating skills. Bringing opposing sides together, discussing differences, giving in on some points while holding fast on others, all in order to bring about change, are the components of negotiating. Interactional and analytic skills are the bases of negotiating. Listening to opposing sides and articulating concerns and positions assist the loosening of stalemates or, conversely, the gaining of resources for client systems. Clearly making our point known, stating how far we are willing to go, and then remaining committed to our cause are further hallmarks of the skilled negotiator (Folberg and Milne, 1988). All this implies an in-depth knowledge of the situation with which we are working, thus, analytic skills further explicate negotiating skills.

The Collaborator and Networker Roles

Bringing people together, finding commonalities among them, identifying interests and needs, and coordinating available resources fitting together to forge new helping systems for people are the part and parcel of the joint roles of collaborator and networker. The two roles are discussed together because their definitions are similar and because the skills called upon to enact both roles are shared.

Collaboration

Collaborative efforts are built on trust and mutual agreement, with people working in a joint effort to address problems. Social workers collaborate with each other to meet client's needs. Case Example 4.2 illustrates the concept of collaboration.

Networking

Networking occurs on three levels: (1) personal/professional/peer, (2) organizational, and (3) community. On a personal level, one may network with others at professional meetings—NASW, ABSW—or one may serve on community boards and participate in volunteer work with other agencies and have the opportunity there to network. Personal networking allows a social worker to establish informal linkages with key people in the community and in the professional world. One's own professional career may be enhanced through networking. In addition, personal networking helps a social worker gather resources for clients and may also help facilitate appropriate actions for the benefit of clients.

Networking at the peer level often begins during one's student years. These peer relationships often continue into professional life. Peer reviews that begin in

---

CASE EXAMPLE 4.2

Flynn Middle School

Della is employed at Flynn Middle School, which has received a special grant to develop a program for AIDS awareness in the schools. It is up to the social worker to call together a team of professionals and students in order to define the problem with which they are working, to develop materials to distribute for AIDS awareness, to decide on direct service activities, and, finally, to agree on project evaluation techniques. Della enlists the assistance of a number of people in the school: the head of the biology department, the school nurse, the school counselor, the art teacher, and the president and vice-president of the student council. Together they decide on the scope of the problem as it affects their middle school and decide to focus only on educational materials. Brochures and other teaching materials must be developed. The biology teacher agrees to present the medical material about AIDS, including etiology and the state of the search for a cure. The school nurse will obtain information regarding AIDS prevention, including safe-sex information. The social worker agrees to put the material together in a brochure, while the biology teacher takes on the additional responsibility of developing appropriate teaching materials. The art teacher agrees to do a layout for the brochure as well as to work on illustrations for the biology teacher's materials. The social worker is the catalyst who brings this group together in order to help meet student needs by developing an AIDS prevention program.

school sometimes continue into professional life in such arenas as peer consultation.

Representatives from agencies and organizations network. Agency people come together to discuss critical social issues such as widespread substance abuse, increasing teen pregnancies, and school dropouts. They may share information regarding programs, services, and skills applicable to problems. They may also discuss gaps in services, discerning where new services are needed and where existing services can be altered. Networking vis-à-vis agencies and organizations has long-term positive results for client systems.

Networking within and among agencies leads us to understand more fully our clients' needs to network on their own behalf. In fact, an important component of networking extends to helping clients discern their networks, enhancing their own networks, and enlisting them in difficult times. Working with at-risk families involves identifying clients' social support networks so that after an intervention from a social agency is over, the client is left with a stronger support system to use in an ongoing way (Tracy, 1990, pp. 252–258).

At the community level, networkers tap into resources and systems to persuade people in key positions to involve themselves in a cause or a solution to a problem. A social worker may bring client systems' needs to the awareness of those in power in order to create additional helping systems for clients. It is not unusual for networkers to bring together factions in communities to work together to solve community problems.

Collaboration and Networking Skills

The skills that apply to collaboration and networking are: (1) identifying mutual goals, (2) analyzing strengths to develop relationships, (3) negotiating labor responsibilities, and (4) building coalitions. These four skills are more precise uses of all the primary skills: analytic, interactional, and action.

It is well to note here that both collaboration and networking do not rely only on the identified skills. And, because they are closely related to other roles—advocacy and social brokering, among others—the skills are used across roles. When one is engaged in a particular role, one is not limited only to the skills identified with that particular role. In fact, in actual practice, the social worker ought to call upon other skills from similar social work roles.

Identifying Mutual Goals

We know that collaboration and networking include the use of groups, and we call upon our analytic skills to discover through the group process just what our mutual goals are when we are collaborating and networking. The establishment of mutual goals is dependent on the ambience of the group. Group cooperation is an essential component of collaboration and networking and is reached through the establishment of working relationships (Compton and Galaway, 1989, p. 598).

Analyzing Strengths and Relationship Building

Group trust is an outcome of collaborative relationships. Trust involves knowing what one another's strengths and weaknesses are and disallowing differences to obstruct the work of the collaborator and networker. We respect differences rather than projecting blame to those who seem most different for what may not be accomplished in the collaborative effort. Then group trust can be obtained.

Relationship building includes the building of group power. Often when we work collaboratively, particularly when our focus is upon seemingly overwhelming social problems, we feel powerless against the tide that so often seems to run counter to social work aims. "We can only effectively carry out something we believe possible" (Compton and Galaway, 1989, p. 599). The reinforcement of individual strengths as well as the recognition of where one's authority lies defines group power. We need to use the power we already have to work toward our collective goals.

Negotiating Work Responsibilities

All collaborative and networking efforts demand a division of labor so that the agreed upon goals can be met. It is necessary to discover the strengths of those participating in the collaborative effort, as well as recognize potential sources of conflict and disagreement, before the actual work can be meted out. Dividing the labor calls for skillful handling of people's feelings while the social worker is working toward a quick resolution so that work can begin (Parsloe, 1981). When we know and recognize strengths, the division of labor seems to come about almost magically because we already know what we have to offer the group; and, if tasks are clearly delineated, then division of labor can be a natural process. However, when competition and conflict are present, there will be a vying for position in the hierarchy of the tasks. We noted earlier that skills are not divided equally among social work roles. For example, collaborative and networking efforts may call forth conflict-resolution skills that we usually associate with the role of conflict manager.

We may need to divide labor responsibilities among various professionals as we use the collaborator/networker role. Professionals from various arenas bring different perspectives on people and on how problems ought to be solved (Compton and Galaway, 1989, p. 600). When you read the section on conflict manager role, you will see that it is important to know how to resolve conflict even in seemingly collaborative arrangements. When such differences arise, conflict and competition follow closely behind. Unless differences are resolved, the cooperative effort fails, and the needs of the client system (the focus of our work) go unmet (Holder and Wardle, 1981, p. 124).

Coalition Building

The collaborator/networker may be called upon to develop longer-lasting groups that are able to cooperate and work together to form a united front on a given issue. Coalition building results in alliances that seem to last over time. Coalition building is most successful when focused on a single "burning" issue (Mchaffey and Hanks, 1982).

The interactional skills that underlie coalition building skills are manifested in group meetings and include: (1) focusing on a single issue, (2) limiting discussion of other areas on which there may not be agreement, and (3) reaching consensus on direct actions in which the group is to involve itself.

The act of forming coalitions implies forming alliances with groups representing various purposes and backgrounds but which share a common interest. Group differences demand that the collaborator focus on what brings a coalition together, clarifying and reinforcing the issue that brought coalition members together in the first place.

Because of the various nature of coalition members, group discussion tends to wander off in disparate areas. Unless guided by a strong leader, the group differences will emerge and the coalition the social worker is trying so hard to solidify will fall apart. It is essential to keep differences at a minimum.

Coalition building is accomplished for a purpose; therefore, the collaborator/networker needs to work quickly toward agreement on what the coalition will do now that it is formed. Only direct action can keep a coalition together. If there is no action, the differences within the coalition will emerge quickly. Direct action with immediate success is, of course, the most sought-after outcome. An example of coalition building explains more clearly what is involved in the skill.

The Enabler Role and Skills

In the enabler role, social workers work directly with individuals, groups, and families whose concerns lie in their interactions with others as well as in their own personal adjustment to their situations. Enablers do just as the role describes: they seek to assist others to find their own strengths, to use their strengths on behalf of themselves and their families in order to bring about change and/or balance in their lives (Compton and Galaway, 1989).

The enabler's work is built upon a helping relationship with client systems. Sometimes we define enablers as counselors. Working with others regarding their emotional lives and their relationships with others is both interesting and complex. For example, enablers must be able to call upon analytic skills to develop the understanding of a client who is experiencing troubling times. In addition, enablers must be particularly adept at using interactional skills.

We focus on several enabling skills that grow out of analytic and interactional skills and that seem essential to developing the helping relationship necessary to carry out this important social work role. Those skills are: (1) empathy, (2) focusing and paraphrasing, (3) questioning, and (4) partialization. We spend proportionately more time discussing empathy than the other enabler skills because we believe it is one of the cross-cutting skills in social work. Empathy is fundamental to each role that social workers enact and its presence allows the other enabler skills to become manifest.

CASE EXAMPLE 4.3

Tri-County

During annual budgeting, the Health and Human Services Committee of the state legislature votes to reduce Medicaid funding overall and to eliminate Medicaid funds for abortions. Those who are interested in maintaining higher levels of payments for Medicaid are diverse, but add to that a diversity of groups that support choice, and forming a coalition appears to be an overwhelming task. Nonetheless, the social worker on staff at the Tri-County Welfare Reform Coalition, a volunteer organization with a mission to bring about social justice and funded by local church groups and grants from national foundations, attempts to do just that. The Welfare Reform Coalition is made up of people from various church groups, from welfare rights organizations, and from social service providers. Some are pro-choice; others are not. How can a consensus be found on this difficult issue?

The social worker brought the coalition together. Additionally, people from the medical establishment were invited to participate in an action because physicians and other health care providers expect deep cuts for their services. The social worker was well prepared for the meeting. She had written an agenda which was distributed to the participants as soon as they arrived for the meeting. It was a good turnout; nearly fifty people were present. The social worker began the meeting with a brief introduction of the problem they were facing: across-the-board cuts in Medicaid funding, affecting service providers and recipients alike. She hoped that by immediately naming the problem she would minimize the possibilities of pro-choice and antiabortion individuals arguing over their positions and thereby breaking up a very fragile coalition. She decided that by adhering to the agenda, focusing on the loss of funding, and leading the group to decide upon a direct action, all the while emphasizing their common mission—social justice—she might get a consensus on an action.

Indeed, within 30 minutes, the group decided on offering testimony to the Health and Human Services Committee the following week. Representatives from the various groups would choose one person to write and deliver testimony. The social worker would orchestrate the event at the state capitol, making sure of the exact time and meeting place. She also arranged transportation.

The action would not have been possible were it not for the social worker's quick and decisive actions. No time was given to divisiveness. The action itself further coalesced this group, and although all funds were not restored to Medicaid, a compromise was reached.

Empathy

Empathy refers to the human capacity to reach out to another, verbally and nonverbally, and to be closely in tune with the feelings of another person or groups of persons. Using empathy allows us to understand others in the true light of their human dignity and worth.

Inherent in empathy is the ability to make an appropriate response to another's cue, a response that conveys understanding to the other. Like all skills, empathy requires appropriate action that is clear and straightforward. Although we are concerning ourselves now with the emotions and feelings of others in our discussion of empathy, we still cannot rely only on our feelings to identify whether or not we are skilled at empathy. Only those with whom we are working can attest to our skills, because the actualization of the skill is absolutely dependent on how another person has received our efforts.

Empathy calls for sensitivity and interest in the person with whom one is engaged. We try to "tune in" to another or to "be with" someone (Shulman, 1979). We attempt to experience the client system's world through their eyes. Characteristics of empathy include: (1) unconditional acceptance, (2) openness in receiving, (3) recognizing the double layers of messages (their content and their feeling components), (4) accurate processing of information, and (5) clear and concrete feedback to the other (Rogers, 1951).

Unconditional acceptance means accepting another's humanity, ways of relating, values, and all the nuances of another that make up a person's character and personality. Unconditional response does not mean one must like everyone, nor does it mean one must approve of anyone. However, one must be able to acknowledge another's very being and find it comprehensible. Unconditional acceptance is only achieved through a deep understanding of human behavior within a humanistic, interactional perspective. It is difficult to achieve and is based, to a large extent, on one's level of self-knowledge and one's degree of comfort with people of all kinds.

Openness in receiving another's communication grows out of unconditional acceptance. When one can truly acknowledge another's point of view and the validity of someone else's experience, then one may be open to receive his or her communication. Again, openness is based on acceptance of oneself, with all of one's own unfinished emotional "business."

All communications have two layers: content and feeling. Hartman and Laird (1983) call the layers digital communication and analogic communication. We talk about what happens to us, events in our lives, and circumstances that brought us to the condition or situation in which we find ourselves. We relay problems and even make interpretations of those problems. All the while we are communicating, we are also bespeaking our emotions, our feelings about what we are saying, about what happened to us, and about how we got where we are. Hearing the double layers of all messages is a critical component of empathy.

We need to accurately process the information we receive from others in order for empathy to be felt and used by another. Processing the information is done both internally and in a give-and-take with the person with whom we are engaged. We think quickly about what the client has said, trying to understand the content of the message and the depth of feeling. We may confirm our understanding of the message by responding. For example, if a client relates a painful experience, the social worker must acknowledge that client's pain in a verbal response. If a client's mother has died, and he is relating his feelings around his loss, the social worker may say, "It sounds as though your loss has brought you a great deal of pain," or "You are feeling alone and adrift in the world." Each of these responses may acknowledge the client's profound feelings at the loss of his mother, but only he knows whether or not the social worker has accurately processed his message. He may agree or disagree and usually indicates this by going on with more discussion, correcting the social worker's response and clarifying his feelings, or he may simply stop trying to express his feelings because he does not feel he has been heard. The client may also feel the social worker has reached him, but being understood is such a new experience that he may need to stop the interchange because it is fraught with too much feeling. Again, if one is processing a client's message correctly, one will understand the meaning of the client's response.

Choosing the exact feedback to give to a client is a complex task. One does respond verbally, but one must be accurate in the timing—that is, one needs to create the feedback that the client is ready to hear at that time. Helpful feedback can only be achieved if the preceding components of empathy are already set in place. Other conditions involved in accurate feedback are knowing when to speak and when not to and choosing the words with which the client can understand and identify.

It is well to stay away from professional jargon. Social workers should use the sort of language that the other person is used to hearing. At the same time, one must be true to one's own identity. It would be ridiculous to take on a teenager's slang in order to "relate" to the young person. It would not be genuine, and the client would know this immediately.

Indeed, the response the social worker gives back to the client (feedback) needs to be genuine, verbally and nonverbally. One's verbal responses are genuine if one's words are one's own, neither condescending nor false. Perhaps more important than the verbal responses in reaching for genuineness are the nonverbal responses. Nonverbal response is communicated through behavior, "body language," eye contact, and facial expression. All of these give way to the depth of one's understanding and one's ability to be genuine. By behaving attentively, keeping appropriate eye contact, maintaining an interest in your client as though there is nothing more important in the entire world at that moment are the ways we transmit to our client systems our understanding and our genuine caring.

Focusing and Paraphrasing

Relationships with client systems must be grounded in empathy, but social workers need other interactional skills in order to help move the client system toward resolution or balance regarding the client's concerns. Focusing discussion with clients so that important issues are addressed while less significant ones are dropped assists the client system's forward movement. The social worker is able to focus with the client by paraphrasing what the client is saying, "using fresh words to restate the client's message concisely" (Hepworth and Larsen, 1986, p. 130). As enablers, social workers hear what is most important, allowing the client through focusing and paraphrasing to look intensely at a particular issue. The following interchange between a social worker and an individual client illustrates this point.

Focusing and Paraphrasing: An Illustration

Mike (client): Sometimes it's hard to gather my energy to continue talking to you. There are so many things that come into my mind when I'm driving here, and when I get here I think I can't tell you everything; it would take up

all the time we have, and I know that I'm not going to have money to continue seeing you, and yet I have to get some relief, and I have to know about
how I can help my son because he's still the most important person in the
world to me.

Vera (social worker): It's very hard for you to know what's bothering you
most, but you do know that you need to get your own feelings straightened
out so you can be a real support for your son.

The client's statement has many layers of meaning and concern. It is a statement that demands the enabler to focus upon what is most important and para-
phrase the key component of the message. She is able to do this by mentally
sorting through the statement and finding the center of his concern—his own
confusion and his fear that his confusion will impede his ability to be a good
father to the son he loves so much. By focusing and paraphrasing (in the context
of empathy), Vera, the social worker, helps Mike move toward resolution and
greater balance in his life.

Questioning

The art of questioning is a delicate one, calling for great skill. Questions must
be used to obtain information from clients for assessments, and questions must be
used to further the social worker's understanding of the situation, not to mention
the client's understanding. However, it is not recommended that social workers ask
too many questions—this approach does not succeed. Asking the right and the
relevant questons is the key.

There are generally two types of questions: closed questions and open questions. At times, one finds it necessary to ask closed questions. One may need specific information: age, date of birth, number of children—all sorts of background
information an agency may need to determine eligibility or program fit. Social
workers need to know when closed questions are appropriate and not bring closed
questioning into situations that really require open-ended questioning.

Open-ended questions encourage freer expression from clients. Hepworth
and Larsen (1986) tell us there are two kinds of open-ended questions: those that
allow for unstructured responses and those that call for structured responses.
Open-ended questions that call for unstructured responses may be stated in the
following ways: What would you like to talk about? How can I help you? The
client is free to begin anywhere and go anywhere with such an open question.

On the other hand, structured open-ended questions point a client in a particular direction or toward a particular problem: How did things go this week with
your son? The client is focused on his relationship with his son, but is free to go
anywhere within the confines of that particular structure. It may be important to
begin interactions with clients with questions, but as time with them increases,
questioning often becomes less useful.

Social workers need to be very careful about the use of questioning because
the skill is misused. Beginning social workers ask not only the wrong questions,
but far too many. Good questioning is based on social workers having sufficient

understanding of the profession's knowledge base in such a way that it can be used to further work with clients.

Partialization

Empathy, focusing, and paraphrasing and questioning all help us enable clients to partialize their concerns and problems. People who are in need of social work services have large concerns, many of them layered and often complex. Helping people separate concerns into manageable, solvable components is *partialization* (Shulman, 1991). The client gives the social worker a great deal of information, much of it regarding the weighty nature of the problem being worked on. The social worker helps the client dissect that overwhelming situation into parts that can be worked on with the client system.

When people are too overwhelmed by their own problems, they lose their hope for solving the problem. There are so many stresses, so many worries. It is up to the enabler to discover, through the use of enabling skills, the problems most pressing, to separate greater concerns from lesser concerns, and to help the client decide what is most important to begin work on. Partializing helps the client gain mastery over a situation because the situation becomes more manageable; it is not an all-encompassing fog that hangs over an entire life.

Partialization helps the client begin the work of problem-solving. Only after dividing a problem can one decide what part one ought to work on first. McMahon (1990, p. 32) urges social workers to work with clients to distinguish among what needs to be done first, second, third, and so on. She rates problems according to a change-potential score. Problems that can have immediate success ought to be focused on first, and those with the least chance of working out can be handled later. We believe this is a valid way to begin work with a client system, but it must be used with caution. Some problems, even after partialization, are so troublesome that no matter how difficult, they must be handled immediately. Child protection work demands that social workers partialize problems, but frequently they must first work with the problem that is the most dangerous and life-threatening to the child client.

The Conflict Manager Role

All system sizes experience conflict when they are in stress, and this is the condition most often experienced by clients who seek help from social workers. Social workers see clients during crises when the atmosphere is charged with emotion. Feelings are heightened; people are on edge; and conflict explodes (Bisno, 1988). Conflict stems from situations in which people think the resources they need and want are scarce. Fears generate around whether or not the scarce resources will be available, and fears give way to conflict.

We expect conflict in a heterogeneous culture marked by competing values, various cultures, and differing views of the world. Given our diversity, we cannot avoid conflict. What we must learn to do as social workers is manage conflict. There are three fundamental types of conflict: intrapersonal, interpersonal, and group conflict (Deutsch, 1973). Having an understanding of each sets the stage for the acquisition of skills an adept conflict manager must have.

Intrapersonal Conflict

Conflict experienced internally by an individual is *intrapersonal*. We are torn between choices, alternatives or courses of action. We are not sure which way to turn. Values may be in conflict; we may be trying to settle within ourselves what we think and feel is right or wrong. Every person experiences intrapersonal conflict, but it is inevitable when we are confronted with a crisis in our lives.

Interpersonal Conflict

Conflict between and among two or more people is *interpersonal*. The sources of conflict may be competition for scarce resources—time, money, attention, love—or disagreements based on conflicting values, norms, and expectation. People who live together in a family system inevitably experience interpersonal conflict. Parents disagree and argue; children are at odds with each other and their parents. As with intrapersonal conflict, interpersonal conflict is more likely to be present in stressful situations (Deutsch, 1973).

Group Conflict

Group conflict can exist both within a group itself (*intragroup conflict*) and between groups (*intergroup conflict*). To illustrate intragroup conflict, consider the morale of workers in an adult protective services unit. The social workers employed there are bickering; unit meetings are ladened with tension and backbiting. The social work supervisor recognizes the conflict and uncovers deep resentment about a variety of issues that boil down to stress reactions related to work overload. There are too many cases and not enough resources.

Intergroup conflict involves the same elements as interpersonal conflict but is even more complex because it includes conflict not only among individuals, but also among groups.

It is not unusual to find intergroup conflict in a neighborhood in which people from different ethnic backgrounds live. Values, cultural habits, socioeconomic positions, and "turf" may all be issues in intergroup conflict. Understanding the inevitability of conflict is the very first step in managing conflict.

Conflict Management Skills

Even though social work generalist skills cut across roles, it is important to have an understanding of the major skills that make up social work roles. Conflict management skills are not bound inextricably to the conflict manager role, but they are most characteristic of that role.

Listening to Each Point of View

The social worker listens to all sides involved in the conflict to hear their points of view, acknowledging the importance of how each party frames the problem, along with validating each party's stake in the problem. If the conflicted party sees the problem as a lack of resources, while the opposing group views the problem as someone following incorrect procedures, the social worker sees immediately that initial misunderstandings exist.

Clarifying Each Point

Social workers seek to clarify every point that each side makes. During conflict, emotions run high, and people state opinions or positions that are not easily understood. By employing empathy to clarify positions, the social worker can help to provide accurate feedback. In clarifying each point, it is important to filter out the extraneous anger and "old baggage" that really do not relate to the conflict at hand.

Defining the Problem

Effectively managing conflict demands that the social worker define the problem causing the conflict. Certainly this is difficult because there are usually so many issues, differing viewpoints, norms, and values that one must sift through to pinpoint the source of conflict. On-the-spot analysis is called for, and this is complicated because defining something in the midst of chaos takes great concentration.

Recognizing Clues of Conflict

When working with client systems, social workers are apt to ignore clues of conflict. Too often, because we want people to feel good and to like each other, one can tend to gloss over gestures that indicate that conflict is in the air. But this ignorance sows the seeds of future discontent and makes the resolution more difficult.

Avoiding Win-Lose Outcomes

The presence of winners and losers lays the basis for future conflict in a family, among groups, or between two individuals. When working in such situations, social workers should strive for an outcome in which both sides experience winning in some way and feel they were heard (Gerstein and Reagan, 1986). Social workers should identify common ground in the conflict and build on this to reach a solution. In a family situation, common ground may be the entire family's love for each other. No one really wants the family to fall apart, because they all love each other. Yet the differences among them are tearing them apart. The skilled conflict manager helps the family to find what binds them together to find a solution in which the family can remain together and all the members can feel they kept the family together, even if each had to give up something to reach its goal. In this situation, no one would lose; everyone would win.

Encouraging Cooperation

We attempt to engage all parties to work together and cooperate. Most likely, this means not competing for identical resources. Most social workers understand how hard this is because it seems as though the resources to which most of our client systems have access are scarce indeed, and conflict among groups competing for the same scarce resources furthers the problem. Reframing the conflict into a win-win situation mitigates the negative outcome that would ensue from fighting over scarce resources.

Creative conflict management is an important role for social work generalists. As conflict managers, the social worker may even seek to create conflict from time to time. Creating conflict and then managing it may help us reach one of the larger goals our profession sets down for us: creating more just social structures in society through empowering people who do not share equitably in resources. Redistributing resources means sharing power, and those who have power often do not want to give it up. As advocates and activists, we must use conflict and then manage it in order to bring about needed changes.

Summary

All roles and skills are used relationally according to the needs and backgrounds of the client systems with whom we are working. We do not choose specific roles and skills because we particularly feel comfortable with them. We use them specifically because they are called for in a situation.

At the same time, how we use roles and their related skills is dependent on the backgrounds of the client. We must become familiar with our client systems' culture, lifestyles, language, and so on. For example, when working with families, we may see them in our offices, in institutional settings, or in their own homes. We must find a comfortable situation for ourselves based on understanding if we are to relate to people where they are. In other words, if a social worker is fearful and anxious because he or she is making a home visit in strange surroundings, it is doubtful whether he or she will be able to understand a family's experiences or concerns. The social worker needs to make careful preparations if he or she is to be successful with the roles and skills that will be employed in the case.

CASE EXAMPLE 4.4

Joint-Use Land

Consider the example of the Navajo and Hopi Native American tribes in northeastern Arizona. The United States government granted to the Navajos a large reservation that happens to completely surround the Hopi reservation. When there were clear signs of conflict between the two groups, the federal government gave each group permission to use the other's land. The government glossed over the conflict between the two groups and did not address the fundamental needs of both groups: the need for more land and the need for economic justice. The two tribal groups fought against each other rather than cooperating and turning their energy toward the institutions of the dominant society that keep the Native American people impoverished.

Traditional values may come into conflict with social policies.

Imagine you are preparing for a home visit with a troubled family. You need to be familiar with the neighborhood and the family's ethnic and cultural background. A white social worker entering a Puerto Rican neighborhood who has no understanding of the Spanish language or Puerto Rican culture cannot possibly be empathic, nor can that social worker create an atmosphere in which trust can grow. Use your analytic skills to develop an understanding of human diversity and contextual diversity, both of which are important for the genuine carrying out of social work roles.

You have been introduced to the many roles social work generalists use in their work. The skills that accompany these roles were described and examples were given to illustrate them. Generalist roles and skills are used when we engage in work with our client systems. You will see later in the book how each role and the skills accompanying the role are actually used in the steps of the planned change process.

The remainder of this chapter is devoted to an explanation of an interactive perspective on change. We show you how an open and dynamic world view enhances your work with individuals, families, groups, communities, and organizations.

THE CRYSTAL MODEL: PROCESS OF PLANNED CHANGE

Generalists use change to assist client systems to reach their goals. The change process is the "how to" in social work practice (McMahon, 1990, p. 32). We are adding yet another dimension to the problem-solving process, moving problem solving out of its traditional step-by-step methods with which most students are familiar. We move the process into the systems perspective and call it the "Crystal Model: Process of Planned Change."

We rely on the traditional steps in problem solving: problem identification, data gathering, assessment, contracting, designing and planning, implementation, termination, and evaluation. However, we frame them differently to take into consideration the dynamic quality of the clients' lives as well as the ever-changing world in which we live when a new day can bring a whole new set of variables to any given situation.

Phases

The Crystal Model, as seen in Figure 4.1, is the process that comprises the generalist practitioner's primary task, change. In principle, change is an orderly process, but when applied to the ongoing complexity of people's lives, it can easily appear chaotic. Social work students need to understand the inherent orderliness of the change process, but they must also learn something of how it is affected by the real-life context in which it must be applied by the generalist practitioner.

FIGURE 4.1 Crystal Model Process of Planned Change

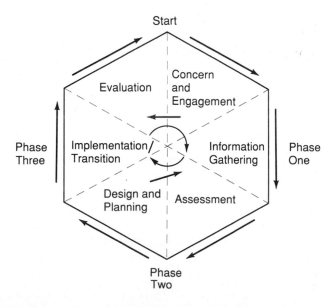

Dewey's Reflective Arc is the seed from which the Crystal Model has grown, but the idea itself emerged as a result of tedious examination of countless visual representations of the process dynamic until we selected the crystal, an everyday object, but one with many interrelated facets. The crystal seems an appropriate visual metaphor for the relationship between the various phases of a process which may move backward as well as forward and may proceed on several fronts simultaneously, but at different rates.

We mean for you to learn the step-by-step process of problem solving, but we want you to learn it in a new way. The "Crystal Model" is used to illustrate change dynamics. Crystals are marked by both order and complexity. There are many sides to a crystal, and they grow according to their underlying conditions. At the same time, the crystal is a whole. Each facet is dependent on another facet. Together, the facets make a crystal, one that is organic, growing, and changing. Using the crystal as a teaching model seems to be the most appropriate way to illustrate how one phase of change is related to another, as well as how we are engaged in problem solving with a variety of system sizes, sometimes simultaneously.

The beginning phase encompasses identifying problems and/or areas of concern, contacts with the client system, building relationships, and gathering infor-

FIGURE 4.2 Crystal Model of Planned
Change by System Size

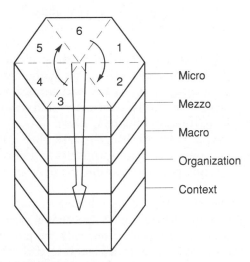

Legend:

1. Area of Concern/Engagement
2. Information Gathering
3. Assessment
4. Design and Planning
5. Implementation/Transition
6. Evaluation

mation relevant to the area of concern. The change process begins even before we see the client system, when we are planning for the initial contact.

Identifying the area of concern/problem is concurrent with beginning our client contact. Most initial work with client systems centers around defining the reasons for social work involvement, and the clients' views are most important. Defining the area of concern takes on more complexity when we take into consideration the type of services the agency renders—that is, the agency helps define the area of concern, and the profession's goals define areas of concern.

Unless clients and social workers are engaged in the process of change, little progress will be made. The manner in which we begin contact, the nature of our ongoing contacts with people, and the quality of the professional relationships we build determine the success of the change process.

Beginning our work, defining the areas of concern, and building relationships are accomplished while we are gathering relevant information. Often our first direct contact with a client is centered around the collection of information. We may need to gather information to determine an elderly woman's eligibility for chore services or a youth's readiness to leave a residential treatment program and reside in another setting. How we collect information, the procedures we use, and the explanations we give to people all play a part in the quality of the beginning phase of the Crystal Model of change. In fact, the quality of the work done during this phase often determines the success of and subsequent work, or even whether there will be any ongoing work. Unless the initial phase is successful, there will be no second phase.

The middle phase includes three steps: (a) assessment and analysis of the situation, (b) designing and planning for the forthcoming change, and (c) contracting with the client system.

Assessment is at the heart of generalist practice. In this step, the area of concern is appraised, examined, and explained. The result is the assessment that guides all further activity in the change process. The assessment should be based on sound human behavior and social environment theory and well-documented results of systematic inquiries (Greene and Ephross, 1991).

The plan that is developed in order for change to take place is based on the assessment. A sound, accurate assessment that explains the area of concern is the best insurance policy for a successful plan and, in time, the positive change the client wants and needs.

Engaging the client system and who else must change in the assessment and in the designing and planning for change is another essential ingredient in the Crystal Model. Working toward change involves not only the professional social worker's expertise, but also the focal system's willingness to effect change. Thus, the contract that is agreed upon by the social worker and the client system becomes another key feature in the Crystal Model process of change. Contracts may be verbal between clients and social worker, but the written contract offers greater accountability and clarity of roles and tasks.

Implementation, evaluation, and transition comprise the ending phase of the process of the Crystal Model. "Where the rubber mets the road" is an apt description of implementation. The social worker and the client system have assessed, planned, and contracted for change. Putting that plan into action—a plan that is based upon an accurate assessment—is the implementation step in the Crystal Model.

The stage must be set early in the Crystal Model, but we usually consider evaluation in the context of ending the change process. Evaluation of practice and program evaluation are both ongoing and depend upon continuous monitoring throughout the change effort.

Monitoring must be carried out systematically to ensure that sound data and correct methodology are used. When effective monitoring takes place, the findings that are generated in the evaluation step can be used to help us understand our own practice skills and the strengths and weaknesses of the programs used to bring service to client systems.

Transitions refer to the changes that take place when our work with client systems comes to an end. In an effective change effort, client goals have been met, and it is time to move on.

The way in which client systems "move on" is dependent on the quality of the service provided and the quality of the professional relationship. An effective plan that was well implemented leaves client systems in an enhanced position with their area of concern or problem having been addressed and resolved. The generalist must be prepared to work with people as individuals or as members of groups, families, communities, and organizations. Sometimes a generalist works with an individual, a family, and a small group simultaneously, all of whom make up the client system. In such cases, the area of concern/problem and the resolutions sought may be matched, but the social worker is likely to be at different stages in the change process with each client grouping (see Figure 4.3). The Crys-

FIGURE 4.3 The Crystal Model: Process of Planned Change. One client system's crystal may represent many other similar client systems. This process is used in all change systems including the focal and action systems.

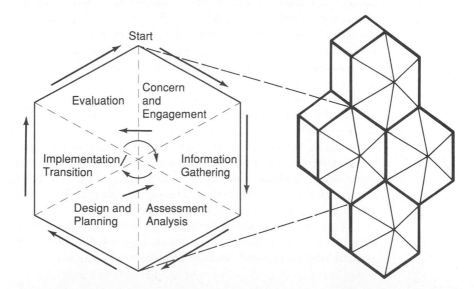

tal Model makes it simpler for the student to visualize this complexity, illustrating how one may be in the initial phase of the change process with one part of the client grouping and in the middle phase with another. Thus the Crystal Model helps us realize how the change process, although orderly, is not necessarily linear.

In addition, the model helps students grapple with the complexity of scenarios in which the social worker and client must backtrack to an earlier step in the process. This occurs when the client begins to identify new concerns or strengths, see problems in new ways, or develop deeper and more trusting relationships with the social worker during the course of the change process. Properly addressed, this can allow the social worker and client to explore a variety of new options (See Figure 4.2).

The change process must be open enough to allow the social worker and the client to be in several phases at the same time. For example, you and your client may be gathering information even while you are making an assessment. The very act of making an assessment brings forth more information to include. In addition, there are times when the social worker and the client must backtrack to an earlier step in the change process. This happens when the worker and client identify missing pieces of information or the client views information in a new way.

Reflections of the Change Process

Every actor in the change process may intuitively see the problem from his/her own perspective. In Figure 4.4, we see an overview of the steps in the change process, overlayed with all of the roles involved in the process. It is the job of the generalist social worker to put the area of concern in focus and see behind the "mirror," or problem. The client systems see themselves reflected in the problem. Through assessment, the generalist identifies who must change, which may or may not been seen by the client system. The focal system, that is, who must change, is behind the mirror and may not be aware of the pain the client is experiencing. The social worker, through empathy and information gathering, enters the picture as reflected in the mirror. Together, the client and the change system are reflected on the goal. A contract is made between the client and the change agent within the change system. The plan and implementation carry them to the goal. The action system supports the change agent and client's goals.

Let us look more closely at Figure 4.4. Find #1, *concern,* in the lower central area. The change system views the problem as a concern. *Information* is gathered (#2) by the change system and *assessed* (#3) in terms of the focal system's impact on the client system's ability to reach its goals. A *contract* (#4) is made between the social worker and the client. The *plan* (#5) for change emerges from the assessment and is *implemented* (#6) with the help of the action system to achieve the client's goal. The client and social workers *evaluate* (#7) the process and to what degree the goal has been reached. Throughout the process, there is *mutuality* between the social worker and the client system.

While we have presented the change process step by step, remember there may be ministeps going on at all times. Figure 4.4 demonstrates how different systems view the problem and are involved in the process.

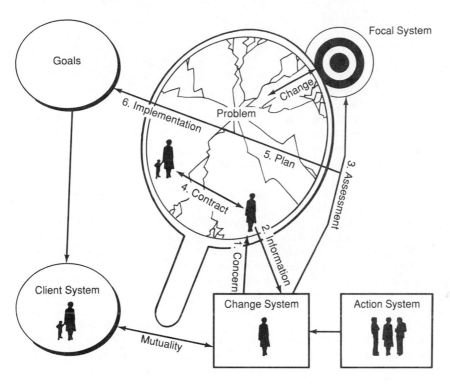

FIGURE 4.4 Different Perspectives on a Problem: Reflections on the Change Process

The following case illustrates the change process, incorporating the Crystal Model and the reflections on the change process.

CASE EXAMPLE 4.5

Mrs. Jones

Mrs. Jones came to the Neighborhood Service Organization (NSO) for immediate assistance. Her fourteen-year-old son, Billy, had run away the previous evening. She has neither seen nor heard from him. She talked to his friends, but they say they do not know where he is. She doesn't know if the NSO can help her, but since the agency is on her block, she figured there is no harm in trying.

A student social worker, Eric Thompson, is the initial contact at the agency. A generalist in orientation, Eric knows that Mrs. Jones needs immediate assistance regarding her son's disappearance. He listens to her fears

and gives her phone numbers of the Youth Assistance Bureau and of the local police precinct. He offers to let her use his phone and wonders if she would like to be alone or if she would prefer his presence during the calls. She invites him to stay. Her call to the Youth Assistance Bureau eases her mind. The contact person there explained the frequency of such occurrences, but urges her to call the police. She does and is both pleased and frightened that there are no reports on him. Mrs. Jones decides to go home and wait there for her son in case he calls.

A few hours later, as Eric's work day is end-

(Continued)

CASE EXAMPLE 4.5   *(Continued)*

ing, he receives a call from Mrs. Jones. Her son is home. He had stayed at a friend's home and has no explanation for his behavior. Mrs. Jones is very concerned and wonders if there will be any help for them at the agency. Eric makes an appointment for the following day.

Eric thinks over the day's events on his way home. He knows there are many youths in the neighborhood who are headed for trouble. He knows the Jones boy's behavior is symptomatic of possible problems ahead. He also knows that as a generalist he ought to see the problem in its fullest possible context.

During the interview on the following day, Mrs. Jones and her son agree with Eric regarding the many youths who are in the same situation as Billy Jones. Billy talks about the absence of meaningful activities, his boredom with school, his anger and disrespect for many of his teachers, and his dim view of the future. Billy confides a great deal in Eric. Apparently, the relationship Eric is building is meeting some of Billy's needs.

After some time, Eric, Billy, and Mrs. Jones agree that offering some services especially designed for youths in the neighborhood is appropriate. During the course of the interview, they identify needs for tutoring, substance abuse education and treatment, and part-

time work. The junior high school in the neighborhood is notoriously unresponsive to the broader needs of students, and most often the kids view the school as a jail rather than as a place to learn.

Eric knows he is on to something. He recalls his generalist framework and the Crystal Model. He knows he might be working simultaneously with Billy and some other kids in the area. He also knows he will have to involve other people on the agency staff. The junior high school principal might be part of the focal system behind the mirror. He also knows that other agencies and social workers in the area will be part of the action system. Eric may be playing the roles of enabler, advocate, and collaborator, as well as that of conflict manager. He needs to call upon a number of skills to help him play these roles. Eric knows for sure that the issue he has identified goes beyond working with Billy alone or even Billy and his family. He and his agency will be working on multiple levels of practice with different sized systems. He remembers the Crystal Model and starts putting it into practice, seeing the issues from many perspectives. These include the client, the focal system, the action system, and his own agency.

CONCLUSION

We have provided you with a brief introduction to the Crystal Model. Seeing how change is multidimensional and interactive adds to our understanding of what can be done to bring about positive outcomes for clients. Social workers need to use specific skills while playing carefully chosen social work roles. In order to do their best work, social workers need to operate within a process of planned change.

The next part of this book begins the unfolding of each of the steps in the change process as seen through the Crystal Model. At the beginning of each chapter, we review the steps and how the step on which we focus in that chapter is related to the other steps in the change process. We use many case examples to illustrate how roles and skills are effectively used in each step.

References

Bisno, Herb. (1988). *Managing Conflict*. Newbury Park, CA: Sage Publications.

Compton, Beulah, and Galaway, Burt. (1989). *Social Work Process,* 4th ed. Belmont, CA: Wadsworth, pp. 598–600.

Corrigan, Paul, and Leonard, Peter. (1978). *Social Work Practice Under Capitalism: A Marxist Approach*. London and Basingstoke: Macmillan Press.

Deutsch, Morton. (1973). *The Resolution of Conflict, Constructive and Destructive Processes*. New Haven and London: Yale University Press.

Dewey, John. (1933). *How We Think: A Restatement of the Relation of Reflective Thinking to the Educational Process*. Boston and New York: D.C. Heath.

Folberg, Jay, and Milne, Ann. (1988). *Divorce Mediation: Theory and Practice*. New York: Guilford Press.

Gerstein, Arnold, and Reagan, James. (1986). *Win-Win Approaches to Conflict Resolution*. Salt Lake City, Utah: G.M. Smith.

Greene, Roberta, and Ephross, Paul. (1991). *Human Behavior Theory and Social Work Practice*. New York: Aldine de Gruyer.

Hartman, Ann, and Laird, Joan. (1983). *Family Centered Social Work Practice*. New York: Free Press; London: Collier Macmillan, p. 76.

Hepworth, Kean H., and Larson, Jo Ann. (1986). *Direct Social Work Practice: Theory and Skills,* 2nd ed. Chicago, IL: Dorsey Press, p. 130.

Holder, Dave, and Wardle, M. (1981). *Teamwork and the Development of a Unitary Approach*. London, Boston, and Henley: Routledge and Kegan Paul, p. 124.

Mahaffey, Maryann, and Hanks, John (eds.). (1982). *Practical Politics: Social Work and Political Responsibility*. Silver Spring, MD: National Association of Social Workers.

Mahon, Maria O'Neil. (1990). *The General Method of Social Work Practice,* 2nd ed. Englewood Cliffs, NJ: Prentice Hall, p. 32.

O'Neil, Maria. (1984). *The Generalist Method of Social Work Practice*. Englewood Cliffs, NJ: Prentice Hall, p. 325.

Parsloe, Phyllida. (1981). *Social Service Area Teams*. London: George Allen and Unwin.

Rogers, Carl. (1951). *Client Centered Therapy, Its Current Practice, Implications, and Theory*. Boston: Houghton Mifflin.

Shulman, Lawrence. (1979). *The Skills of Helping: Individuals and Groups*. Itasca, IL: F.E. Peacock.

Shulman, Lawrence. (1991). *Interactional Social Work Practice: Toward an Empirical Theory*. Itasca, IL: F.E. Peacock.

Tracy, Elizabeth M. (1990). "Identifying Social Support Resources of At-Risk Families." *Journal of Social Work, 35*(3), 252–258.

United Way of America Services Identification System I (1972). Alexandria, VA: United Way of America.

Identifying Areas of Concern and Engagement

OVERVIEW

We presented an overview of the Crystal Model in the previous chapter, but some review may assist your incorporation of this first phase into the context of the entire change process. The Crystal Model represents a systems approach to social work practice at the same time that it is embedded in traditional problem solving.

Although it is similar to problem solving, the Crystal Model contains a new twist. We conceive of the process in much the same way that we envision systems—that is, dynamic, forward-moving, and complex. Beginning in a positive manner with clients in the first phase of the Crystal Model heightens the likelihood of success in the remaining phases of the process. However, even while our work begins in the first phase, some components of other phases may also be used on behalf of client systems, showing that appropriate steps may be taken in a nonlinear fashion. Once the first phase is completed, while we are likely to move on to the next, there are situations which require that we backtrack to the first phase. The nature of problem solving in the real world fits more closely with the Crystal Model than does the traditional approach simply because real problem solving is never neat and tidy.

In this chapter, we define and analyze the first phase of the process. We discuss the roles and skills that are attached to each phase and illustrate, by way of the model, what systems are involved in this phase. We give examples throughout the chapter and end with a summary, identifying key concepts.

IDENTIFYING AREAS OF CONCERN

Areas of Concern and Engagement make up the first phase in the Crystal Model. Each is a distinct step in the phase, yet they are carried out simultaneously; hence, they are treated as one phase in the process, although we discuss them separately.

This phase in the process is sometimes referred to as problem identification. Many of the same components present in a more traditional approach are in our conceptualization. However, we see important nuances regarding how the situations that clients bring to us are defined.

Moving away from defining all concerns as problems helps free the process of helping for both client systems and change systems. Focusing on areas of concern, with problems as one possible component, helps change systems move away from blaming the victim. We tend to blame those in our society who have a problem. We are not negating the complexities and even the existence of problems that client systems have; we are pointing out broader and more compassionate ways of viewing the "baggage" with which our clients are burdened.

Competency

To support the goal of becoming a competent generalist social worker, we will include with each phase of the Crystal Model the Baer and Federico (1978) competency that relates to the purpose of this phase. You may wish to review all of the competencies as discussed in Chapter 1.

The first competency is to identify relationships between people and social institutions that need to be initiated, enhanced, restored, protected, or terminated (Baer and Federico, 1978, p. 86). Our focus in this chapter is on understanding the concerns in the relationship between people and institutions in a manner that is congruent with social work values.

Defining Areas of Concern

An *area of concern* becomes apparent when a belief, principle, or value is violated or when boundaries are crossed in systems. All size systems hold values. The profession of social work has codified values in its system of ethics. In other words, an individual or group may either have their values violated or see where values may be violated. Some violations are clear, such as abusing a child, while others are less obvious or are in conflict with the rest of society, such as providing social services to the mentally ill or to criminals.

The issues clients bring to social workers for help are areas of concern. Areas of concern may be problems or they may be the way in which systems, including client systems, interact with other systems.

When we are defining areas of concern—that is, the issues brought to our attention regarding our clients—we consider who "owns" the definition. In other words, is the area of concern defined by the client, by the agency, by the focal system, or by the profession? Discerning which definition is most prominent helps us understand the client system's concerns. If the agency is defining the concern, then we need to stand back and analyze just what the agency is saying about clients in general. Likewise, if the client is defining the area of concern, we need to understand how other systems interacting with the client system may define the area of concern.

For example, a client who, as part of the focal system, is mandated to see a social worker as a condition of parole, sees his or her situation in quite a different light from the court which referred the client. Thus, analyzing the "players" who contribute to the definition of the area of concern becomes essential.

Barriers in Identifying Areas of Concern

Far too often, social workers have a narrow view of the social situations that bring clients to professional help. We mentioned the limitations of a narrow problem definition. We think understanding the limitations of that focus is critical and deserves further elaboration.

Blaming the Victim

Three common pitfalls accompany a restrictive view of problem identification. First, when areas of concern are seen only as problems, the personification of the problem is placed on the client. In other words, the problem-bearer becomes the problem-causer when, in reality, the problem-bearer may be the victim (Ryan, 1971). Most of us are familiar with the "blaming the victim" syndrome, which deflects blame from the most powerful to the least powerful.

Ryan gives an example of this syndrome in the following vignette:

Mothers As "Victims"

In the housing units, posters were placed throughout the units with the caption that read, "Good Mothers Do Not Allow Their Children To Eat Paint." Children, by nature, place items in their mouths. It is normal and desirable behavior, and stopping them is virtually impossible. Poisonous or potentially poisonous substances should not be available to children. The mothers did not make the paint available to the children. Rather, landlords used lead-base paint, and mothers were blamed for the unconscionable acts of others. Placing blame on the least powerful (the mothers) deflected the blame from the most powerful (the landlords). When we narrowly define situations as problems only, we risk blaming the victim.

Failing to See Potential

Second, when we look at issues only as problems, we fail to see the potential of developmental approaches to problem solving. For example, child protection is a major concern in child welfare. However, the social services we provide are usually limited to investigating, detecting, and verifying individual cases of child abuse and neglect. After abuse and neglect is verified, action is taken to protect at-risk children through specialized services in specific incidents. While protecting children is both necessary and admirable, framing the needs of at-risk children in a narrow problem definition of abuse and neglect fails to assist children to develop their full potential in a safe and nurturing environment (Thomas, 1990). It is, at best, a "band-aid" approach with no consideration given to the broader needs of children, let alone to our ethical mandate to prevent conditions that encourage child abuse and neglect in this society. The prevention of at-risk conditions must be fully incorporated into our everyday work.

Danger of Labeling

Third, problem identification may become routine, and we may fall back on labeling rather than differentiating among individual client systems. Routinizing problem identification frequently happens when the agency interacting with a client system has a set view of client problems and situations. Earlier in this chapter, we pointed out the importance of analyzing the players while defining areas of concern. The agency players have a profound effect on how we see client concerns.

Our own limitations are also barriers in understanding the areas of concern clients bring to us. We fall back on myths, constricted viewpoints, and easy answers from time to time when we try to understand what our client's concerns really are. Case Example 5.1 illustrates the point.

In summary, the area of concern perspective allows us to examine the problem

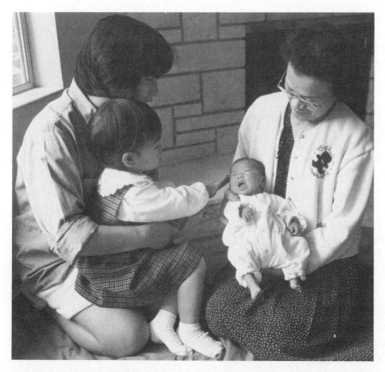

Generalist social workers identify potential in all systems.

CASE EXAMPLE 5.1

Joel

Joel is working in an outreach program in a community and has been assigned the task of working with a group of adolescent boys who are fifteen and sixteen years old, are low-income, and who are members of ethnic minorities, both African-American and Hispanic. Helping them learn how to use each other as sounding boards and, eventually, as actual helpers in their own solutions to problems, crises, and developmental tasks is one of his goals. However, he is growing impatient with their seeming lack of direction and attention to their group agenda. His ongoing analysis brings him to the conclusion that the group is simply not motivated—they really do not want to grow and develop. This is a harsh judgment, indeed, but not uncommon, especially in relation to certain groups in society: low-income, minority male adolescents among them.

Joel speaks to his supervisor about his frustration. After some exploration, he sees that the problem lies not with client motivation, but rather with the organization of the group itself. He hypothesizes that the absence of an indigenous group leader—an element of great significance among adolescent groups—may be the real concern.

Rather than resorting to the labeling of a group as unmotivated, Joel recognizes his role in creating a group that was bound to fail because he did not organize the group in a manner commensurate with the needs of the group. In this example, he saw that problem identification had become routinized because of a narrow focus on observable behavior. Seeing structural inadequacies allows us to see the basis of the group's difficulty in working on its agenda and saves us from focusing blame on a particular group.

situation without blaming the victim and encouraging us to see the broader picture of client needs. The perspective mitigates against a superficial, easy answer to account for the conditions client systems find themselves experiencing.

Differing Perspectives on Areas of Concern

Before we can help client systems, we must identify the major issues or areas of concern that clients bring to our attention. In fact, that is the major goal of this component of the first step: to identify areas of concern. Identifying areas of concern is somewhat more complex than simply finding out from clients what is bothering them. In fact, it is a multilayered process that involves the following: (1) the client system, (2) the agency from which service is offered, and (3) the profession of social work. Before we begin our discussion regarding how to identify areas of concern, let us digress for just a moment so that we can understand what each "player" brings to the process.

The Client System

Clients come to social agencies for help, and they are also mandated by authorities (usually the courts) to seek help. Having already introduced you in Chapter 3 to the differences between voluntary clients and those who do not seek help on their own, involuntary clients, you can imagine the vast differences between the two groups regarding how they view the reason or problem that brought them to the social worker in the first place. The voluntary client may well define his or her area of concern as a problem, while the involuntary client may see the problem not of his own making, but rather belonging to an external system — school, court, and so on. In general, voluntary clients are more willing to become engaged in the helping process, while involuntary clients may be considered "potential clients," at least in the beginning of the process (Pincus and Minahan, 1973).

We have more to say on working with voluntary and involuntary clients, but the first step in recognizing how one works with both groups is the understanding of the different ways each client system views the reasons or areas of concern that led up to seeing a social worker.

The Agency

Agencies also see the reasons for which clients seek or receive services in a number of ways. Imber-Black (1988, p. 74) talks about the "myths" that larger systems — that is, agencies — have regarding the clients, especially families, whom they serve. For example, an agency operates from a particular theory of behavior that tends to categorize all people who are served by that agency. He gives the example of the child welfare or family agency that tends to perpetuate the common belief that all abusing parents were abused children. That may quite often be true, but it is not true for everyone. Taken to extremes, and this sometimes happens, the agency then views every person who had been a victim of abuse as a probable abuser. The real concerns brought to an agency by an adult child of an abusing parent may go unrecognized because an unsubstantiated belief undermines the real nature of the client concern.

Myths regarding racial and ethnic minorities determine how an agency sees the concerns or problems such persons from different groups bring with them. All sorts of "unexamined cultural attitudes" (Imber-Black, 1988, p. 75) set the stage for how individual persons' concerns, in fact, their very lives, are defined. The dominant culture may define problems quite differently from a minority culture viewpoint.

We need to know what belief system the agency is working under when we work with our clients. Of course, such knowledge is not always possible, but we think that by understanding the conditions under which social work services are offered helps us keep an open mind.

The Profession of Social Work

The profession of social work defines what its areas of concern are through its publication of professional literature, through public speeches by members, through the National Association of Social Work's goals, and through the individual work of professionals. As a profession, social workers tend to see their work in broad terms — enhancing the well-being of persons; enhancing relationships among people; and creating humane services and social structures in society. The profession sees its work in broad strokes throughout society (Reeser and Epstein, 1990).

Summary

Practitioners translating those broad strokes often get bogged down in the barriers their agencies erect and in their own limitations. We know how difficult it is to keep in mind the "big picture" or the context from which our clients come as well as the "big picture" of what social workers are supposed to do. Sometimes our work seems almost too much, and we revert to seeing every client in a stingy rather than generous way, focusing on weaknesses rather than on strengths. A step toward mitigating that tendency, especially in view of the overwhelming social problems with which social workers become engaged, is found in how we define the reasons we are working with people in the first place.

We put our efforts into helping people because we believe they can change and grow and because we believe society can improve. We cannot allow narrow definitions to limit us and our perspective. We firmly believe that a first step toward keeping the "big picture" involves the way in which we view the people and the situations with whom and what we work.

Even while putting forth this point of view, we do not negate the difficulties people bring with them when they are clients or potential clients. Social workers work with people who have many strikes against them, who are under tremendous stress, and who are in pain—physical and emotional. At the same time, they work with human beings whose strengths are legion. We cannot forget their troubles; but we are remiss if we fail to see their strengths (Saleeby, 1992).

Preparatory Steps in the First Phase

Problems, troublesome situations, and dysfunctional systems, as well as potentials for growth, are intricate, demanding enormous attention. Prior preparation helps the social worker greatly. We usually prepare for situations by knowing as much as we can before we meet with someone or before we enter a new situation.

Preparing during the beginning phase leads us back to examine our knowledge base and to put into practice what we know. Specifically, in the beginning phase we urge you to reacquaint yourselves with two concepts we have already introduced, but we now put them into the Areas of Concern step. These two concepts are Contextual Diversity and Human Diversity.

The concerns that people bring to us and of which we, as social workers, are aware must be examined in the context of diversity. Real understanding means moving away from narrow foci, whether it may be the problem perspective or a perspective limited by cultural, lifestyle, regional, and social class myopia.

Contextual Diversity

Contextual diversity refers to the differences in the physical and social environments in which people live and which, in turn, affect their concerns, problems, and limitations. Contextual diversity can stem from differences in geography, social class, and type of habitat; for example, urban, suburban, or rural. We are concerned about contexts mostly because they account for differences in how societal resources are distributed, and we know that distribution of resources is a key factor in understanding how people experience their lives.

Human Diversity

Human diversity issues ought to be accounted for in one's preparatory work. How does belonging to a particular ethnic group affect participation in resource distribution in society? What impact do racial differences have on getting basic needs met in society? What is the effect of sexual orientation on daily living? All of these questions arise from our understanding of human diversity and how diversity relates to the concerns of clients which you as a professional social worker identify (Montiel and Wong, 1983).

Summary

Identifying the areas of concern begins with identifying the violation of a client's, society's, or social work values, or with identifying the potential for growth that has been blocked. By viewing problems as concerns, we can more easily avoid blaming the victim, failing to see potential, and labeling. We need to learn how each system views the area of concern, whether it be the client, the agency, the focal system, or the professional. In the next chapter, we will present how to gather information on concerns and strengths from each system. We begin the process by understanding how concerns may relate to the contextual diversity of clients. The next step in this phase is to engage each system so we can begin to gather information on the area of concern.

ENGAGEMENT

Engagement refers to our efforts to assist client systems, focal systems, and action systems to become involved in the change effort. People need to have some stake in change or it is unlikely that positive changes can take place. Engaging relevant parties in the process is essential.

Two major goals of engagement are: (1) to begin contact with the client system and (2) to establish professional relationships that engage all systems in the change process (Shulman, 1992). We begin our discussion by focusing on the ways initial contacts are made. We then delineate specific strategies to begin contact and thus, engagement. In addition, we discuss how professional relationships are built, showing how to develop relationships with client systems, action systems, and target systems.

Initial Contacts

We remind you that clients come to social workers in two ways: (1) the client initiates the contact (voluntary), or (2) the social worker as a representative of a sanctioned, legitimate agency begins the engagement (involuntary).

Voluntary Clients

Voluntary clients come to social workers on their own. They seek help out of their own discomfort or concern. For example, a family with a chronically ill child is referred to an agency working with families of children who have the same dis-

Social workers develop relationships with each person in the client system.

ease. It is likely that the physician treating the child made the referral. The physician, most likely, strongly recommended the contact, but, in fact, the contact was entirely voluntary. No one told the family they must seek help. They are doing so because they recognize their need for support, information, or additional resources.

How they view the problem or area of concern, their desire for assistance, their openness to problem solving, and their belief in the possibility of change are all descriptive of their position as voluntary clients.

Involuntary Clients

Clients who are seen in social agencies by social workers because they are forced to are called involuntary clients. For a variety of reasons, their interactions with societal institutions are problematic, and they are involuntarily sent for social work help. For many social workers, working with involuntary clients makes up a large portion of their practice (Cingolani, 1984, pp. 442–446). Services are mandated by courts, schools, and child welfare agencies. Clients may have many service and resource needs, but they have not identified them as such. The worker making contact with the involuntary client system is left to do that. According to Johnson (1989, p. 171), "Unwilling clients often do not see the need for service, do not believe help is possible, or have difficulty in developing a relationship with the worker." The contact between the client system and the social work generalist is quite different when the client is involuntary.

Engagement Strategies

There are several important strategies to consider when the engagement process begins, and the social worker is making the first contact with a client system, an action system, or a focal system. All three systems are dealt with early in the change process: the focal system must change for the client system to change, and the action system must be mobilized for the change process to begin. Therefore, it is important to gain an expertise in working with all three systems.

In the following discussion, contact strategies for client systems and then for action and focal systems are presented.

Client System Contact

Direct versus Indirect Contact   If the worker initiates the contact, a decision regarding whether the contact is indirect or direct is required. *Direct contacts* are those in which the worker and the client system meet, face to face, or at the very least, on the telephone. By contrast, *indirect contacts* occur when the social worker sees someone other than the client system. The direct approach is the most economical in terms of time, but it may violate cultural traditions and/or reduce the influence of the worker to produce change later on in the helping process.

The initial contact really does set the stage for all of the ongoing work. For example, within certain traditional cultures, such as the Arabic culture, direct contacts by an opposite-sex person may be inappropriate. For example, a female social worker working with a family may have to first speak to the man rather than the woman, and this may not be appropriate.

Family structures vary from culture to culture. For example, within the Cambodian culture, a direct contact with the family without going through the clan leader is deemed rude and intrusive and likely makes initiating a helping relationship difficult. In such a case, saving a little time in the beginning by making direct contact may actually prove to be a detriment in the long run. Therefore, when beginning your work with client systems, considerations related to ethnicity, culture, and gender are all important. Knowledge of client systems as groups and further knowledge of intergroup relationships will help reveal just how to proceed with clients.

First Impressions   The first impression the social worker makes when meeting the client, action, and focal systems is critically important in the helping process. Contact opens the other system's boundary, an act not to be taken lightly.

In some ways, a social worker is intruding in another's space, and he or she needs to be conscious of the basic human worth and dignity of others when beginning the change/helping process. We can never take back first impressions, and therefore, in making contact, we should be careful to initiate an appropriate strategy.

The first time you knock on the door and introduce yourself to a family, the change process begins (Golan, 1978). If you genuinely believe in the family's worth and capacity for good and you are confident, you already have initiated the change process. There is a good likelihood that the family will build a relationship with you.

If you have made an appointment to meet the client, the client, likely, has done a considerable amount of thinking about the initial contact and may have built up prejudices and fears to which you must be sensitive so that they can be diffused within the first few minutes of meeting.

Setting   We see client systems, action systems, and focal systems in a variety of settings. The locations impact upon our work and become a determining factor in our ability to engage these systems.

We often see client systems in their own homes, otherwise known as *home visits* (Wells and Biegel, 1991). Although social work is historically associated with home visits, we see clients in their own homes because it assists in the change process. We believe greater understanding between us and our clients can take place if we make home visits. Frequently, our visits to clients' home environments help us make better assessments and interventions with our clients, and we know that if done thoughtfully, respecting clients' rights to privacy, that successful engagement is likely to occur.

At other times, we see clients in more neutral settings, or depending upon the service offered, clients come to the agency. Meeting clients in other settings — hospitals, schools, even courts and jails — impacts on how our work proceeds. The agency in which you are employed may have developed an ambiance that welcomes clients. On the other hand, some agencies provide a setting that seems more hostile than warm. For example, if you are to conduct a board meeting, you want a formal setting to engage the board in a businesslike manner. If, on the other hand, you are engaging a group of elderly people for an activity in a nursing home, you might put up balloons and decorations to communicate a lighter atmosphere. You simply need to be aware of the importance of the setting and choose the setting that fits the purpose of your work, thus enhancing the engagement process.

Outreach   *Outreach* implies making contact with persons who may not be aware of or consider that they have problems or an area of concern. Outreach services should be shaped in such a way that they correspond with the comfort level of client systems (Jones, Magua, and Shyne, 1981). For example, if you are going to work with Hispanics living in a barrio in East Los Angeles, perhaps you would rent a storefront and staff the program with indigenous community leaders. These leaders can provide initial screening and information. They also know when to refer the family or individual to your agency for more extensive help.

Outreach may also include enhancing community awareness regarding areas of concern that are urgent, requiring that both focal and action systems are likewise engaged. The extensive problems of many low-income families and children, chemical abuse, and poverty, itself, are all areas of concern so compelling they demand outreach programs, not only to meet the needs of those already in distress, but to prevent further erosions in the community.

Focal and Action Systems Contact

Not only do we make contact with the client systems, but we also make contact with focal and action systems. When we initiate contact with the focal and action systems, we need a somewhat different strategy from our contact with client systems.

Timing of Initial Contacts   Although social workers are nearly always working under pressing situations, it is helpful to initiate contact with these systems when there is no crisis that either party is experiencing. For instance, initiating contact with an agency going through an accreditation review may not bring the outcomes you desire simply because this is a critical time in the life of the agency. The social worker should try to initiate contacts with agencies under the most positive of circumstances. You may be able to do this through professional meetings and informal contacts.

Leveraging   It is helpful to obtain prior information regarding the status of an individual or system you are engaging. Contacting a *leverage person* — that is, a person with influence — may be beneficial. In working with larger groups and boards, it is important to make contact with influential persons who can help facilitate change. Likewise, when working in a community, you will want to identify influential persons. Influential people are not necessarily those who hold highly visible elected positions.

Texas Campaign

While participating in a campaign in rural Texas communities, a member of PACE, the political action arm of the National Association of Social Workers, learned that the grocery store owners exercised considerable influence over elections by controlling the major advertising budgets of the small-town community newspapers. If the newspaper supported a candidate whom the grocery store owner did not support, advertising, and thus, the newspaper's largest source of revenue, could be withdrawn. Therefore, grocery store owners turned out to be an important initial contact on the campaign trail.

Engaging Factions   Lippett, Watson, and Westley (1958, pp. 21–48) suggest numerous contacts may be necessary in order to approach different factions within an existing group or organization by using a multiple-entry strategy. In other words, a social worker needs to make contact with not only the dominant subsystem but also the other factions as well. Initially, it is helpful if all the subsystems agree to cooperate in the proposed change effort. Therefore, one may need to identify several key leverage people in different subsystems or factions for one's first contacts. The order in which these contacts are made should be considered.

For example, if one wants to raise private money from the local civic organization for a homeless project, a multiple-entry strategy may be the most effective approach. Consider the possibility that there are strong subgroups in the organization, or that the president is a figurehead who takes his lead from someone else. If this is the case, one may choose to go to the person with real power, then the president, and then meet with each subgroup, establishing a relationship with each group. Social workers who fail to use a multiple-entry approach when appropriate and fail to understand systems usually come away empty-handed.

Building Relationships

All contact and engagement strategies fall by the wayside if the social worker has not developed professional relationships with the various systems with which he or she is interacting—the client system, the focal system, and the action system. Relationships are at the heart of social work, and the change process is dependent on the quality of relationships that social workers are able to form. Next, we consider the importance of relationship building in the Area of Concern and Engagement phase of the Crystal Model.

Social work techniques and the use of professional self are both necessary for change. A substantial amount of research indicates interpersonal skills are most closely related to successful change (Fischer, 1978, p. 191). Relationship building begins at the time of the contact and continues throughout the change process. Relationships are established with the client system, the focal system, the action system, and, of course, within one's agency or organization. Maintaining relationships through the change process requires continual attention and special skills.

The Client Relationship

Relationships with client systems are based on mutual trust and the client's belief in the worker's genuineness, nonpossessive warmth (Rogers, 1951; Fischer, 1978, p. 191), and professional capabilities. Empathy needs to be a part of every worker-client relationship. Understanding situations from clients' points of view is essential to any ongoing work. Worker-client relationships are directed toward the needs and wants of the client system, not of the worker. These relationships carry a certain amount of authority, regardless of the setting where they are carried out, and they are time-bound and controlled. Authority is derived from the knowledge, experience, and skill base of the worker (Rubenstein and Block, 1982). Social workers are prepared to assist people at many different levels, and their authority results from their expertise. Client systems see social workers through their own experience and through their own needs and concerns. Our effects on others are not always what we assume. Case Example 5.2 illustrates the point.

Social work relationships do not go on forever. They are purposeful, directed

---

CASE EXAMPLE 5.2

A Parenting Skills Class

A group of mothers of developmentally disabled children were learning parenting skills from a young social work student who was not a parent himself. Toward the end of the year, the student mentioned that during the year he had been self-conscious about the fact that he did not have children, yet he was helping the women in the group who were parents of special needs children. Surprisingly, the women quickly assured him that they thought he was an authority because he had realized early in his life not to have children and endure all the difficulties they were facing!

The experience cast a new perspective on the young worker's view of the client-worker relationship building process. He realized that continuous clarification and openness helps dispel the unspoken messages, expectations, and viewpoints that go on within professional relationships.

---

toward defined client needs, begin when the work begins, and end when the work is finished or when client systems decide to terminate the relationship. Social worker–client relationships are also controlled. Although social workers see clients in a whole variety of settings, from homes, to hospitals, to schools, to agencies, the purpose is always clear. The social worker conducts himself or herself in light of the problem or area of concern identified. It is a relationship directed toward the client. Relationships with client systems often begin during a crisis, as is seen in Case Example 5.3.

During the relationship-building process, the social worker can help the client meet some immediate needs and clarify each person's role. Throughout the crisis, the social worker should treat the client system with absolute respect and understand that the client system has information that is necessary for the helping process.

CASE EXAMPLE 5.3

The Crist Family

The Crist family is moving from Michigan to California, looking for better-paying jobs, when their car breaks down in St. Louis. They misestimated the costs of the trip and are out of money after having the car fixed. Mr. Crist comes to the Catholic Social Services Office, exhausted and looking for help. Paul, a first-year social work graduate student, greets Mr. Crist with respect and explains that he had helped several families in the Crist's situation already this winter. After discussion with Mr. Crist, Paul moved quickly to locate a shelter for the night and to identify some sources of money for gifts and loans to the Crists so they could continue their trip the following day. While Paul saw the Crists only twice, he engaged them and developed a relationship in just two days. Mr. Crist assured Paul they would never forget him.

At other times, the social worker builds the relationship in a less charged atmosphere. Nonetheless, basic principles remain when one goes about building professional relationships, crisis or not.

Steps to Relationships

The following steps help social workers develop system relationships:

1. Effect some small concrete change as soon as possible.

2. To gain trust, be trustworthy. Meet deadlines, acknowledge lines of authority, recognize others' expertise, be consistent, be honest about disagreement. Maintain this stance even when you meet resistance.

3. Have high expectations of yourself and others—we often get what we expect.

4. Nurture and esteem building—demonstrate by direct and concrete actions that you care about the client's needs. For example, make sure the room is comfortable for a group meeting, or consider serving food in an early morning meeting.

5. Clearly state your role and purpose. Explain how you and the system will participate together in the change efforts.

6. Maintain basic respect for the system. Use the first or last name as wished by the person. Respect time, boundaries and personal dignity. (Lloyd, 1980, pp. 45–50).

Relationships with Involuntary Client Systems

Working in agencies that exert authority and social control is common practice in social work and requires us to work with persons who have not requested our help. Although we have discussed both voluntary and involuntary client systems, the differences regarding how we each approach our work with both bear continuing clarification. Pincus and Minahan (1973, p. 57) refer to involuntary client systems as potential clients. In some cases, clients are required by authorities to work with social workers. Involuntary clients are (1) parents of abused and neglected children, (2) adolescent status offenders, (3) criminal offenders, (4) agencies that are under investigation or regulation by a state or federal agency, or (5) communities that may be mandated to provide certain services that leaders do not feel are necessary. Usually, the social worker possesses some level of authority in work with involuntary clients.

Authority

Agencies that offer services are public or quasi-public and are sanctioned through law. In private or voluntary agencies, a social worker can only suggest strategies, but if you are a social worker in a correctional facility, you may have legal authority to order the client to follow a certain plan.

With this authority must come the understanding of how to use the authority and how to engage the client in a relationship (Schlosberg and Kagan, 1988). This requires the social worker to balance the use of authority with the attempt to gain legitimate sanction with the client system. One needs to have a clear definition of one's social work role and be aware of one's responsibilities to the state or public agency. It is imperative to inform your clients just where your authority begins and ends and how you will function within these limits (Rubenstein and Bloch, 1982). It does little good to threaten involuntary clients, and if one states what the consequences of a behavior are, one must be prepared to follow through. By being straightforward with the client and not apologizing for the possible necessity of using authority, the social worker usually will avoid testing by the client system.

Additionally, in developing a relationship with an involuntary client, it is important to delineate which decisions the social worker must make and which decisions are open to the client system. Once a decision is made, it is important to resist the client system's efforts to change this decision through manipulation. On the other hand, it is important that the social worker defend the client system's right to make his or her own decisions. The social worker should stand by those decisions. If the client system can demonstrate through appropriate behavior that the social worker has reached an incorrect decision, then that decision can certainly be changed. It is important in working with involuntary clients that social workers demonstrate that their authority is humane, consistent, and fair to all parties (Hardman, 1960, pp. 3–10).

Relationships with Hard-to-Engage Clients

Another group of client systems with whom it is difficult to develop a working relationship are clients who are distrusting or afraid to become involved. Many of these clients are isolated and may have had a history of being "burned by agencies." Sometimes it is hard to reach clients or community groups who do not want help from the state or federal government and are strongly independent.

Fearful Clients   Hard-to-engage clients in small systems may be mentally ill, physically ill, fearful of personal relationships, or wary of authority. Traditional techniques of engagement may not work with such clients. Therefore, the social worker should be creative and willing to use unconventional strategies or techniques and depart from the usual principles we have delineated in this chapter.

First impressions are important with hard-to-engage client systems. They often make judgments quickly and interpret situations based on negative histories with agencies. To engage the client, the social worker needs to be a warm, considerate, giving, and dependable person, and, in a sense, he or she should be a good senior partner figure to the client and focal system, loving but firm (Sheafor, Horejsi, and Horejsi, 1991, p. 193). As a senior partner figure, the social worker needs to be sure that the client system does not develop an ongoing dependency, yet it also means that the social worker may do more home visits and become more personally involved with the client system by accepting some gifts and by observing birthdays and other holidays.

Hard-to-Reach Groups   At the medium-system level, engaging a hard-to-engage group may include arranging the meetings for a group of day-care mothers and ensuring that each member has transportation. By helping with these very basic functions, the social worker is taking on the group's dependency needs and helping the client system understand that he or she is safe and considerate (Kowal et al., 1989). The social worker communicates to the client that he or she has something that the client needs and wants and is willing to tune in to the needs of the group. In addition, the social worker wants to identify leverage persons within the group and engage them in the same way. Their importance in the group is to counteract the client system's distrust and fear of help from an outside person and provide assurance that your relationship is neither superficial nor temporary.

Frequency of Contacts   At all levels in engaging hard-to-reach client systems, it is important to have frequent contacts. We know that the more frequently people come in contact with one another, the less likely they hold prejudices and distrust each other. Therefore, frequent phone calls, face-to-face meetings on the client system's turf, and informal, written notes help to maintain contact. Additionally, if the client system experiences a crisis, it is helpful if the social worker can be there at that time. Great bonding and relationship building can take place with client systems during emergencies.

Racial and Cultural Differences   With hard-to-engage client systems, the social worker needs to be tactful and aware of any statements that might be misconstrued by sensitive client systems (Benjamin, 1987). In one such example, a white social worker was working with the issue of perceived racism within a school system with a group of African-American mothers from the inner city. He needed to be aware of their perspective. He strictly avoided anything that might be misunderstood as criticism of their group. Therefore, although he felt from their statements that the entire school system was racist and against them, he withheld those comments until he had developed their trust and they had faith in his judgment. Then he helped them identify specific, key individuals who could effect change and ensure that racist policies are eliminated in the school.

Expectations   During the relationship-building time with hard-to-engage client groups, it is important that social workers do not place excessive demands or expectations on them. Case Example 5.4 illustrates the point.

The case demonstrates the need to move slowly with client systems who are hard to engage in certain contexts.

System Brutalization   Hard-to-engage clients may have a history of being "brutalized" by human service providers. *Brutalization* is treating clients without respect or sensitivity to their needs. Large public agencies may "lose track" of clients or move clients from one worker to another. Brutalization generates helplessness, and clients may need to test a social worker, taking an extended period of time before they will trust the social worker to make changes in their lives. They may feel that their situation is hopeless, and you must be patient and understand

---

Case Example 5.4

An Adoptive Child, David

Ella is a school social worker with a generalist perspective whose client is David, a newly adopted eight-year-old boy. Ella makes frequent contacts with the child both at home and at school. She also is in touch with the teacher. Ella explains to the teacher that he ought to avoid placing extra demands on David because the child is expending a great amount of energy grieving over the loss of his biological family and adjusting to a new adoptive family.

Ella helps the teacher understand that although the teacher is there to provide an education, he should wait until a meaningful relationship has developed and he becomes sensitive to David's needs before placing the same demands on the adopted child as he does on other students. Ella further explains that the teacher should not be permissive, just that additional demands should not be made.

---

that the progress toward effecting change will be slow (Paster, 1986). During this time, it is helpful to reinforce any positive actions the client system might show or strengths they may possess.

Physical Contact   Making appropriate physical contact with the hard-to-reach client is not unusual. Within limits, it is acceptable and useful to be openly demonstrative in your caring for the client, as long as clients are comfortable and you do not exceed professional boundaries. For example, when working with a group of emotionally impaired children who are in a residential program, you may give the children hugs, take them by the hand to show them something, or even restrain them if they begin acting out. Physical contact with clients must have meaning for them and be helpful to them. Social worker gratification is never the reason for physical contact with clients (Cormier and Cormier, 1985).

Self-Disclosure   A social worker may also disclose some information about himself or herself that is appropriate. Self-disclosure can help clients see the social worker as an authentic human being rather than as a representative of an impersonal agency (Hollis and Woods, 1982, p. 114; Sheafor, Horejsi, and Horejsi, 1991). On the other hand, social workers ought to examine their own motivation for self-disclosure. Sometimes, when social workers disclose information about themselves, they become overly identified with the clients, feel guilty about having said too much and, in turn, are simply ineffective. Clients are much more interested in their own needs and in their own lives than they are in the social worker's life. Hear what the client is asking and respond to the client—to the underlying message as well as the overt message. Case Example 5.5 further explains the principle.

Summary   Hard-to-engage client systems can prove to be some of the most fulfilling cases. Working with a low-income, single mother with three dependent

CASE EXAMPLE 5.5

Understanding Self-Disclosure—Sandra

Sandra is a young social worker who is working with a group of parents who have disabled, chronically ill children. Sandra is unmarried and has no children. The group is working hard on learning alternative parenting skills, sharing their own concerns, and dealing with their own fears. One member of the group asks Sandra if she has children. It is appropriate for Sandra to tell the group she is not a parent. However, the real meaning of the question ought to be responded to. It is likely the group is really wondering whether or not she knows enough of the reality of parenthood to be effective in working with them. This is the real question, and Sandra needs to respond to it.

children and watching her grow during the professional relationship into an independent, effective parent and bread-winner is, indeed, satisfying.

Effecting change with community leaders and influencing them toward an understanding that it is a community necessity to provide social resources (Kahn, 1966) are equally rewarding. The key to success across the various system sizes with which social workers work is the quality of one's relationships and one's willingness to do what is necessary and perhaps what is unconventional to engage hard-to-reach clients (Sheafor et al., 1991, p. 193).

Relationships with Action Systems

Of all action system activities, perhaps the most important is maintaining and building quality relationships with the other people who are going to effect change with the client system. Initiating these relationships is usually more effective under neutral circumstances, when there is no pressure. While we feel we never have enough time to do the initial relationship-building with agencies, it will save us hours and help our client systems more if we do take the time. One new generalist social worker, for the first few months on the job, kept a list of the people with whom he routinely came in contact and with many of the clients with whom he was working. At the end of the month, he had a list of seventeen persons whom he routinely called every two to three weeks, whether he was working with a client system or not. Not only was this a useful way of maintaining a relationship with workers and agency staff, but it also provided him a comprehensive view of the community and the kinds of systemic problems that might be just over the horizon.

Scheduling regular staffings or meetings, depending upon the size of the client system, maintains contact with the action system. Staffings are an important component of many residential treatment programs and sometimes happen on a daily basis. In other situations, such as with community organizational groups, staffings pull together outreach workers on a weekly or monthly basis and could be an important way of maintaining quality relationships and quickly eliminating misunderstandings.

Frank honesty, along with an ability to clearly state one's case while not projecting failures to others, assists one's relationships with action systems.

Wells (1989) discusses how she initially formed relationships within the school system where she worked as a social worker. She stresses the critical importance of working out relationships in order to begin work within that system. It seemed as though she had to choose between strict adherence to her professional role and being effective within the school system. For example, she allowed certain school personnel who did not have a direct contact with her work to staff family cases. While this raised confidentiality issues for her as a social worker, she realized that questioning this practice to an authoritarian school principal would preclude her continued effectiveness within the school system in that community.

Relationships within the organizations where we work, in a more general sense, are explored later in this book when we talk about professional issues and the future of social work. These issues include dating coworkers, working together as a team under stressful situations, and office politics.

Relationships with Focal Systems

The *focal systems* are those systems that need to be changed so that client systems' goals can be met. The relationships we have with focal systems are often adversarial.

For example, a school principal may be a focal system when working with the homeless population. Homelessness involves many school-age children, and placing them in schools so their educations are not interrupted is usually a primary goal for homeless families. However, school administrators are not always willing to allow transient children to participate and may place barriers in the way.

The social worker is committed to link clients to the resources they need, and when an "immovable object" such as a school administrator is encountered, it is

---

CASE EXAMPLE 5.6

Board Misunderstanding

The chair of a community board had failed to invite the new chair of the nominations committee for the board to its monthly meeting. The nominations chair-elect knew about the meeting from various people in the community, and she knew it was important for her to attend. However, the board meeting came and went, and she had not been officially invited. She could have just let it slide, thinking that the chair had forgotten. But instead, in a very polite way, she inquired whether the board meeting had taken place and why she had not been invited. The chair said he had asked the staff to invite her and had been assured that she had been invited. A possible misunderstanding was quickly resolved, and at the next board committee, the nomination chair-elect was invited and learned about the board's needs. If she had not inquired, or if she and the chair had not had a good relationship, she would have been left out and could have projected many false assumptions, when, in fact, it was simply a staff person's oversight in failing to make a telephone call.

not unusual for a social worker to experience anger toward the person. Angry feelings can create problems that will only further stand in the way of obtaining resources for clients. Maintaining a professional stance in this sort of relationship helps us to depersonalize the process. Emotions are less likely to become entangled in confronting or trying to influence the focal system if the social worker presents his or her professional self, not personal feelings.

Developing Relationships   The most critical factor in developing relationships actually comes from the way in which one uses one's professional self. If you genuinely like people and want to help them, this attitude comes across to others. They can feel your energy, your positiveness, your optimism. Because your persona affects client systems, it is important to genuinely know yourself. If you are feeling down and discouraged on a particular day, if possible, do not go out to develop new relationships. You should develop new relationships when you are positive and at your best. In this perspective, think of how you get to know someone. What are the steps you go through? What works and what does not work for you? Again, do a brief self-assessment to understand your personal strengths of developing relationships.

Some of us do a much better job developing a relationship with a large group or an agency than we do with individuals. Understand what your strengths and weaknesses are in developing relationships, and improve areas of weakness while you take joy in the strengths you have. In examining the strengths and weaknesses you bring to relationships, consider the other systems with which you are interacting. You may be an expert at understanding the agency's regulations, purpose, and your role as a generalist social worker. On the other hand, the client system may be afraid, unsure, and unclear about the legal authority you have.

You want to tune into where the other person is coming from and begin active listening and developing your relationship (Shulman, 1992). We do not mean to imply you ought to just let the client system or the focal system ramble, but, instead, direct the discussion as you develop the relationship. This includes formulating a contract stating what you can do and how you will do it and asking the same from the client, the action, and focal systems.

Building trust begins as early as setting the time for the next appointment and discussion of what you will be doing. You may be afraid and unsure of yourself while your clients trust you implicitly. Tune in to the other system's perspective of the relationship and expectations.

Summary

Relationship development and maintenance is an aspect of the helping process in which one's professional self plays a major role. Understanding that relationships need to be established with the client system and the focal system as well as within one's own organization should lend a focus for one's efforts. And, it is important to understand that the timing of developing those relationships may vary, depending on whether one is working in a crisis situation or in normal times. Where and how one initiates the relationship and how successful one is in developing a relationship with the leverage person in that system will go a long way toward dictating the success one has in the change process.

The personal attributes one displays in the relationship, such as generally liking people, and the enthusiasm one expresses add to one's success when carrying out generalist roles and skills. We will discuss specific roles and skills associated with the Area of Concern and Engagement phase. But, roles and skills cannot be effective unless one is able to establish meaningful relationships.

ROLES AND SKILLS IN PHASE I

Enabler and Conflict Manager are the two social work generalist roles most frequently associated with identifying Areas of Concern and Engagement. Although both roles have been introduced, further descriptions and examples enlarge upon this phase of the change process. In addition, the skills linked with the roles in this phase are also discussed.

Enabler

The major goals of the Area of Concern and Engagement phase are: (1) identifying areas of concerns, (2) engaging systems, and (3) building relationships with client systems, action systems, and focal systems to facilitate the entire change process. All three goals can only be reached when we put into action the enabler role with its accompanying skills.

Enablers work toward engaging client systems in the solutions of problems and enhancing their own capacities. They are excellent communicators who use empathy, good listening skills, appropriate questions, supportive comments, and advice giving that is limited and appropriate. They help people identify their concerns in parcels, rather than in overwhelming wholes. They encourage people to express themselves, and all of their work is aimed at building trust.

In a trusting relationship, people are able to take some emotional risks, and may be able to find creative solutions to their concerns. Acting as an enabler with involuntary clients and hard-to-reach client systems is no easy task because trust is difficult to build. The enabler is willing to go slowly when necessary and to find innovative and unconventional means as they work with people.

Conflict Manager

We pointed out that conflict is commonly present when we begin our work with client systems, action systems, and target systems. The precipitating factors that bring clients to social workers and that bring social workers to client systems are often stressful, contentious, and discordant; therefore, we are called upon to manage the conflict inherent in beginnings (Parad, 1965).

Conflict managers deal with conflict swiftly and directly. They understand its nature and possess the communication skills necessary to ease tension so that problems and concerns are identified and professional relationships are built.

Skills Associated with Enablers and Conflict Managers

All three skill categories are called upon in Phase One of the Crystal Model. We use our analytic and interactional skills, and, in the following discussion, we specify skills in both categories—analytic and interactional—that are essential in this phase of the change process. We begin with several analytic skills and then proceed to interactional skills.

Identifying Performance Discrepancies

When areas of concern and problems are brought to our attention, the ability to identify performance discrepancies—an analytic skill—regarding the focal system assists our progress through Phase One. Very often, focal systems exhibit discrepancies between actual performance and what they or others may expect. The following example throws some light on the need for this skill when working with communities.

As concerned citizens, we expect communities to provide social services to their populations. When this does not happen, we see a possible area of concern. In East Branch, a medium-sized community in the Midwest, low-income people are not taking advantage of existing services because public transportation is very limited. The community is not meeting its obligations to provide societal resources appropriate to the needs of the community. This is a case of performance discrepancy.

Performance Discrepancy: Families   Small systems such as families also experience performance discrepancy. For example, in most cultures, when a family member dies, kin and close friends are expected to grieve openly. If an individual does not live up to his or her familial/cultural expectations, a performance discrepancy exists. Family members question the relationship of the silent person to the departed relative, and queries arise regarding the appropriateness of behavior. The source of the problem or discomfort is mysterious to everyone. All that is known is that a family member acted in what appeared to be an inappropriate manner.

Performance Discrepancy: Community   Performance discrepancies become clearly exposed and highlighted during a crisis. Consider a small midwestern community that is fairly homogeneous. If a neighbor confronts a tragedy such as a burned home, a particular sort of response is expected, given the nature and size of the community. It is likely the informal resource system will respond, and families and friends will help rebuild the home or meet in some other way the needs of the family experiencing the tragedy.

Such a response is likely out of the question if the home is in a tenement district of a large city. We expect societal resources to be employed to take care of the crisis. Neither community response is better. It is not only individuals who manifest performance discrepancy. As you analyze areas of concern and problems, you need to look at how larger systems—families, communities and organizations—behave.

A crisis lets us see how a community responds, whether actions match stated values.

Diversity We need to examine how we identify performance discrepancies in the context of diversity. What is appropriate and expected for one group may not be for another. What happens in rural Iowa may not happen in Chicago. People may experience the same losses, but community responses are expected to be different. Likewise, the response to the death of a young loved one in an Arabic culture can be considerably different from the response of a young person's death in a northern European family. We need to be able to see real performance discrepancies that contribute to areas of concern and problems and those issues that may be appropriate given a specific culture or context.

Identifying Frequency and Duration

Identifying timing, frequency, duration, and extent of an event, condition, problems, and reports constitutes a meaningful skill in Phase One. The frequency with which a particular condition occurs is important in identifying areas of concern. If a child is slapped by a parent who is enraged at a specific behavior the child exhibited, and this happened once in five years, we treat the incident quite differently when a parent who is in a rage hits a child weekly. The child who is hit frequently is likely more at risk than the child who had one terrible experience. That parent may even come to appreciate the limits of parental tolerance.

Identifying a condition or problem's duration must be done effectively during this phase. We need to ask how long a situation has been going on. For example, spouse abuse that is experienced during courtship, frequently after marriage, and even after divorce is abuse of long standing, and its duration helps us identify the concerns to be assessed.

It is not unusual for prolonged community problems to come to the forefront in a community crisis. To illustrate this point, consider a community in which substance abuse and suicide among young people are long-standing problems. For the most part, such situations go largely unnoticed until a child of a prominent person is effected. The child of a politician or a corporate executive commits suicide and, suddenly, the city council, the media, and the entire community identify teen suicide as a major concern. Along the same order, there was little concern about crack cocaine until it crept into the suburbs and wealthier communities. At that point the drug takes on serious proportions.

Identifying Priorities

As we identify areas of concern, we must place them in a priority listing. We know we cannot do everything at once, and furthermore, some problems are simply more pressing than others.

Concerns that are life-threatening are obviously first on our priority list. After that, priorities reflect client systems' expressed concerns. We listen to clients while not imposing our priorities on them.

The priorities of larger societal systems such as governments and corporations may be at odds with social work's priorities. In social work, we deal with critical issues that seem to go unaddressed by the political establishment and even by society at large. For example, parents in low income families do not obtain decent employment; young people do not receive adequate education; vocational education is neither broad nor accessible. Long-term poverty results from flimsy investments in human beings, and society continues to shortchange our youth and our families. Identifying societal priorities and then setting about changing those most critical to our professional purpose are legitimate social work activities.

Creating a Helpful Atmosphere

When we begin working with client systems, action systems, and focal systems, we cannot forget the importance of setting up an atmosphere in which helping can begin. Creation of such an atmosphere is preparatory to putting interactional skills into practice (Benjamin, 1987).

If we are seeing people in an office, chairs are arranged so that conversations can proceed openly. Usually, social workers do not sit behind desks, but talk with clients face-to-face, without artificial barriers. We make sure that our desks are clean, free of clutter, and absent of material containing confidential information on any client. It is also important for our office to be neat and professional-looking. It is disconcerting to talk to a helping person if all one sees is disarray. When social workers see clients in their own homes, they must treat the clients' homes with respect. The social worker arrives on time, uses the door the client designates, and sits where invited to sit. Be aware of boundaries within person's homes. For example, there is little reason for a social worker to go into a client's bedroom unless visiting a child or ill person. If food and drink are offered, a social worker decides whether acceptance will assist in relationship building or will detract from it. When a social worker creates a helpful atmosphere, the stage is set for effective helping.

Listening   Areas of concern are identified because they are brought forth by clients, by the community, by the agency or by professional concerns. In that light, listening is the key interactional skill necessary for that process to begin (Egan, 1975). We listen to what others have to say, and we hear, observe, and even "hear" what the nonverbal persons are expressing. Do not be afraid of silence when working with clients. Some concerns are very painful; and words are simply hard to find. At other times, people are confused and really do not know what to say. Beginning work on problems is both frightening and overwhelming, and we need to listen carefully, even to the silences.

Empathy   Listening allows us to respond to client, focal, and action systems verbally and nonverbally. These responses are the manifestation of our empathy skills. We discussed this skill in the last chapter. We raise it again because its use is so critical in this phase. We cannot begin to build relationships with people if we do not display empathy. People will not feel we understand, and trust cannot be built without understanding and faith in people who are offering help.

Questioning   We often begin our work with clients with questions. We must know whether or not ours is the correct agency for them to be involved with; we need to know who they are and what their concerns are. Questions are always necessary. We urge you, however, to be quite cautious with questioning and not to overdo its use. Ask as many open-ended questions as possible. Naturally, there are times when closed questions must be asked, but open questions can help us identify concerns and build relationships much more effectively than closed questions because the client is volunteering more information that will surely be of help.

Application of Skills

Practice illustrations can become vehicles for integration of the phases, roles, and skills. Following are two case examples that illustrate work in this phase of the change process. Both case examples focus on two agonizing concerns in our society: child abuse and homelessness. The first case example illustrates our work with smaller systems, yet emphasizes the need to engage larger systems even while we are working with individual families. The second case example addresses homelessness from a larger-system perspective while engaging the real concerns of families who are homeless. Read them, concentrating on the beginning phase of work, identifying areas of concern and engagement. After reading Case Example 5.8, identify the members of each system and think about how the social worker raised concerns and engaged each system.

CASE EXAMPLE 5.7

Hubert Family

Chris Hubert, age 10, was referred to social services because he disrupts his classroom constantly, and today the teacher noted bruises on his arms and neck and one under his eye. She is concerned but does not know what to do about Chris's behavior. The school social worker contacted state social services. The social worker from social services followed up on the situation by first visiting Chris at school, and then by making a home visit.

Prior to direct contact with the client system, the social worker speaks with her supervisor. They discuss possible resources in the community, and the social worker thinks about what she knows regarding child abuse, the conditions surrounding it, as well as ways to investigate it.

The social worker visits Chris in school. Chris says his father beat him. He indicates that this was not the first time it has happened. The social worker calls the mother for an appointment within twenty-four hours when the father is not present. A home visit is arranged.

During the initial visit at home, the social worker explains her role with social services. She inquires about the severity of abuse, its history, duration, and frequency. She attempts to discover Mrs. Hubert's view of the injuries and discerns her strengths.

Results of the initial visit lead the worker to continue her contact with the family. In order to understand the situation at home, Mr. Hubert needs to become involved. Likewise, the teacher who sees Chris every day needs an understanding of how to be helpful to him. Mr. Hubert is part of the focal system. He needs to change in order to help Chris. The teacher is willing to help, so she and the school social worker become part of the action system.

The meeting with Chris's dad takes place at home with the mother and Chris present. The worker inquires about the abuse, and urges Mr. Hubert to consider the ramifications of his behavior. Mr. Hubert does not want to lose Chris to foster care, nor does he want to be prosecuted for child abuse. He states there is pressure from work.

The conversation with Chris's teacher centers around helping her increase her understanding of the child's behavior. The teacher is afraid other students have put Chris in a "loser" role. The focus must be on changing the school environment so that Chris will feel welcome and comfortable in the classroom. The worker identifies the other members of the action system as the Mental Health Center where she plans to refer the family and the homebase service program. The school social worker needs encouragement to change the atmosphere at school so that it is generally more accepting for Chris and children in his circumstances. The Mental Health Center and homebase program offer parenting skills and counseling that have proved helpful for couples like the Huberts. The social worker contacts both the school social worker and a social worker at the Mental Health Center describing the family's needs and her view of the situation.

CONCLUSION

In this chapter, we discussed how to identify areas of concern. We examined how to initiate contact with the various sized systems with which social workers may work, including the client system, action system, and focal system. Contact is engaging that system and opening the boundaries of that system.

We explored how to bring one's professional self to the helping process through relationships. Relationships are developed with the client system, focal system, and action system as well as with various organizations. Treating client

CASE EXAMPLE 5.8

Esse

The generalist social worker employed by the Community Services Center raises a concern regarding the absence of quality, affordable housing and programs for the growing homeless population in the community based on new census data and a report by graduate students at the local university. The worker contacts the Homeless Union, the client system.

The Homeless Union is a loosely organized group of homeless people. Thinking that the absence of affordable housing is only one component of their concern, she interviews leaders of the organization. She collects statistics regarding the extent of the problem. Her agency needs to know how many people are homeless, the conditions under which people are now living, and what the Homeless Union thinks the agency and community can do to address the concern. She brings her concern to the Executive Director and other staff to study during a regular meeting. They agree that contacting a large foundation in the community, the Esse Community Foundation, is a first step toward effecting this concern.

The Esse Community Foundation has a history of involvement in the most salient issues of the day, yet has done nothing regarding the homeless. The regular staff meeting at the Community Services Center also focuses upon what sort of contract with Esse they should seek as well as the internal resources the agency is willing to commit. Tackling this problem is a major thrust of the agency.

After the initial agreement from her agency, the social worker sets up an interview with a reporter from the local newspaper, hoping the media will cooperate to inform the community of the growing problem regarding housing and homeless people. The newspaper responds, publishing a story that very week.

The worker at the Community Services Center identifies the focal system: the Esse Community Foundation Board president. Her area of concern with the foundation is in the form of a question: Is the foundation doing all it can to assist the homeless? Believing the answer is no, a meeting is set up with the Presi-

dent of the Foundation Board and the Executive Director of her agency. This meeting is in preparation for a larger meeting with the Foundation Board. Information regarding the extent of the problem is shared and inquiries are made regarding the extent of knowledge by the Foundation of housing and homelessness.

Knowing other systems must change in order to change the conditions in the community, the agency social worker designates the City Council as well as the entire community as other members of the focal system. The City Council has not concerned itself with this problem, and the initial contact takes place with a "friendly" member of the Council focusing upon how to win support of the entire Council.

The community at large is simply not aware of the concerns, although the initial newspaper article did generate some interest. The agency people call a press conference to further discuss the situation. They also call meetings with various community groups, particularly church groups to gain support. The agency is attempting to raise the consciousness in the community.

At this point, the social worker and the agency are not sure who will comprise the action system. It is hoped that other agencies and community groups will join the efforts, including the Esse Foundation.

The City Council meets and decides to table concerns regarding housing and homelessness. The Esse Community Foundation, in reaction to the Council rebuff, decides to contract with the Community Services agency to further study the housing problem. The staff at the Community Services agency and the Homeless Union see this commitment as a beginning, and they decide to accept a contract, moving forward with the issue. There is no assurance that the Community and City Council will develop appropriate concerns and resources, but the agency and client are willing to go ahead in light of the seriousness of the conflict with their mission—quality housing for all.

systems with respect by acknowledging client strengths is a guiding principle in relationship building.

The case examples of beginning work with client and focal systems are meant to provoke discussion and to illustrate what generalist social workers do with different sized systems. They also serve to portray the common skills and roles that generalists use regardless of the systems with whom they are working.

References

Baer, Betty L., and Federico, Ronald. (1978). Educating the Baccalaureate Social Worker: *Report of the Undergraduate Social Work Curriculum Development Project.* Cambridge, MA: Ballinger, p. 86.

Benjamin, Alfred. (1987). *The Helping Interview: With Case Illustrations.* Boston: Houghton Mifflin.

Cingolani, Judith. (1984). "Social Conflict Perspectives on Work with Involuntary Clients." *Journal of Social Work, 19*(5), 442–446.

Cormier, William, and Cormier, L. Sherilyn. (1985). *Interviewing Strategies for Helpers,* 2nd ed. Monterey, CA: Brooks/Cole.

Egan, Gerald. (1975). *The Skilled Helper: A Model for Systematic Helping and Interpersonal Relating.* Monterey, CA: Brooks/Cole.

Fischer, Joel. (1978). *Effective Casework Practice: An Eclectic Approach.* New York: McGraw-Hill, p. 191.

Golan, Naomi. (1978). *Treatment in Crisis Situations.* New York: Free Press.

Hardman, Dell. (1960). *The Functions of the Probation Officer, Federal Probation,* 9/24/60, pp. 3–10.

Hollis, Florence, and Woods, Mary E. (1982). *Casework: A Psychosocial Therapy.* New York: Random House, p. 114.

Imber-Black, Evan. (1988). *Families and Larger Systems.* Guilford Press, New York, p. 75.

Johnson, Louise. (1989). *Social Work Practice: A Generalist Approach,* 3rd ed. Boston: Allyn and Bacon, p. 171.

Jones, M., Magua, S., and Shyne, A. (1981). Effective Practice with Families in Protective and Preventive Services: What Works? *Child Welfare, 60,* 66–79.

Kahn, Alfred. (1966). *Neighborhood Information Centers.* New York: Columbia University School of Social Work.

Kowal, L., Kottmeier, C., Ayoub, C., Komives, J., Robinson, D., and Allen, J. (1989). Characteristics of Families at Risk of Problems in Parenting: Finding from a Home-Based Secondary Prevention Program. *Child Welfare, LXVII*(5), 520–538.

Lippett, Ronald Watson, Jeanne, and Westley, Bruce. (1958). *The Dynamics of Planned Change.* New York: Harcourt, Brace & World, pp. 21–48.

Lloyd, June C. (1980). *Placement Prevention and Family Reunification: A Handbook for the Family Centered Service Practitioner,* rev. ed. Iowa City, IA: National Resource Center on Family Based Services.

Montiel, M., and Wong, P. (1983). A Theoretical Critique of the Minority Perspective. *Social Casework, 64*(2), 112–117.

Parad, Howard J. (ed.). (1965). *Crisis Intervention: Selected Readings.* New York: Family-Service Association of America.

Paster, O. D. (1986). A Social Action Model of Intervention for Difficult to Reach Populations. *American Journal of Orthopsychiatry, 56*(4), 625–629.

Pincus, Allen, and Minahan, Ann. (1973). *Social Work Practice: Model and Method.* Itasca, IL: F.E. Peacock, p. 57.

Reeser, Linda Cherrey, and Epstein, Irwin. (1990). *Professionalization and Activism in Social Work: the Sixties, the Eighties and the Future.* New York: Columbia University Press.

Rogers, Carl. (1951). *Client Centered Therapy, Its Current Practice, Implications and Theory.* Boston: Houghton Mifflin.

Rubenstein, Hiasura, and Block, Mary Henry. (1982). *Things that Matter: Influences on Helping Relationships.* New York: MacMillan.

Ryan, William. (1971). *Blaming the Victim.* Pantheon Books, pp. 22–23.

Saleeby, Dennis. (1992). *The Strengths Perspective in Social Work.* White Plains, NY: Longman.

Schlosberg, S. B., and Kagan, R. M. (1988). Practice Strategies for Engaging Chronic, Multi-Problem Families. *Social Casework, 69*(1), 3–9.

Sheafor, Bradford W., Horejsi, Charles R., and Horejsi, Gloria A. (1991). *Techniques and Guidelines for Social Work Practice,* 2nd ed. Needham Heights, MA: Allyn and Bacon, p. 193.

Shulman, Lawrence. (1992). *The Skills of Helping Individuals, Families, and Groups,* 3rd ed. Itasca, IL: F.E. Peacock.

Thomas, George. (1990). "'Bottomed Out' in a 'Bottom Up' Society: Social Work Education and the Default and Recapture of Professional Leadership in Child Welfare." Paper presented at the Council of Social Work Education 36th Annual Program Meeting, Reno, NV.

Wells, Carolyn Cressy. (1989). *Social Work Day to Day: The Experience of Generalist Social Work Practice.* New York and London: Longman.

Wells, Kathleen, and David, Baird E. (eds.). (1991). *Family Preservation Services: Research and Evaluation.* Newbury Park, CA: Sage Publications.

Information Gathering

OVERVIEW

Phase Two of the Crystal Model focuses on gathering information about the area of concern and the related systems that may be involved in the change process. We focus on information gathering early in the change process because our work with client, focal and action systems must be based on accurate information, gathered in a fair, scientific, and humane way. The information that is collected becomes the basis of assessment, designing and planning, implementation, and, finally, transition and evaluation.

Information gathering in the Crystal Model sets the stage for more specific data-gathering procedures that are applied to *microsystems* (small systems), *mezzosystems* (medium systems), and *macrosystems* (large systems and organizations). It is also important to know how to gather information from the focal system and the action system in order to learn as much as possible about a client situation before moving into the assessment phase. Finally, we also discuss in this chapter the social work roles and skills frequently used in information gathering.

THE CRYSTAL MODEL PROCESS OF PLANNED CHANGE AND INFORMATION GATHERING

In the change process, information gathering provides us with the basic data for the work that will take place on behalf of our client systems. Although information gathering takes place largely in Phase Two of the Crystal Model, it is continuous, like all the other steps in the process. New information may have to be incorporated at any stage in the change process, even though the bulk of information has already been collected. The structure of the Crystal Model process reinforces an openness to collecting information whenever something new and relevant enters the picture.

Competency

The Baer and Federico (1978) competency that relates to the purposes of this phase of the Crystal Model emphasizes collecting information to identify where the "relationship between people and social institutions needs to be initiated, enhanced, restored, protected or terminated" (p. 86). Implicit in this competency is the ability to interview, observe, record, listen, and even to use computer technology in order to retrieve the kind of information that will be helpful to client systems. In addition, information gathering must include ways in which client systems participate in data collection. Social workers collect information from involuntary and voluntary clients, from action systems, and from focal systems. As we have stated, all of these systems are relevant to the change effort.

Purposes of Information Gathering

Successful information gathering has two major purposes: (1) understanding the client, focal, and action systems and their perspectives of the concern, and (2) provision of a base for assessment, planning, and change (Johnson, 1992, p. 220). It should be understood that to be successful, information gathering must be detailed, and this requires a considerable amount of time. Frequently, in an effort to alleviate the pain experienced by client systems as quickly as possible, social workers can be inclined to begin "helping" before they understand the situation that exists within and around a client system. Instead, social workers should take the time to actively listen, to observe, to read, to ask questions, and to talk to people who are involved in the situation the client is facing.

The Interview

The most commonly used technique to gather information in social work is the direct, traditional social work interview. According to Cormier and Cormier (1991, p. 172), the interview is used frequently "because of its practicality in applied settings and its potential efficiency." Pincus and Minahan (1973) state that the interview is the most important tool in data collection, yet overemphasis on this technique has often ruled out other modes that could be used in its place or to supplement or complement the interview (p. 134).

The interview is a systematic, purposeful interaction between at least two people—the interviewer and the interviewee. In the social work profession, the interviewer is usually the social worker, while the interviewee is the client system, the focal system, or the action system. Even other social workers who are part of the change system are interviewees. Although interviews are much more than "conversation," verbal communication is the basis of the interview.

Interviewing Environment

Interviews take place in social work offices, in homes, or in other institutions or organizations such as hospitals, schools, or factories. The place where the interview occurs can have a significant impact upon the content of the interview. Too often, social workers gather information at their convenience in the environment in which they are most comfortable. Given the person-environment focus of social work, gathering of information in places such as the social worker's private office seems illogical. Unless one is working in a residential treatment program, a hospital, or a school, the social worker's office is unconnected to the lives of clients. Home-based services to children and families and to the elderly rely on the home visit in all aspects of service delivery, including information gathering. Taking a cue from such services that support the person-environment focus, we recommend "out-of-the-office" visits as much as possible.

General Components of All Interviews

According to Gorden (1987, p. 5) all successful interviews are collected by three "elementary forms of human activity: empathy, participation and observation." All three are used simultaneously, although the level of intensity varies according to the structure and purpose of the interview.

Empathy   Earlier in the book, we refer to empathy as a "cross-cutting" skill, fundamental to every role and every phase of the change process. Social workers must use this central skill if they are to collect accurate data. We must listen with the "third ear," hearing the covert as well as the overt meaning of the client system's statements. Only if we truly listen will reliable data be assembled.

Observation   Effective social workers must be keen observers. Much is learned from direct observation of people in their environments. Social work knowledge regarding observation is drawn from anthropology, the discipline that relies most heavily on the skill (Bernard, 1988).

The skilled observer is able to discern the meaning of nonverbal cues from voice tone to dress of those being observed. Anthropologists rely on participant observation to gather data. They must learn the language of the people they are studying, including the everyday vocabulary, the slang, and the idioms. Anthropologists must become "explicitly aware" of the details the people and the culture exhibit. The ability to remember particulars, such as the color and style of a person's clothing or the manner in which simple tasks are performed, is an example of "explicit awareness" (Bernard, 1988). Social workers need to adopt the practices of anthropologists and translate them for use in social work.

Videotaping is sometimes used in family sessions to provide information to the social worker as well as feedback to the family. In some cases, videotaping has even been used while interviewing in the home. While this is intrusive, it is amazing how families become used to the videotaping and drift back to their natural reactions to situations.

Participation   Social workers are not really participant observers because they are actively engaged in the change effort. However, when collecting data, social workers must approach client systems with the openness of the participant observer, with well-honed observational skills.

Clients may best be understood if social workers actually attend group meetings where they are present, move in with the family, or go to school with the

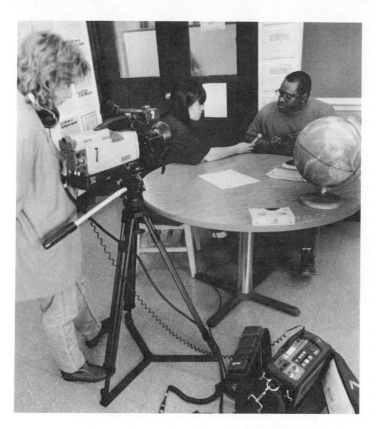

*Videotaping generalist practice
helps social workers better
observe nonverbal behavior.*

child, so that the social worker can see their world through their eyes as well as observe their behavior. Although it is usually not possible or desirable to resort to such extremes, social workers can leave their offices and observe their clients in more natural surroundings. This greatly enhances the quality of the information that is collected.

Interviewing Patterns

Two predominant patterns of interviewing exist in social work. Interviews with clients can be open, in which the agenda is set by the client system and no particular forms must be completed. Structured interviews, on the other hand, are laid out before the client and social worker interact. Social work interviews are frequently a combination of open and structured interview formats. A brief description of each type of interview follows.

Open Interviews   Although information gathering is always purposeful, the open interview contains unlimited possibilities. With the client setting the agenda, the social worker usually begins with a question or a statement such as "Can you tell me what is troubling you?" or "Perhaps you'd like to tell me what's on your mind." With open beginnings, the client can start exactly as he or she desires. The social worker must be especially attentive to the nonverbal communication in open interviews and respond empathetically.

Case Example 6.1, which features an interview with Lisa, a nine-year-old girl, by a school social worker, held during a walk on the school grounds on a sunny, fall afternoon, demonstrates the open interview.

The open interview allows the client system to set the agenda. Even the time it takes and the manner in which information is put forth is up to the client. Many interviews are less open than the example with Lisa and her social worker. However, even when agendas are set by both the social worker and the client, the ingredients of the open interview can be present. The social worker took her lead from Lisa. As the information gathering phase ensues, it is likely the social worker will be more directive, knowing that information that can form the base for the assessment needs to be gathered.

Structured Interviews   Often questions are a part of structured interviews and have been formulated long before the initial contact with a system in which information is to be gathered. As a college student, if you have applied for student housing or financial aid, you may be familiar with the structured interview format. Social workers are expected to obtain information from clients vis-à-vis forms—that is, the structured interview. Often the social worker fills out the form in the presence of the client system. The social worker can spend more time on particular components of the form than others, can respond with empathy to the client's concerns and, generally, can be relatively flexible and open in the conducting of the structured interview.

We caution against excessive questioning. Questioning can be intimidating,

---

CASE EXAMPLE 6.1

Lisa

Social Worker: Sometimes it's easier to talk when you're outside of the school building.

Lisa: I guess so. (Lisa is very quiet, walking slowly with her head down, shoulders slumped.)

Social Worker: Your teacher told me that you said you wanted to talk to me. Is there something special on your mind today? (They stop, looking at the trees at the edge of the playing field.)

Lisa: Yes. But I can't talk about it. (Lisa is very quiet, giving her response almost in a whisper.)

Social Worker: Things that mean a lot to us or are scary are hard to talk about.

Lisa: Yes. (Lisa takes a deep breath. She looks more relaxed.)

Social Worker: When you feel like talking, I'll listen. (They continue walking.)

Lisa: I feel like talking, but I don't know how.

Social Worker: Just start where you want to. We've got lots of time.

intrusive, and can drive people away. On the other hand, we cannot gather information without asking questions. We encourage you to explain the use of the questions you ask during data gathering and to focus upon, to the extent possible, open-ended rather than closed questions. Do not ask unnecessary questions and try to disperse questions between other sorts of verbal communication.

Social histories, risk-assessment scales, application forms, and eligibility forms are just a few of the many forms (structured information gathering techniques) employed by social workers. The following example of a structured interview form is drawn from broad areas identified by the United Way of America Service Identification System (1972). Its purpose is to facilitate information gathering from an individual or family seeking service from a United Way agency. The social worker has this form in her possession, shares it with the client, and together they complete the form. The social worker can ask open-ended questions under each heading, combining that structure with open interview formats.

1. *Income.* In our society, a person's source of income is very important. Without income, a person's options are greatly limited. Therefore, we need to gather information about the person's financial situation.

2. *Basic needs.* The client system's basic needs include housing, food, clothing, protection from others, and access to other services through equal opportunity.

3. *Health.* What is the person's health, both physical and mental? What insurance or other options does the family have for adequate health care?

4. *Education.* What is an individual's educational attainment or training level? In the case of a child client, what is the education process like? Does the child have learning disabilities or other problems that might impede educational progress?

5. *Individual and family development.* The individual and family development area includes family dynamics, strengths, and weaknesses. What traditions are important to the family? How does the family support the development of its members?

This same structure is used to obtain information from agencies and ultimately about a community's human service system.

The benefits of structured interviews are that they provide us with guidelines without predicting people's responses and that they offer the most efficient way of collecting direct information.

Systems Perspective on Information Gathering

We use the two-pronged approach to gather information: (1) data gathered directly from the client system, and (2) data gathered from sources and systems external to the client. We also need an overall perspective that will help us see the whole picture when gathering data.

The systems perspective helps us make sense of the complex situations in which we work. The act of gathering information from various people at different times, sometimes under adverse circumstances and often under stressful conditions, requires that we use a perspective that helps us make sense of competing, sometimes contradictory, data. The systems perspective helps us accomplish our goal because its focus is on the interaction of the person or persons and the environment and takes into consideration the continuous change that systems undergo. In other words, we have a broad view of the situations that clients are experiencing, and we are not undone or confused by the changing nature of the client situation that may even involve new or revised information.

Think of the systems perspective and information gathering as the sense organs of the change effort. If we do not collect accurate information (if we are myopic), we cannot help people change in the ways they want and in the avenues that will increase their opportunities in life. As we have said, collecting correct information is essential for a successful change effort.

The strategies we employ to collect data are embedded in the systems perspective. Put yourself in the position of a social worker in an agency, seeing a client for the first time. Upon first hearing of the client's concern, what was your reaction? Your impulse may be to begin an assessment too soon, before information from many quarters has been collected. Before you act upon the identified area of concern, there may be additional information that needs to be gathered from a number of sources. The systems perspective should guide us toward a broad view of the client system's area of concern.

The three goals of information gathering using the systems perspective are: (1) identify all the systems potentially involved in the situation or concern, (2) remain sensitive to human and contextual diversity, and (3) focus on client strengths and opportunities as well as risks.

Identifying All Systems

Client systems may be families, individuals, groups, communities, or organizations. Obviously, identifying all the systems involved in a large community change effort is more complex than identifying all the systems that are relevant to a single family. There is a need to identify all levels of systems involved, from microsystem to macrosystem, and also to identify the change, the action, and the focal systems. We employ the two-pronged approach when we begin collecting data on all systems involved.

We remind you that the approach includes: (1) all systems that affect the client system and that the client system identifies, and (2) the systems from which we must gather information to form the basis for the assessment. Obviously, there are overlaps between the two. Many of the systems the client identifies are relevant to the assessment, but we need to go beyond the client viewpoint if we are to gather all the relevant information for a sound assessment.

Client System   Case Examples 6.2 and 6.3 — the former involving an individual and the latter, a community — serve to illustrate the point.

CASE EXAMPLE 6.2

Mrs. Olga Barnes

Mrs. Barnes, seventy-four years old, is brought to the intake social worker at the Mountain View Health Facility by her daughter, Jane Fields. Ms. Fields is concerned about her mother's ability to live alone and maintain her own health. Her mother is suffering from emphysema, and can easily contract pneumonia and other pulmonary diseases. In addition, Mrs. Barnes has osteoarthritis.

The social worker, Jeanne Valdez, begins to gather information regarding Mrs. Barnes's health from Mrs. Barnes, Ms. Fields, and, later, from reports from Mrs. Barnes's physician and physical therapist. Ms. Valdez' approach is to collect information from Mrs. Barnes's perspective, in order to determine whether or not she can live alone and maintain her own health. When it is time for the assessment, Ms. Valdez also wants to observe Mrs. Barnes in her own home and gain a bet-

ter understanding of her neighborhood, friends, and family. Therefore, Ms. Valdez seeks this information through a home visit, observation of the neighborhood, and research on available action system organizations and services that might be available to Mrs. Barnes. These may include Meals on Wheels, Friendly Visitors, In-home Health Care, and Specialized Transportation.

After collecting the information specific to Mrs. Barnes's health and the other systems, Ms. Valdez has the information to form a better understanding of the client's situation as well as the basis for the assessment, and, later, the plan for helping Mrs. Barnes meet her goal of maintaining the highest level of healthful independence, whether that be in a nursing home or in her own home with numerous supports.

Change System The agency, through its regulations and policies, frames the practice context. Service to clients is always dependent on the agency. Before any change effort is begun, the social worker needs to be familiar with all aspects of the agency, including its goals, its funding, its geographic service area, as well as numerous other facts.

Focal System Basic methods of gathering information are employed when applied to the focal system. Those who are participants in the focal system may differ from the client system in their level of commitment to the change effort. Consider the case of Mrs. Barnes. Although she is the client, we know that in order for a successful change to occur, her daughter, part of the focal system, has a great deal of important information to share. Likewise, the neighbors, who may have to pitch in by calling on Mrs. Barnes more often if she is to remain in her own home, have a great deal of pertinent information to share with the social worker. Their obligations to Mrs. Barnes are quite separate, but the change effort will be much less successful without input from both parties.

Action System What groups, organizations or individuals will be involved in establishing the change effort? The action system must be mobilized on behalf of the client system, and information from that system is an essential component

CASE EXAMPLE 6.3

Blanca Island

Blanca Island, a small Texas community on the Gulf coast, is experiencing a tourist boom and an economic system shift from fishing and agriculture to tourism. Condominiums are being built along the beach, and fast food and convenience stores are opening. In the community, the small, two-lane roads are crowded and congested with traffic, and many old-time community folks are afraid that these new, fast-life tourists will bring drugs, crime, and other evils from the city.

An ad hoc community group, consisting mostly of community "old-timers," engages the services of a community social worker to assist them in gaining some control over what feels to them like a community that has lost its way.

Even in such a small community, there are multiple systems involved in the situation from which a social worker will need to gather information. The social worker identifies the following groups and individuals from which relevant information must be gathered: the city council, the school board, the officers and sailors at the Coast Guard station, the fisher-men, the restaurant and motel owners, the owner of the ferry to the mainland, new residents at the island, and the "old-timers" who hired the social worker in the first place.

The concerns the social worker focuses upon in information gathering are both crime or potential crime, economic growth, and preservation of the environment and of a pleasant way of life. Undoubtedly, conflicting perspectives will be presented if the developer in the community, school superintendent, and local residents (to name but a few) are consulted. Therefore, for each person, group, or organization contacted, the social worker makes a list of questions that need to be answered.

The information the social worker gathers must come from the perspective of the group that originally identified the concern, but must include many other systems, including objective, empirical data likely found in the local library, in order for an accurate assessment, followed by effective change, to take place.

of the data collection strategy. If Mrs. Barnes is to remain in her own home, she may need Meals on Wheels. The social worker obtains Meals on Wheels's schedule, reimbursement procedures, and other data that may contribute to the change effort. All related systems involved in the change effort must be engaged in the information gathering phase.

Sensitivity to Human and Contextual Diversity

Another approach in developing this first stage of the information collection strategy is to be sensitive to diversity issues, whether they relate to human or cultural differences. The anthropologist collects information as a participant observer only after the language has been mastered and the explicit details of the situation are taken into consideration. The social worker, who is culturally competent and sensitive to diversity issues, employs his or her awareness of diversity in information gathering. Case Example 6.4 raises issues pertinent to this discussion. This particular case has much to offer the student who is learning generalist practice, and we refer to it in later chapters, particularly in relationship to assessment.

CASE EXAMPLE 6.4

The Roanhorse Family

The Roanhorses are a Navajo Native American family living in a large southwestern city for the past four years, having moved there from the Navajo reservation. The nuclear family is composed of the father, Joe Roanhorse, 33; Mary, his wife, who is 32; and the children, Alex, 12; Ellen, 10; and Mark, 6. Joe received his Associate of Arts degree in welding from the Navajo Community College on the reservation and is motivated to make a good life for his family off the reservation. He has had a drinking problem off and on.

Mary has an eighth grade education and, like most Navajo women, is very knowledgeable of Navajo rituals. Alex is in sixth grade and participates in the Boy Scouts through the Kit Carson Boy Scout Council. Ellen is in the fourth grade, and Mark is in the first grade.

Put yourself in the place of a social worker with the Human Services Department in this city. This referral was on your desk when you came to work on Monday morning:

Alex Roanhorse was picked up by the police at 11:30 p.m. last night (Sunday) on Broadway Street (a main drag through an older part of town), about three blocks from the railroad tracks, just across from downtown, in a lower-middle-class neighborhood. Alex was with a "gang" of seventeen- and eighteen-year-olds who were "Anglo" and Hispanic. He was taken home by the police and referred to Social Services for neglect. Alex and his parents feel he did nothing wrong or out of the ordinary.

Alex and the other boys were walking down the street about fifteen minutes before a neighbor telephoned the police that some kids threw rocks through her window.

The father, Joe, is having a difficult time keeping a foot in the "Anglo" world, working as a welder, and at the same time, maintaining his link with the Native American culture of the reservation. He is bored because he is not around other Navajos and is not fully accepted by his co-workers or neighbors. Therefore, he does not have much to do. Mary feels out of balance and is not able to get in touch with what is going on because it is all so new, com-plex, and fast. However, within the family dynamics, there are no observable problems.

This is the second time the parents have had contact involving the police. The first time was five years ago when the police in Grants, New Mexico, picked up their three children from a pickup truck; the parents were on a twenty-four-hour drinking binge. The children were placed in a residential group home overnight; the parents came and got them the next day. Social Services warned them not to go on these drinking binges again.

The description of the referral is brief, and you realize you will need to collect additional information in order to be helpful to the Roanhorses. Before your initial contact with the family, you develop some questions you know will need to be answered:

1. Are there other Native Americans in the area?

2. What services are there for Native Americans?

3. Why did Joe leave the reservation?

4. What are the economic implications for the family?

5. What strengths does the family have?

6. What are the implications of being Navajo in an "Anglo" world?

7. What is the extent of contact with the extended family?

8. What is the employment rate for welders in Albuquerque?

9. What data is available to support the assertion that Joe is "bored."

10. What Navajo rituals are critical to the Roanhorses?

All of these questions imply using the systems perspective for information gathering with particular emphasis upon sensitivity to diversity issues. Your cultural sensitivity will serve you well when we discuss this case once again as an illustration for assessment.

Strengths, Opportunities, and Risks Perspective

The social work profession is set apart from other helping professions because of the manner in which it initially views client systems. We focus on a person's strengths rather than on weaknesses; on what clients are capable of doing for themselves rather than on their disabilities. When we collect information on clients, we must remember this principle that distinguishes social work from other helping professions.

By identifying and learning more about the strengths of a system, we will be able to complete a fuller assessment and provide more options to the client system in the change process. The Roanhorse case was presented to a group of beginning social work students. Although their questions were penetrating regarding the family and its situation, they were framed in a perspective that failed to understand Alex's cultural diversity and the fact that the Roanhorses were not "bad parents." The students failed to go beyond the fact that Alex Roanhorse was referred for being out past curfew. Their focus was on his "acting out." In other words, the students' questions were not framed from a "strengths" perspective, but rather from a deficit perspective.

In gathering information, we must collect information that indicates the risks the client system may be experiencing. It may be important to frame our questions in terms of what risks any family or person, given the situation the client finds himself or herself dealing with would experience. For example, any Native American family that lives many years on a reservation and then moves to a large city is bound to experience stress. Each family experiences the transition differently, but all families endure strains.

The systems information collection strategy should be formulated before the actual collection begins. How do you, as a student, go about gathering information for a term paper? Do you walk into the library and start reading every book on the shelf, or do you target your investigation and only collect information about the subject area assigned? Use the same techniques when you begin to collect data to begin the change process.

In addition, we urge you to take advantage of the technological advances in the age of computers and information retrieval. While we have made comments regarding ethical issues and computer technology, it is essential to understand and have access to the technology that is available. Not only will you be assisted, but you will be empowered to use your knowledge on behalf of client systems. In designing your information collection strategy, be creative. Consider the whole picture, take into account human diversity, and appraise client strengths as well as their risks.

Collecting Information from Small, Medium, and Large Systems

Maintaining a systems perspective, social work generalists collect data from microsystems, mezzosystems, and macrosystems. Nonetheless, concrete procedures used to collect data from different sized systems vary according to size. Common sense tells us that collecting data from a community differs from data collection procedures used in working with an individual. For example, when information is collected from an individual, the systems perspective guides the collection, although procedures and focus are tailored to the individual. In the following discussion, specific information collection methods applied with individuals, families, groups, communities, and organizations are presented.

Collecting Information from Individuals and Families (Microsystems)

The most commonly used technique in gathering information from microsystems is the traditional social work interview. While we rely on the interview to yield substantial information, reliability and validity regarding information are increased when more than one method of information collection is used (Sheafor, Horejsi, and Horejsi, 1991, p. 213). Pincus and Minahan observed that the direct interview is the most important tool in data collection, yet overemphasis on this technique has often obscured other modes of data collection that can be used in place of the interview or to supplement or complement it (1973, p. 134). As a student in your practice class as well as in your field agency, no doubt you have practiced, or will practice, the direct verbal interview. The important thing to remember is that there are other ways of collecting information, and you should be open to them.

Objective and Subjective Information

Before proceeding to a discussion of the tools used to gather information from individuals and families, some basic considerations regarding information collection with individuals and families should be discussed. The social work interview is always defined in relationship to empathy, observation, and participation. There is no proxy for each component. Framing our interviews around these three essential components, we collect data that is both objective and subjective.

Objective data refers to facts such as names, dates, number of people in family, residence, occupation, health, and so on. Objective data must be collected, and often we rely on the structured interview for such information.

Subjective data consists of impressions, interpretations, feelings about situations or people, opinions, and verbal and nonverbal cues. Social workers listen acutely to verbal and nonverbal cues when collecting information, especially in small systems, when in-depth attention is possible.

There are a number of verbal cues that can be interpreted as subjective information. For example, tone, inflection, and pacing all influence our understanding during the interview. To understand nonverbal cues, we must rely on our observational skills. A person's posture, walk, eye contact, and general affect are all taken into consideration.

Noting discrepancies between what a person says and the manner in which it is said adds further to our understanding during information gathering as subjective data. Case Example 6.5 illustrates an important discrepancy between a client's

CASE EXAMPLE 6.5

Phil Stone

Phil enters the room with his eyes darting around to every corner and piece of furniture. He looks at the social worker, Janet Lewis, and then turns away, focusing on the floor.

Janet: Hi, my name is Janet Lewis, the social worker here. Maybe we can talk awhile and see how we can work out something for you. It's scary to come to a new city and then end up in a place like this.

Phil: Maybe some kids are scared around here, but not me. I'll be outta here before the day is over.

Janet's observations and the first interchange between Phil and her demonstrate an enormous discrepancy between what Phil's nonverbal cues are and what he is saying. The social worker does not confront him with the discrepancy, but she files it away in her own mind as she collects information that later will contribute to an assessment.

words and the feeling or meaning that may be attached. In this case example, the interview takes place in a runaway shelter in a large midwestern city. Phil is a seventeen-year-old youth, a stranger to the city, who arrived at the shelter the previous evening.

Dynamics between and among People

How people interact and talk to each other are both vital ingredients to note during information gathering. We call what goes on among people in their relationships dynamics. The same nonverbal cues that are observed when working with individuals are important when gathering information about families. When collecting information in families, the social worker needs to notice the following: eye contact, posture, dress, overall affect, and how these nonverbals affect others in the family. For example, observing distance between people, interruptions, and reactions to verbal statements and behaviors gives us information regarding dynamics between and among people. Case Example 6.6 illustrates the point.

Environment

The client's environment must be understood if a comprehensive assessment is development. Gathering data regarding the environment is essential. For example, a hospital social worker, serving an elderly client who may need placement, must investigate the client's living situation prior to hospitalization to help her client determine the best placement after hospitalization.

Having already gathered information regarding the client's physical condition, including her mobility, the worker visits the client's home. Will the elderly client be able to maneuver around in the home? Are there steep stairs that must be climbed or is there a bedroom and bath on the ground floor? In addition, the social worker checks the neighborhood, including accessibility to friends and neighbors, shopping, and transportation.

CASE EXAMPLE 6.6

The Marshall Family

John Fleming is a social worker making a home visit with the Marshall family. He is collecting information for the assessment. The family consists of Denise Marshall, her new husband of seven months, Bob, and Denise's two teenage boys, Mark and Ryan. They are seeking help from Everett County Family and Children's Services because both boys are very unhappy with Bob and would like their mother to leave him. Denise, Mark, and Ryan had lived as a family for five years after the boys' father deserted them and before Bob moved in last year.

John enters the family home, begins the interview, and finds the family seated in the living room in the following configuration. Bob is seated on a chair on the far right of the room, while the two boys are on a loveseat on the left of the room. Denise is sitting on a chair, close to the boys, but facing Bob. John,

the social worker, takes note of their seating arrangement and continues to observe the family members' reactions to each other.

When Bob speaks, Mark and Ryan look at each other, then the ceiling and the floor. They whisper to each other while Bob talks. However, when their mother is explaining the problem, the boys are attentive to her. Each boy speaks almost unintelligibly, their reactions consisting mostly of grumbling. Denise glances at Bob and then at the boys, then finally at John, the social worker.

All the reactions the Marshall family exhibits with each other are noteworthy. John must order them to make sense for the assessment. He responds to the family's behaviors empathetically, nonverbally while he observes and participates in the interview. How would you record all that John observes?

See Figure 6.1.

Context

A family's culture and traditions must be appraised, in relation to the change effort during the information gathering phase. For example, a family with a fundamental religious orientation may have distinctive requirements when accepting their teenage daughter's pregnancy. How the parents view her behavior and how the daughter feels about her situation in view of the family's religious orientation are considerations in information gathering.

FIGURE 6.1

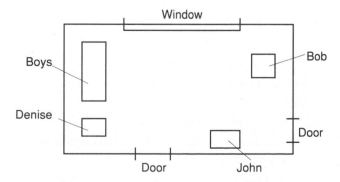

Subjective and objective data, dynamics, environment, and context are all factors to be attended to during the information gathering phase. However, nothing is more important than what the client system reports as their experience, how they feel, what they say, and what they want. We assist in information gathering, but the clients and other related systems provide the vital information.

The Social History

Gathering data from an individual may entail a structured interview. The social history is the most commonly used data gathering technique. Many social workers must complete social histories with their clients from time to time. Social histories are used within agencies by the professionals therein to develop an assessment and a plan of action. Social histories are seldom shared with clients, but more recent thinking regarding this long-standing practice is changing, and some social workers do share the histories with their clients. In fact, social workers report success in doing so.

Social histories contain both "the raw data and the worker's assessment or thoughts about the meaning of that data" (Sheafor, Horejsi, and Horejsi, 1991, p. 215). Our focus in this chapter is on the collection of the "raw data." An example of part of the social history (Siporin, 1975) on which we gather information follows:

Personality of the Client

A. Personality: "What are the dynamics and how are they organized within the individual? What determines his characteristic behavior and thought? What determines his unique adjustment to his environment?" (Allport, 1955).

B. What are the client's (a) capacities, and (b) functioning? What is the historical development? What is the current status of functioning for each of the personality dimensions below?

1. *Physical Functioning*: (as related to personal capacity and functioning).

   a. Circumstances of birth, early and later physical development.

   b. Constitutional conditions. Energy level, sex, and other drives.

   c. Disabilities, illnesses, personal health habits.

   d. Current status of health and self-care.

2. *Intellectual Functioning*:

   a. Intellectual level, and source of information.

   b. Cognitive style and flexibility.

   c. Creativity level.

   d. Characteristics of memory and recall

   e. Perception of, orientation to, and consciousness of, reality, persons, and things.

      f. Judgment.

      g. Predominant assumptive beliefs about reality, people.

  3. *Emotional Expressive Functioning*:

      a. Temperament: warm, cold, excitable, phlegmatic.

      b. Characteristic traits: sensitive, shy, envious, self-centered, exact, decisive, self-confident, rigid, good-humored, introverted, extroverted.

      c. Impulse-control and emotional stability.

      d. Empathic ability and skill.

      e. Conscience: nature and degree of development. Moral character and value system to which individual subscribes.

      f. Self-direction: Autonomy, self-responsibility, spontaneity, initiative.

      g. Nature and intensity of fantasy and dream life.

      h. Predominant emotional reaction pattern or mood: optimism, pessimism, enthusiasm, rage, depression, anxiety, fear. (Siporin, 1975, pp. 371–372.)

If we were collecting information on a person's childhood, the social history should also include information on interactions at school, activities, friends, and how often the client system moved from city to city or within a community. Their early adulthood and their education are also areas on which information is collected. The client should be questioned about the impact of major family events. Crises and life tasks, such as health and medical problems, finances, divorces, and how the individual and family responded are other clusters of information to gather when obtaining a social history.

The length and depth of a social history varies greatly. Most generalist social workers focus on the social components of functioning—that is, interactions with others—while psychiatrists, who also complete social histories, focus on biological and intrapersonal functioning. Depending on the setting in which you are working, you may focus on particular time periods in the life of your client or special problem areas. For example, juvenile probation officers, in completing a social history, concentrate on childhood and family history, while a social history of an elderly client focuses on middle and later adulthood.

Adoption Application

To further your understanding of information gathering with small systems, the following adoption application is presented. Information is collected on aspects of the couple's (or single person's) life, as well as the systems related to the applicants. The information collected on the following form becomes the basis for assessing the family's capacity to adopt, as well as to help the child find the most suitable family.

Prospective Adoptive Parent Structured Interview Form

Name _____

Address _____

Phone _____

   I. Family Description

     A. Height

     B. Weight

     C. Physical description

     D. Color of hair and eyes

     E. Affect

     F. Manner

     G. Articulation

  II. Family Background

     A. Parents

        1. Name and ethnic background of each parent

        2. Length of marriage (and number of marriages, if applicable)

        3. How did your parents get along?

        4. Personality characteristics of each parent

        5. Education of each parent

        6. Employment of each parent

        7. Hobbies of each parent

        8. Your relationship with each of your parents

     B. Siblings

        1. Names and ages of your brothers and sisters

        2. General information about each

           a. Married? How many children?

           b. Education

           c. Your current relationship to each

 III. Childhood Experiences

     A. Your general feelings

        1. Overall, good or bad? Why?

        2. Discipline

           a. Type of discipline your parents used

           b. Just or unjust?

        3. Relationship with siblings

B. Activities

   1. Extracurricular (hobbies, sports, camping, music lessons, scouts, etc.)

   2. As a family (vacations, outings, etc.)

C. Values

   1. Religious

   2. Personal

D. Birth place

IV. Education

   A. Level of education attained

   B. Feelings about education

V. Cultural background

   A. Ethnic background

   B. Strength of cultural ties-traditions.

VI. Armed Services

   A. Branch served in

   B. Length of time in service

   C. Quality of experience

VII. Employment

   A. History of

   B. Feeling about (Are you happy in your career?)

   C. Future

VIII. Marital Relationship

   A. Number of marriages and how long in each?

   B. Courtship (How long did you date, how long were you engaged, etc.?)

   C. What qualities do you like in your spouse?

   D. What qualities do you dislike in your spouse?

   E. What has been your biggest adjustment to married life?

   F. Communication—(How are decisions reached?)

   G. How would you describe your marriage? Why?

   H. How do you view your role within this marriage?

   I. How do you view your spouse's role within this marriage?

   J. Sexual relationship—are you sexually compatible?

   K. Of the roles you play (spouse, parent, lover, employee, child, sibling, friend, etc.), which do you consider to be most important? Why?

      L. Please identify a crisis in your family and describe how the family dealt with it

IX. Self

      A. Goals (and how you plan to meet them)

      B. Current values, moral code, religious beliefs

      C. Strengths

      D. Weaknesses

      E. Hobbies (or spare time activities; what do you find satisfying, meaningful, and enjoyable?)

      F. Stress (What causes you stress; how do you handle it?)

X. Children

      A. Number of children currently in household

      B. Number you would like to have

      C. Past experience with children (younger siblings, baby sitting, youth leader, Sunday School teacher, etc.)

      D. Child-care options (If you work, who would care for your children?)

XI. Lifestyle

      A. Current (Are you happy with it?)

      B. Goals

      C. In what area of the country/world do you desire to live (Urban, rural, near relatives, etc.)?

      D. What type of relationship do you have with relatives, friends and neighbors?

XII. Finances

      A. Monthly income

      B. Monthly expenses (rent/mortgage payments, car payments, insurance, outstanding bills, etc.)

      C. Do you see yourself as a spender or a saver?

      D. Do you see your spouse as a spender or a saver? (Sallee, Adoption Study Form, 1985)

Other information is collected on the family, including a criminal records check (to ensure no child abuse has occurred), letters of reference, and information collected from other family members and friends.

An adoption worker may need to explore areas of concern or particular strengths in more detail, depending on the individual family. The uniqueness and individuality of each situation must ultimately be explored no matter which data collection tool is employed.

When using a form, the social worker collects the information as it presents itself, not necessarily in a sequential format. As the worker interviews the couple, he or she may ask about the extended family. The social worker then can more naturally ask questions about siblings as found in II.B. under Family Background. By using empathy and questioning skills, information can be more effectively collected, allowing the social worker to develop a helping relationship.

We have presented two examples of the structured interview in relationship to information gathering. It is important to decide what will most efficiently and accurately help you obtain information to begin to formulate your assessment. In addition, you want to ensure that the client system will feel comfortable during what can be rigorous and detailed questioning.

Other Techniques

There are two other techniques used in information gathering with individuals and families. They employ innovative means to gather data and can bring forth relevant and detailed information.

Client Self-Monitoring   Clients' self-monitoring may best take place when the social worker supplies a form or log to help them structure the information they are gathering. For example, in a direct interview with a family with a mentally retarded child, a social worker may be told that when the child becomes frustrated, she breaks windows and mirrors in the family home. The social worker wants to know how often this happened. The family is unsure just how often it happens, but has a sense it occurs with regular frequency. The social worker provides a log on which the family monitors the child's behavior. The information from the log assists the family clarify the extent of the problem and renders a baseline from which the social worker can later measure success of various interventions.

Other methods of self monitoring have come about because of more sophisticated technology. They include biorhythm feedback, taking the client's blood pressure, and other physical monitoring. Some states have experimented with in-home detention programs in which an inmate is allowed to live in his or her own home and go about routine work or education during the day. The former inmate is continuously monitored by a listening device strapped to the leg, informing correctional officers of the inmate's whereabouts. While this latter approach certainly raises ethical issues around coercion and excessive control, it illustrates the sophistication of modern technology.

Graphic or Visual Techniques   Gathering information with clients while using graphic or visual techniques can bring immediate feedback to the client, further the information gathering process, and support a systems perspective on information gathering. Collecting data while developing a visual depiction opens up the data gathering phase. In gathering information for assessment on families, Satir (1972) used *family sculpting*.

In family sculpting, the family members are asked to place each other and themselves spatially in relationship to one another. If a father puts himself to the side of the family, perhaps in the doorway, on the way out, a picture is created for a family that surpasses the power of words. In fact, the power of the visual representation is in its capacity to go beyond the spoken and written word. In today's world, in which visual representation, vis-à-vis television, is so commanding, our use of the techniques is growing.

Working with families and individuals, such graphic techniques as the eco-map and the genogram are often used. Both the social worker and the client system receive a first-hand picture of the client's view of family and environment. We discuss in detail these two techniques in Chapter 7, on Assessment.

Collecting Information from Groups

Gathering information from groups most often begins when the group begins. Of course, there are exceptions, especially using the Crystal Model of change to understand how our work is accomplished, because information that is relevant can be introduced at any time during the change effort. Whether one is working with task groups or treatment groups, gathering information with complete awareness of group dynamics is imperative. Sometimes we equate group dynamics with social systems (Toseland and Rivas, 1984), and that parallel fits with the focus of this book. Our aim in data collection is to explore roles, interactions, subsystems, and boundaries. There are a number of techniques we can use in gathering information on groups, including sociograms (visual representations), participant observation, and group interviews.

Roles

All persons in groups play various roles, depending on their function and status within the groups. Understanding roles helps us gain awareness of relationships among people. In fact, roles are behaviors that define how we relate to each other. One has a role only in relationship to roles that others play. People play roles in relationship to their own personal qualities as well as their status within the group. Power within the group is usually held by those with the highest status—the leader, the group facilitator, and so on. There are an unending number of roles to which people adhere in groups (Henry, 1991). However, in collecting data regarding groups, we are looking for the outcomes for individuals and the group as a whole when particular roles are experienced.

For example, many groups designate someone as the scapegoat. The scapegoat gets blamed for problems and imbalances within the group. This is not a pleasant role to play for the individual to whom it is assigned, but the scapegoat can also further the process or work of the group and can save other group members from negative experiences. The social worker gathers information related to roles within each group, and that information is very helpful in a group assessment.

Interactions

Collecting data regarding the interactions between and among group members in an orderly manner will add to the breadth of the assessment. Every group member interacts with other groups members and the quality of the verbal and nonverbal communication is noteworthy. Observing verbal and nonverbal cues is no different from collecting data on communication patterns within families or even between the individual and the social worker. We look for the same prompts; it is just more complicated with groups because the social worker must keep up with a number of different people. That is why techniques that are especially suited to the group are so important.

The group affect or climate is linked to the interactional patterns within groups. Groups can be characterized as warm or cold or any degree between the two extremes, and the qualities of group interactions affects this emotional component of the group.

Subsystems

All systems are made up of subsystems. Every group has subgroups, the equivalent of subsystems. Two people within a group may have a special attraction to each other that may have some effect on the group process and progress. We usually refer to the subgroups as dyads, triads, and cliques (Toseland and Rivas, 1984). The subsystems are likely in flux, but gaining information regarding major subgroups is important.

Boundaries

Groups, as well as individuals, families, communities, and organizations have boundaries. Group boundaries set limits for group behaviors, attitudes, and

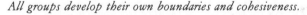

All groups develop their own boundaries and cohesiveness.

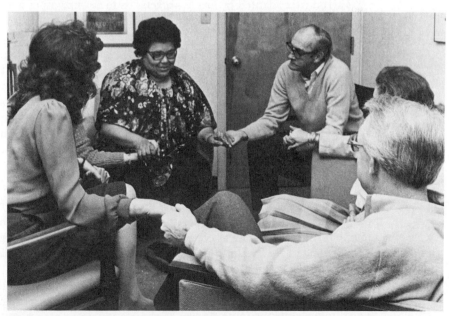

membership. The rules or sanctions within groups, what is tolerated, and what is unacceptable are pieces of information we collect about boundaries.

Some groups are open and accept new members easily, allowing them to manifest their own unique styles of relating to each other. Other groups challenge the addition of new members, making entry difficult, if not impossible. Those groups are closed.

Within the group membership, there are various levels of cohesiveness. Membership in the group may be very important, and people are attracted to one another. There may be a real desire to maintain a group. Groups with high degrees of attraction are cohesive. People in such groups may believe they share common goals and values. In addition, there may be members in the group who have a high status, and people want to be in the group simply because of the individuals who are members. Understanding group boundaries is critical in data collection.

Techniques to Gather Information from Groups

When gathering information from groups, the characteristics groups described above are the focus of our procedures. The most common ways of gathering information from groups are through the use of graphic or visual techniques, group interviews, and participant observation. The techniques are applied to groups in ways similar to our application with individuals and families.

Sociograms

Preliminary research related to data gathering and assessment supports the effective use of visual representations. In gathering information about groups, the sociogram is a traditional method, used originally as a research tool (Moreno, 1953), and later adapted by group workers. Its focus, like other graphic presentations, is about interactional patterns among group members. It is a means to organize the complex data that comes out of groups in which subsystems, boundaries, roles, and interactions can present almost overwhelming information. In a sense, the sociogram is a snapshot of interactions at a particular time. Other graphic presentations are the eco-map, used with groups and families; the mutual aid network map, that maps the relationships people have with resource systems; and any other technique that summarizes data pictorially (Hartman, 1978; and Cheers, 1987, pp. 18–24). Immediate pictures of the client system's world are brought forth. This information is used to develop the social work assessment.

Participant Observation

When we gather information from groups, there is a great likelihood we are participants in the group. Our participation, of course, is related to the helping role, but, nonetheless, we are certainly participants. Gathering information while participating in the group calls for adherence to the professional role, so that we understand our influence on the group process.

We may act as an enabler, facilitating communication by encouraging people to define themselves, their needs and goals within the group setting. Our professional role permits us to be present in the group and to gather data.

Group Interviews

The same techniques used with individuals are used with groups when interviews are conducted—empathy, participation, and observation. We collect the information in summary forms, collecting information around group dynamics. When interviews with groups are conducted, the group must understand the purpose of the interview. If information is being collected for future assessment, the group is informed.

In group interviews, the social worker may ask a similar question to every member of the group. The group, both individually, and as a whole, hears responses and those initial responses encourage further discussion. The group, itself, forms the outcome of the interview. Ideas and opinions may change during the course of the interview. The social worker keeps the group members informed about the salient points of the process throughout the interview. Group interviews are rich sources of data gathering.

Gathering Information from Organizations

When we think of projective techniques for information gathering, we usually think of the psychologists' use of the Rohrschach (the ink-blot test) that gives information regarding personality. While we do not use psychology's projective techniques, social workers certainly use projective techniques to gather information, even with larger systems.

For example, when working with a board of an organization, we may ask the board members to write down what their goals of the organization would be if all the problems of the organization were solved. Another information gathering technique with boards is to ask members to write headlines regarding their organization for their newspaper ten years in the future.

Gathering information from organizations requires prior planning. Techniques are developed that suit the membership of the organization. For example, if you are gathering information along strategic planning for an organization, you may ask task groups within the organization to develop "wish lists." What characteristics do they want their organization to have? What sort of financial picture is most helpful to the organization? Where would they like their energies to be focused in the coming months and years? The social worker is gathering information to assist in a future assessment with the board.

Gathering Information from Communities

Survey Questionnaires

Survey questionnaires elicit client responses to questions that are generated by the social worker or the agency serving the client where the social worker is employed. They are used to gather information about community needs, organizational development, or program and practice effectiveness. In fact, according to David Royse (1991), the National Research Council in publishing a report by Adams, Smelser, and Treiman declares " 'the survey is the most important information gathering invention of the social sciences'" (cited in Fienberg, Loftus, and

Tanur, 1985, pp. 547–564). Although we generally think of surveys only in terms of research, and then we go on to consider research as a separate entity in social work and social work education, we encourage you to end those sorts of generalities and stereotypes and to regard the survey as simply another tool to gather information. There may be times when it is not only the best tool to use, but it may be the only reasonable one. For example, if you are collecting information on the needs of a community, you cannot expect to gather data that are usable if you do not develop a way to collect enough data to give you a picture of a community at a given time. Talking to a few people, without consideration of what you want to know, may give you impressions, but the information you ought to have to assess the needs in a community cannot be collected haphazardly.

There are two general types of surveys: exploratory and descriptive (Royse, 1991, p. 103). Exploratory surveys are to explore an area of concern or problem. The social worker may want to get prevalent viewpoints on perceived problem areas in a community and will construct a questionnaire to gather such data. On the other hand, descriptive surveys enumerate or describe characteristics of a population. An agency may need to know client characteristics of its service population (Royce, 1991). Both are legitimate uses of the survey questionnaire.

We may mail questionnaires, use the telephone, or administer them to groups or individuals face-to-face. The response rate is obviously much higher when done face-to-face, but the cost in time and personnel is also high. How you administer the survey is dependent upon a number of considerations.

ROLES AND SKILLS: INFORMATION GATHERING

The farther we move into the Crystal Model Process of Planned Change, the likelier it is that we will use multiple roles. Roles most prevalent in the first phase—area of concern and engagement—are further used in the second phase—information gathering.

The major roles associated with area of concern and engagement are enabler and conflict manager. Both are essential in the beginning, including the information-gathering phase, because the enabler role incorporates building trust so that professional relationships can be built. The beginning stages of working with client systems are often fraught with conflict; therefore, managing conflict early in the process is requisite to a positive start.

Given that caveat, two additional roles and associated skills are linked to information gathering. The roles presented here, in addition to those of enabler and conflict manager, are broker and collaborator. The specific skills called upon in data collection in addition to those discussed regarding area of concern and engagement are questioning, recording and documentation, and computer skills.

Social Work Generalist Role: Collaborator

Bringing two or more people together to work on behalf of the client is known as collaboration. Social workers work in teams, collaborating with each other and other professionals, and social workers collaborate even when employed in different agency settings in order to bring about the most effective change for clients. Working together is essential in the information-gathering phase.

A great deal of information is gathered from sources other than the client, including agencies that may have served the client in previous years, and agencies or organizations that are serving the client presently. Of course, you need a release-of-information form signed by the client system before agencies will discuss or release any information. Comprehensive information gathering encompasses the collaborator role.

Social Work Generalist Role: Broker

The other role closely related to this phase is brokering. The goal of the broker role is to link client systems to the services they need (Compton and Galaway, 1989). In order for meaningful linkage to take place, appropriate information must be gathered, not only from the client system, but from systems related to the client (focal and action). The broker is a key role for the social work generalist, and as such is tied to all the remaining phases in the change process.

Skills Associated with Phase Two—Information Gathering

Questioning

Information cannot be collected without using questions. The process itself relies on questions. As professional social workers using structured or unstructured formats, we are aware of the categories or subject areas of information that need to be collected. We lead the process, partly through our questioning. Yet, we encourage you to use questions as infrequently as possible.

Questioning does not encourage elucidation or enlargement unless it is framed in empathy. Therefore, even questioning must be done within an open, caring, concerned atmosphere.

Keep questions simple, and, if possible, open. Explain the use of the questions, why certain material must be discussed, and how the answers to the question clients share will be used. The asking of "why" questions is discouraged. The answers almost always produce a sort of "intellectualizing" and sometimes even defensiveness. In either case, "why" questions do not really help us find much out that is useful about our clients. In addition, "why" questions detract from a positive climate.

Sometimes we ask direct questions that demand a straightforward answer. Other times we may ask questions that bring up underlying concerns or problems. Social workers may use questioning with projective or indirect techniques. With an individual, the social worker may ask the client to complete a sentence or ask for a description of a picture of a family. Indirect questioning helps us understand an individual's perspective on his or her relationships with others (Hepworth and Larsen, 1986).

Recording and Documentation

Keeping track of the information collected is no easy task, but, in some form or another, the information we have gathered must be organized. The assessment that follows information gathering and later guides the change effort with the client relies upon accurate recording of the information we have collected. The social worker must immediately differentiate in his or her records between fact and opinion and between intuition and findings based on critical thinking.

Accurate recording and documentation begin with excellent writing skills. Social work educators do not teach writing, per se, although most educators are aware of the crisis in American education regarding students' difficulty with the written word. Taking our cue once again from anthropology, we believe the surest way to develop good writing skills for recording in social work is to begin through the taking of detailed notes in the field. In social work, we call this technique *process recording*.

Process recording forces us to differentiate among statements clients make, our feelings regarding the interactions that take place between our clients and us, and the analysis we might develop, based on the meeting between the social worker and any other system.

Early in the history of the social work profession, process recording was the preferred method of recording (Wilson, 1980, p. 18). Presently, with greater concern for efficiency as well as client rights, process recording is used as a teaching tool. In our way of thinking, process recording is a necessary step in learning how to be a competent practitioner and is particularly important in the information-gathering phase.

Wilson (1980) suggests a format (Figure 6.2) for process recording that utilizes a legal-size paper, divided lengthwise into three columns. The first column is

Figure 6.2 Process Recording

Field Instructor	Client-Student Dialogue	"Gut" Feelings
3/15/94	3/9/94 Ms. James arrived fifteen minutes late. She quietly came in the room and sat in the far chair in a closed position—looking at the floor.	I was upset that she was late again yet I remembered the buses don't always run on time.
You are learning how to overcome your discomfort with silence.	I asked her how she was feeling. She said nothing for about thirty seconds and then in a very low voice said "Not good."	I was worried about her silence, but waited.
Your prompting helped her release her feelings.	I waited another 30 seconds and then asked "What isn't good?" She said "I lost my job again. That stupid system of last hired first fired isn't fair. . . ."	I agreed with her—it wasn't fair.

left blank, to be filled in later with the field instructor's comments. The middle column (the widest one) contains the client-student dialogue. The student is encouraged to write down as accurately and as completely as possible all the dialogue that transpired between the two. The column on the far right is used for recording "gut-level" feelings. Here the student is expected to record (immediately after the student-client interaction) his or her own feelings regarding the social work interview.

When students complete process recordings during their field placements, they not only gain awareness of their own behaviors and how they impact on clients, but they also become better writers and more skilled information gatherers because they are forced to focus on details and to remember as much as possible regarding what happened in the client-student interaction. As a teaching tool for the field, we do not know of any technique that comes close to teaching what the process recording does.

Process recordings are most often used with individuals but can be adapted to use with groups, other professionals, including supervisors, committee meetings, and community gatherings.

Other recording and documentation skills build upon success in process recording. Once you have become a keen observer, an empathic listener, and a pointed questioner with the ability to remember what has happened and then to write your process recording accurately, other forms of recording and documentation will flow.

In social work practice, you will be expected to complete *summary recordings* of various kinds. Recording forms are usually adapted by individual agencies, although funding sources and the state and federal governments may require standardized forms. Summary recordings are more brief than process recordings and do not include line by line dialogue between the worker and the client. Instead, summary recordings highlight the most important behaviors, impressions, and outcomes related to the client system. The focus is on the client, not on the student as learner. Progress notes, periodic summaries, and diagnostic reports are all examples of summary recordings (Wilson, 1980, p. 110).

Some government programs require specialized recording styles, and often the recording is done on the computer. The development of computer skills, especially word processing and information retrieval, are important.

Documentation of client outcomes and worker interventions are related skills in information gathering. Social workers are expected to possess the ability to evaluate their own practices and to contribute to the evaluation of the programs in which they are working. Documentation is a part of that expectation. We begin accurate documentation in the information-gathering phase. The accuracy of our documentation affects our ability to evaluate the impact our actions have had.

Social workers are often required by the change system to document their actions with client, focal, and action systems. Keeping simple statistics, keeping track of your work by way of a daily log, and collecting baseline data for later evaluation are all components of documentation.

When recording or documenting, we recommend the use of dictaphones or tape recordings. Social workers complain of never having enough support staff, and this is certainly a reasonable grievance. Using dictaphones and tape recorders to record does not require staff. Agencies will not listen to the pleas of social workers unless we are prepared to use the equipment that clerical support relies upon.

Computer Skills

There are few universities today that do not require computer literacy as a basic competency for the college graduate. Computer skills are especially important in social work. From the computerized classification systems found in libraries to the vast storage of information found in departments of social services throughout this country, social workers need to be computer-literate.

Your own gathering of data from clients and related systems may involve using word processing at a social agency in order to facilitate record keeping. Realizing that you are storing confidential information in a large system that may be privy to a number of people ought to cause you to type with not only care, but with clarity and brevity. Although we can store information with ease, the reality is that the information stored is too accessible. The growing reliance on information systems, thus, puts the onus on the individual social worker to safeguard the client's privacy rights. The development of computer literacy is essential (Heerman, 1986).

Other Issues Pertinent to Information Gathering

Using the Knowledge Framework

Every phase in the Crystal Model relies on the knowledge base of social work practice. We cannot ask appropriate questions, record our interactions with clients, or even keep track for the purpose of documentation without using the knowledge base. Referencing the Crystal Model, position the information collected into the following components of the framework: the general issues client systems experience, the opportunities and risks of each system, and the systems with which we must interact in order to collect data.

Using Existing Written Material

Frequently, a beginning social worker inherits a caseload from a previous worker. Reading through the written material on each client system is an essential launching point, not only for the new social worker as a means to acquaint herself or himself with the agency's purpose, but also as a way to know the clients with whom the worker will be engaged.

You may read a client's file before or after the first interview. Some social workers prefer to meet the client system before knowing anything about them in order not to assume any of the prejudices the former worker may have had. While this action may help the social worker, it may frustrate clients because they have already given someone else all a great deal of information and may not want to go over "old business." How existing material influences work with clients depends on the social worker's professional judgment.

Written policies and minutes from board meetings contribute to the understanding of organizational issues. In addition, written organizational plans (strategic planning for an entire organization) and reports published by the agency may contain critical information on community systems.

Value and Ethical Issues

Information gathering raises confidentiality issues. Wilson (1980) recalls that earlier in the profession's history, maintaining confidentiality was relatively simple. "As long as social workers kept their mouths shut and 'didn't blab to their clients,' confidentiality was considered maintained" (Wilson, 1980, p. 181). With computer technology and federal and state regulations regarding privacy and records, confidentiality today is a complex topic.

How much of the information we collect will actually remain confidential? When information is placed in records that are later stored in data banks, the limits to confidentiality are considerable. Therefore, care regarding just what information ought to be placed in the record is recommended (Albers and Morris, 1990). At the same time, clients have the right to their records as a result of the Federal Privacy Act of 1974. This means that what you write in a client's record may, at some later time, be seen by the client.

For some more traditional social workers, the Privacy Act is the object of much criticism. However, in the social work process this text advocates, we see the client's right to the record as a strength. The process of change, the process of helping are shared experiences—shared by the social worker, the client, the focal system, and the action system. When change is sought, whether one is a voluntary or involuntary client, what the social worker writes in the record, at the very least, should be available to clients. Otherwise, the mutuality we support is a pretense. The real confidentiality issues deal with others, outside the systems engaged in change, who may obtain records to which they do not have rights.

Students are encouraged to take every precaution when collecting information on client systems. Do not take records home; do not leave records in your car; do not leave records displayed in your office for others to see; keep records under lock and key; and destroy any private notes you may have regarding clients.

When case examples are brought to class for discussion, disguise the names and all other identifying information of those involved. One never knows when a client may be known to another student. Process recordings that are used only for teaching should be destroyed when they are completed. Never turn in a process recording to your instructor with undisguised names. You are privy to information about clients that you must guard steadfastly. Maintaining confidentiality is an important principle for social workers.

Information in Flux

The information gathered regarding clients is always in the process of change. What is true today may not be true tomorrow. Information is correct only at a given point in time; every aspect of information collected is potentially irrelevant. Therefore, you must be continuously open to new information, to nuances regarding information and even to complete contradictions regarding information already collected. Developing an appreciation for the volatility of information is a further step in becoming an effective generalist practitioner.

CONCLUSION

Information gathering takes place early in the change effort and is the bridge to the assessment that follows. Our perspective on information gathering, the procedures used to collect data, and the roles and skills employed in the process all contribute to whether or not its outcome is successful. A successful outcome is determined by the quality of the assessment, the design and plan, and the implementation, evaluation, and transition in the change process. Of course, the most telling outcome comes from the client system's perspective: were the goals attained; is change secured; and has improvement in social functioning taken place?

Information gathering orders data for the next phase of the change effort: assessment. In the following two chapters, you will be introduced to the purposes of assessment, and the procedures, roles and skills needed to accomplish this next important phase.

References

Albers, Dale, and Morris, Richard. (1990). Conceptual Problems in Social Workers' Management of Confidentiality. *Social Work, 35*(4), 361–362.

Allport, Gordon W. (1955). *Becoming: Basic Considerations for a Psychology of Personality.* New Haven: Yale University Press.

Baer, Betty, and Federico, Ronald. (1978). *Educating the Baccalaureate Social Worker: Report of the Undergraduate Social Work Curriculum Development Project.* Cambridge, MA: Ballinger, p. 86.

Bernard, H. Russell. (1988). *Research Methods in Cultural Anthropology.* Newbury Park, CA: Sage Publications.

Cheers, B. (1987). The Social Support Network Map As An Educational Tool. *Australian Social Work, 40,* 19–24.

Compton, Beulah, and Galaway, Burt. (1989). *Social Work Processes,* 4th ed. Belmont, CA: Wadsworth.

Cormier, William L., and Cormier, L. Sherily. (1991). *Interviewing Strategies for Helpers,* 3rd ed. Belmont, CA: Brooks/Cole, p. 172.

Gorden, Ray L. (1987). *Interviewing, Strategy, Techniques and Tactics,* 4th ed. Homewood, IL: Dorsey Press, p. 5.

Hartman, Ann. (1978). Diagrammatic Assessment of Family Relationships. *Social Casework, 59,* 465–476.

Heerman, Barry (ed.). (1986). *Personal Computers and the Adult Learner.* San Francisco: Jossey-Bass.

Henry, Sue. (1991). *Group Skills in Social Work: A Four Dimensional Approach.* Itasca, IL: F. E. Peacock.

Hepworth, Dean, and Larsen, JoAnn. (1986). *Direct Social Work Practice: Theory and Skills.* Homewood, IL: Dorsey Press.

Johnson, Louise. (1992). *Social Work Practice: A Generalist Approach,* 4th ed. Boston: Allyn & Bacon, p. 220.

Moreno, Jacob L. (1953). *Who Shall Survive: Foundations of Sociometry, Group Psychotherapy and Sociodrama.* Beacon, NY: Beacon House.

Pincus, Allen, and Minahan, Anne. (1973). *Social Work Practice: Model and Method.* Itasca, IL: F. E. Peacock, p. 134.

Royce, David. (1991). *Research Methods in Social Work.* Chicago: Nelson-Hall, p. 103.

Royce, David. (1991). Report in the National Research Council by Adams, Smelser, and Treiman; cited in Fienberg, S. E., Loftus, E. F., and Tanur, J. M., (1985). Cognitive Aspects of Health Survey Methodology: An Overview, *Milbank Memorial Fund Quarterly/Health and Society, 63*(3), 547–564.

Sallee, Alvin L. (1985). Adoption Study Form.

Satir, V. (1972). *People Making.* Palo Alto, CA: Science and Behavior Books.

Sheafor, B., Horejsi, C. R., and Horejsi, G. A. (1991). *Techniques and Guidelines for Social Work Practice,* 2nd ed. Boston: Allyn & Bacon, pp. 213, 215.

Siporin, M. (1975). *Introduction to Social Work Practice.* New York: MacMillan, pp. 371–372.

Toseland, Ronald W., and Rivas, Robert F. (1984). *An Introduction to Group Work Practice.* New York: MacMillan.

United Way of American Service Identification System. (1972).

Wilson, S. (1980). *Recording: Guidelines for Social Workers.* New York: The Free Press, pp. 18, 110, 181.

Chapter 7

Assessment_____

OVERVIEW_____

Phase Three of the Crystal Model—assessment—is the focus of both this chapter and Chapter 8. The systems perspective, with an emphasis on cultural competence, is the organizing framework for assessment. We review the Crystal Model in relationship to assessment and enumerate the competencies or outcomes related to assessment. We define the purposes of assessment, describe the process and product of assessment, and learn how values, theory, and research interconnect with clients' experience in assessment. This chapter ends with practical formats that undergird all social work assessments, regardless of the size of the client system. In Chapter 8, we build on the assessment foundation presented in this chapter by discussing specific assessment tools relevant to small, medium, and large systems.

What Is Assessment?

What is assessment, and what can this investment of time do for us? *Assessment* is defined as a professional statement and process which makes sense of the information collected by applying theory, research, and analytical skills to an area of concern. The professional assessment statement is intended to facilitate an in-depth understanding of the area of concern based on one's professional knowledge. As Berger and Federico (1985, p. 13) state: "Perhaps the best way to see the impact of knowledge on practice is through assessment." The basis of social work's professional knowledge is gleaned from the social and behavioral sciences and from the ways in which this knowledge is organized into a social work perspective.

As social workers, we are concerned about gaining more information and knowledge in order to make effective decisions that are in the best interests of our clients. "Knowing in the light of reason and knowing in the light of experience are surely two of the candles with which we can light the darkness" (Siporin, 1975, p. 219). Effective assessment provides us with a structure to bring light to many social problems which otherwise may remain in the dark. The assessment process informs us about the relationship between variables on which we gather information.

Assessment and the Crystal Model

In the Crystal Model, assessment plays an invaluable part. Appropriate and thorough assessments can only be developed if previous steps in the change process have been followed. For example, contact must have been initiated with client systems and focal systems. Information must have been collected regarding all systems involved in the situation. In this effort, the social worker focused not only on stresses and problems but also on client systems' strengths. Now, as we move into the assessment phase, we will use the information gathered to help understand the area of concern.

Assessment, design, planning, and the contract form the middle phases of the Crystal Model and are tied closely together, yet each is a separate step. An accurate and useful assessment of the situation identifies where change needs to occur. Design and planning, then, enable us to identify goals and objectives and appropriate options that might be used during the implementation phase. The contract phase allows us to negotiate the roles and responsibilities of all those involved in the change process. A quality assessment helps assure an effective design and plan, thus enhancing implementation and successful change.

The assessment phase of the change process employs the Crystal Model's centrally located dotted lines more than any other. The dotted lines represent the blending of the change phases. According to the model, the assessment stage begins after collecting information. In the real world, it may begin with the initial contact with the client system, continuing throughout all phases. To put it another way, our initial contacts with clients provide information and impressions that will be incorporated into the assessment. Later, as we obtain feedback from clients, we may alter the assessment.

COMPETENCIES

The competencies that relate to assessment are drawn from the work completed by Baer and Federico (1978, p. 86) and by Harold Lewis (1982, pp. 121–124). The Baer and Federico competency that relates to assessment is presented in the first item in the list below, and remaining items highlight the competencies defined by Harold Lewis.

1. *Assess situations where the relationship between people and social institutions needs to be initiated, enhanced, restored, protected, or terminated.* An analysis of information collected about vulnerable and discriminated-against populations whom social workers serve is included in this competency. The competency implies that some groups do not adequately have their needs met, and therefore, change must occur. Analyzing the relationship between people and institutions is a critical ability generalist social workers should possess. In addition, it

is necessary to understand how knowledge regarding human behavior in the social work environment supports the assessment process.

2. *The ability and skill to make accurate decisions and plan for action in uncertain situations.* A common concern regarding social work practitioners is their difficulty in making decisions, particularly in controversial situations. Too often, people in social work positions without social work training base professional decisions on their own life experiences, which by their very nature, are narrow. For example, a worker whose client system is a family from an ethnic and socioeconomic level different from that of the worker has little personal knowledge on which to base decisions. Yet, a knowledgeable and experienced generalist whose education has provided opportunities to learn theories of human behavior and research on transcultural counseling should be able to make more accurate decisions. This worker ought to be better equipped to effect change in difficult and uncertain situations. Accurate decision making for action is an ability you will want to acquire in your field placements, by observing experienced workers, and by discussing your experiences and observations with the field instructor.

3. *Be aware of knowledge available to explain situations and what can be done about the situations.* The ability to employ knowledge in the change process does not mean a direct application of theory to action. In social work, we will never resort to using a recipe that can be applied to each client with whom we work. There is a tremendous amount of knowledge available to you, from interactions with people as well as knowledge gained through reading professional literature. Professional literature must be evaluated if it is to be used effectively to help us understand and work with clients.

Knowledge can be gained through attendance at seminars and workshops. Current trends as well as new practice models in social work practice are often first presented in workshops. In addition, an ongoing dialogue with fellow students and colleagues can contribute to an understanding of research findings, theories, and emerging concepts that can be integrated with your generalist social work practice.

4. *The skill to use analytical process instruments and methods of deduction.* The Crystal Model is an analytical process model because each step implies a careful understanding of the complex material that must be translated into planful action. There are numerous assessment instruments found in the literature that are available to social workers. Methods of deduction are logical reasoning steps that you are introduced to in the study of philosophy. Becoming an analytic thinker implies using problem solving or deductive reasoning steps.

5. *The ability to describe a situation in operationalized terms by ordering parts or variables according to a theoretical framework.* Generalist social workers should be able to make sense of the information that is collected. An analysis or assessment of an area of concern is of little use if we are unable to communicate this assessment to client systems or target systems. In addition, in order to maximize the use of supervision and consultation, we need to have the ability to communicate the dynamics of the problem, orally and in writing. Social workers are expected to keep accurate records of their work and are sometimes called upon to present their assessments in public forums, such as in court, where the ramifications of assessment are critical. An entire family's future may be determined by the accuracy of the social worker's assessment.

6. *Knowledge of how to draw accurate conclusions based upon the information gathered.* Drawing accurate conclusions is based upon the best knowledge available about human beings and their environment. It is obvious that you must have in-depth knowledge of theory at your fingertips. Beyond this, you need to understand how to draw accurate and relevant conclusions based on the available knowledge. It is critical that during the information-gathering stage you have identified facts rather than assumptions.

7. *Know how to employ and use feedback to correct assessment on an ongoing basis.* Assessment is a continuous process from the beginning of the Crystal Model through evaluation. Although assessment is a separate step in the change process, there is room for feedback that may alter the assessment. Assessment provides a type of evaluative function by identifying the desired situation with the client system.

8. *Knowledge of the contextual and human diversity constraints which differentially affect people and groups.* Contextual and human diversity issues are applied in our assessment. These may identify constraints and differences which affect people and groups in various ways. Compare how the environmental contexts of people differentially affect assessments. An elderly woman with no car who is living a considerable distance from services presents a far different picture from another older woman who resides in assisted-living facilities in which services are readily available. In both situations, the contexts of environment determine what we may be able to provide for them.

Likewise, diversity, based upon culture and ethnicity, alters assessments. A social worker assigned to work with a group of Native American women who are in substance abuse recovery must understand differences in engagement strategies. Approaching a male member of the tribe to set up the group may enhance the possibilities of its effectiveness. The gender of the worker also impacts upon the beginning phases. These and other differences must be taken into consideration, or effectiveness may be undermined.

9. *The ability to assess the strengths of the client system.* Assessing the strengths of a client system and holding the value of the worth and dignity of a client system may be one of the most critical aspects of assessment. Because social work practice has partly grown out of the medical model, which looks for symptoms or problems, uncovering strengths is sometimes difficult. Many human behavior concepts differentiate between dysfunctional and normal behaviors. Social work uses the concepts but in developing an assessment, focuses upon how people adapt to situations. In an assessment, we need to be able to value strengths in every client system with which we work. Looking at what might first appear to be a negative attribute of a client system, from another perspective it may be reframed as a strength.

For example, an eighteen-year-old boy who is about to become an unwed father may be very stubborn about not allowing the mother to receive an abortion during the first trimester. While this may be viewed as a problem, the stubbornness and conviction of the young man may be seen as a strength in other areas, in which this behavior could help him achieve his goals.

Actualizing Competencies

Assessment competencies are largely focused upon the development of analytic skills. Such skills are waxed through our own individual thought processes, then tested and shared with colleagues and clients. Students have the added opportunity of testing their analytic skills in the classroom. During the assessment phase, you will utilize the knowledge you have learned from other disciplines, particularly the psychological, sociological, and biological sciences. Accurate assessment demands the use of theory, research, and our own practice experience. When analytic skills are employed based upon our knowledge base and our experience, the next step is placing all components into a framework that helps organize what we have learned. The organization of knowledge and experience is fundamental to each of the assessment competencies.

The Importance of Assessment Competencies

Too often, assessment is given scant attention. Several studies and the experience of social work practitioners (Sallee, Marlow, and Eastman, 1989) have identified ineffective or no assessments as a major concern in child welfare practice. The problems clients encounter because of poor assessments are associated with social workers not acquiring the analytic skills necessary to complete helpful assessments and to using inadequate and unvalidated assessment tools.

In mental health services, tools to determine the mental status and quality of life issues of clients are in short supply. In our rush to help people, if we do not attend to assessment, we may move directly from information gathering to the solution.

By deemphasizing assessment, we fail to use much of the knowledge available to implement effective change. Assessments may be based on worker hunches and common sense (practice wisdom) rather than on careful analysis drawn from knowledge areas. While practice wisdom is considered important in social work practice, without social-science-based assessments, we resemble volunteers or lay persons rather than professional social workers. A key need in social work practice is the development of valid and reliable assessment tools that practitioners can use to enhance the change process.

GENERAL CHARACTERISTICS OF ASSESSMENTS

Characteristics of the assessment phase include mutuality, individualization, and the creation of multiple options for the client system. The client system is regarded as an expert on the area of concern, collaborating with the social worker to develop an assessment. Thus, the work is based on mutuality. Although assessment may follow designed formats and are developed in the context of the social work knowledge base, each assessment is also unique because all client systems are different. Finally, the assessment is the basis for planning and, as such, ought to render as many options for reaching client goals as possible.

Assessment Skills

Assessment employs both interactional and analytic skills. We depend on our communication abilities to gather information that will be mutually considered by the client and the social worker. However, assessment's focus—the analysis of data to set the stage for change—is weighted heavily toward the use of analytic skills. The two basic analytic skills called upon in assessment are called "seeing into" skills and "seeing through" skills. We have borrowed these two terms from Siporin (1975, p. 222) who defines assessment as a process of "social perception and cognition" that results in "seeing into" and "seeing through." We "see into" client systems' concerns and problems and we "see through" barriers to change.

"Seeing into" Areas of Concern

The social worker has defined the area of concern and gathered information relative to it. In assessment, a further step is taken. One looks into the area of concern, applies one's knowledge base, and develops an understanding regarding the background of the situation, the extent of the concern, the depth of the concern to those affected by it and a clear definition of the area of concern provided by the client system. With detailed analysis, you will understand what the problem or concern consists of and what might happen if no change occurs.

Again, we refer to Siporin who suggests why "seeing into" client systems concerns is necessary. "Assessments can tell us . . . primary points regarding client systems:

1. How the area of concern is defined and by whom.

2. What explanations are suggested by theory or research which can help us understand the systems, their interaction and possible direction they may go if there is no intervention" (Siporin, 1975, p. 221).

"Seeing Through" Clients' Concerns

Only if we see beyond the area of concern or the problem definition will we have the ability to help our client systems. We must see the possibilities for change rather than the impossibilities. All persons, families, groups, organizations, and communities have strengths that can be used for change. We need to focus on those strengths, even while we recognize the barriers so that change can occur, not just superficially but for an extended period. Siporin sheds further light on "seeing through" the areas of concern. He suggests we find:

1. "What needs to be done to set things right? What change needs to occur? What resources are needed for what ends and goals?

2. How can the intervention program be monitored to ensure the plan stays in effect?" (Siporin, p. 221).

Assessment: Process and Product

Quality assessment is a process which results in a product. The process is the manner in which we make sense of the facts and their interrelationship. The recording of the process is the product, the assessment statement. Each is considered in the following discussion.

Assessment As Process

The process of developing an assessment is as critical as the assessment's product—that is, the written statement. Engaging the client in a mutual analysis of the area of concern contributes to a greater possibility for positive change (Nelson, Landsman, and Deutelbaum, 1990, pp. 3–21). People begin to understand their own problems, stresses, and strengths during assessments.

The assessment step, when well-executed, automatically becomes a process in which activities directed toward positive change can continue. A social worker engages a family referred to home-based services to prevent foster-care placement. The social worker works with the whole family, engaging them in the assessment process. The presence of the social worker in the home along with the change in focus of activities in the family once the social worker has entered the family system put a change process into effect. Thus, although the worker and the family may not be "solving problems" per se, the process of change has already begun.

A further illustration can be found in Case Example 7.1. Through the assessment with her social worker, Christy Raymond articulates her hopes for the future, her fears, and her strengths. The social worker encourages her to dream, to go after something for herself, and all the while she is connecting Christy's facts with facts gathered from other sources. The process, in and of itself, is helpful to Christy.

The Professional Statement

The product produced in assessment is the professional statement. This is a written document, worked out with clients, often becoming part of our recording. Producing a product is necessary because assessments are used to determine client eligibility for service, method of payment, type of service, and fit with the agency. You may be asked to present an assessment of an individual or family in court, and a written assessment is required. Other professional and social work colleagues often are privy to your assessment.

Assessments are produced with the change system's abilities to assist the client and with the focal and action's systems' analysis that is intended to facilitate an in-depth understanding of the area of concern.

THE ROLE OF RESEARCH AND THEORY IN ASSESSMENT

An assessment connects the relationship of knowledge of human behavior obtained through research and theory with specific facts regarding a client system that were obtained in the information gathering phase of the change process. In

CASE EXAMPLE 7.1

Christy Raymond

Christy Raymond, eighteen years old and African-American, completed the eighth grade in a large midwestern city in which the tax base had eroded significantly. The schools, supported largely through local property taxes, had suffered a terrible decline in the past twenty years, as the middle class, both Black and white, had moved to the suburbs. Inequities between suburban and urban schools are recognized locally, but the federal government, unconvinced that the nation as a whole may be at risk because of substandard schools in a variety of cities across the nation, leaves the problems to the localities (Kozol, 1991).

Christy, a product of an inner-city school, is the mother of two children and is unable to read well enough to pass even a driver's test. Her math skills are no better. Unable to obtain a decently paying job, she receives Aid to Families with Dependent Children (AFDC).

The neighborhood in which Christy lives is low-income, isolated and clearly segregated. Her landlord does not put money back into the building in which she lives but instead uses the building as a tax write-off. He, like many absentee landlords, benefits from segregation, unenforced city codes, and the social and political isolation his renters live with every day.

Ms. Raymond is embarrassed because she cannot read, but has admitted her lack of skill to her income maintenance case worker and has said she would like to return to school. She is serious about her desire to improve her condition in life.

Social science data point out that segregated communities lack essential resources, even maintenance of housing codes. The neighborhood's isolation cuts off Christy from the resources she needs, and even if she were able to obtain employment, it is likely she would be hired in a service position that pays minimum wage. The professional assessment statement takes in human behavior theories and social science research findings, including the relationship of her socioeconomic status to her opportunities in life.

At the same time, the professional assessment statement does not neglect Christy Raymond's individuality, her particular ways of coping, and her strengths that may be gathered during the change process.

---

addition to practice wisdom, one of the major ways we establish the theoretical relationships between facts we have gathered is through applying research findings to our assessment. In order to apply research results to assessment, we need to have the skills to evaluate journal articles and research studies. An assessment should combine both components (client experience and knowledge).

Combining Research and Theory with Client Experience

An assessment of a client system that does not intertwine client experiences with a breadth of knowledge will not be helpful. For example, a statement that poverty, racism, and sexism created an inner-city African-American youth's problem may be true, but in and of itself it does not give us any clear information on the relationship between these variables and their impact upon his particular family. We need to understand how these environmental forces impact on the family and the youth with whom we are working. In so doing, we assess how a family has coped

Professional statements are used with social work colleagues.

with racism, sexism, and poverty, and hence our focus includes a client system's strengths.

As social workers, we are concerned about gaining more information and knowledge in order to make effective decisions. Assessments that lack a sound theory and research base are inadequate professional statements. On the other hand, the assessment lacking the client system's perspective is, likewise, ineffective. The combination of the general (knowledge gained from theory and research) with the particular (information obtained regarding the client system) are the essential components of the written assessment—the professional statement. The professional statement, including the client experience, examines the relationship between variables in the area of concern. The Christy Raymond case example explicates the need to combine theory and research with the client's unique experiences.

Making Your Way through Research Articles

Navigating professional literature so that the research findings that you discover are useful in working with a client involves the following steps: (1) understanding the major types of research, (2) understanding the general format of most research articles, and (3) knowing how to assess quality in research presentations. Each step is an explication of the general analytic skill, "seeing into."

The Major Types of Research

According to Nowak (1981, p. 68) and Grinnell and Williams (1990, pp. 170–171) there are three major types of research studies. Classifying the research findings you are using into one of these three areas is the initial step in using research effectively, because the scope and limits of the research findings are first predicated on what type of research was employed. In other words, you must measure how you will use research findings, in part, based on the type of research that was conducted. Each type is briefly discussed below:

1. *Exploratory studies* examine areas that are heretofore largely unexplored in the literature. Although the designs and methodologies employed in exploratory work are varied, they are usually flexible and informal, often utilizing small samples. Exploratory studies are often on the "cutting edge" of a problem area and are aimed at gaining insights for further work.

2. *Descriptive studies* picture a problem area, a population, a situation or an event. We may know more about an area when descriptive designs are used, and the knowledge gained in descriptive studies leads us to a point where more rigorous research designs might be utilized.

3. *Explanatory research* may use knowledge generated from exploratory and descriptive studies. Hypotheses are tested and phenomena or events are explained in a cause-and-effect or relationship manner.

The Format of Research Articles

Research articles are usually presented in a general format. An abstract at the beginning of the article provides a brief one- or two-sentence problem statement on why the study was done, a description of what was completed and found in the study, and perhaps a brief description of implications for practice. By reading the abstract, you can quickly review numerous articles to assist you in finding the one most relevant to your client system. The abstract can also be used as a measuring stick to see if the paper accomplished what was promised in the abstract.

Most articles begin with an introduction and brief history of the problem under consideration, including a literature review so that you can understand work that has preceded the findings you are reading.

Once the history is presented, description of the extent of the problem is usually presented. The methodology utilized in the research follows. Since this area explains how the data was collected, careful attention ought to be given to its appropriateness.

The findings that result from the study are presented next. Results of statistical analyses, including the logic of the results, are presented. Implications of the study help us learn how to use the research findings. Perhaps a great deal more becomes known about a population group similar to your client's, or you may understand the results of a particular program upon a client group. In either case, the findings and implications can be directly utilized in our assessments.

Assessing Quality of Research

Not all research is applicable, nor is all research sufficiently rigorous and of high enough quality to use in assessments. Your critical analysis of the research areas is imperative before using the findings to inform your own assessments of client systems. Nowak (1981, p. 77) offers fourteen checkpoints to use in assessing the reading of a completed research report. Since each is equally critical, we present them in their entirety.

1. Is there a careful and clear statement of the problem?
2. Is there significant evidence that the investigator did a thorough review of the literature?
3. Is the scope and method of the study stated clearly and concisely?
4. Is there clear and appropriate table and graphic information?
5. Is there an accurate and careful statement of the findings in a way that the readers' questions will be answered?
6. Are the findings discussed in a meaningful and relevant manner?
7. Does the investigator present the data base for conclusions drawn?
8. Are there distortions of bias evident in the report?
9. Are the limitations of the study clearly stated?
10. Is the content and style of the report appropriate for those who will be reading the study?
11. Is the report written in an interesting manner?
12. Is the language of the report understandable?
13. Were the rights of the human subjects (if any) protected?
14. Were the implications for social work practice clearly enunciated?

Reading research carefully and accurately is of paramount importance. Generalizing to a client system without a critical review is dangerous. Knowing how to use research, how to assess it, and then how to apply it to client systems is a major component of assessment.

VALUES AND ASSESSMENTS

Assessments help client systems and social workers organize information, analyze experience, and place clients' unique situations into a broad context. At the same time, they are value-laden. Values influence assessments for two reasons: (1) they are intrinsic to all persons' experiences, and (2) they are woven into the human behavior theories that undergird assessments. The key is to have an understanding of the meaning of the values that influence each assessment.

Clients' Values

We must consider clients' values regarding their situations, their problems, their own view of distress, and we must accept the reality that our values may differ from the values of our clients. Differences must be understood so that value conflicts between the worker and the client do not impede the assessment process.

Case Example 7.2 portrays the impact of a value conflict on the assessment process.

Social workers assess client systems in relation to their environmental constraints, barriers, and opportunities. When we introduced Case Example 7.1, featuring Christy Raymond, our discussion regarding her landlord, the inequities of the tax laws which allow him to profit from Ms. Raymond's inadequate housing, and the deplorable state of affairs in society in which adequate housing for low-income people is not available, we are explicating a social value that supports just and humane social structures. No assessment is unrelated to values, nor should it be. It is important, however, that assessments be underwritten by social work values.

When we analyze client circumstances from a strengths perspective, we are actualizing the social work value that supports the worth and dignity of each individual. That social work value, in turn, helps us accept differences between ourselves and clients.

Viewpoints regarding people, their backgrounds, ethnicity, gender, and even their problems are value-laden. Levy (1976) describes values as preferred understandings of people. That is, we can choose to see people through our biases that hold us back from real understanding, or we can choose to see people as unique individuals, coping with their environments in their own ways.

The client values, of course, are central in the assessment phase. When conflicts arise between a social worker's assessment of the situation and a client's assessment, values are likely the source of the conflict. In Case Example 7.2, which involves Carl Benson, the value conflict between worker and client system was made clear. Working out that value dilemma is imperative if Carl is to go on working with the task group.

In assessment, we must realize values are a product of our own culture and experience, just as the clients' values are. Cultural differences may greatly affect

---

CASE EXAMPLE 7.2

A Task Group

Carl Benson is working with a group of mothers of children with cerebral palsy. They have been meeting together for a long time, having accomplished many wonderful goals and gaining much support from each other. The spring fundraiser is in the planning process, and this group has been assigned a major task. Carl is participating in the group this evening because the group needs to develop a plan to carry out its assignment. The members of the group spend most of their time socializing and talking about their children in a way that Carl hears as "gossipy." Clearly, Carl's value is to ensure the group has objectives and meets its goals. The group members, on the other hand, value the opportunity to share and support each other. If each party—the group members and Carl—were asked to assess the group at this particular juncture, no doubt the assessments would be quite different. Assessments that are not mutually agreed upon, with shared values, are discouraged.

assessments, if they are not grounded in a thorough discussion with the client system. DuBray (1985, pp. 30–37) found in a study of Native American M.S.W.s a significant difference from white social workers on three of four major values. Cultural competence is one approach to use to ensure we make few errors in assessment.

Cultural Competence and Assessment

Attaining cultural competence in assessment utilizing the "ethnographic" approach in both data collection and analysis of information (Green, 1982, p. 91). The ethnographic approach is predicated on the worker's having extensive knowledge of the cultural or ethnic group with which he or she is working. Such knowledge includes familiarity with language, beliefs, values, and customs, as well as appropriate demographic data.

Using the knowledge base in a sensitive, helpful way is equally important in one's quest for cultural competence. James Leigh (1989) suggests adapting the ethnographer's "cultural guide" role when working with persons whose background differs from one's own.

The cultural guide seeks to understand another's culture and, in so doing, values the culture. Leigh gives the example of an African-American young man

Knowledge of language, beliefs, values, and customs is critical to accurate assessments.

who is referred to a social worker. Rather than focusing on his "problem" behavior, the social worker, instead, enlists the young man's point of view on the area of concern. "I want to learn from you as much as you will teach me about Black children your age in school, how they survive or fail and what they say about the school system" (Leigh, 1989).

By becoming a cultural guide, the assessment immediately becomes a process based upon mutuality. Establishing openness in the assessment process has marked, positive effects on the way in which information is analyzed by both the worker and the client system. The focus, immediately, is on strengths and sets the stage for the action phase—implementation—that follows quickly on the heels of assessment.

Assessments and Professional Values

Assessment provides us with a framework of reference that enables us to feel connected to others. It is unnecessary to "reinvent the wheel" each time we examine a new problem. What we learn through research, presentations, consultations, supervision, and journal reading enables us to develop a frame of reference that helps us make sense of the information we have gathered and enhance our professional development. Thus, our direct work with clients is enhanced, and we find greater meaning in our profession, placing a premium on our own professional development.

Stressful Situations and Assessments

Working in public agencies is stressful, taking a great deal of energy that diverts us from effecting change. When we develop accurate and thorough assessments, we are more focused on our work, resulting in greater changes for clients. Social workers also benefit because they are more likely to see positive results with clients when thorough assessments are accomplished. Burnout among social workers is greatly reduced when the social worker feels his or her work has meaning and significance (Shulman, 1991).

PUTTING AN ASSESSMENT TOGETHER

Assessment is a complex process that contains several essential steps. In order to develop an assessment, you may find it beneficial to follow these steps:

1. Have a framework for analysis of information in mind. We suggest the Framework for Planned Change (Chapter 3). This framework focuses on: (1) general issues, (2) client system's at-risk conditions, (3) client system's conditions of opportunity, (4) a continuum that places client system's concerns on a continuum from risk to opportunity, and (5) systems involved in the change effort (change, client action, and focal systems).

2. Review the area of concern and pinpoint the essentials. By so doing, you are setting boundaries that, in turn, help you use your time well.

3. Use a systems perspective in data collection in collecting relevant information. Specifically, the systems perspective in data gathering includes: identifying all systems potentially involved in the area of concern, remaining sensitive to human and contextual diversity issues, and focusing on client strengths and opportunities as well as on risks.

4. Apply a systems' focused assessment tool that utilizes Siporin's two essential elements of assessments: "seeing into" situations and "seeing through" barriers to change.

The following vignette dealing with a homeless family demonstrates the steps:

CASE EXAMPLE 7.3
The Prices—A Homeless Family

1. Using a Framework for Analysis

A. *All systems have general issues with which to contend.* The mounting numbers of homeless has become a national disgrace in the United States. The Price family is temporarily housed in a church shelter. They are part of a "revolving shelter system." Churches in the area have formed a homelessness coalition, and they open their facilities to homeless people. The downside of their effort is that people staying in their shelters must be moved every five days to a new church shelter. An agency oversees the system, but it is far from satisfactory. Basic needs are met, but children do not attend school and social brokering for clients is minimal.

The reasons for the Prices' homelessness are likely to be numerous. Funds for public housing were significantly reduced during the 1980s, resulting in the loss of thousands of units of housing across the country.

All homeless people, regardless of their families, personalities, sex, job preparation, or any other factor must contend with the general fact that affordable housing in this country is not available for all those who need it.

B. *All systems are at risk.* Homeless families, of course, are at risk because they are vulnerable, not only to the environment, but also to illness, crime, violence, and prejudice. The Prices are further at risk because Bill and Arlene Price are both addicted to alcohol and neither has specialized job skills. They are African-Americans, dealing with daily discrimination and oppression and attempting to balance their dual perspective.

C. *All systems have opportunities.* Bill and Arlene Price show a stubborn determination to stay together as a family in spite of their problems. They have weathered great hardship and despite many strikes against them, when they seek help, they seek it as a family. This is a wonderful opportunity for the social worker to focus on family unity as a client strength.

D. *All systems are on a continuum from risk to opportunity.* The parents' determination to maintain the family unit is a strength that must be reinforced immediately so that it does not become a risk. For example, if the social worker ignores their determination, seeing only the family's liabilities, the security the family has created with each other could be undermined. Likewise, the risks may themselves turn out to be opportunities. If Bill and Arlene free themselves of their denial related to their alcoholism, there may be treatment centers the entire family could be housed in while they obtain help. Admitting to a problem can, in and of itself, become an individual and family strength.

The continuum concept reinforces the need to act immediately with client systems because the precarious balance between risk and opportunity is made more apparent. While we do not encourage you to act without thinking, we do urge you to be on your toes, starting where the client is, when the client is ready to begin.

E. *All systems are involved in the change effort.* Focal systems, action systems, and the change systems are all part of the framework used to analyze the Prices situation. In order for the Prices' immediate needs to be met, the Prices need to be housed in a shelter in which more services are available. Pressure must be placed on other shelters to accept them. The Prices have school-aged children who need to be educated, and the couple is in need of alcohol treatment. The social worker will be looking at all related systems during their assessment.

2. Focusing on Essentials

After choosing a framework for analysis, focusing on essentials in your information gathering enhances the assessment. In the Price case example, the focus was on the here and now because the Prices' need for immediate help was so evident. As important as knowing about the Price family background is knowledge about possible substance abuse, and this will in fact be necessary if the Prices do seek help for their alcoholism. Develop your assessments following the above guidelines and thorough assessments will likely result.

Areas of concern are most apt to develop when system needs are not met and during transitions which, inevitably, all client systems experience. Furthermore, problems usually arise in the course of one system interacting with another system.

3. Using Systems Tools to Assess Data

The first component of the systems perspective in data assessment that is applied to the Price family deals with the identification of all systems involved. For the Prices, information should have been gathered from their own perspective on potential resources and systems that relate to their condition.

We have mentioned the importance of client input, and its importance is reemphasized. While effective assessment demands an unbiased understanding of the area of concern, we carefully listen and consider the client system's explanation. Who knows better than the Prices regarding both their needs as well as their potential resources? Inclusion of the client system's perspective is crucial to both assessment as a product and assessment as a process. While we add to the client's outlook from our professional knowledge base, we respect their in-depth understanding of the area of concern.

The focus we use for doing assessments is a systems understanding. While we focus on client systems, action systems, and target systems in terms of their general issues, risks, opportunities, and their position on the continuum from risk to opportunity, resource systems (informal, formal, and societal) must be considered in relationship to the client system. Within those systems are critical issues, and to understand those issues we must look at problems using a broad-range focus. Each resource system can prove to be either helpful or inadequate—that is, a risk or an opportunity for the person or family. In addition, these resource systems interact with each other. Informal resource systems' (neighborhoods, families) support for societal resources (schools, fire protection) is crucial to community well-being, which, in turn, affects the quality of life for individuals. Consideration of resource systems is an important part of any assessment.

Human and contextual diversity issues are always woven into a systems perspective on assessment. The fact that Mr. and Mrs. Price are members of a minority group that has been historically, as well as presently, at risk in society is a fact. How they cope with ongoing discrimination and the particular local discriminatory conditions that may exist in alcohol-treatment programs, housing, and job training are all information to be considered in the assessment process.

(Continued)

CASE EXAMPLE 7.3   *(Continued)*

Underlying all ways of gathering data is the focus upon strengths. The Framework for Planned Change and a systems perspective on data gathering have that principle implicit in all their aspects. The Prices are not looked upon as a family without strengths. Instead, the very fact that they remain together as a family, despite the overwhelming odds against them, is a strength that permeates every step of the assessment.

4. Using Systems Assessment Tools and Techniques

Assessment techniques that require an over-arching view of client systems, target systems, action systems, and resource systems contain a systems or ecological perspective. Such techniques should help you, as a student, "get started" on assessments. You may not apply them in every agency setting, but their principles must be applied, regardless of setting.

You can apply these techniques to the Price family, but we are presenting another family for your consideration, to give you more experience and actual application of systems techniques.

In each of the techniques presented below, there is a focus on systems and on their inter-relatedness. A complete picture of the area of concern along with a direction for change are inherent in each technique.

THE GENERAL ASSESSMENT PLAN

Initial Comments

The assessment process can resemble a giant sponge, soaking up information, regardless of its usefulness, if we do not have a plan to guide us. In the previous chapter, we emphasized the importance of having a purpose for collecting information. The same rule applies to assessment—use information in a purposeful way. Focusing our efforts results in a clearer understanding of the dynamics of the situation and helps us use time effectively.

We have developed a generalist assessment tool that can be used with any size system: the Generalist Process Assessment Tool (the GPA model). For individuals, families, and small systems, we have a broad knowledge base that has promoted the use of agreed-upon assessment outlines and protocols. Large groups, bureaucracies, and communities are areas of great attention in social work, yet assessment tools are not nearly as well developed as they are for smaller systems. The following tool is comprehensive, focusing on all systems related to the client system.

Generalist Process Assessment Tool (GPA)

The Generalist Practice Assessment Tool integrates the systems approach and the values of generalist practice with knowledge and theory. The Generalist Process Assessment tool includes the components of the Framework for Change introduced earlier. In fact, the GPA is an extension of that framework that integrates a new concept, the social worker's vision of the client's area of concern, with all the facts gathered during information gathering. (See example of GPA, Figure 7.1.)

FIGURE 7.1 Generalist Process Assessment Tool:
GPA for Tanya Marshall

General Issues	At-Risk Conditions	Opportunities	Vision of the Social Worker
Low-income	Female head of household	Mother is strong, healthy, and positive	Identifies strengths of client system
AFDC recipient	Teen mother	Special grants available for mother for college	Identifies strengths of action and focal system
Urban dweller	Father not present	Good relationships in family	Willing to intervene with larger systems
Transporation concerns	Financial contributions are sporadic	Mother has GED & ACT score of 18	Sees relationship between client situation and community concerns
Shopping limitations	AFDC cut	Quality child care is available, hard to access	
Child-care facilities are limited	Child-care facilities are inadequate	Responsive police department	
	Bus transportation is limited		
	Shopping in distant suburbs		
	Isolated neighborhood		
	"Crack" houses		
	Poor housing (rats present on premises)		

The social worker's vision embraces the facts, the connections among the variables that are only visible by "seeing into" and "seeing through" the area of concern and the possibilities for change. The social worker's vision, incorporating data from all sources, becomes the assessment.

CASE EXAMPLE 7.4

Tanya Marshall

1. General Issues

The system of concern that presents the initial problem is the family system—a small system. Tanya Marshall is a nineteen-year-old mother of two children. The children's father is not present in the household, although he occasionally makes contributions to the family. Tanya is fond of him, but thinks he is immature.

Like many young women in her situation, Tanya receives Aid to Families with Dependent Children and would like to complete her education, but finding quality child care is very difficult. Her mother had been caring for the two children, ages two and three, but she is finishing her own college education and does not have time. Tanya cannot bear to leave her children in the child-care facility the Department of Social Services will pay for be-

(Continued)

CASE EXAMPLE 7.4   *(Continued)*

cause it is crowded, and she thinks the owners are only interested in money. She spent one day at the child-care facility and was appalled at the noise level generated by the television that was always playing and the loud voices of the child-care workers. She took both children home.

Her neighborhood is isolated from shopping and decent transportation. Recently, she waited forty-five minutes for a bus to take her to a shopping center in a suburb where she liked to do her food shopping. At that store, prices are better, produce is fresher, and she is treated with dignity by the check-out people when she presents her food stamps.

Tanya and the children live in a second-story flat that has seen a better day. So far she has not been bothered by rats, but she lives in fear because her neighbors have told her about rats in the alley behind the house. Several houses down from her, there is a "crack" house. People are coming and going all day and all night. At night, gunshots interrupt the silence, and Tanya sleeps with both children thinking she can protect them from the violent world that surrounds the family.

In a word, there is nothing unusual about Tanya's everyday life. Thousands of women in every city throughout this country live in similar surroundings and face similar challenges. We have all read about or experienced firsthand this story. Tanya's is an individual life that presents its own set of risks and opportunities, yet they are shared in countless ways with women in similar circumstances.

2. At-Risk Conditions

The issues Tanya and the children must face contain potential at-risk conditions. In general, families in which a woman is the head of household are financially less well-off than families in which men are present. In addition, teenage parents, as a group, have two strikes against them because their earning power is greatly limited and their own emotional and mental development is in flux. Ta-

nya's status is a potentially at-risk situation from the beginning.

We already know that the child care she has located is of low quality and that her neighborhood is isolated from basic societal resources. Being aware of at-risk conditions related to the targeted system helps us narrow down problems to be solved and allows us to economize on time and effort.

3. Opportunities

Although the odds appear to be against Tanya and her family, there are a number of strengths. Tanya, herself, is the major strength in the system. She is healthy, intelligent, young, and positive. She takes good care of the children, even though they try her patience and she becomes tired of meeting their needs. She knows that obtaining outside help will ease her way.

There is assistance available in the community, but it is difficult to access. Quality child care exists, but she has not yet found it. There are special grants available from the state and federal government to assist her to obtain the college education she wants. Although she graduated from an inner-city high school in the adult education division, she recently took the American College Testing program (ACT) for college entrance and scored 18, a decent score by any standards.

Tanya's mother is busy with her own life, but she talks by phone regularly with Tanya, and Tanya can call her any time of the night or day. The children's father is not around much, but Tanya's attitude toward men is generally positive, and she looks forward to having a permanent, intimate relationship someday.

4. Vision of the Social Worker

Building on these conditions of opportunity depends on the social worker's vision. For example, if at the onset of meeting Tanya, the Department of Social Services social worker views the client system as helpless and dependent with few recognizable strengths, it is doubtful that any positive which might develop for the family can be reinforced.

If, on the other hand, the social worker's vision includes a view of a family with potential, there is a greater likelihood that resources for the family can be accessed and their situation will improve.

The vision of the social worker includes identifying other systems which require intervention or may become potential clients. Tanya is not in a unique situation. The worker might begin to help other families like Tanya's band together to obtain the resources they need. For example, quality child care ought to be available in her neighborhood. The city health department ought to be alerted to the rat condition that surrounds Tanya's home. The police should be dealing with the "crack" house down the street from Tanya. Many families live in similar conditions, and social work generalists must see the big picture—the one beyond the client system.

Circles Maps

Circles maps (Heus and Pincus, 1986, p. 175) are used to organize information for assessment. The maps are constructed in a paper-and-pencil exercise by first naming an issue and then breaking that issue down into subparts. Subparts are written on a large piece of butcher paper and circles are drawn around each one (Figure 7.2).

Areas of concern, at-risk conditions, and conditions of opportunity are all identified for each client system, target system, and action system.

The circles maps can help to logically organize information you have gathered. They also help to prioritize information while stimulating our intuition. They help us break out of linear thinking. The circles map becomes a way to visualize an infinite variety of "part-whole configurations" (Heus and Pincus, 1986, p. 176).

Tanya Marshall's circles map connects systems in which she is involved or would like to be involved in: job training, child care, AFDC, her extended family, and her neighborhood. By connecting the circles and discerning their location in relationship to each other as well as the distance between circles, we begin to see relationships and associate general goals Tanya has. Although mapping is very useful when working with families and larger systems, an assessment must be translated into a narrative so that it can be shared with others who are involved in the change process.

Writing an Assessment

The written assessment is the assessment's product. Formats vary depending upon system size, the agency requirements, and the purpose of the written assessment. Even when we are required to complete our written assessments in a predetermined format, we must be careful not to be limited by that format. For that reason, we presented general assessment techniques that are broadly inclusive. As a student and beginning social worker, you may find it helpful to first analyze the process in your own words and in a fashion with which you are comfortable, and

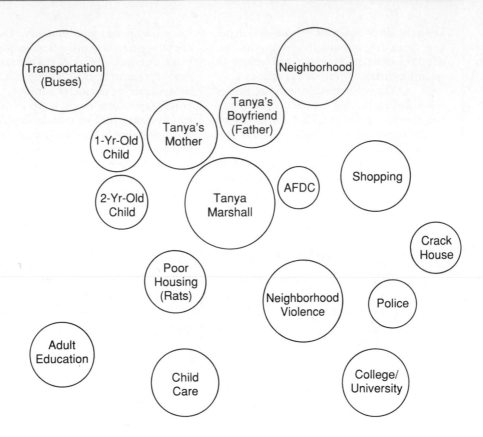

FIGURE 7.2 Circles Map for Tanya Marshall

then reduce it to the required format. A good written assessment should provide answers to why and how phenomena are connected. It should not include superfluous information, unrelated to the plan or to the implementation phase.

Put yourself in the role of the reader who knows little or nothing about the situation. Understand that the reader may represent different audiences. For example, one audience may be your supervisor, another audience may be a judge, and another audience may be the client system. It is likely the supervisor will want to see a more detailed and fully described assessment while most judges will be satisfied with a summary version of an assessment. The client system's written assessment should be jargon-free and well founded in facts.

The professional assessment statement is useful in the supervision process as a check on our objectivity. The professional statement is an understanding of our personal and professional observations and assessment. As part of the assessment, we need to organize our own life-views with our professional knowledge and understanding. This can be an intellectually demanding and emotionally stressful test (Lewis, 1982, p. 64).

The professional statement in the assessment phase should help you answer the question, What am I to do in the planning the implementation phases? It should help you decide the question, What am I to do now? How am I to act and why?

The following major steps in the generalist assessment process can help guide the overall assessment (Sallee, Sandau-Beckler, and Ronnau, 1990):

Major Steps in the Generalist Assessment Process

Step One: Identify the following:

1. Change system
2. Client system

Step Two: Use the following to identify pertinent information to include in your assessment:

Social Worker/Agency
Client System   _____

Context   _____

History   _____

Contextual
Issues   _____

Strengths   _____

Informal Resources   _____

Formal Resources   _____

Societal Resources   _____

Developmental Stages _____

Level of Functioning _____

Systems Dynamics
(Boundaries,
Structure,   _____
Communication,
Feedback, Hierarchy, _____
Bureaucracy, and so
on)   _____

Step Three: List and prioritize the *additional* areas of information you would explore with this client system in order to complete your assessment (for example, missing information). Along with each item, indicate how you would collect this information (for example, ask client, use formal assessment tool, interview extended family member, examine case records, and so on).

Additional Information Needed	*Collection Methods*
1. _____	1. _____
2. _____	2. _____
3. _____	3. _____

Step Four: List and prioritize the major issues of concern.

Step Five: Determine from your assessment the following:

1. *Focal system*
2. *Action system*

CONCLUSION

Assessment, Phase Three of the Crystal Model, centers on an analysis of the information collected on the area of concern. We made sense of the information we collected around each system. We attempt to "see into" the situation in order to gain in-depth understanding of what we are focusing on and to "see through" barriers to change in order to realize changes that might be or can be made.

While there is a major stage in the change process reserved for assessment, it is also an ongoing process throughout the helping process. Assessment is a phase that includes the client system's participation.

We employ knowledge generated from theory, research, and practice as a base to understand the situation and the interaction among variables we have identified. We also employ empirically tested instruments and practical techniques to help organize and assess the information. Using validated instruments for assessment contributes to the knowledge base in social work and assists individual social workers to compare their work with others in the field. Practical techniques guide our assessment so that important facts and considerations are not ignored.

Even though we encourage the use of validated instruments, good assessments individualize each client system and each assessment becomes a new experience taking into account the unique aspects of that situation. Assessment helps us make decisions necessary to move forward with the change process. In Chapter 8, assessment instruments applied to small, medium, and large systems are presented. The generalist employs a systems focus in every assessment to ensure a broad understanding of the area of concern.

References

Baer, Betty L., and Federico, Ronald. (1978). *Educating the Baccalaureate Social Worker: Report of the Undergraduate Social Work Curriculum Development Project.* Cambridge, MA: Ballinger, p. 86.

Berger, Robert L., and Federico, Ronald C. (1985). *Human Behavior: A Social Work Perspective,* 2nd ed. New York: Longman Press, p. 13.

DuBray, W. H. (1985). American Indian Values: Critical Factors in Casework. *Social Casework, 66,* 30–37.

Green, James W. (1982). *Cultural Awareness in the Human Services.* Englewood, NJ: Prentice Hall, p. 91.

Grinnell, Richard M. Jr., and Williams, Margaret. (1990). *Research in Social Work: A Primer.* Itasca, IL: F. E. Peacock, pp. 170–171.

Heus, Michael, and Pincus, Allen. (1986). *The Creative Generalist: A Guide to Social Work Practice.* Barneveld, WI: Micamer, pp. 175, 176.

Kozol, Jonathan. (1991). *Children in America's Schools.* New York: Crown.

Leigh, James. (1989). "The Ethnographic Interview," given to Wayne State University students, Detroit, MI.

Levy, Charles. (1976). *Social Work Ethics/Charles S. Levy.* New York: Human Science Press.

Lewis, Harold. (1982). *The Intellectual Base of Social Work Practice.* New York: The Haworth, pp. 64, 121–124.

Moreno, Jacob (ed.). (1960). *The Sociometry Reader.* Glencoe, IL: Free Press.

Nelson, K., Landsman, M., and Deutelbaum, W. (1990). Three Models of Family Centered Placement Prevention Services. *Child Welfare, LXIX*(1), 3–21.

Nowak, Mary Jane. (1981). How to Read Research Critically. *Information and Referral,* 3(2), 68, 77.

Sallee, Alvin L., Marlow, Christine, and Eastman, Kathleen. (1989). New Mexico: An Example of Federal Court-Ordered Foster Care. *Foster Care Journal,* February 1989.

Sallee, A., Sandau-Beckler, P., and Ronnau, J. (1990). Class notes. Las Cruces, NM: New Mexico State University.

Shulman, L. (1991). *Interactional Social Work Practice: Toward an Empirical Theory.* Itasca, IL: F. E. Peacock.

Siporin, Max. (1975). *Introduction to Social Work Practice.* New York: Macmillan, pp. 219, 221, 222.

Chapter 8

Assessment of Small, Medium, and Large Systems

OVERVIEW

This chapter focuses on the assessment of small, medium, and large systems. As we saw in the last chapter, general system assessment provides us with a description from a theoretical and research base of what is happening at a rather broad level. While this provides critical information, we may need to assess the subsystems in more detail. We also need to be familiar with the tools used by change systems, such as mental health centers, community councils, or schools. Therefore, we present in this chapter specific assessment techniques and tools for each size system. While this is far from an exhaustive list, it does provide the major frameworks generalists and the action system usually use. We begin with small systems.

ASSESSING SMALL SYSTEMS

Because we often work with individual clients, we must understand the assessment process as applied to them. However, we must be sure to include an ecological understanding and systems perspective in the assessment of individuals in order to take into account individual differences and the contextual and human diversity issues that further differentiate people. "Despite social work's long standing commitment to a person in an environment perspective, much of social work practice is directed toward changing individuals. This orientation derives in part from the profession's knowledge base and in part from its organizational political context" (Kagle, 1988, p. 35). Of course, helping individuals change does not negate the person in environment perspective. The information that is gathered to build an assessment on an individual must include data from the individual's social environment.

Individual Assessment Components

Generally, there are eight factors that are considered in an assessment of an individual. These are:

1. The client and focal systems' resource systems, and the interaction and inadequacy of each.

2. The client's strengths and skills.

3. Physical and medical history, if critical to assessment.

4. Psychological assessment, utilizing appropriate instruments.

5. Contextual issues.

6. Human diversity issues.

7. Brief social history.

8. Potential for change of the focal system and the client's motivation to address resistance and barriers to change.

In an assessment of the individual, it is important to state conclusions and the logic used to reach that conclusion. A summary is helpful to rekindle one's memory when meeting later with the client or focal system. It is important to remember to individualize and to be aware of human diversity issues (Austin, Kopp, and Smith, 1986, p. 280).

By relying heavily on psychological theories, the social work profession has given more attention to changing people than to addressing change in their environments. With the person-in-environment perspective in mind, we present some examples of how to assess individuals.

Assessment Approaches

In clinical work with individuals and families, social work has a long history of assessment, beginning with the approaches presented in Mary Richmond's *Social Diagnosis* (1917). Over the years, a number of approaches to assessment have been developed, varying with theoretical perspectives and technology. Mattaini and Kirk (1991, pp. 260–266) have identified six major types of assessments of small systems. These include (1) psychosocial, (2) classification systems, (3) behavioral, (4) computerized, (5) ecosystems and visualization, and (6) expert systems. As generalists, we need to be familiar with these types of assessment, yet we are not expected to be able to use all of them.

Psychosocial assessments are usually made by inference and are best used by specialists in clinical work. These specialists are usually M.S.W.s, psychologists, or Ph.D. counselors who may make up the action system.

Classification systems group types of behaviors, diseases, or other features related by a similar characteristic. Classification systems organize the information we collect and provide an assessment that indicates the most appropriate implementation. Social work generalists have not fully embraced classification systems (Kirk, Siporin, and Kutchins, 1989, pp. 295–307), partly because they focus on differences and problems, and partly because they categorize and label people.

The DSM III-R (American Psychiatric Association, 1987), a manual in which mental disorders and illnesses are described, is an example of a classification system. Behavioral assessments record observed behaviors unique to each person. For the generalist, behavior or cognitive assessments may work well for individual clients, yet it is far more difficult to use behavior assessments for broader systemic analysis (Mattaini and Kirk, 1991, p. 262).

The use of computers in assessment is growing. Although most computer systems simply speed up the use of scales and classification systems, some applications have been made with graphic assessments (discussed below). Computerized assessment packages allow the clinical specialist to use a number of scales with a client without the delay of time a manual system would require. Yet, computerization does not overcome the limitations of classification systems discussed above.

Ecosystem and graphic visualization is based on a systems description and, therefore, fits best with the generalist perspective. The use of graphics may expand assessments while still providing a depth of understanding (Mattaini and Kirk, 1991).

Expert systems have been developed from work on artificial intelligence, in which experts develop decision programs, such as risk scales for child abuse. These assessments work best when there are few options to be considered. Sometimes in computerized risk assessment, clients themselves may enter information directly through the keyboard.

While there are several approaches to assessing individuals, we believe the systems approach with graphic presentation is best suited to generalist social work practice. What has been missing is a way to make systems assessments practical. With resource systems, the Generalist Process Assessment, circles map, and the general guidelines we provided in the last chapter and in more detail in this chapter, you will be able to complete complex, in-depth assessments with small, medium, and large systems.

Resource Systems in Assessment

As we see in the major steps in the generalist assessment process, examining the resources of each system is a cornerstone of this phase. One way to avoid "blaming the victim" (Ryan, 1976) is to look at the individual and his and her interaction with resource systems. As we discussed in Chapter 3, the individual's interaction with resource systems helps us understand his or her situation in a broader light. In assessment, we look at the individual's or family's interaction within the informal resource system — family, friends, neighbors — and how adequate the informal resource system is in meeting the family's needs. These needs consist of, primarily, tangible goods, emotional support, and information. While information and tangible goods are easier to assess, assessing emotional supports is far more complex.

Understanding the individual's interaction with the formal resource system and the adequacy or inadequacy of the formal resource system is fairly straightforward. Are there organizations or groups that can provide resources to this individual? If not, how can he or she become a part of an organization and benefit from its resources? These are the key questions in assessing formal resource systems.

CASE EXAMPLE 8.1

Mrs. Smith

Mrs. Smith is a seventy-nine-year-old white woman who was fairly active until recently, when she fell and broke her hip and was required to use a walker. Her daughter, family, and friends believe she should be in a nursing home. Mrs. Smith wishes to stay at home with support services. The change system provides case management from Comprehensive Coordinated In-Home Care (CCIC) (Medicaid Waiver).

General Assessment Grids (GAG) I and II

In order to structure and make sense of the complex information we have collected on different size systems and themes, we have designed a grid. The general Assessment Grid I (Figure 8.1) addresses systems, and Grid II (Figure 8.4) charts themes. Grid I charts the change systems and resource systems for an individual or family client system. Both strengths and inadequacies of each resource system are described.

Grid II helps us see themes that are developed for client systems. These include history, context, human diversity, developmental stage, and organizational culture. We will use Grid II later in this chapter in an example on developing a group home.

Case Example 8.1 illustrates this point and uses the General Assessment Grid I (GAG-I), which presents the change roles and resource systems by different size systems.

Psychological Assessment

Development Assessment

Developmental psychology is concerned with how individuals change and grow over time. Developmental theory addresses language development, cognitive development, and social development. Scales have been constructed that help us assess one's progress through developmental stages. For example, if we are assessing an individual child whom we think may be developmentally delayed, we may compare the child's development with the age norms for motor skills, using the Denver Developmental Screening Tests (LeVine and Sallee, 1992). This test would tell us that 90 percent of all babies have learned to sit without support at 7.8 months. Comparing this child's vocalization, another aspect of development, with the norm, we learn that hearing speech stimulates the baby after a certain point. For example, deaf infants stop babbling at about six months of age, whereas hearing infants continue to diversify their babbling experimentation (LeVine and Sallee, 1992). Other aspects of language include sentence development, including vocabulary acquisition. Understanding some aspects of language development is important when a child is assessed who may have some developmental problems.

Cognitive behavior assessment is usually based upon Piaget and his colleagues' work. According to Piaget, adult intelligence is qualitatively different from that of a child, but all levels of intelligence are defined in terms of adaptive

FIGURE 8.1 General Assessment Grid I: *Systems.*
Assessment Question: Placement of Mrs. Smith

System	*Micro*	*Mezzo*	*Macro*
Change	Social worker's knowledge of elderly.	Co-workers and supervisor.	Agency setting policies.
Client	Mrs. Smith independent.	Other elders.	CCIC policy and procedures & procedures.
Focal	Mrs. Smith's daughter.	Friends and neighbors.	Community support for case management—i.e., doctors, nursing homes.
Action	Individual social workers in other agencies.	RSVP—Mobile meals. Homemaker.	Network of services for elderly.
Resources*			
Informal	Daughter is very involved. Wants best for Mrs. Smith. Not familiar with case management.	Friends and neighbors think nursing home only option. Supportive, involved.	Church's support of case management. TV publicity. Word of mouth.
Formal	Mrs. Smith member of AARP.	Monthly meetings. Uncomfortable because others have health.	Strong advocacy group nationally, but not always in tune with low income senior needs.
Social	Completing difficult forms with Mrs. Smith at agency.	Team meetings.	Getting agencies to deliver services in timely fashion. Complex regulations and forms create mistrust.

* Address inadequacies and strengths of resource systems. Identify barriers.

thinking and action. Children arrive at the adult stage by going through four major stages of conceptualization: (1) sensorimotor, (2) free operational, (3) concrete operational, and (4) informational operational. All these variables related to cognition are considered in the child's assessment.

When assessing social development, the beginning of personal social skills, such as using the toilet, dressing oneself, sharing toys, and so on are considered. These social skills differ greatly from culture to culture, so assessments are generated in a cultural context. Eric Erikson's work (1963) furthers our understanding of social development. The first stage of social development, according to Erikson, is trust versus mistrust. This stage of socialization can be broken down into target behaviors. Trust versus mistrust includes spontaneous smile, awareness of strange situations, and separation anxiety, behaviors we see in infants under one year. As an example, deviation from these expected behaviors should be a signal to look closely for potential problems.

A critical part of development includes the growth of the parent-child bond or parent-infant bond. Some social work clinicians believe that the infant's well-being is determined by the quality of the relationship that is established between the parent and the child, commencing at the infant's birth (LeVine and Sallee, 1992). In assessing a child, the parents' physical and social contacts with the infant are investigated. Not many years ago, after the birth of a baby in a hospital, the mother was permitted only to glance at the newborn while the father may have peered through the nursery window. In most hospitals today, parents have immediate and continued contact following delivery. Some studies have shown that infants under this latter type of care score better on tests of physical and mental development at one year of age than babies who did not have extended contact (LeVine and Sallee, 1992). Therefore, in an assessment of a child, it may be critical to look at parent-infant bonding.

Developmental theory tells us that in assessment it is most critical to understand the disruption of normal developmental processes. Such a disruption may include physical factors such as perceived problems during pregnancy, low birthweight, or exposure to drugs or diseases during pregnancy (LeVine and Sallee, 1992). Problems such as the loss of a parent through divorce or death or the severe physical illness of parents can affect children's development. Child-rearing that is too lax or too severe may also create problems for the child. In assessing a child developmentally, the child's biology, temperament, physical condition, and social environment are all reviewed.

In social work assessments, we attempt to focus on theories that are empirically tested (Shulman, 1991). Because our personal experience involves parenting, sometimes our own biases get in the way of understanding how children grow and develop. Child development is one of the areas in which personal experiences and common sense may lead to assumptions that cannot be supported. In assessing a person's development, all the systems that may have created abnormal development are taken into account.

Adolescence creates major changes, including moving to a different school, developing a new peer group, exploring roles, interacting with the opposite sex, and a transitioning to adulthood. In young adulthood, an individual begins to cut the strings to the family and establish new roles and relationships. These may include becoming a college student, a roommate or a spouse. In entering mid-adulthood, the individual begins a new career and the roles that go along with that and begins to join formal organizations. In many instances, middle adulthood includes divorce and remarriage. Later adulthood includes promotion, job changes, perhaps career shifts; having children go off to school, and perhaps returning to school and becoming a "nontraditional student." The late-adulthood stage includes retirement, and, with declining physical abilities, loss of independence (Garvin and Seabury, 1984).

Psychological Tests

Generalist social workers are not prepared to administer psychological tests, but they are often expected to refer clients to psychologists whose training includes the administration and interpretation of tests. If you are working with a client system in which a psychological test is either ordered or in which you think test findings will assist the client, you may need to work with the client to prepare him or her for the testing experience. In addition, it is not uncommon for social workers to discuss with clients how the results of tests will be used. The testing experience is frightening to most people, and receiving emotional support is most helpful.

There are hundreds of psychological tests used in assessments. The purposes of several of the most commonly used tests are summarized below. Again, we remind you that you will not be administering tests, but their use is so extensive in developing individual assessments in hospitals, schools, community mental health agencies, and child welfare agencies — all places in which generalists work — that we believe some familiarity with them is essential.

Intelligence Tests

The Wechsler Intelligence Scale for Children, Revised, and the Stanford Binet Intelligence Scale are two of the most popular tests used to measure intelligence (LeVine and Sallee, 1992). IQ scores are assigned, depending upon the results of the tests. Both tests are administered to single subjects and are lengthy and expensive. Nonetheless, they can offer important information for assessments. For example, intelligence tests are used to determine the presence of childhood schizophrenia and autism, mental retardation, or organic brain damage (Sattler, 1974). Unfortunately, it is widely agreed that IQ tests are misused. Test conditions affect the outcome of tests, and more recently, a great concern was raised regarding cultural biases inherent in the tests. Interpreting IQ tests must be done judiciously.

The Wechsler Intelligence Scale for Adults is frequently administered to measure the intelligence of adults. It is also administered to single subjects.

The Bender-Gestalt is a frequently administered test for children, evaluating the possibility of brain injury and assisting clinicians to differentiate between behavioral disorders that are psychiatric in nature from those disorders which are neurological (Koppitz, 1962, p. 71). Widely accepted scoring systems have been developed, making this an especially useful test.

Achievement Tests

Most children experience achievement tests at some time during their school experience. You may be working with children who are experiencing academic failure, and assessing their level of academic achievement is essential to complete an individual assessment. Two commonly used tests are the California Achievement Test and the Metropolitan Achievement Tests. Specific diagnostic tests are often administered in math, reading, language development, and spelling.

Measuring school readiness may demand the use of achievement tests. Two important ones are the Boehm test of basic concepts and the Denver Developmental Screening Test.

Results of achievement tests assist in the assessment of possible learning disabilities. The Frostig Development Test of Visual Perception and the Illinois Test of Psycholinguistic Abilities are both reliable and valid and have been normed to a broad range of children in different ethnic groups. The field of academic testing is complex, and trained persons using sophisticated instruments must be called upon to provide the information needed to assess a child's academic deficiencies.

Personality Inventory

The Minnesota Multiphasic Personality Inventory is a personality assessment widely used for many years. It can be administered individually or in group settings. People who are sixteen years old or older with at least six years of schooling are able to complete the inventory (Graham, 1977). The test was originally developed to diagnose patients as discrete psychiatric types. It is now used simply to draw inferences and assist in understanding of behaviors.

Sociometric Scales

A variety of sociometric scales can be used to measure social behavior among adults and children. Sociometric questionnaires provide information about human interaction. Children who feel isolated in school may be given a sociometric test to determine the level of interaction in a classroom. The results of a sociometric scale may assist a client to see an alternative view of his or her problem. For example, a woman may report she has no friends, yet neighbors and acquaintances say they feel they are her friends and attend meetings with her and interact with her in a number of ways. The plan for this client may be to assist her to gain a more realistic view of her interpersonal skills. Sociometric scales are often used in group settings and will be discussed more extensively when we take up group assessments.

Family Assessment

The ultimate question we want to answer in assessing an individual is, why does one behave as one does? Of course, to truly answer this question, we must explore the individual's physical and psychological make-up and the social environment, including the family, as well as peer groups and those with whom one interacts in the community and neighborhood. Therefore, while we focus on the individual in this assessment, a thorough assessment could never occur using a generalist perspective without looking at these other systems. Having said that, we will now move forward and examine another small system: the family.

Family assessments are more complicated than individual assessments because more information is collected and must be placed in an orderly way to enhance our understanding of the family system. Although there are forty-three identifiable theories of family theory (LeVine and Sallee, 1992), family systems theory is most closely associated with the generalist model. Families are critical in the development of individuals and are the basic social unit in society. Understanding the importance of family to the internal functioning of the individual and to the social relationships of all people forces us to consider both intrafamily and interfamily relationships.

Family Assessment Tools

The choice of assessment tools is essential in determining how we will make sense of a family. The generalist must decide, for example, whether it is better to assess each individual member of the family or to use a standardized assessment of the family unit. A subjective assessment that is not tied to theory will, of course, lack any comparative information and is subject to insensitivity to cultural or unique characteristics of that particular family. On the other hand, an assessment that is totally standardized may fail to note the uniqueness of this family. As we know, families exist in complex environments and standardized tests cannot measure all the variables that impact on families.

Relationships

Intrafamily Relationships Using family systems theory, family interactions are first assessed. As a unit, the whole family differs from each of its members, but each person affects each of the other family members. In addition, specific transactions are analyzed such as how the family solves problems, how the family deals with conflict, and how the family yields to individual taste and behavior. In addition, how families communicate, both verbally and nonverbally, is considered. Assessing communication is a key way to gain insight into the family situation (Kerr and Bowen, 1988).

Families are critical in the development of individuals and are the basic unit of society.

Many families are resistant to change and seek to maintain a balance, even if the balance is causing pain and unhappiness for individual members. Families, like individuals, pass through developmental phases that must be assessed (Kramer, 1985). Each phase has critical points that are potentially stressful, and the manner in which families meet developmental crises needs to be considered in a family assessment.

Interfamily Relationships Interfamily relationships include family interactions with extended family, their community, and resource systems. The quality of such interactions provides an understanding of the family's capacities to survive in the world beyond its doorstep. For example, family interactions with the school give some indication of parents' abilities to protect their children if the school is not meeting the children's needs. On the other hand, the parents' interactions with the school may also indicate the family's capacity to deal with information that may be helpful to a child.

From a Health Perspective

One way of assessing families is to compare the healthy way families function and assess how far from this healthy norm the client family is. According to the health orientation, highly functional families are determined by the following:

1. There is a power balance that is understood and accepted by all family members.
2. Each member has rights, and autonomy is encouraged.
3. Each member can tolerate separation and members support each other through losses.
4. Family members perceive reality in compatible ways.
5. All family members are free to express their feelings (LeVine and Sallee, 1992, p. 158).

Family Life-Cycle Assessment

Using the family life-cycle, the family's developmental stage is assessed. The transition from one stage to another is often critical in the life of a family and may explain both new strengths and problems within the family. Family developmental stages are:

1. Courtship Courtship is the dating and exploration of roles prior to matrimony. Friendships between individuals are established with the intent of expanding to a permanent relationship. During this time, the young adults explore sexual and moral behavior with the opposite sex.

2. Marriage and Couplehood Marriage as an institution publicly identifies the formerly unattached adults as a couple. Young adults are then separated from their nuclear family as they form their own family. This requires new role identifications and adjusting to a partnership role. Alternative forms of couplehood may include gay or lesbian couples. During this stage, young adults have to adjust their idealistic views of marriage and couplehood to the realities of compromising and relating on a day-to-day basis with a partner. At the same time, extended family adjust their relationship to the couple. Close contact during this time may expose incompatibilities. This may create a divorce, or, on the other hand, it may help to develop a more intimate relationship with the new partner.

3. First Child   With the birth of the first child, a new role emerges—that of parent. In addition, the role of spouse changes. The alteration and interruption of sexual relations during pregnancy may create problems. Bonding and attachment are critical for the child, but the presence of a new family member with demanding emotional needs places stress on the marriage unit. The advent of a new child in the family creates a different living situation for new parents as they adjust to limitations on privacy, the need for child care, and the fact that the previous diad is now a triad, with all the attendant complications. Within the community, having a child sometimes increases the status of the couple.

4. Growth of Children   During this stage, the older children go off to school and begin to establish contact with their peer groups. Children develop their own roles and begin to pass through their developmental phases. The child begins to learn behaviors, not only at home, but also in the community. During this time, the child relies upon the parents' actions and words for guidance. The use of discipline becomes critical during this stage. The parents' use of affection at an age-appropriate level is important to both parties. At this stage of development, economic resources may be limited and further responsibilities placed on the parents. The parents' careers may be reaching a point at which the parents are gaining more responsibility at work, which also creates stress in the family.

5. Departure of Oldest Child   During the child's adolescence, peer groups compete with the parent in the moral development and the youth's allegiance. As in the stages of individual development, this is the time when the oldest child may lack knowledge and experience regarding sexuality and relations to the opposite sex. Children may display sibling rivalry on a more intense level as they compete with each other and assert their independence. As the oldest child leaves home, the family is open to stress when the strings are cut and major role redefinitions take place. This is also a time when the parents may be changing careers or moving into leadership positions at work and in the community.

6. The Empty-Nest Stage   This stage is reached when all the children in the family have left the home and the couple returns to a dyad. The couple has to redefine their relationship and are also looking toward retirement. But, there is also stress created by this phase. The couple may feel isolated, and, with retirement, may have more leisure time yet fewer acquaintances and friends available to them. As the adult children have children of their own, the parents are redefined in the role of grandparents. The major changes and the losses that affect a couple in this stage may be tempered by the positive feelings of a lifetime of shared experiences. The death of one partner changes the family, but the life of the family continues, albeit in a new way.

These are some limitations of using the family life-cycle in assessment. The first is that today, about 60 percent of all children born can expect to live with only one parent for some time during their lives (LeVine and Sallee, 1992, p. 156). The mythical concept of the two-parent American family is rapidly changing. In addition, the family life-cycle as described does not reflect all cultures, as many cultures, such as the Native American and Hispanic cultures, because the nuclear family that the life cycle approach describes is much less important. In addition, tasks and expectations for each phase in the life cycle differ from culture to culture.

Ecomaps—Family Systems

Similar to the circle maps are *ecomaps*. Hartman refined Bowen's family systems theory and developed ecomapping (Sheafor, Horejsi, and Horejsi, 1991, p. 232). In ecomapping, we use a paper-and-pencil exercise with the family. The social worker asks the family to draw a map of their relationships within and external to the family. The ecomap can give attention to many of the areas addressed in the family assessment outline, including the family composition, the marital status, family structure, job situation, use of community resources, use of societal resources, use of informal resources, sources of support and stress, and interactions with the community. The family is asked to draw circles on a large piece of paper and connect the circles with a set of lines that are previously coded. For example, a stressful or strongly negative relationship is represented by a line of dashes. A positive relationship may be a solid line. Individuals within the family are represented by a circle for a woman, a square for a man, and so on, and their ages and names can be written in. The family can then map out different systems for each person. For example, the father might write down his job within a circle and connect his box with the job with the positive arrow. Problems and positive situations can be identified in this manner for each member of the family. Thus, the discussion of the ecomap with the family begins the assessment process. Ecomapping is helpful in assessing families in a number of situations, ranging from reasonably well-functioning families when they are adopting children or when they are working out new relationships in a recently blended family, to families experiencing serious problems.

Case Example 8.2 illustrates how the ecomap is a valuable tool in documenting relationships, available resources and the individual or family's environment as a whole. (See Figure 8.2.)

Genograms

Another form of map is the *genogram*, also developed from Bowen's work (LeVine and Sallee, 1992, p. 164). A genogram gives a historical perspective of the family, going back several generations. This helps to identify issues and themes that survive across generations (McGoldrick and Gerson, 1985). Families

CASE EXAMPLE 8.2

Ecomap for Jason

Jason is a twenty-five-year-old, gay, white so-cial worker in a rural midwestern state. He has been working for three years at a social services agency in the area of adult protection. He has a B.S.W. degree from a private liberal arts col-lege in the capital city of this state. He lives outside a small town on a farm 42 miles from the county seat, where he works.

Jason recently experienced some discomfort with a "gay-bashing" incident in a local coun-try-western nightclub that he and his partner frequent. Until the incident, in which he and a group of college friends were taunted by some locals, he was unaware that anyone even suspected that he was gay. In order to be dis-creet, he lives alone on his farm and sees his partner on weekends in the capital city. Infre-quently, his partner will come with a group of friends from the city to visit and camp.

The nightclub incident brought great dis-tress to Jason, because it raised fears that someone at his place of employment might discover that he is gay. He worries that the ad-ministrators or public officials who oversee his department will fire him if they know that he is gay. He is sure that no one on his staff talks about gay clients on their caseload, and he has never participated in a discussion in the office about varying sexual preferences. His immedi-ate supervisor appears tolerant but has not sought out any training or consultation on the subject. He also wonders if some of the client systems know that he is gay. He feels sure that most of his clients and their families are unin-formed about gay issues.

Jason sought help from a gay and lesbian services agency in the capital city. He and his social worker did an ecomap of his resources. Following is his ecomap (see Figure 8.2):

> *Work or Employment:* Jason described a tenuous relationship with work. Although he loves his job, the insecurity of not know-ing the potential repercussions of the ad-ministration finding out that he is gay makes it difficult to feel settled. Jason is

paid $26,000 per year and has full medical, disability, dental, and vision insurance. He also has an agency-paid retirement plan.

Parents: Jason has had some difficulty since the time that he first acknowledged to his parents that he was gay. His mother is supportive and stated that she always suspected that he was gay. His father, how-ever, has withdrawn from Jason. The father fears repercussions from family members if Jason openly acknowledges that he is gay. Jason has one sister who also knows about his sexual orientation and she is very sup-portive. Although she has met his partner, his parents have not. They plan to meet him in the near future.

Partner: Jason has a positive relationship with his partner, although it has not always been monogamous. This has led to some discussion and concern about the risk of HIV. Both get tested regularly for the virus as well as practice safe sex. His partner is a nurse with a good income and a supportive family. They have been especially support-ive since the gay-bashing incident.

Friends: Jason has many good friends from college, both gay and straight. In his rural community he socializes only with some staff members with whom he occasionally spends time canoeing and camping. They constantly want to line him up with single women in the area. He feels some guilt that he doesn't share information about his relationship with his partner with them.

Housing: Jason lives on a picturesque farm on a small river. His farm land is rented out and the income covers the farm payment. He has a three-bedroom farm home with a garden.

Community: Jason describes liking the peace and quiet of his neighborhood. His only concern is that the community atti-tude toward diversity is not very tolerant. Although his community is rural, it is lo-cated sixty-five miles from the capital city.

Social Welfare: Jason has no needs at this time to relate to the social welfare system. He is comfortable seeking government-funded services at the gay and lesbian agency. He feels assured that his anonymity will be secure at this agency. He also feels they will understand his concern for potential discrimination.

Legal System: Jason and his partner have had positive contacts with his lawyer who was recommended to him because of his sensitivity to the complexities of gay partners. A mutual will has been written by Jason and his partner.

School: Jason is interested in working for one more year and returning to get his M.S.W. He hopes to take a leave of absence from his current job at that time. He is interested in returning to this rural area. He worries that the agency may not give him his leave of absence if they find out that he is gay. This may be used as a more subtle form of discrimination. School will also be very expensive for Jason, and he is currently saving money for this. He will not be eligible for financial aid because his pay is too high for much assistance.

Health Care: Jason is in good health. He routinely gets medical check-ups and HIV testing. He has full medical coverage with no co-payment. He goes to the university medical school in his state for medical check-ups.

Church: Jason has a stressful relationship with his church. The church does not believe in or condone homosexuality. He has left the church, angry at both the church's teachings and at God. He has been experimenting with a more liberal church that does not hold the same beliefs as his former church; however, his parents are opposed to his joining this church.

Extended Family: Jason has a very traditional extended family. Only a cousin who was his close friend in college knows about his being gay. He and the cousin, who is also gay, usually meet at family gatherings. Jason's parents frequently are asked if their son is dating or serious about anyone.

Recreation: Jason lives in an area with lakes, streams, and many hiking and camping opportunities. He enjoys camping, canoeing, and water sports. He enjoys country-western music and enjoys dancing.

Case developed by Patricia Sandau-Beckler, 1991. Used with permission.

---

are asked to draw what amounts to a sophisticated family tree. Not only are names and dates of births and deaths included in the genogram, but also patterns of interactions and areas of concern are coded. For example, one may find that numerous marriages are a relatively common experience in a family. Grandparents, parents, and siblings may have experienced divorce. Sometimes certain diseases seem to cross generations. It is not uncommon to find alcoholism in several generations of a family.

Scaling Procedures

Using the characteristics of a healthy family, scaling procedures have been developed to determine the potential of how well a family may deal with a crisis. The Parent Attachment Structured Interview (PASI) is a way of gathering and understanding how closely the child is bonded to each parent (LeVine and Sallee, 1992). Some examples of the questions which are asked of the child are: Who likes to put you to bed? Who was too tired to play? Who helps with your homework?

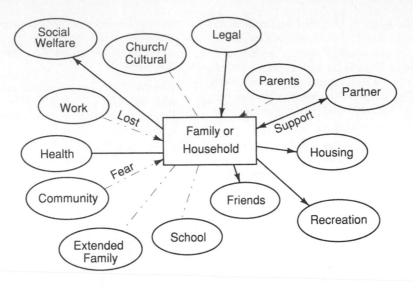

Legend:

1. Connections where they exist.

2. Nature of connections with a descriptive word
   and/or by drawing different kinds of lines:

   ———— for strong
   — — — for tenuous
   — · · — for stressful

3. Arrows along lines signify flow of energy,
   resources, etc.

4. Significant people are circles.

FIGURE 8.2 Ecomap for Jason

Who breaks promises? The answers to these questions help us determine the range and degree of positive and negative attachments.

An example of another clinical family assessment tool is one developed by Costell and Reiss (Reiss, 1980). In this procedure, family members are asked to sort a set of cards. The family members are placed into separate booths and, by using earphones and microphones, they may communicate during the performance of the task. The clinicians assess how the family works as a group or as individuals. The answers to these questions are objectively measured.

One of the difficulties of using standardized tests in family assessment is that it is difficult to explain to the family what the results actually mean (Taynor, Nelson, and Dougherty, 1990). Another difficulty is the difficulty of classifying families whose members have varying lifestyles.

Guideline for Family Assessment Narrative

Based upon a review of the theories discussed above as well as others, we have developed guidelines for family assessment. As introduced in the previous chapter, information that has been collected is assessed using the following areas.

1. In the first section of the assessment, the family life-cycle phase and the potential for growth or stress in each phase are determined. Using the family life-cycle approach, the social worker examines the relationship of the couple, including their roles, the division of power, and the division of labor. The children's developmental stages and their interaction within the community are evaluated. Children's roles, children's birth order, and the family's use of resources are noted.

2. The second broad area of assessment includes the family's patterns of interaction. Family structure is a critical area to assess, and within that context questions are asked about decision-making patterns, parenting types (democratic or authoritarian), communication patterns, and family make-up. It may be important to know whether or not the family is a biological grouping or a blended or remarried family.

a. Another area of interest is in regard to individuation. Are the children and parents able to express themselves and still be accepted in the family? Does the family do everything as a unit, or are individuals able to do things separately? Do the children have a strong sense of self-identity? How is affection shared between family members at age-appropriate levels? Are the children allowed to mature and grow at appropriate developmental stages?

b. Assessing interaction and communication is a way of understanding the family. How does this family resolve conflicts, and who begins the conflict resolutions? Are conflicts addressed or "swept under the rug" and ignored? Do the family members clearly understand each others' positions and feelings? The manner in which a family deals with a crisis explains a great deal about their dominant pattern of interaction. For example, when there is a problem, can the family adapt to resolve the problem? How does this family restore equilibrium after a crisis? What resource systems does the family bring to their own aid in dealing with a crisis?

3. The third major area of assessment is the family's environment, beginning with the home. How is the home arranged; are there shared bedrooms, and so on? What are the arrangements of the bathrooms? Is there privacy? Expanding to a wider circle, what are the parents' views of the neighborhood, and what are the contextual constraints upon the family, including such things as transportation and child care. What societal resources are available to the family in the way of police and fire protection, school and recreational activities? Other environmental considerations may include the family's socioeconomic status. What is the family's interaction with the extended family, and how are they viewed by the community and their neighbors? Finally, as part of the environment, we take into account human diversity such as ethnicity and culture. What impact do these have on the family?

Questions raised in the Roanhorse case example provide us with a general family assessment that guides us to a more in-depth assessment of strengths and problem areas that the social worker and the family may identify.

CASE EXAMPLE 8.3

The Roanhorse Family

We introduced you to the Roanhorse family in the last chapter. Alex, age twelve, had been picked up by the police late at night, with a gang of boys. Mr. Joe Roanhorse and Mrs. Mary Roanhorse had moved to the large city from the reservation where Mr. Roanhorse works as a welder. There has been a "drinking problem off and on." The Roanhorses are highly motivated to make a good life for their family. The identified area of concern began when Alex was arrested for a curfew violation. He had been running with a gang of boys several years older than he.

The "gang" of boys is "an accident waiting to happen." What resources are available in the city to help these boys? What is the potential for this gang of boys?

In doing an assessment, take note that Alex is involved with the "Kit Carson" Council of Boy Scouts. Kit Carson helped round up Navajos and move them to Fort Sumner, New Mexico, where thousands of them died. How do you think that makes Alex feel? In social work, one must look at a client's ethnic group's historical development and be ethnically sensitive.

What is normal parenting for Navajo children? Native American children are expected to function on their own at a much earlier age than white, hispanic or Black children. Alex's staying out late at night may be the urban way of growing up and testing his manhood. In the Navajo tradition, parents are noninterfering, partly because they rely upon the extended family to assist in child-rearing and partly because of the trust Navajos have in one another. Staying out late and hanging out with older boys may simply be an urban adaptation from a more tribal way of life. Alex was not trying to see these boys as friends; it was a

way of getting out on his own and testing himself in the new world.

This Navajo family had been transplanted from the reservation into the urban life. It was a new experience for Mr. Roanhorse to work for someone else rather than working on his own and collectively for the tribe. Owning personal property rather than collectively owning land and property is also new. To Native American children, it is important to be in touch with their elders on a daily basis. In this case, where are the elders? When does this family see them? And what stress does this cause the family financially and emotionally? This is a family with one foot in one culture and the other foot in another culture.

Mark is six and has just started school, now for the first time, leaving Mary at home by herself for most of the day. What are the implications? Joe received an Associate of Arts degree, a major accomplishment. He has finished all the college possible on the reservation, indicating a strong support system on the reservation. Because of his high education level, he is likely connected to a high status in traditional tribal hierarchy and, thus, is quite capable. Given that, why did they move to the large city? Perhaps Joe wanted to make more money and saw this as the way to do it, but he still was pulled by the old traditions. This may be the crux of his ambivalence about his new situation.

The conflict is likely based on contextual issues rather than interpersonal issues. The family gets along well and they are not dysfunctional. Alex's behavior is not the issue. He is only doing what is normal for a Native American twelve-year-old boy, except that he is not on the reservation. He is living in an urban setting, and the way he has decided to live is to befriend boys who are much older and stay out late at night. This is acceptable to his family.

Based upon this assessment, a plan could include connecting the family with resources and other Navajos in the community, although they probably already know where these families are. The concept centers around bringing these families together—they share the same customs, language, and success in making the transition from the reservation to the city.

Summary

Individual assessments are dependent upon the purpose of the social work intervention and the goals of the agency that is servicing the client. Certainly, the client's risks and opportunities must be understood. Beyond that, assessment is clearly a function of the nature of the client's concern or problem.

In assessing families, we find the importance of looking at the internal working of the family and how the environment and the contextual issues impact on the family. An assessment of the family is incomplete if we leave out any one of these. Assessment of the family's stage of development is important in understanding the family. In addition, the family patterns of interaction need to be assessed in a logical and organized way to help us understand the family. Finally, the quality of the environment and how the family makes use of resource systems provide us with a broad understanding of the family. The tools available to do this are numerous. Examples include the ecomap and the genogram.

ASSESSMENT OF MID-SIZE SYSTEMS

Overview of Group Assessment

When launching a group assessment, an initial differentiation between task groups and treatment groups must be made. The major role and function of a task group is to complete a task that is usually related to a subject outside the group. An example is a group of students who are planning to build a float for a homecoming event. There is a clearly stated task, and the members complete the task, which is then a product shared with the campus community.

A treatment group's primary function is to help bring about interpersonal change within the members. Examples of treatment groups range from self-help groups such as Weight Watchers International and Alcoholics Anonymous to therapy groups with mental health patients. While the purpose and functions of these groups differ, much of the assessment of the groups is similar. For an accurate assessment, we look primarily at three systems: the individuals that comprise the group, the group as a whole, and the group's environment (Toseland and Rivas, 1984, p. 162).

While there are many ways of assessing groups, depending upon the practitioners theoretical perspective, we will primarily use the systems approach. First, we begin by assessing the individual members of the group. This begins when we are forming the group and continues throughout the course of the group. The following factors are considered: What can this individual contribute to the group? What problems does each person bring? The actual group process allows us to further assess the functioning, communication, and social skills of each individual. The assessment of the individual falls along the same lines we discussed earlier regarding individual assessment. However, an added technique is by having other members of the group share their observations on the individual. This process may be helpful in the individual members' development as group members.

Role Plays

Role playing is an effective way of assessing individual members of the group. One group member is asked to act in a role that is similar to a real-life situation. Another group member is then asked to respond to that role. The social worker bases part of the assessment on the group member's probable behavior outside of the group. These role plays are sometimes referred to as *simulation tests* and can be used in measuring the skills of a number of different client groups (Toseland and Rivas, 1984, p. 171). The limitation of this approach is that it is used in a controlled environment, and the members are acting. Also, effective role playing takes extensive preparation and thought before it can be used effectively.

Group Dynamics

Tools for assessing the group's interactions as a whole are more complicated than assessment of individuals within groups. Group behavior and function are referred to as *group dynamics* (Cartwright and Zander, 1968). Group dynamics include the following:

1. *Communication interaction patterns.* How the members communicate with each other is important in assessing the group. People communicate using language that is their code for thoughts put into words. Words can never be heard exactly as the speaker meant. Distractions occur while the message is being spoken, and there may be other activities, noise, and so on that pull attention away from words.

The receiver's previous experience affects how a message is heard. The message is received, probably not exactly as the speaker meant; but, nonetheless, it is received. Then feedback occurs. The receiver becomes the speaker and responds to the message. Again, distractions appear, and the original message is altered in some way. The quality, tone, and extent of communication make up communication interactions within the group. Assessing communication is integral to a full assessment of group functioning.

2. *Group cohesion.* Another indicator of group dynamics is group cohesion. Group cohesion refers to the level of attraction members have to the group and its purpose. This can be measured by both attendance levels and the group's functionality. In a cohesive group, there is usually a great amount of interaction among the members. Goals are quickly agreed upon and achieved, and the expectations of the people in the group are met (Henry, 1991).

How group members communicate is an important group dynamic.

3. *Social control.* The third element of group dynamics is *social control.* Social control refers to the ways in which the group, as a whole, exerts pressure upon its members to comply and conform with certain values and behaviors. Social control contributes to the group's ability to function in an orderly fashion. It is identical to the function of social control in society at large. Social control determines the norms expected in the group, the roles individuals play, and a person's status in the group.

4. *Group culture.* The final group dynamic is the group's *culture.* Group culture emerges slowly as the group develops over a period of time and refers to shared values and traditions that emerge from the group experience. Assessing group dynamics using these four elements helps makes sense of quite complex interactions.

Sociograms

Sociograms measure the group as a whole. In the sociogram, individuals are represented by circles, and their interactions are coded on a continuum from positive to negative. Sociograms help us identify subgroups, positive and negative relationships, and frequency of interaction (Moreno, 1960). Figure 8.3 is an example of a sociogram with a code. In a sociogram, one would use a code appropriate to the

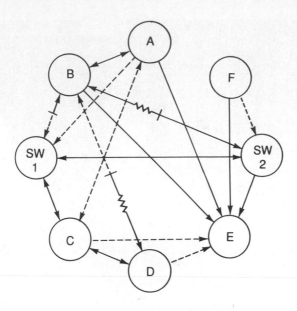

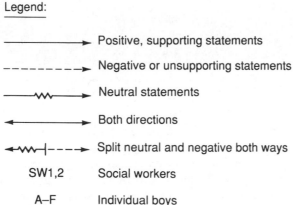

Legend:

—————————▶ Positive, supporting statements

– – – – – – –▶ Negative or unsupporting statements

———〰———▶ Neutral statements

◀—————————▶ Both directions

◀〰—|– – –▶ Split neutral and negative both ways

SW1,2   Social workers

A–F   Individual boys

FIGURE 8.3 Sociogram to Identify Subgroups and
Leadership

nature of the group and the purpose of the assessment. In Figure 8.3, a sociogram
of a group of adolescent boys during one meeting is presented. Information on
the type, the number, and the flow of statements made by each boy and the social
worker is gathered. We can assess subgroups and leadership (at least for this session) from the diagram by analyzing the statements made by all the members. By
studying the statement patterns, it is obvious that three subgroups emerged during this session. One consists of B, A, F, and E, another of C and D, and the third
of the two social workers. The leadership role is played by E and social worker 1. A
derivation of the sociogram is the Bales Systematic Multiple Level Observation of
Group (SYM-LOG). The SYM-LOG is a way of diagramming a group's interaction
on several levels. In this assessment, group members are placed (on paper) within

four quadrants and their leadership in roles outside the group is simulated. This process is helpful, but it does take a number of hours to learn to use it effectively. The assessment of a group's dynamics is a critical part of understanding how to plan for implementing a course of action, whether the group is a task group or a treatment group.

Assessing the Group's Environment

It is important to know the group setting in order to complete a group assessment adequately. What is the physical set-up of the meeting room? Who is involved? If the group takes place in an agency setting, what constraints are placed upon the group? Since all groups take place in a community, we need to assess congruence or lack of congruence with community norms. Is the meeting place accessible to the members, and, finally, is the community interested in the problem that the group is addressing (Toseland and Rivas, 1984, p. 189)?

Assessing Group Process

In part, group process can help to understand the group's goals and purposes. There are a number of methods available to determine group process. In a task group, we may review minutes, and in treatment groups, it may be necessary to speak to the group leader. Additionally, we can ask individual members about the group's goals. This can be accomplished either verbally or in a written form. We may become privy to latent or hidden goals within the group. Conducting individual interviews may help to develop a plan to address such issues.

Identifying the roles individuals assume is another important piece of information in understanding group process. Some of these roles may assist the group to move toward goals; others may detract from forward momentum (Heap, 1977).

Group development is an ongoing phenomenon, and we assess the group's stage of development at any time during the life of the group. However, the beginning phase consists of the period when the goals, objectives, and rules are stated. The second phase occurs when the group begins to learn about each other and conflict emerges. Out of conflict, an integration of purposes grows. The next phase is characterized by a reorganizational process. Goals and objectives are redefined, and group structure and norms are renegotiated (Henry, 1991). The fourth phase occurs when the group begins to function and maintain itself. The fifth and last phase is the termination phase. The most critical phase of group development, and, therefore, the phase to which most attention must be paid, is the third phase, in which reorganization and redefinition take place. The management of conflict and the methods used to work together are critical to the positive functioning of a group.

Group Boundaries

Social workers are always concerned about boundaries; that is, the interface between one system and another. Groups need boundaries to maintain their integrity, but boundaries must not be permanent. Therefore, assessing group boundaries gives us important information. For example, the extent of interaction among group members outside group meetings is boundary information. When there is interaction outside group time, the boundaries of the group actually change. We may want to encourage boundary changes. For example, a generalist social worker is working with a group of mothers who abused their children. They are interacting with each other and drawing support from one another. Through their transactions, the need for external resources outside the group becomes apparent. They decide to set up a babysitting co-op among themselves. Their boundaries have extended outside the group. An assessment should contain information on group boundaries (Heap, 1977).

Group Assessment Outline

Assessing any system involves obtaining information on both content and process. Group process presumes the manner in which the group operates and the content, task, or subject matter upon which the group is working. Following is a general outline for assessing group process, whether the function of the group is task or treatment.

1. *Interaction.* Interaction is a significant component of group process. It is essential to know the level of interaction among members. Some members may dominate discussions. Some members may be ignored, while the contributions of others is valued. Those whose level of participation is low may be ignored. Apart from participation, per se, we need to be aware of a less tangible aspect of interaction—influence. How others react to various participants will determine their levels of influence.

2. *Decision making.* The quality of decision making sheds light on group process. What sorts of discussions ensue and are discussions used as a basis for decision making? On the other hand, does the group simply vote without prior discussion of issues? Is the decision-making model autocratic or democratic? When certain decisions are made, do some members support the decision, while other members do not? How are the persons in the minority treated by the group once the decision is made? Answers to these questions add to the group assessment.

3. *Roles.* What roles do the individuals assume? Are they leadership or follower roles; or are they gate-keeper roles, which keep the process flowing? Are the roles positive or negative? Do some people take on the role of synthesizing or summarizing the information? Does someone keep the group on track and focused on the topic of discussion? Again, the answers become the content of the group assessment.

4. *Boundaries.* Do the members of the group get along with each other? Do people want to come to the group? Is everyone able to share their ideas without being judged or shut off? Is there support in the group for individuals? Are group members able to share their thoughts and feelings in a safe environment? How are

conflicts resolved in the group? What are the norms in the group, and how are the people who deviate from the norms of the group treated?

Answering these questions helps us assess the group and its ability to function. A helpful aid might be to use the following contrasting list of ineffective versus effective indicators as a group is assessed. These examples will help guide your assessment.

Effective versus Ineffective Indicators

Functional Group	*Ineffective Group*
Participation	Low involvement
Leaders will influence	Little leadership
Democratic	Autocratic
Peace makers	Little commitment
Sharing of decision making	Decision making without
Gate openers	checking
Constructive conflict	Gate closers
Inclusive	Exclusive
Full airing of concerns	Group think

Summary

Group dynamics consist of the group's interaction, cohesion, social control, and group culture (Heap, 1977). Assessment of the group goes on throughout its development, but is most critical in the beginning and, as it begins to develop cohesion, in the reorganizational phase. It is also important in assessing a group to look at its environment and the acceptance of the group within the community.

ASSESSMENT OF LARGE SYSTEMS

Community Assessment

Generalist social workers work not only with individuals and families, but with groups and large systems, such as communities. Because the information on community assessments is diverse and far-ranging, we have decided to provide an overview of the important aspects of community assessment.

A useful framework for looking at complex communities are the three models of community organization practice developed by Jack Rothman (Cox, Erlich, Rothman, and Tropman, 1974). Although these are practice models, inherent in each is a unique view of community. For that reason, the models can be used to represent varying views of community assessment.

Three Models of Community Organization

Rothman identifies twelve selected practice variables for each of the three models. In this discussion, selected variables have been chosen to assist in assess-

CASE EXAMPLE 8.4
Model A, Locality Development

Jane Mills has been employed as a family-life extension agent in rural Utah to work with communities for the purpose of enhancing their capacities to solve their own problems. Her first step is to collect information to determine whether or not community members are lacking problem-solving skills. She begins by visiting with key persons in the community. She also gathers some objective data such as voter turnout and the number of persons who attend the city council and school board meetings. She determines there is very little participation from the community. Through the completion of planned interviews, Jane finds that most people are either not comfortable with the technicalities of the democratic process or they do not understand them. Based on this information, Jane assesses all the communities in her area and begins to design and develop a plan.

ing communities. Because each model defines the variables from a different perspective, familiarity with the basic premise of each model is important. In addition, each model does not fit with every social agency. Therefore, linking a social-agency type to a model is preliminary to understanding its use in assessment.

The type of agencies usually found using Model A, Locality Development, include settlement houses, community development agencies, the Peace Corps, health associations, and consumer groups. Community councils, city planning boards, the federal bureaucracy, and environmental planning organizations most often use Social Planning, Model B. Social Action, Model C, has been used primarily with welfare rights organizations, social movement groups, the women's movement, and African-American, Hispanic, and Native American Civil Rights organizations.

In each agency, a particular model guides the type of community organization activity, and, therefore, the form of assessment one would use. Model A might find a social worker employed as a neighborhood worker or a family-life extension agent. With the increase in the number of volunteer organizations, the social worker might be as a facilitator of town halls or other community-wide voluntary agencies. Model B, social planning, employs social workers as planners and analysts. Model C employs social workers as local organizers or community organizers.

Assessment Variables

Once the social worker is clear on the type of model he or she will use for implementation and understands the model his or her agency employs, the social worker then selects the appropriate perspective to complete the assessment. The social worker will have collected information on community and on broad economic, political, and educational problems.

Community Structure   The first variable consists of the assumptions made by each model concerning community structure and problem conditions. In

Model A, Locality Development, the neighborhood in which one is working may be overshadowed by oppressive systems and therefore lacks positive relationships with the external systems. Individuals may feel isolated and disillusioned. Perhaps the community has been the place where intense industrialization and urbanization has occurred, with little attention paid to their impact on social and family relations (Ross, 1955, pp. 80–83). The community may be tradition-bound and ruled by a group of leaders who are knowledgeable in the democratic process. The people may be characterized by leadership as illiterate, lacking skills and understanding of the democratic process (Rothman, 1974, p. 29). The information one would have collected involving locality development provides the basis for assessing whether the neighborhood or community does fit with these assumptions.

Model A's assumptions concerning the community structure closely parallel those of developing communities or countries. Therefore, the community's needs include the development of a whole community infrastructure. This is very similar to the approach employed by the Peace Corps in countries all over the world.

The social worker working in a social planning capacity has very different assumptions regarding the community structure. From the social planning perspective, a number of substantive social problems or conditions that require change are identified. These may include homelessness, unemployment, inaccessible welfare benefits, transportation, or the absence of recreation facilities. These concerns have their origin in urbanization and are seen in the decay of cities' infrastructure as well as in social programs (Warren, 1963, p. 14). The list of community concerns is almost endless, and the topics continue to change, although the underlying problems remain the same.

Social work generalists employed in a social action capacity and utilizing Model C probably view the community as a division between those who have privilege and power and those who are oppressed and powerless and who suffer social injustices and exploitation (Rothman, 1974, p. 29). Historically, social workers are often identified with people who are the least advantaged in society.

CASE EXAMPLE 8.5

Model B, Social Planning

Cindy Boyd has been employed as a Social Planner I in the Human Services Department in San Bernadino County, California. San Bernadino County is geographically one of the largest counties in the United States, with large population centers on one edge and rural areas in the rest of the county. Cindy's first assignment is to work on the lack of transportation for the elderly to social service agencies. She has collected information from the Census Bureau on how many elderly live in different areas of the county and what the distance is from each area of the county to social ser-

vices agencies in San Bernadino. She also has identified the resources for transportation in each area and the most efficient mode of transportation. In some areas, this might be the train; in other areas, bus service; while in still other areas, a van might be more appropriate. She assesses which is the most appropriate form of transportation in each part of the county to meet each client's needs. She collected information through a survey form mailed out to a selected sample of the elderly. She uses the statistics and reports to help her begin to develop an assessment.

CASE EXAMPLE 8.6

Model C, Social Action

Harry Rictor is employed by a civil rights organization to collect information and assess the needs of African-American state employees. He identifies how many Black state employees there are and the types of positions in which they are employed, as well as their advancement rates as compared to their white counterparts. Using Model C, Social Action, he comes to the conclusion that while the door to Black employment in the state bureaucracy has been opened just a crack, in fact, the power is not really being shared in decision making on key issues. Harry reviews the history of the civil rights movement and how the government, through undercover operations, attempted to discredit Black leaders, including Martin Luther King. Based on Harry's assumptions that current practices are unfair and that there is an unjust sharing of power, he begins to assess how well organized African-American state employees are in order to gain more control over their own destiny.

Boundaries of Client Systems   The makeup of the client system varies according to the models. Model A, locality development, will include the total geographic community and all the people living in it. Model B, Social Planning, sometimes includes the entire community or parts of the community, including neighborhoods in the community. Model C, Social Action, identifies the client system by the community or group of individuals being exploited or suffering from social injustices. Therefore, such groups may be, but are not limited to, ethnic or cultural groups, Vietnam veterans, or women. Understanding the boundary definitions that are expected within your organization, of course, is critical before you can collect and assess information.

Summary

Assessing communities is a very complex and expensive process. By identifying the type of community organization process in which you may be involved, such as locality development, social planning or social action, you will be able to more efficiently analyze the information you have collected on the community in a useful form for the type of implementation allowed by the agency or setting by which you are employed. The assumptions regarding the community structure and who the client system is will help you in this assessment (Jennings, 1982).

Organizational Assessment

Communities and neighborhoods are complex systems and, as such, are difficult to assess. Organizations are also complex and because they are usually part of the action system or focal system accurate assessment is essential. On some occasions, you may find an organization as a client system.

Organizational Goals

An important source from which to collect information on an organization is its goals and objectives. Organizations have stated as well as unstated goals which drive their overall direction and operation (Hasenfeld, 1983). After we have identified these goals and objectives, we begin to assess how close the organization is in adhering to these goals and objectives. Individuals in organizations may not be part of the focal system, because their stated goals and objectives of meeting the client system's needs are not being achieved, and therefore, are targets for change.

On other occasions, we may feel that the organization should include the client system in its goals. For example, the assessment of organizational goals and objectives may also reveal methods that are not efficient or humane in its operation.

At still other times, the same organization may serve as part of the action system for helping meet the client system's goals. To use this organization most effectively as part of the action system, we need to be aware of its resources and capabilities. This may be as simple as knowing which individual workers you can count on within that organization to do certain things. For example, in a child welfare agency, perhaps there is one individual who works well with young, sexually abused girls, while another individual in that organization works effectively with runaway boys. The networking skills you employed prior to working with this particular client system will help you identify these individuals and then assess how to use that organization most effectively on an individual-by-individual basis.

Culture

Organizational Culture   Just as culture is important to understand when assessing families and individuals, organizational culture is also important to assessment. Organizations have values, beliefs, and traditions that need to be assessed when planning for change (Smith, 1970). The organizational culture may be set by the board of directors of organizations and, therefore, collecting information regarding board membership is necessary. Board members are often sought out because of the status and success that they have attained. While this can be helpful and may be needed to move the agency forward, it may also give a distorted value base and perspective to the organization because the values and life experiences of board members are not congruent with the values and life experiences of clients.

An agency's board president may hold traditional beliefs regarding families that influence his or her view of the work being done in the agency. If his or her authority is pervasive, the result may be a distorted view of what constitutes a "healthy" family. This, in turn, may have an impact about clients.

In Case Example 8.7, Casa de Familia, the agency's culture is reflected in its physical environment. The plush offices were in contrast to the agency's setting in a low-income area. Other physical indicators of the agency's culture are the number and size of interviewing rooms, the decor and size of the waiting rooms, and even the quality of the restrooms for clients.

CASE EXAMPLE 8.7

Casa de Familia

The Casa de Familia agency is a community mental health center designed to meet the needs of a catchment area 90 percent of whose population is Hispanic. It is located in a small community next to a large southwestern city. The program's stated goal is to provide mental health services in a culturally sensitive manner to the individuals living in the catchment area.

John Sanchez, B.S.W., an employee of the Community Council, received a number of complaints from social workers throughout the community that Casa de Familia was failing to meet the needs of Hispanic persons living in their catchment area. These social workers asked him to approach the organization. The Community Council served as a planning organization and has a particular expertise in evaluating and helping to facilitate change in organizations. Mr. Sanchez met with the executive director, Ms. Smith. Her office environment was rather plush and in a new office building located on the edge of "old-town." Ms. Smith worked with Mr. Sanchez to set some ground rules for the process, which included allowing Mr. Sanchez to review records and visit with agency staff.

In the information-gathering stage, Mr. Sanchez did a spot-check of client records and also reviewed personnel folders and the agency's annual report. In the annual report the stated goal was to provide mental health services with the specialization as substance-abuse treatment for individuals living in the old-town area. Mr. Sanchez found that 92 percent of the clientele were "Anglo" and from the neighboring large city. In fact, most clientele drove right past their mental health center, located next to the state university, and came to the "barrio" to receive substance-abuse services. Mr. Sanchez was able to do follow-up interviews with a small number of former clients of Casa de Familia and found that these clients did not wish to be seen in the large city mental health center, since they were concerned about confidentiality.

People living in the neighborhood were not receiving services. Upon reviewing personnel records, he found only two Spanish-speaking employees, both clerical staff. The "Anglo" employees were well intentioned and sensitive, but they did not speak Spanish nor were they particularly knowledgeable about Hispanic culture. In addition, Mr. Sanchez thought that the office decor might discourage neighborhood individuals from using the services, as they may assume that the services were too expensive.

The assessment suggests a need to reframe the agency's implementation of their goals and objectives. In fact, their actions appear to be contrary to their stated goals. Mr. Sanchez structured the facts he observed and presented them to Ms. Smith. Together they began to design and plan changes.

Morale is an important variable in most organization's cultures (Hall, 1972). Morale is rarely static within an organization, varying in relationship to the quality of relationships of people within the agency. Morale is manifested in a number of ways, including working conditions, compensation levels, and the feeling of success that the workers have in working with their client systems. The social worker's opportunity to do quality social work often correlates to high morale in an agency. While compensation is important, it is usually ranked lower than these other factors. We need to assess whether workers are supported in their activities or are ridiculed by superiors for mistakes. Morale is an important aspect of assessing the culture of an organization.

The agency's definition of client potential and client problems must be included in an organizational assessment. Are clients seen as sick, deviant, or without potential? Or, conversely, are they defined as persons capable of making changes that are positive. Such information adds to the assessment's breadth.

Public agencies that employ non-social workers in a social worker role have a culture that is far different from that found in private organizations that are professionally staffed (Hasenfeld, 1983). Morale is often lower in public agencies; clients are defined negatively, and staff interactions may be conflictual. Understanding the whole of the agency culture contributes to a thorough assessment.

Organizational Structure   Assessing organizational structure helps us understand how the organization functions and the quality of its work (Smith, 1970). The social worker needs to obtain information on the formal structure of the organization, including the board makeup, the organizational chart, and the division of labor. The budget allocations, and the official policy and procedures of an organization are used in the assessment. Although these documents may not describe how the organization functions on a day-to-day basis, they give us valuable information regarding the purposes of the agency. This information may be collected through interviews with staff, clients, administrators, and board members.

Important aspects of structure that will not be found in written documents are lines of power and influence; although an individual may occupy a box on an organizational chart as a symbol of authority, in actual practice, he or she may have very little power. Authority must be sanctioned by those above and below someone in a hierarchical organizational structure.

Hierarchical arrangements are not always the most conducive to working with persons. How the structure helps carry out the goals and objectives of the organization is part of the assessment. If the goal of an organization is to produce machines, it may be structured much differently from an organization whose function it is to help other organizations raise funds and develop strategies. Organizational structure includes formal and informal structures, both of which are included in the analysis that leads to the assessment (Garvin and Seabury, 1984, p. 162).

Host Organizations   Social workers are frequently employed in host organizations, and, as such, organizational assessment presents special challenges. Host organizations are those in which professionals, other than social workers, are the primary service deliverers and usually possess most of the power. Hospitals and school systems are examples of host organizations. Most hospitals are directed by physicians, and educators control most school systems, yet social workers can influence the amount of power that these other professionals have through generating community support, sanctioning their authority, or controlling information (Smith, 1970).

In assessing host organizations, the social worker must have developed quality interactions with decision makers in the organization. The decision makers may be organized as committees or teams, making the use of group assessment techniques necessary.

Organizational Development   Organizations grow, develop, and go through stages just as do individuals and families. In Phase Two of the Crystal Model, information on the age of the organization, its funding security, and its history is collected. These variables help us determine the organization's stage of development. Certainly, in the beginning stages, organizations may not be as well organized, yet they may be able to respond more quickly to community concerns. Established, mature organizations may be very strong and stable yet slow to respond to new trends or needs.

When working with a family in attempting to obtain services from an organization, it is important to determine whether the difficulty in obtaining the service from the organization is related to the stage of development of that organization or from a major dysfunction within the organization. If the agency just opened and is devoting a large percentage of its time to raising funds to continue service, that may be normal for the developmental phase through which the organization is going. Yet, if the organization is well established and has a board of directors that does not have the same values concerning meeting new problems that may be controversial in the community, such as AIDS, then we may have more of an organizational concern. The importance in differentiating between these two stages of development will become even more apparent as we look at planning for change within organizations. The way in which the focal system is addressed will be far different, depending upon the organization's stage of development.

Interorganizational Relationships   Just as social workers develop working relationships with individuals and other organizations, organizations, too, develop relationships. Community councils or health and planning councils help to coordinate and facilitate interagency or organizational coordination in relationships. With the limited resources available in most communities for delivering social services, the quality of the interorganizational relationships may prove critical to how well persons are helped in a community (Cox et al., 1974). If agencies are willing to give and take and not be slaves to turf battles, then the social-service dollar and the expertise in the community can go much further toward helping clients.

An area of coordination critical to assessment involves agency boundaries. Systems have boundaries that may or may not be discernible to other systems. Agency boundaries that are clearly articulated are much more helpful than those that are less well defined or closed. For example, a nursing home interacting with a hospital will need to have an open boundary for receiving patients from the hospital through discharge planning. There needs to be a clearly articulated agreement between the hospital and the nursing home on the level of care expected and the level or health of the patient at the time of transfer.

Some agency's boundaries are closed, meaning that particular potential clients are refused service. While most public agencies are required to serve all eligible clients, caseloads are so high that effective service is less likely offered. This needs to be taken into account in developing the plan for the client system. Private agencies, which often can control the number of clients served, may provide higher-quality service because of their lower caseloads, but a plan for implementation may include how to get the client serviced without a detrimental waiting

---

CASE EXAMPLE 8.8

Group Home Development

The following case example illustrates the second part of the General Assessment Grid (GAG-II) (Figure 8.4) in which history, context, human diversity, development, and culture are considered.

A state social service planner believes a community needs three group homes because of the high number of children placed in homes around the state. She contacts a youth and family agency director to see if the board will consider developing homes.

---

period. Organizational boundaries are important to assess, whether working with an individual client system or in helping to facilitate interagency cooperation.

Summary

Generalist social workers look at the whole situation of a client system. That includes in-depth assessment of various sized systems. Although generalist assessments are never neat and tidy, the General Assessment Grids are tools to sort out and make sense of the important systems. In the next chapter, designing and planning for change based on assessment are presented.

FIGURE 8.4 General Assessment Grid II: *Themes.* Assessment Question: Readiness of Youth and Family Agency to Begin Group Home

Client System Themes	Micro	Mezzo	Macro
History	State planner sees need. Executive director is innovative and wants agency to grow.	Board is well established and works well together.	Community is growing fast and services have not kept up.
Context	Youth and family agency staff experienced.	Agency organization strong.	Multicultural growing community with growing awareness of social problem.
Human Diversity	Staff 80% white. Sensitive to cultural issues.	Proposed residences. 50% Hispanic. 50% white.	White population increasing, but 75% of low-income are Hispanic.
Developmental Stage	Planning stage with executive board.	Board planning committee.	Unaware at this point.
Culture (Organization)	Executive director concerned about morale.	Staff becoming bored.	Youth and family viewed positively by community.

CONCLUSION

Generalist assessment of microsystems, mezzosystems, macrosystems, and their interactions is critical to the success of the change effort. Unfortunately, due to its complexity and difficulty, it is often minimized in or eliminated from the assessment process. In our rush to help, we may fail to assess adequately and plan for change.

In the previous chapter, we introduced the concepts and competencies of assessment. In this chapter, we have introduced a number of techniques, tools, and models for specific assessment of individuals, families, groups, communities, and organizations. We have drawn heavily on related disciplines and, at times, on clinical social work. Social workers need to know about most of these and they use them with supervision. The General Assessment Grid is a generalist tool used by the B.S.W. and first-year M.S.W. student.

In assessment, it is important to "realize what you do not know." It is critical to select and use assessment perspectives and instruments deferentially and with respect for one's knowledge limits. Assessment builds the foundation for designing and planning. Having made sense of the information we have gathered on the area of concern, designing the plan follows.

References

Austin, M. J., Kopp, J., and Smith, P. L. *Delivering Human Services,* 2nd ed. New York: Longman, p. 280.

Cartwright, Dorwin, and Zander, Alvin (eds.). *Group Dynamics: Research and Theory.* New York: Harper and Row.

Cox, F., Erlich, J., Rothman, J., and Tropman, J. E. (eds.). (1974). *Strategies of Community Organizations: A Book of Readings,* 2nd ed. Itasca, IL: F. E. Peacock.

Diagnostic and Statistical Manual of Mental Disorders, 3rd ed., revised. Washington, DC: American Psychiatric Association, 1987.

Erikson, Erik. (1963). *Childhood and Society,* 2nd ed. New York: Norton Press.

Garvin, Charles D., and Seabury, Brett A. (1984). *Interpersonal Practice in Social Work: Processes and Procedures.* Englewood Cliffs, NJ: Prentice-Hall, pp. 134 and 162.

Graham, John R. (1977). *The MMPI: A Practical Guide.* New York: Oxford University Press, p. 7.

Hall, Richard. (1972). *Organizations: Structure and Process.* Englewood Cliffs, NJ: Prentice-Hall.

Hasenfeld, Yeheskel. (1983). *Human Service Organizations.* Englewood Cliffs, NJ: Prentice-Hall.

Heap, Ken. (1977). *Group Theory for Social Workers.* Oxford and New York: Pergamon Press.

Henry, Sue. (1981). *Group Skills in Social Work: A Four Dimensional Approach.* Itasca, IL: F. E. Peacock.

Jennings, Joanne G. (1982). "Needs Assessment and the Planning Process: Three Needs Assessment Methodologies Demonstrated on the Local Level." *Dissertation Abstracts, 18*(4), no. 1373.

Kagle, Jill. (1988). "Overcoming 'Person-Al' Errors in Assessment." *Arete,* Winter *13*(2), 35.

Kerr, Michael, and Bowen, Murray. (1988). *Family Evaluation: An Approach Based on Bowen Theory.* New York: Norton.

Kirk, S. A., Siporin, M., and Kutchins, H. (1988). "The Prognosis for Social Work Diagnosis." *Social Casework, 70,* 295–307.

Koppitz, Elizabeth. (1962). *The Bender Gestalt Test for Young Children.* New York: Grune and Stratton, p. 71.

Kramer, Jeannette. (1985). *Family Interfaces: Transgenerational Patterns.* New York: Brunner, Mazel.

LeVine, Elaine, and Sallee, Alvin L. (1992). *Listen to Our Children: Clinical Theory and Practice,* 2nd ed. Dubuque, IA: Kendall/Hunt, pp. 31, 33, 45, 46, 51, 156–160 and 164.

Litwak, Eugene, and Hylton, Lydia. (1961). "Interorganizational Analysis: A Hypothesis on Co-ordinating Agencies," in Etzioni, Amitai (ed.), *A Sociological Reader on Complex Organizations.* New York: Holt, Rinehart and Winston, pp. 339–356.

Mattaini, Mark A., and Kirk, Stuart A. (1981). "Assessing Assessment in Social Work." *Social Work, 38*(3), 260–266.

McGoldrick, M., and Gerson, R. (1985). Genograms. *Family Assessment.* New York: W. W. Norton.

Moreno, Jacob (ed.). (1960). *The Sociometry Reader.* Glencoe, IL: Free Press.

Reiss, D. (1980). "Pathway to Assessing the Family: Some Choice Points and a Sample Route." *The Family, Proceedings of the 1979 Annual Meeting of the American College of Psychiatrists.* New York: Columbia University Press.

Richmond, Mary. (1917). *Social Diagnosis.* New York: Russell Sage Foundation.

Ross, Murray G. (1955). *Community Organization: Theory and Principles.* New York: Harper & Brothers, pp. 80–83.

Rothman, Jack. (1974). *Planning and Organizing for Social Change: Action Principles from Social Science Research.* New York: Columbia University Press, p. 29.

Ryan, William. (1976). *Blaming the Victim,* 2nd ed. New York: Vintage Books.

Sattler, Jerome. (1974). *Assessment of Children's Intelligence.* Philadelphia: W. B. Saunders.

Sheafor, B., Horejsi, C. R., and Horejsi, G. A. (1991). *Techniques and Guidelines for Social Work Practice,* 2nd ed. Boston: Allyn & Bacon.

Smith, Gilbert. (1970). *Social Work and the Sociology of Organizations.* London: Routledge and Kegan Paul.

Taynor, J., Nelson, R., and Dougherty, W. (1990). "The Family Intervention Scale: Assessing Treatment Outcomes." *Families in Society: The Journal of Contemporary Human Services, 71*(4), 202–210.

Toseland, Ronald W., and Rivas, Robert F. (1984). *An Introduction to Group Work Practice.* New York: Macmillan, pp. 162, 171, and 189.

Warren, Roland L. (1963). *The Community in America.* Chicago: Rand McNally, p. 14.

Chapter 9

Designing, Planning, and Contracting for Change

OVERVIEW

Designing, planning, and contracting for change are the components of Phase Four in the Crystal Model. In this chapter, each element of Phase Four is examined and case examples are presented that relate to this phase. Before we begin the detailed discussion of each step in this phase, we review how designing, planning, and contracting fits into the Crystal Model. The professional purpose and social work generalist outcomes related to designing, planning, and contracting are also described.

Designing, Planning, and the Crystal Model

By this time, you are knowledgeable regarding the Crystal Model—its dynamic qualities and the interrelatedness of each step in the change process. The designing, planning, and contracting phase follows the assessment phase and is only successful if an appropriate assessment has been accomplished. The connections and patterns of the client, change system, and focal and action systems are all analyzed in the assessment and subsequently included in the designing, planning, and contracting phase.

In addition, the skills one uses in engagement—identifying the area of concern, relationship building, and information gathering—are vital to this phase. For example, one cannot possibly implement a plan unless a professional relationship has been established, and one cannot contract unless one has gathered the pivotal information necessary for a meticulous assessment. In fact, the professional purpose of designing, planning, and contracting is determined in relationship to the previous steps and sets the stage for the later stages in the Crystal Model.

Professional Purpose of Design and Planning

The design step enables you to conceive, in your mind, a creative and effective plan for change. During the planning phase, we delineate goals, objectives, and tasks. In the contracting phase, the social work generalist operationalizes the plan into an agreement with the client, focal, and action systems.

Design's purpose is to aid in the process of devising objectives and tasks that assist client systems in reaching their goals. In the design phase, we draw from the assessment and lay out what we are going to do in the implementation phase.

Planning ought to help us develop a method to achieve ends. The plan outlines the procedures to be used when the change is implemented. In the design and planning phase, we should develop far more options than we can implement. While design calls for freely generating ideas that enhance fresh ways of understanding systems, the plan is far more rational and practical (Johnson, 1989, p. 298).

The purpose of the contract is to spell out the tasks that each person or group involved in the change effort must carry out in order to fulfill the client system's goals. In the contract phase, the plan is documented with the client, focal, and action systems. Siporin (1975) suggests formalizing the plan into a "deliberate, rational process that involves the choice of actions that are calculated to achieve specific objectives at some future time" (Siporin, 1975, p. 251).

The design, planning, and contracting stage is a time of mutual work between the social workers and the client system, focal system, and action system. Its overall purpose is to make use of the assessment (Phase Three) so that change can be implemented and client goals can be attained. In fact, if you use our bridge metaphor, you can imagine design as finding the best way to build the bridge. The plan is the formularization of the design into specifics. The contract, metaphorically, determines how and when the bridge will be built.

COMPETENCIES

There are three competencies related to designing, planning, and contracting for change. Baer and Federico (1978) articulate competencies that they present as the expected behaviors of a social work generalist. We include one of the Baer and Federico competencies in our discussion of designing, planning, and contracting, and we have added two others, borrowed from Lewis (1982). The Baer and Federico (1978, p. 86) competency that relates to planning is:

1. *Develop a plan for improving the well-being of people based on the assessment of the problem situation and exploration of obtainable goals and obtainable options.* In the designing and planning phase, we use the results of our assessment to identify goals and objectives as well as available options for change. In addition, values, ethics, and effective change methods are all identified and organized in the planning process. Our social work values and ethics guide the development of the plan. Furthermore, the change methods that we decide to employ ought to have been proven effective by others or through evaluation of our own practice.

Lewis (1982, pp. 121–124) articulates competencies relevant to designing, planning, and contracting.

2. *To plan for action in uncertain situations.* An ingredient of what sets a professional helping person apart from a lay person who cares about others is the ability to plan for change in situations without benefit of personal experience. A seasoned social worker, whose education has provided him or her with an understanding of cultural issues, human behavior theories, and use of research can develop effective plans for action in difficult and uncertain situations.

3. *The ability to negotiate and develop workable agreements with client systems, actions systems, and focal systems.* This competency refers to contract development. A professional social worker outlines the contract, in writing, including a description of the roles and responsibilities of all parties in the change process. The skills to write a contract that clearly states goals, objectives, tasks, skills, and a timeline, all necessary to bring about the planned change, are part of this competency.

DESIGN

Design is, above all, a creative process that connects the assessment with the plan. We cannot have a plan without designing one, and using our creativity is imperative, given the real world in which we work with a variety of people from diverse backgrounds and infinite individual differences. Whether we are working with a community services agency facing a budget crisis or an elderly person trying to obtain additional basic resources, each design is unique, fitting the distinctive qualities and concerns of the client system.

What Is Design?

Think of the designing process as a kaleidoscope. Children are fascinated for hours (as are adults) by the multitude of patterns that can be created by the change in focus as one looks through the kaleidoscope. In the design phase, we need to look at our assessment from a variety of perspectives and from different foci.

Our general approach in design is to connect ideas in a variety of configurations. In the information-gathering and assessment phase, our goal was to make sense of the information collected. Now we move from assessment to forming ideas about what can be done to meet the client system's goals.

Preliminary Steps

Design involves four preliminary steps that help ensure creative options, the foundation of design.

1. *Plan ahead.* Before meeting with the client system, it is important to develop some questions which help elicit clients' ideas.

Planning in partnership with a family.

2. *Mutuality.* We need to work closely with the client and action systems to generate the design and the plan. The worker may have ideas for objectives, but it is equally critical to understand the client system's ideas. For example, a group of low-income women living in a rural area have been brought together by a social worker to design ways they can achieve mutual support and aid. The social worker may anticipate that the women want to enhance their financial status, yet the social worker may be surprised to learn that they want, in fact, more street lights and neighborhood security. Certainly, both of these important goals—increased finances and greater security—can be explored.

3. *Review the assessment with the client system.* We need to restate the assessment and ask the client system questions regarding its present goals. How would you like to see things develop in the next six months? Are there conflicts within the family that you would want to resolve? Where would you like to see this agency in one year and in five years? Try to help the client system frame the answers into goals which then can be distilled or broken down into manageable objectives.

4. *Drop biases.* To be most effective in developing options in the design phase, we need to forget our biases regarding our own expectations of client groups and find new ways to approach the area of concern. For example, we must avoid our tendency to see all situations framed as problems. We should focus on client strengths, rather than weakness, utilizing comprehensive and positive assessments.

Cultural and gender biases must further be addressed in design. What may appear to be a creative design based on our own background may not fit with the client system's view of the world. Recognizing our own barriers helps us overcome bias.

Biases based on misunderstandings regarding organizations and communities must also be challenged. It is not unusual to feel animosity toward large bureaucratic systems. However, understanding how bureaucracies work and putting aside our own negative experiences with them will help us develop flexible and broad-based designs with our clients.

The client system is, of course, just one part of the overall change process. We will also want to explore options in working with the focal system, through mutual cooperation, confrontation and/or negotiation. Effectively using the action system is also explored in the design phase.

Design Tools

Several tools or techniques are recommended to help us creatively design change. Heus and Pincus (1986, p. 327) believe flexible tools, visually presented and containing new ideas, are design's foundation.

Brainstorming

Brainstorming is a tried-and-true process for generating creative ideas. We brainstorm in a group setting, using all the creative power we can muster. According to Heus and Pincus, there are four simple rules that should be followed in brainstorming because they help create an environment that is conducive to creative thinking (Heus and Pincus, p. 332).

The first rule for proper brainstorming is to defer judgment. We wait before we decide how to use an assessment. Quick judgments can result in designs that are negative and fault finding. By deferring judgment, ideas that we know are not practical, those that may have been first seen in our kaleidoscope thinking, when given time to gel, may spark a practical solution. We want to list all possible ideas first, before making judgments or practical choices.

Brainstorming's second rule is to free one's imagination. Think outrageous or outlandish thoughts that are usually considered impractical. While these ideas may create snickering or even laughter throughout a group, eventually they may help to generate a practical and workable option.

The third rule is to aim for quantity. The more ideas we are able to generate, the greater the chances are that we are going to find a useful one. When using brainstorming in a large group, one reaches a plateau—that is, a dry spell without new ideas. Just a word or two of encouragement or a little comic relief may be enough to again begin the flow of ideas. Encouraging an outrageous idea may also help to get the ideas circulating.

The fourth rule is to piggyback ideas. In other words, build on the ideas that others have already stated. A synthesis of ideas creates brand new options that may prove useful.

As one proceeds through the brainstorming process, record the ideas, written as accurately and as quickly as possible so all participants can read them. Butcher paper, a large chalkboard, and, if agreed to by all parties, a tape recorder can be used to record the session to ensure that the group does not miss any important ideas.

After the ideas are recorded, one can begin to look for patterns and a blue-print for change. Ideas from the group are combined, creating a distilled list of options. Also, during this phase, one eliminates the "outrageous" ideas.

What If?

We do not always have the luxury of working with others to create designs. On our own, using our own mental imagery, allowing our minds to flow and entertain any possibility, we may invent new prospects for change. "What if _____; then can we _____?" Of course, we may engage the client system, focal system, or action system into dreaming "what if."

Incubation

Most designs need a period of incubation during which they are set aside, while we go on to something else. Upon returning to the situation, we may see the concern from different perspectives. For example, students are encouraged to write term papers several weeks before they are due, then set them aside and return to the paper in a few weeks (Heus and Pincus, 1986). When the papers are viewed again, mistakes, poorly constructed sentences, and absence of clarity are much easier to detect. The student has allowed ideas to incubate, casting new light.

Circle Map

The circle map is a technique to help visually clarify our ideas and link them, perhaps creating new thoughts (Heus and Pincus, 1986, p. 338). After ideas have been generated in brainstorming, we write them down on a piece of paper and begin to circle and connect them. Patterns emerge that may become solutions to the area of concern we have identified. The circle map can be used to highlight the resources and strengths the client system brings to the change process.

Case Example 9.1 illustrates the technique.

McSherry Family Circle Map

To begin the circle map of the McSherry family, the social worker began with the family and placed them in the center of the issues, concerns, and ideas. The McSherrys' main concern, homelessness, shares the center circle. The Community Homeless Task Force, the social worker, and the McSherry family sat down together to work out their main concerns and ideas to solve some of the McSherrys' concerns.

Figure 9.1 illustrates how the group identified five main concerns or issues that needed to be addressed first. These are: housing, steady employment (maintaining income), family budget, family issues (concerns, emotional needs), and health issues. Working from each of these five circles, the team was able to design

CASE EXAMPLE 9.1

The McSherry Family

The McSherrys, a homeless family, contact the Rescue Mission for food and a place to stay. After receiving emergency food and shelter for a day, they are referred to a generalist social worker in a community development agency. The social worker collects information on the family, including strengths and areas of concern. Mr. McSherry is a skilled craftsperson, but the family became financially overextended and fell several months behind on rent and other commitments, including· health care.

Based upon the assessment, the social worker convenes the Community Homeless Task Force (the action system), made up of various agencies, to design and, later, to plan a change with the McSherrys. After presentation of the situation and introducing Mr. and Mrs. McSherry, the group and the McSherrys

brainstorm ideas which, through the circle map, are refined into a plan. The McSherrys and the Task Force generated as many solutions to their situation as they were able. The ideas, as well as continuing concerns, were written on a large piece of paper. The circle map for the McSherrys illustrates connections among economic conditions in the community, the family's spending patterns, their loss of health insurance, and their hope to win the lottery.

The task force continues the process for each of the other change systems—the action system and the focal system. The interaction of all three systems, including the client system, is laid out in a visual map. Completing the circle map leads to a plan that will be formulated in a more structured format.

FIGURE 9.1 McSherry Family Concerns

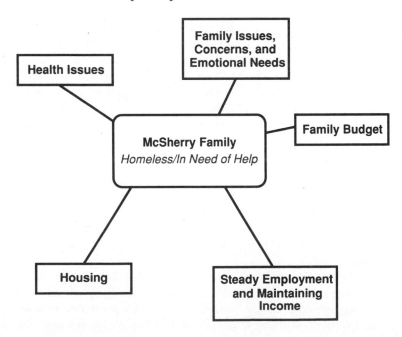

resources, referrals, suggestions, strengths within the family, and other issues that needed to be dealt with.

The circles that branch out from the five highlighted circles in Figure 9.2 reflect the brainstorming and creativity of the team. This circle map gives the team a place to start planning implementation with the McSherry family. By using the circle map, the McSherrys are able to look at their concerns as well as help visualize possible routes to their desired goals.

Creativity

The design phase calls for creativity, even establishing "outrageous" options. Brainstorming, "what if," incubation, and using the circle maps are ways to gain

FIGURE 9.2 McSherry Family Circle Map

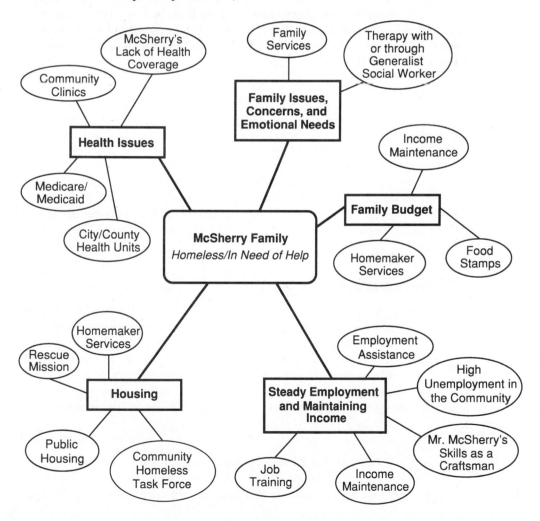

options that can be turned into practical solutions. There are other tools you can use and even devise yourself.

Brainstorming and the circle map must be done in groups, while "what if" can be used when one is working alone with the client system during the design phase. Use the principles in brainstorming, "what if," and the circle map: be creative, consider all alternatives, engage in kaleidoscope thinking, and attempt to present all the data in some sort of visual representation (Heus and Pincus, 1986). The client systems will find visual maps, whether they are circle maps, ecomaps, or any other sort of graphic representation, helpful.

Summary

We want you to break the rules of conventional thinking that move the systems we are working with to new, yet viable options. Once the design is in motion, we develop a plan in which everyone in the change effort can participate.

The group goes through this process for each of the major change systems—that is, the action, focal, and client systems. The assessment of these three systems' interaction leads to a plan which they will formulate in a more structured format, the contract.

PLAN

The plan operationalizes the design. We take creative ideas and state them so that all parties can understand and use the plan. Clients must understand the plan; and action and focal systems, likewise, must understand the plan. The change system must also have full understanding of the plan. For example, if a social worker leaves his or her place of employment and a case must be transferred within an agency, the new social worker can quickly understand what needs to be done in the implementation phase. Thus, an effective plan can inform everyone involved.

Operationalizing the Plan

In order to operationalize the plan, identify the goals, objectives, tasks, skills, and tools needed to implement the change. Sorting out these steps helps organize the plan. The steps range from broad to specific. The McSherry family (Case Example 9.1) shares goals, the most general component of the plan. To ensure the Mc-Sherrys' goals are reached, objectives must be agreed upon, followed by the specific tasks to accomplish. In the following section, each component of the planning phase—goals, objectives, tasks, skills, and tools—is briefly defined.

Goals

A *goal* is a declaration of intent or outcome (Heus and Pincus, 1986, p. 340). Social work students usually share a common goal—completing the social work degree. You may have decided on this goal through career counseling. You connected your desire to work with people and your interest in social justice. You realize social work education will facilitate your work. Putting your hopes and desires together helped you determine a professional goal — a social work degree. To obtain your goal, of course, you must advance beyond identifying what you want.

Social workers help the client system, the action system, and focal system identify their goals. Successful change is dependent upon the three systems' cooperation.

Objectives

Goals are broken down into objectives that are conceptionalized and written in measurable terms (Sheafor, Horejsi, and Horejsi, 1988, p. 306). Objectives are more immediate than goals. For example, completing specific social work courses and mastering the content must be accomplished before the degree is awarded. However, in order to complete even one social work course, you must engage in a number of learning tasks. Combining tasks with objectives leads to the social work degree.

Developing and writing objectives, deciding on tasks and applying them with tools and skill to our client systems are the heart of this phase in the Crystal Model.

Developing and Writing Goals

The goal is the desired outcome for the entire change effort. Making that goal concrete, reasonable, and obtainable depends on one's relationship with the client system, their motivation and capacity for change, and one's ability to move them through the change effort. Helping clients articulate their goals is part of our work (Maluccio, 1979). The goal is also a restatement of the area of concern, stated positively and suggesting a solution. It may be the opposite of the current state of affairs, reflecting a condition to move toward rather than away from. Case Examples 9.2 and 9.3 clarify this point.

In Case Example 9.3, we correct for goals that are too broad and abstract.

Developing Objectives

Developing objectives from broadly defined goals is more successful when specific criteria are met. Eight steps in the developing objectives that help put the plan into action are:

CASE EXAMPLE 9.2

Leonard Parks

Leonard Parks is drinking. Perhaps his goal is to stop drinking. However, a goal stated in positive terms includes the hoped for outcome may assist Mr. Parks. The following goal state- ment is more helpful: Mr. Parks would like to feel more in control of himself and stopping drinking will help make that possible.

CASE EXAMPLE 9.3

The Robertsons

The Robertson couple's goal is to become more effective and caring parents. June and Harold Robertson are not satisfied with their parenting skills, wanting to improve them. A narrower, more concrete goal statement follows. The Robertsons will increase the effectiveness of their parenting strategies and demonstrate more empathy toward their children within a given time period.

1. The objective starts with the word "to" and is followed by an action verb.

2. The statement specifies a single key result that will be accomplished.

3. The statement specifies a time by which it will be accomplished.

4. The objective is as specific and quantitative as possible, and therefore is measurable and can be verified.

5. The statement is readily understandable by the client system and others who will be involved in the implementation.

6. The objective is realistic and obtainable while at the same time representing a significant challenge.

7. The objective is agreed to by the client system and the social worker without pressure or coercion.

8. The objective is consistent with the values and ethics of social work and agency policies and procedures (Sheafor, Horejsi, and Horejsi, 1988, p. 308).

The objective statement answers, who will do what, by when, to what extent, under what conditions, and how? The objectives should have a reasonable chance of success and should be related to changes that can be evaluated. Objectives will become part of the written, working agreement—that is, the contract.

Writing Objectives   One way to learn how to write objectives is to differentiate between poor and helpful objectives. The following examples are based upon the concerns mentioned above in the Robertsons' case: improving upon parenting skills.

1. *Poor*   "Be better parents to the children."

   Helpful   "Attend a ten-week course in effective parenting and score 80 percent on a simulation effective parenting test at the conclusion of the course."

2. *Poor*   "The family will receive counseling for substance abuse."

   Helpful   "The father, the identified substance abuser, will attend ten substance abuse counseling sessions in the next two months and will reduce his consumption of beer by 75 percent by the end of the two months."

3. *Poor*   "The family will get along better and have fewer fights."

Helpful   "The family will report they feel better about themselves as a family unit and the number of outbursts or yelling will be reduced by 50 percent at the end of a month of intensive, in-home family sessions."

Writing Specific and Time-Limited Objectives   From these three examples, you notice that good objectives are specific and time-limited, containing measurable outcomes. At times, social workers identify the activities the client will engage in, such as attending counseling sessions, but fail to mention the outcome of what those sessions ought to provide. For example, in child welfare, we often see "abusive parents will be referred to ten sessions of parent counseling" (Sallee, 1983). Nothing in the research shows that simply attending ten sessions of counseling will keep parents from abusing their children.

What we want to focus upon are changes in behavior, and family relationships and to ensure that the children will be safe. Thus, we might formulate objectives such as, "The parents will attend ten counseling sessions to become better parents and will demonstrate caring discipline and rewards for good behavior as observed by the social worker, using a behaviorally anchored scale." Time limits are especially important in child welfare work because children's needs must be attended to quickly. The child's vulnerability must be recognized and acted upon.

Writing Positive Objectives   Helpful objectives are written in a positive format, emphasizing a reduction in negative behavior. For example, with abusive parents, we focus on increasing behaviors that are positive, such as spending more time with children, rather than ending abuse, an objective that focuses on the negative.

Tasks

Tasks ferret out the discrete actions necessary to achieve the objective. The task might include completing written assignments and tests with passing grades. Accomplishing your task depends upon such skills as library research, literature analysis, and test-taking skills. In addition, you need tools, including textbooks, journals, video tapes, and role plays, to reach your long-range goal.

Tasks are specific, discrete action steps that must be taken in order to meet objectives. Laura Epstein (1980) identified seven types of tasks. Due to the complexity of the helping process, tasks do not necessary flow directly from objectives. Therefore, generalist social workers may want to have identified an array of task options. Epstein has enumerated these as follows.

1. *Unique tasks.* These are tasks that are necessary for a one-time effort—for example, Mrs. Smith's cousins will apply for licensure as a relative foster home.

2. *Recurrent tasks.* These are tasks that are necessary to be repeated—for example, Mrs. Smith will take her child to day care on time every day this week.

3. *Unitary tasks.* Unitary tasks are those that are even though may be a single action require a number of steps—for example, Mr. Peralta will prepare a grant proposal for Title IVE funds.

4. *Complex tasks.* This is when two or more discrete actions are required which are closely related—for example, a mental health agency will explore several possible funding sources and determine the effects of each funding source on their relationship with the family services agency.

5. *Individual tasks.* These are tasks to be carried out by one person—for example, Mr. Cole will bring the printed agenda to the board meeting.

6. *Reciprocal tasks.* These are separate but are interrelated tasks that are completed by two or more individuals, usually through an exchange—for example, Mr. Toney will refrain from using physical discipline with Joey, and Joey will verbalize what is bothering him rather than sneaking out of the house at night.

7. *Shared tasks.* These are tasks that are completed by two or more people. These individuals are accomplishing the same thing—for example, Mr. and Mrs. Smith will both meet with the social worker three evenings a week for marriage counseling in their homes (Epstein, 1980, pp. 202–203).

While Epstein developed the task-centered approach primarily for working with individuals and families, these tasks can also be used with groups, organizations and communities as you can see in the examples above.

Barriers and Constraints

From our analysis of the area of concern, we should have been able to identify conditions that can be changed, (barriers) and situations that are beyond our capacity to change (constraints) (Simons and Aigner, 1985, p. 72). The plan needs to address how we work with the client, focal, and action systems to overcome barriers while working within the constraints of the given situation. The Miller family's adoption (Case Example 9.4) illustrates the design and a plan which overcame barriers and recognized constraints.

Issues in Designing and Planning

Individuals and Families

Successful planning with each size system is contingent on a successful and accurate assessment. Familiarity with assessment tools in general (Chapters 7 and 8) and those used particularly with the client system is essential. We use assessment tools that lend themselves to workable plans. Risk assessments used in child welfare have the added desirability of linking goals, objectives, and tasks because they usually deal with specific behaviors that must be curtailed in abusing families. Risk assessments also address strengths in family systems that can be translated into goals, objectives, and tasks (Washington State Department of Social and Health Services, Division of Children and Family Services, November, 1987).

CASE EXAMPLE 9.4

The Miller Family

Jane and Larry Miller were asked by a birth mother (who lived 200 miles away) to become adoptive parents of her yet-to-be-born child; in effect, an open adoption. An adoption study was conducted by Ms. May, the social worker who recommended to the court that the Millers be approved for an adoptive home placement. The child was born prematurely, before all the legal work could be completed.

Based on her knowledge of human development, Ms. May, the social worker, knew it was critical for the Millers to be with the baby as soon as possible to begin the bonding process. This assessment was supported by research indicating the importance of early bonding between parents and infant. Yet, the Millers could not have the child live in their home until they were officially approved for a placement by the courts. Official approval would take six days. The baby could not live with the Millers in their home during this time.

Ms. May faced several constraints, including 200-miles distance and the time of five or six days to complete the legal work. As an experienced social worker, Ms. May was knowledgeable regarding the law. By telephone conference call, she brainstormed with the Millers and the attorneys to design a plan to have the biological mother place the child with a mutual friend's family in the same community in which the Millers resided. The Millers then would live with the friend for the six days, during which time they would be able to begin to bond with the baby. This design was completed in the matter of an hour or so, and the plan developed. The attorney, the biological mother, the friends and the Millers all agreed to the plan and how to overcome the barriers within the existing constraints.

Groups

When designing and planning with treatment or task groups, it is always important to come to a general agreement on the group's purpose. Obviously, the group's purpose determines the goals and objectives (Henry, 1991). For example, if you are working with a group of substance abusers, you know that recovery will always be a component of goals and objectives.

Group discussion can assist in determining the group's goals and objectives. Members may be asked to share their individual goals so that group goals can be formulated. Other, more directed means of determining goals and objectives are also helpful with groups. For example, the group leader may ask each person in the group to write down his or her goals and objectives. Each person is subsequently asked to read his or her list while the leader writes them on a flip chart, large enough so that everyone can see. No discussion is allowed at this point. Once the ideas, goals and objectives are listed, the floor is open for discussion and the group tries to come to a consensus regarding goals and objectives.

For a treatment group, the goals and objectives might be focused toward each individual's personal growth in that group. On the other hand, a task group might identify a group goal of raising $5,000 for prevention programs for adult abuse and neglect.

Just as with individuals and families, it is critical in the formulation of goals and objectives to achieve a mutual understanding of those objectives with all parties (Reid, 1978). The plan and the specific tasks to be accomplished are more complex in a group setting and, therefore, time is spent on receiving feedback from each person in the group on the objectives and tasks. Group support for the plan is critical if we are to have successful implementation.

Communities and Organizations

In communities and organizations, a substantial amount of time goes into developing plans, publishing them and receiving feedback in order to build a consensus before moving forward with implementation. Timelines or flow charts can identify sometimes literally hundreds of tasks that must be accomplished in order to implement change.

Methods for designing and planning change at the community and organizational level include flow charts and Program Evaluation Review Technique (PERT) charts. A PERT chart, first developed by the United States Defense Department for the building of nuclear submarines, is a process of charting a variety of activities that occur simultaneously. Ultimately, the activities come together to meet the overall goal. For the Department of the Navy, this included building the hull in one geographic location, building the nuclear generator in another, and then wiring and putting the plumbing in the hull in such an order and sequence that once the hull and the generator arrived, the job could be quickly and efficiently completed.

A great many tasks at the community level are as complex as building a submarine and involve even more systems organizations. Therefore, a PERT chart is helpful to give us an overall road map of all the activities and tasks to be accomplished when and by whom.

For example, a fundraising campaign by the United Way of America identifies the major phases of the campaign and then breaks each phase down into different tasks. Each task is completed in sequence. Employees in large corporations are contacted immediately following a general community-wide media campaign. In fundraising, it is often said you need to present your message five to seven times in different forms before you can expect to receive any action.

Analogies for Designing and Planning

In order to describe the process of designing and planning, we present two illustrations through as analogies to reinforce your learning regarding this phase.

Writing and Producing a Play   Designing the plan can be compared to writing a script for a play. The playwright develops an idea, which in the Crystal Model is analogous to identifying the area of concern. The playwright researches his or her subject.

Playwright Mark Medoff, in writing the Tony Award–winning Broadway play *Children of a Lesser God,* wanted to explore the world of the deaf. He met with deaf persons, studied the subject, and gathered information. In reading the play, we know he developed a theme and vehicle (the play) in which to present the world of the deaf to a broad audience. He wrote the dialogue, putting his ideas and creativity into the script. He took into consideration the length and structure, deciding on three acts, each with different scenes. Before the play was presented to a wide audience, a dress rehearsal was staged in which the playwright and actors received feedback from the audience. Through this process, Professor Medoff incorporated changes into the play before it went into its final form. The actual production of the play is the implementation. The critics' reviews and the size of the audiences serve as the evaluation.

A New School of Social Work Using an architecture theme, this analogy may help you understand the designing, planning, and contracting process in social work. The School of Social Work is outgrowing the physical space provided by the University. The school received additional grant money; thus, student financial aid increased, allowing more students to attend. Concomitantly, the number of faculty and support staff increased, requiring more office, classroom, and lounge space.

The architect meets with the dean and the faculty to gather information about their present and future needs. Moving into the designing and planning stage, the architect takes into account the exterior design of other buildings on campus, and the needs of the faculty and students that influence interior designs.

Normally, architects will ask for a "dream list" specifying the desired sizes of offices, open areas, student lounges and library, and computer and videotape labs. Then a second list of the critical needs is created, identifying the minimum space requirements. The architect takes this dreaming, or design stage, and projects the costs, and comes up with a plan that will more than meet the minimum needs but perhaps is not as extravagant or creative in its design as the faculty and students wish.

The architect must find an open space to locate the building on the campus. Again, the architect solicits input from the faculty and students, which might include issues such as window views, accessibility to the library, parking and distance to related academic offices. The architect takes into consideration all this information as well as other criteria such as location of sewer pipes and utilities.

The architect, through consultation with the state board of regents, will select the site and develop a detailed plan (a blueprint) of the building. This plan undergoes several revisions. It includes a schedule, which will list the construction material, windows, doors, and other features of the building. Then the project is put out for bid by the architect.

A contract is signed after some negotiations with the builder. The contract calls for the contractor to build the building according to the specifications laid out in the blueprints. This, of course, is the implementation of the plan, which we explore in the next chapter.

Just as the building the architect designs can be no better than the plan, neither can the generalist implementation be better than the design and plan. The architect's designs and plans are based on the assessment of the information collected. Similarly, as social workers, we must design and plan change based on our assessment of the interrelationships and patterns we have seen and identified within and external to the client system.

Summary

Analogies help see the process as a whole but do not replace concrete tools to guide us. A planning checklist guides us in completing a design and plan with client systems. The goal statement is written with appropriate objectives listed underneath in a hierarchial manner. We answer the five "W" (who, what, where, when and why) and one "H" (how) questions. We consider tasks, including the type of task, the tools needed, and the date to be completed. We can then measure movement in the implementation phase:

1. The task has been fully completed.
2. It has been significantly completed, which means that we can go on.
3. It is not sufficiently completed.
4. We need to rewrite the tasks and be flexible.

Designing and planning change are critical to effective implementation. Design is a creative approach to developing a plan, while the plan represents a rational judgment of various, identified options. The planning process involves cooperation and collaboration with all of the systems. The plan is mutually agreed upon, and, through the process, we learn more about the client and focal systems' perspective on the area of concern. The plan with every size system needs to be written and agreed upon. In the next section, we introduce the concept of a *contract*, the means by which the plan is translated into activities.

CONTRACTS

Plans work if the people who are being "planned for" participate. Too often, social workers neglect developing contracts with others, believing their own expertise will suffice. Working on mutual designs, plans, goals, and objectives and then formalizing them is the contracting step or working agreement.

What Are Contracts?

In the social work literature, contracts are referred to by various terms. Sometimes they are called working agreements, social service plans; in other places, they are service plans or agreements. No matter what the term or precise definition used for the contract, all include both product and process. The product is the written statement, and the process is how we arrive at the statement. The product and process are often determined by the setting in which we are employed. Contract forms and the process have been developed in the various fields of social work practice, including public welfare, social services, child welfare, adult services, mental health, community councils.

Contract Contents

The basic contents of most written agreements between social workers and other systems should include: (1) major goals of each system, (2) tasks to be performed by each system to achieve the goals, and (3) operating procedures for the change process (Pincus and Minahan, 1973, p. 164). The roles and responsibilities with a timeline are also included. Contracts should be explicit, mutually agreed upon, dynamic, flexible, and realistic (Garvin and Seabury, 1984, p. 176).

Nonbinding and Binding Contracts

The term "contract" may not accurately reflect the process and product in generalist social work practice. It is most often not legally binding. Rather, it is flexible and open to change. If one party fails to meet the requirements as stated in the contract, there is usually no legal ramification.

There are exceptions, such as when the focal system is an involuntary system and has been involved in court cases. These are usually mental health patients, abusive parents, or persons under criminal investigation. As a social worker, you may or may not have input into the contract with involuntary clients. However, you will be responsible for carrying out the contract.

Characteristics of Contracts

There are five general characteristics of working agreements. These include:

1. *Clarification,* in which each party can understand what is expected of him or her, stated in terms of rules and responsibilities and including each party's individual perspective.
2. The contract is *concrete.* It is written on paper and is not subject to question, only interpretation.
3. It is a *mutual process* by which the social worker can better understand the focal system.
4. A contract equates to the *credibility* of the change process.
5. The written document can be *changed* and *amended* and provides for *monitoring* (Garvin and Seabury, 1984, p. 173).

How Contracts Are Used

Contracts serve a variety of occasions, and they have many audiences. Contracts are used within and between agencies and organizations, sometimes as a form of evaluation for accountability. Contracts are used by supervisors to contract with workers regarding their own professional goals. Social workers must understand legal contracts, particularly if they are working with the courts (Maluccio, 1979).

Contracts are useful with groups to develop group goals and rules. Written agreements are used between agencies to clarify working relationships and to provide authority. Whatever the purpose or audience for the contract, the concept is being used more extensively in social work and has become the focus of some research that indicates that the contract is important in affecting successful change (Garvin and Seabury, 1984, p. 171).

Misusing Contracts

The contract can be misused. For example, an inmate may contract to attend group sessions only because it will look good to the parole board rather than for the reasons stated in the agreement. The negative use of contracts usually occurs when the focal system is involuntary because he or she has really not participated in the designing and planning process. Social workers need to change the system so that their efforts in working with involuntary systems are effective (Hoffman, 1983).

There is no reason to believe that an inmate serving time in prison cannot benefit from group counseling for substance abuse. Yet, he or she must have a stake in the treatment, and that stake needs to be recognized for what it is. The same inmate mentioned above, who participates in group sessions only to impress the parole board, may need to hear from the social worker that his involuntary participation is understood and that even within the inmate's negative viewpoint, some positives may come from the group experience.

Contract Process Skills

Building the contract involves skills, particularly empathy and negotiating skills. Not only must the social worker hear the spoken and unspoken messages the client is sharing, but he or she must influence the client to participate in meaningful change (Maluccio, 1979).

Although the use of authority may come into the contracting process with involuntary systems, consequences of participating or not participating in the agreement ought to be made clear. Only when contracts are explicitly stated and then implemented are they useful. Contracts can never be used to threaten. For example, a family has abused a child who had to be removed from the home. One of the terms of an agreement with the family might be to invoke a legal process to terminate parental rights if the parents fail to meet the terms of the working agreement. The statement is not meant as a threat but to inform the parents. Therefore, if they abuse the child, they should not be surprised that their parental rights are terminated.

Contracts with Each System

The social worker enters into agreements with the various change systems. Some of these are very obvious; others are not readily recognized by new social workers. It is important to understand the types of agreements made explicitly or implicitly with each system in the change process.

Change System

If you take a job in an agency, you are entering into a contract with the change system (Pincus and Minahan, 1973, p. 164). You are agreeing to the policies and procedures of that agency. At the time of employment, you may wish to negotiate your contract. You may discuss the policies or procedures that you can accept, as well as those that you question.

Public agencies that operate with the purpose of keeping people away from their agency, rather than encouraging them to use the system have the potential to violate the Social Work Code of Ethics. Such agencies are not evil, but the constraints under which they are operating can negate the real possibilities of your working effectively. You will want to be clear on this point before being employed in such an agency. We are not discouraging you from working in such agencies. In fact, there is no place where educated social workers are needed more. Yet, you must be clear about your purpose and your own professional and personal limits.

The change system, the agency, or organization has a contract with the community, whether or not it is written. Most agencies publish annual reports in which their goals are stated. This report becomes a contract with the community. Agencies also enter into agreements with funding sources and other organizations. If an agency in which you are working is a private, nonprofit agency, it may have agreements for doing contract work for public agencies as well. Third-party payments may also be another type of contract. There are many types of contracts with the change system with which you should become familiar.

Client Systems

The primary focus of our discussion on contracts and working agreements is, of course, between the social worker and the client system. Central to the contract is the agreement on the goals of the change effort. This, in and of itself, defines the client system. As we have seen in the planning process, agreeing on a goal is the necessary first step to be taken before specific tasks and responsibilities are defined to achieve the goal.

Focal Systems

There are overlaps between the client system and the focal system. For the portion of the focal system that is also the client system, there usually is no need for a separate contract. The focal system cannot be composed entirely of the client system, and, therefore, some agreement of ways of negotiating with the focal system is also required. This agreement is usually three sided among the social worker, the client system and the focal system. For example, a family (client system) may contract with the landlord (focal system) to provide a deferred payment plan supervised by the social worker (change system).

Action Systems

A working agreement with the action system may be on a one-time-only basis with a specific client system, or it may be standard operating procedure used with numerous client systems. If you are working with a group of agencies, other social workers, or other non-social-services resources on a given case, it is helpful to come to some agreement.

CASE EXAMPLE 9.5

The Van Meters

A social worker is working with the Van Meter family. Mrs. Van Meter has cancer. Her illness requires radiation treatments on a daily basis. Mr. Van Meter is unemployed. Their car starter is broken. The social worker attempts to obtain funds in the form of a loan to buy a new starter, but is unable to do so. As a creative social worker, she approaches a local car club (part of the action system), which agrees, as a form of community service, to put a used starter in the car. The social worker negotiates an agreement with the car club to determine when they would put the starter in, and how, and on what terms, the family will repay the club for the used starter. The three parties sign the contract. The car is fixed and Mrs. Van Meter can be driven to her treatments by Mr. Van Meter.

Protocols

A standing, working agreement with action systems often includes protocols. These are agreements signed between agencies concerning how certain types of cases are to be handled. It includes the roles and responsibilities of each agency involved. A protocol for child abuse cases illustrates the point. The social worker and police are involved in investigating sexual abuse cases which may later be turned over to the district attorney. The roles of the police and of the social worker are delineated and their tasks clearly stated (Pincus and Minahan, 1973, p. 164). Any social worker or police officer follows the child abuse protocol.

Summary

The contract is built on the design and plan developed in the earlier phase of the change process. All parties and systems need to commit to the agreement. All parties should be involved in developing the agreement, with input from the change, client, focal and action systems.

The generalist social worker is able to explain how to properly develop goals and objectives and encompass the plan within the agreement. The agreement helps to empower the client system. The contract provides caveats for motivating the system toward change. In other words, rewards are received through successful completion of different parts of the agreement. The contract is reviewed by all parties to ensure that all systems' needs are addressed, not just the social worker's. The agreement takes into account the restraints and barriers to the client system reaching their goals.

The contract is specific in its terms and usually is written. The agreement is reviewed on a regular basis and monitored with the client focal and action systems.

Every effort is made to ensure against negative purposes or hidden agendas in the agreement. Particular attention is given to involuntary clients. Finally, the contract is time-limited and may be either (1) short-term, (2) an established working agreement, or (3) a protocol between organizations.

CONCLUSION

Designing, planning, and contracting for change sets the stage for the implementation phase. A well-designed planned change, built on an accurate assessment, will ensure successful implementation. By using an objective and measurable time-limited format, the contract sets the stage for effective evaluation of the change process.

The design portion of the process involves creatively identifying all the possible options and pathways we may need to meet the client's goals. The plan becomes the blueprint for change, with the goals, objectives, tasks, and tools necessary to build a successful change process. The contract is a written agreement with all systems which clearly outlines roles, responsibilities, and time frames for accomplishing tasks. The negotiating process involves mutual goal setting.

An effective design, plan, and contract stage leads directly to constructive implementation. When you read the next chapter, you will find that implementation is putting the plan into action, using the contract as a monitoring tool.

References

Baer, Betty L., and Federico, Ronald. (1978). *Educating the Baccalaureate Social Worker: Report of the Undergraduate Social Work Curriculum Development Project.* Cambridge, MA: Ballinger, p. 86.

Epstein, Laura. (1980). *Helping People: The Task Centered Approach.* St. Louis: C. V. Mosby, pp. 202–203.

Garvin, Charles D., and Seabury, Brett A. (1984). *Interpersonal Practice in Social Work.* Englewood Cliffs, NJ: Prentice-Hall, pp. 171, 173, and 176.

Heus, Michael, and Pincus, Allen. (1986). *The Creative Generalist: A Guide to Social Work Practice.* Barneveld, WI: Micamar, pp. 327, 332, 338, and 340.

Hoffman, Kay S. (1983). "Women Offenders in Social Work Practice," in Roberts, Albert (ed.). *Social Work in Criminal Justice Settings.* Springfield, IL: Charles C. Thomas.

Johnson, Louise. (1989). *Social Work Practice: A Generalist Approach,* 3rd ed. Boston: Allyn & Bacon, p. 298.

Lewis, Harold. (1982). *The Intellectual Base of Social Work Practice.* New York: Haworth Press, pp. 121–124.

Maluccio, Anthony. (1979). *Learning from Clients: Interpersonal Helping as Viewed by Clients and Social Workers.* New York: Free Press.

Pincus, Allen, and Minahan, Anne. (1973). *Social Work Practice: Model & Method.* Itasca, IL: F. E. Peacock, p. 164.

Reid, William J. (1978). *The Task-Centered System.* New York: Columbia University Press.

Sallee, Alvin L. (1983). *Child Protective Services in Bernalillo County: Analysis and Recommendations.* Santa Fe, NM: New Mexico Human Services Department.

Sheafor, B. W., Horejsi, C. R., and Horejsi, G. A. (1988). *Techniques and Guidelines for Social Work Practice.* Boston: Allyn & Bacon, pp. 306 and 308.

Simons, Ronald L., and Aigner, Stephen M. (1985). *Practice Principles: A Problem-Solving Approach to Social Work.* New York: MacMillan, p. 72.

Siporin, Max. (1975). *Introduction to Social Work Practice.* New York: MacMillan, p. 251.

Washington State Department of Social and Health Services. (1987). Olympia: Division of Children and Family Services.

Chapter 10

Implementing Change___

OVERVIEW

This chapter's goal is to illustrate how the social work generalist implements the plan that has been agreed upon by both the client system and the social worker. The components of implementation that the social worker employs are introduced in this chapter: (1) change management, (2) encouraging empowerment, and (3) exercising influence. The chapter ends with an extended case example that shows how a plan is implemented by a generalist social worker.

Implementation is based on the social worker's skills actualized within a social work role. As we have said in previous chapters, the overarching skills in social work practice are analytic skills and interactional skills. Separating the two skill areas is not practically feasible, but it is necessary in the conceptualization of social work practice. Analytic skills underlie assessment, designing, and planning, while interactional skills form the base for implementation—the "doing" of the plan.

Social work roles represent sets of expected behaviors. Within each role, the social worker uses skills that direct professional activities toward the goals the client and the social worker have agreed upon. The roles that are frequently used to explain social work practice and that we have discussed in Chapter 4 are: broker, advocate/activist, enabler, collaborator/networker, conflict manager, and educator.

In professional practice, social workers do not enact singular roles and leap from one to another. Most often, social workers engage in roles simultaneously and then gradually change roles, depending on the situation and need. In fact, both roles and skills are utilized within a larger framework that allows for individual social worker style, situational opportunities, and barriers and system strengths and limitations. In order to gain an understanding of implementation through a larger lens, we have conceptualized implementation along three parallel strategies. These represent the holistic approach to social work practice that is emphasized in the Crystal Model Process of Planned Change. These three strategies, change management, encouraging empowerment, and exercising influence, include the discrete roles and skills that we presented in Chapter 4, but they are framed in relation to cases that explicate the roles and skills corresponding to this phase in the Crystal Model.

Reviewing the Crystal Model

Implementation is the action phase in the Crystal Model and thus of great interest. Throughout our discussion of the other phases, we have cautioned that patience is necessary so that a social worker would not yield to the natural urge to act hastily upon recognizing an area of concern. Only after collecting information, assessing it, creating a design, planning, and contracting is the time ripe for implementation.

The above statement notwithstanding, inherent in the Crystal Model is the notion that implementation is present, to some degree, in each phase. For example, involving a family in an ecomap exercise may help them begin immediate, positive action. Even more pronounced, the very act of a client beginning the change process with a social worker (the engagement phase) is the first significant action. Each phase thereafter has implicit within it the process of change (Lloyd, 1980), but the implementation phase, especially, highlights the process of change.

Implementation, Not Intervention

Generalists work with the action, change, focal, and the client systems. With each system involved, we implement the plan. Implementation does not always equate with cooperation. Remember, the focal system must also change to meet the client system's needs. Implementation reflects a mutual partnership with the client system and portions of the focal system, which may include the client as well.

Therefore, as generalists, we focus on implementation rather than intervention, although much practice literature does not differentiate between the two. In fact, the two are often used identically. We separate intervention and implementation as a way of illustrating basic differences between generalist practice and more specialized clinical practice. "Intervention . . . should consist of a specified way of dealing with a particular problem and should be adhered to, unless, of course, there are compelling clinical reasons for departing from it" (Reid, 1983, p. 655). The clear focus in Reid's definition is on coping with or solving a specific problem. By contrast, implementation implies managing plans, working in teams, and affecting systems. Problems are not always the focus, nor are solutions the only outcomes.

For implementation to be successful, it must flow from the previous steps in the Crystal Model. It also must fit the needs of the client system. Social workers are active participants in the change effort. Our abilities are closely related to the effectiveness or ineffectiveness of change. In previous chapters, we have identified for you the competencies that relate most closely to the phase of the change process we are discussing. We continue with the same format in this chapter, and offer below the social work competencies that relate to the implementation phase.

Competencies

Baer and Federico (1978) identify three competencies relating to the implementation phase of the change process. All imply skills within roles the social work generalist plays. Following the discussion of competencies, we present conceptualizations of role and skill sets connected to implementation.

1. *Enhance the Problem-Solving, Coping, and Developmental Capacities of People.* Building on the strengths of each change, client, focal, and action system is inherent in the activities of social work generalists. The tasks that are planned in the designing and planning for change step are usually directed toward enhancing each system's capacities, especially regarding expertise in solving crises and dealing with stressful situations. Such enhancement considers the unique capabilities of each system and takes into consideration what each system is actually able to do. In other words, tasks not related to a system's capacity to use the tasks effectively are not part of a workable plan because they ignore the individuality of each system. Social work generalists implement plans with the enhancement of each system's strengths in mind.

2. *Link People with Systems That Provide Them with Resources, Services, and Opportunities.* Linking people implies action on the part of the social work generalist. We connect people with what they seem to need and what they seem to want in order for the identified areas of concern or problems to be solved. Linking means not only naming resources, but helping systems take advantage of the resources we point out. It is a complicated skill and is dependent on our accuracy in determining the client goals and our interactive roles and skills in helping clients find the necessary resources.

3. *Implement Effectively on Behalf of Populations Most Vulnerable and Discriminated Against.* Implementation, or the actions of the social worker on behalf of at-risk client systems, is certainly a component of change. This competency takes special notice of who client systems are, who ought to be a part of our work, and, further, implies that there are particular roles and skills that are most useful with vulnerable populations. We believe this to be an exceptionally important component of role and skill building in social work.

Earlier in the text, we discussed relationship building and some of the difficulties inherent in working with populations whose experiences with social services and social work prove injurious. Attention must be paid to previous negative episodes with social service agencies, in order to offer a corrective response. Those most often experiencing such difficulties are people who are vulnerable in society at large and who live within the parameters of economic and social discrimination. Implementing change in a context of poor experiences takes particular skill that must be acquired as one claims competence as a social work generalist.

Empirical Support for Implementation

A great deal of social work practice is at a preliminary stage relative to empirically tested models. In fact, social work practice is largely based on practice wisdom. Scientifically based theories of social work practice are emerging, but there are great distances to cover (Fischer, 1978; Hoffman and Sallee, 1990; and Shulman, 1991). Social work practitioners have a wealth of practice experience, and clinicians who are practitioner-researchers are the wave of the future (Briar and Blythe, 1985). Their challenge is to understand what sort of research methodology fits with the practice models they are testing. Underlying research paradigms must be understood before great progress can be made that will assist the profession to identify what practice models work with whom.

But where are we now as far as roles and skills in the implementation phase are concerned? Overall, things are a bit uneven. Although skills such as social work negotiation and political action are less well developed and researched, other roles and skills, including the roles of social broker and educator, are important features in most social work practice. Applied research conducted by social workers is a growing trend and will enhance social work practice in ways not yet even conceived. In the meantime, we use our tools at hand and keep working away.

The excitement of social change and of individual growth drew most of us to social work. Even as social work practice becomes more empirically validated, individual practitioner style and creativity continue to be important components of successful practice.

Implementing the Vision

The shared vision of the worker and each system is realized during implementation. Without vision, we believe positive and meaningful change is almost impossible to achieve (Maples, 1991, p. 96). We must be able to see beyond "what is" to "what can be." Stating a vision may seem idealistic, yet all professions rely on their visions to realize their goals (Maples, 1991, p. 100). Our aim needs to be to encourage each person to share in the vision and become invested in the change process.

An agency serving the elderly may share a vision that all elderly persons in its area will live in dignity with opportunities to contribute to society. A smaller but no less important vision for an individual family may be that the elderly persons in the family will obtain decent housing located near services and accessible to family and friends.

The absence of vision is often found in public agencies that operate on a bureaucratic model that can mitigate against professional behavior and purposes. For example, compliance with policy and regulation becomes more important than the well-being of persons the agency was designed to serve. Leaders caught up in the crisis in public welfare agencies may not have a vision simply because they have no time to plan for future possibilities. However, agencies that continue to meet their clients' needs adopt an attitude of vision that supports a forward motion in developing new strategies and models for planned change.

Practice Concerns

There are three basic practice concerns that are common in the implementation phase.

1. We must maintain the continued support of the client system for change. This becomes paramount if the client system is also part of the focal system (which is usually the case).

2. Everyone (with perhaps the exception of the focal system) needs to be clear on and invested in the plan—that is, what needs to be done, by whom, how, and the time constraints. This constitutes the contract and must be monitored during the implementation phase.

3. The social worker will need to maintain the commitment of the action system throughout implementation.

These practice concerns are raised throughout this chapter as we examine the change concepts in the implementation process.

The Strategies of Implementation

The professional purpose of implementation is to put the plan into action by exercising social work skills within appropriate social work roles. As stated earlier, the three component strategies are (1) change management, (2) encouraging empowerment, and (3) exercising influence.

Change management represents a combination of roles and skills in the implementation phase. The emphasis in change management is on securing resources for client systems.

Other activities are primarily directed toward empowerment of the client, action, and change systems so that goals can be met. Empowerment may focus on the client system, but is not limited to individual empowerment. Instead, its concentration includes the client system's context—that is, the neighborhood, community, and institutions interacting with the client. Empowerment embodies the notion that each system's strengths are to be recognized and activated in the empowerment process. Strengths are "renewable and expandable resources" that must be enhanced, but take on lives and directions of their own (Saleeby, 1992, p. 8).

The power base we have includes our using our own influence as social work professionals to foster change on the part of the focal system. In addition, we influence other systems, including the client, change, and action systems, to help implement the plan and obtain resources.

Thus, implementation consists of (1) using acquired social work skills and placing those skills within the context of change management, (2) encouraging empowerment of each client system, and (3) exercising influence on every system involved in the change effort to ensure meaningful change. As a prelude to the Case Example, in which these components are expanded, each strategy of implementation is discussed below with relevant roles and skills for each. Figure 10.1 provides an overview and helps us organize the change strategies.

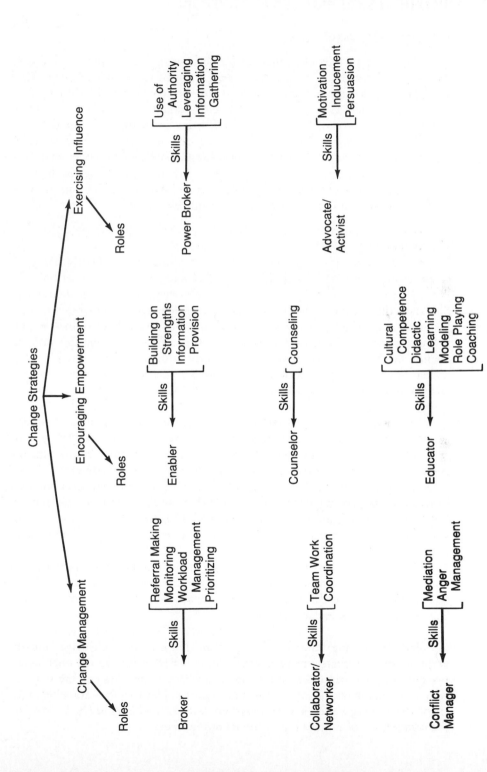

FIGURE 10.1 Implementation

THE COMPONENTS OF IMPLEMENTATION

Change Management

One of the primary roles of a generalist is to oversee the change process and make necessary adjustments. Change management is similar to case management. Case management is a comprehensive process to link and coordinate all involved parties (LeVine and Sallee, 1992). Some practitioners find fault with the title "case manager" and consider it offensive to clients who do not wish to be referred to as "cases" nor as "managed." The use of the term case management, however, is increasing. For our purposes, we focus on *change* management rather than *case* management. We emphasize the management of change as portrayed in the Crystal Model, not the management of people. The major roles that fall under change management are broker, collaborator, and conflict manager.

Broker Role

Brokering is a primary generalist role with an associated set of skills that has as its function connecting resource systems. As a broker, the social worker links the client system to the concrete and service resources they need to meet their needs. Similar to the stockbroker who knows all options of stocks, the social worker must be aware of all of the societal resources available, or at least, how to find the programs and services. Based on the assessment, the social worker, together with the client, matches the most appropriate resource with the client system's need. Sometimes the generalist social worker can provide the service directly, but client systems with many concerns often require a referral.

Skill: Referral Making   A referral is a mini–Crystal Model process. It consists of identifying the client's concern, briefly assessing the concern, planning what resources can best meet the client's needs, putting the client in touch with the resource, and, later, following up to ensure the client's needs were met.

Making a quality referral is a skill much needed by generalist social workers. This skill includes being able to state clearly what the client needs to the community agency. This requires both verbal and written communication skills. Negotiating with the other agency to accommodate the client is another skill inherent in making a referral.

Referral making cuts across all sized systems, although most programs and services are configured to serve individuals or families. To illustrate the breadth of referral options, Case Example 10.1 demonstrates how a referral can occur in a large system and professional arena.

Skill: Monitoring   Monitoring is a major skill used by the change "broker" and is inherent in change management. Not only does it refer to the ongoing activity of "keeping track of" what is happening with the client system, the skill also comprises the change manager's efforts to secure the best resources available to the client. Monitoring is used with every system. Bertsche and Horejsi (1980) organize the components of monitoring in the following steps:

A. Documenting and ensuring accurate flow of information between parties in a timely and professional manner. This may include phone calls, process recordings, videotapes, or letters.

B. Following along with each system as needed so unexpected concerns can be addressed early. For a neighborhood change effort, this might include attending evening meetings or phone calls to leaders.

C. Providing emotional and ongoing support to each system.

D. Serving as a liaison between the client systems and other systems to minimize conflict and increase the flow of information.

E. Assessing the change process according to where everyone had hoped to be in their plan. For example, if a social worker is coordinating the United Way fundraising campaign, and the plan calls for 65 percent of the goal to be achieved by the end of the first month, it is the social worker's role to check the percentage periodically and make sure all of the team leaders are aware of how much the campaign has achieved relative to the plan. (pp. 94–98)

CASE EXAMPLE 10.1

Referring a University to the Council on Social Work Education

Jill graduated from a Council on Social Work Education–accredited B.S.W. program, where she was involved in the reaffirmation process. After receiving her B.S.W. degree, she relocated to a rural community in western Massachusetts that was home to a small private university. At a National Association of Social Workers program unit meeting, several M.S.W.s who served as agency administrators expressed the concern that they were unable to find B.S.W.s for direct service jobs in their agencies. The suggestion was made to approach the local university. Jill was asked to serve on a university-professional planning committee, given her B.S.W. and her experience with the accreditation process.

As the group struggled to conceptualize a generalist curriculum, Jill suggested a referral to the Council on Social Work Education's national office. The staff at the Council referred Jill and the committee to persons in leadership positions in the organization that represented B.S.W. education.

Jill made the contact with the B.S.W. leadership group and asked them to suggest consultants who might help. The committee contacted the several individuals suggested and interviewed them by telephone. The results of the interviews were discussed in the planning group so that a good match between the program needs and each consultant's strengths could be determined.

Next, the first-choice consultant was interviewed again by telephone in a conference call. The results of the interview were positive, and the consultant was offered the opportunity to participate in the project. Availability of times and costs were negotiated until an agreement was reached between the consultant and the planning committee. As a follow-up gesture, a staff member of the Council on Social Work Education called later to see if the group had obtained a consultant.

Monitoring requires the social worker to "keep up" with what is going on during implementation and to share it with all parties. Skillful monitoring implies that accurate, timely flow of information is inherent in the process.

Skill: Workload Management   The broker role concerns itself not only with direct service to clients but also ensuring that workload is appropriately brokered or distributed to carry out the plan. For example, if the plan for a family requires intensive (once or twice per day) in-home work with the family, the social worker cannot have ten concurrent cases. Either the plan has to be reconsidered or the worker will have to negotiate with the agency for a different workload distribution—not necessarily a workload reduction.

Effective use of time is an important factor in work management. Let us assume intensive work with a family at risk of having a child placed in an out-of-home placement can benefit from in-home services offered over a two-month period, thus avoiding foster-care placement. An in-home social worker can likely service two families simultaneously during such a time period. On the other hand, if more traditional office-based services are used, an individual social worker will serve a caseload of ten families per year. Although the intensive in-home services worker serves fewer families at once, over the course of one year, more families are serviced. An average in-home worker serves twelve families per year (two every two months). Therefore, the time issue is related to the distribution of cases, rather than to total number of cases.

Managing workload is especially important when intensive services are offered. For example, if a social worker is working in an agency in which social workers are "on call" for extended periods, effective caseload management is a necessity. Mary, a social worker in a twenty-four-hour program, says she doesn't want to carry a beeper when her children are on vacation from school. At times, she feels overwhelmed by her job and her many strains at home. Her supervisor assists her by arranging that she will not carry a beeper on January 1, January 18, and February 15—that is, the days her children are home. Then the other staff members can work with that list of dates and all staff members can be on call at appropriate times.

Managing workload distribution is the foundation of effective implementation. The manager role extends to one's personal workload and time management as well. Most generalists work in very busy jobs fraught with crisis and lacking in resources. What many clients cite as their greatest dislike is their social worker's inaccessibility (Shulman, 1991, p. 142). One could argue that workload management skills have a dramatic impact on the social worker's availability to the client and other systems.

Effective workload management is like any other training. It is more difficult when one begins, yet after a few weeks, positive feelings and higher performance are realized. Simply extending a work day does not help, as social worker "burnout" sets in, and one is less effective with clients.

Skill: Prioritizing   Prioritizing and knowing how to sequence tasks are critical skills to the broker role. It takes great discipline and focus to stick to a prioritized list each day, particularly when some of the tasks and people with whom one must deal are not pleasant.

Many social work students are already experts at time management and prioritizing, for as working parents they are balancing family, work, field placements, National Association of Social Workers meetings, and classroom work. It has been wryly suggested in some quarters that the way to best manage the federal budget is to put a welfare mother, who monthly gets by with 50 percent of her family's needs being met, in charge. Perhaps we should suggest that "returning students" (that is, older students who have spent some time in the work force) give workshops in prioritization and time management!

Collaborator/Networker Roles

The role of collaborator enhances the spirit of cooperation among systems and social workers, as well as between clients and the resource systems they need. Working together brings the fullest resource possibilities to each system and adds to the possibilities of each system maintaining their resources after the social worker has completed services. Building trust so that mutual agreement among the many parties involved in the change effort adds to successful collaboration.

Networking is a form of collaboration that includes working between services and agencies. Building mutual respect between and among workers at various agencies serving clients improves service delivery to clients; however, high quality relationships are not easily obtained in the hectic, day-to-day world of human services.

Skill: Team Managing   Team managing is an important generalist skill, especially in working with the action system. Bringing people together from a number of different agencies to work as an action system is similar to putting together an all-star basketball team from competing teams. Agencies and organizations are frequently in competition for resources, prestige, and clients. Effective teamwork does not mean everyone always agrees, or that things always go smoothly. "Group think," in which everyone agrees at all costs, can allow individual team members to abdicate their responsibilities, and dangerous warning signals in a case may be bypassed.

Team-managing skills include the ability to form groups of professionals, lay persons, and clients to design and implement plans. Team management can be listed as the ability to:

1. Involve all team members in decision making.
2. Create a division of labor, based upon each person's expertise and strengths.
3. Create an atmosphere where all opinions and problems can be expressed.
4. Negotiate differences of opinion.
5. Expect responsible actions of all members.
6. Ensure all information is shared. (Compton and Galaway, 1989, p. 607)

Team managing is a critical generalist skill.

One technique for working with teams regarding family issues is always to have the family present during all team meetings. Professionals act like professionals and speak with respect regarding the family. Labeling disappears and the family's expertise is more easily recognized.

Team managing requires the ability to communicate effectively, group decision making, monitoring of tasks, developing mutual respect, and the ability to work in complex organizations. Flexibility and trust are also key ingredients for teamwork. The generalist who can identify or develop teams of persons who share a common goal and are willing to work hard with people they respect will be a successful team leader (Johnson, 1992, p. 175).

Skill: Coordination   Coordination brings us face to face with other professions and their myths about social work and vice versa. This, coupled with the "whose client is it?" question, creates a barrier to delivery of coordinated services and prevents the development of a common approach to working with the client system. For example, a group of parents concerned about the high teenage pregnancy rate might obtain a variety of explanations for the phenomenon from educators, priests, police, doctors, and social workers. Moving beyond barriers and coordinating a response to their concern assists the parents toward a broad-ranged understanding and perhaps the development of services to head off the high pregnancy rate.

In one example of effective coordination, a community service system with a highly skilled facilitator brought the leaders of each agency together for two days and, through a number of techniques including community sculpting, helped those influential persons learn more about each other, built trust and understanding, and created a better-coordinated social service system. In the final analysis, coordination appears to be a very simple process, yet the bureaucracies that house our agencies do not work work collaboratively (Lloyd, 1980, p. 144). Through written agreements and informal personal relationships, by respecting other professionals and their agencies, and by understanding the need to invest in coordination, positive, powerful results can be achieved.

Conflict Manager Role

Managing change involves conflict management. Brokering, collaborating, and networking bring about changes that client, focal, and action systems may find unfamiliar and uncomfortable. The conflict that any change precipitates must be understood and addressed in the helping process.

In conflict management, the social worker uses skills to mediate conflicts that arise as a result of self-interest conflicts (Shulman, 1986). Conflicts may include those between the client and focal systems' self-interests or between client and resource systems' self-interests. For example, a family (the client system) has been referred to a psychologist (the action system) by the social worker (change system) for testing. The father in the family says he can only attend the family testing sessions on Saturdays because he works and is too tired after work to attend on week nights. The psychologist's agency is only open Mondays through Fridays, including evenings. Many conflicts may be occurring here that stem from each person's self-interest. It is the task of the social worker to work toward a solution that meets the self-interest of those involved and helps all parties understand their interdependence. Without clients, the agency will not meet its goals; without the testing, the family may continue to experience pain.

Skill: Mediation Shulman suggests a four-step process to mediate among systems, thus resolving real or potential conflict (Shulman, 1982). The steps, mirroring an abbreviated Crystal Model, are: *tune in, come together, work,* and *transition.*

In the tuning-in phase, the worker uses active listening to hear each system's concerns and identify the areas of self-interest each system purports to have. The parties are brought together, and the worker helps them identify areas where work is needed. In the above example, the family and therapist agree they do want to meet for therapy. The next step is to decide upon the location where the parties will do what is necessary to meet the self-interests of each party. In our example, the agency may conduct special office hours on Saturday, or the father may take off work an afternoon during the week. A third alternative may be that the therapist makes a home visit. Once the agreement is made, the social worker leaves the situation (transition), having successfully mediated the conflict regarding schedules.

Skill: Anger Management   More complex situations, in which client systems experience strong self-interests that have lain dormant until change efforts are brought to bear, are frequently faced by social workers. Unresolved pain, anger, and hurt within focal systems can result in outbursts directed toward the social worker or toward others in the client or focal system.

The social service system is large, very complex, and can be intimidating to even the most educated and persistent client. Learning to manage clients' anger directed toward the social worker and all he or she represents is an ongoing challenge. Case Example 10.2 presents a portrait of this challenge, illustrating the anger and pain that follows a tragedy in a foster family.

Encouraging Empowerment

Encouraging empowerment is the second component of implementation of the Crystal Model. Empowerment consists of (1) developing a new perspective on the area of concern, (2) developing new skills, and (3) identifying all possible options. In earlier chapters, we have presented specific ways to do each of these. You may want to review the design section of Chapter 9.

Identifying a client's strengths is also a key to empowerment. By focusing on an individual's strengths, the potential for growth and change present in all human beings is heightened.

Saleebey (1992) cautions against our turning against the word empowerment because of its overuse when he states: ". . . the empowerment agenda is not based on returning power to the people, but on discovering the power within the people (individually and collectively)" (p. 8).

Empowerment is based on clients' finding the resources that are already present within them, learning their own value, and then becoming educated regarding the resources that are available or that need to become available. Thus, the social work generalist enables and educates toward the end of client empowerment. The "flip side" of empowerment involves social workers putting pressure on external systems—focal and action systems—to open their boundaries so that clients can effectively use the resources that exist in communities.

Enabler Role

Enabling is a role that assumes a client system has a number of resources that other systems may not recognize or that are framed negatively. The role of enabling and, thus, empowering focus on the social worker's helping client systems recognize and utilize their own strengths and provide information.

Skill: Building on Strengths   Building on strengths assists social workers and action systems to recognize client and focal system strengths and to provide feedback so they can make better use of their own resources. "To discover that power, we must subvert and abjure pejorative labels, provide opportunities for connection to family, institution, and community; assail the victim mindset; forswear paternalism (even in its most benign guises); and trust people's intuition, accounts perspectives and energies" (Saleebey, 1992, p. 9). The ability to identify

CASE EXAMPLE 10.2

Elsa Covington's Fire

Elsa Covington is a forty-nine-year-old foster mother who has worked for a variety of family and children's agencies for the past twenty years. She has cared for many children and is one of the most loved and popular foster mothers that the public human services agency in a small eastern city now has in their employ. During the Christmas season, a fire broke out in Elsa's home. Two of the four foster children for whom she was caring were killed in the fire. Turner, twenty months old, and Lenny, who was two-and-one-half, died in the fire, while Josie and Tommie survived. The fire was a result of faulty wiring in one room and was accidental. Newspapers showered the tragedy on the front pages and stories of the irony of children being removed from the "dangerous" homes of their biological parents, only to die untimely deaths in foster homes, did not escape the public eye. The deepest anger and rage as well as profound grief were experienced by the dead boys' mothers and by Elsa Covington, the foster mother.

Both biological mothers had been crack cocaine users who were making positive steps toward employment and drug abstinence. The mothers planned to rebuild their lives so that their children could rejoin them. Mrs. Covington was devoted to the children and hoped they would someday return to their mothers.

A crisis team to serve the mothers and Mrs. Covington was immediately constituted in the agency. The team was especially trained to work with clients who had been severely traumatized. The team members were well trained in crisis and anger management. Feelings had to be expressed, but the social workers aimed to keep the anger nonviolent. All parties were heard, and a great deal of time was devoted to working daily with not only the individual mothers involved, but with other women whose children were in foster care. In fact, the team pulled several mothers' groups together for discussions and bonds were formed among the mothers.

Turner and Lenny's mothers were worked with individually as well as in a group with the foster mother. Recognizing the steps in the grieving process as well as the anger the mothers felt, the agency workers offered ongoing support throughout the terrible ordeal. Turner's mother lost control with one social worker, screaming and crying, but because the worker was prepared for the verbal attack, her attentive listening skills helped de-escalate the mother's anger, and she was able to begin to bring some closure to the situation. Turner's and Lenny's mothers continue to feel their tremendous loss, but did not act out toward others, nor did they tend toward self-destruction.

Many months went by before Mrs. Covington began to feel that the whole incident was not her fault. The house was rewired and Elsa agreed that one day, in the not-too-distant future, she may take another child.

Agency personnel gave interviews with newspapers and responded openly to queries, thus averting a defensive posture that may have further exacerbated the situation. In fact, the media was impressed with the work the agency was doing to manage the potential conflict inherent in such catastrophes.

and to build on strengths is more than turning problems into positives. In families, we want to build on strengths in culture, extended family, hobbies, talents, skills, and personality traits. In groups, we want to build on positive relationships, group cohesion on issues, or individual's skills. In a community, we may build on community pride in their high school basketball team or in an elected official or an outstanding agency. We want the system to make use of available resources. In a family, building on strengths may include reconnecting with extended family and reaching out to friends who may become sources of support.

For example, a social worker helps a family about to place an elderly parent in a nursing home to develop an alternative plan. Family members agree to take turns caring for her in partnership with societal resources (Meals on Wheels) and her church group (Compton and Galaway, 1989, p. 531). In this example, the family's strengths are supplemented by community resources.

Skill: Information Provision   When clients confront complex societal systems, enabling may take the form of information about remedies, not accessible in everyday life. In recent years, workers in factories have learned of the legal protection afforded them in the work place. Unions inform their membership regarding developing legislation regarding security in the work environment.

The Welfare Rights Organization empowered thousands of welfare mothers by providing them accurate information on how to apply for Aid to Families with Dependent Children, food stamps, and other programs. In turn, these empowered mothers, with social work volunteers, became enablers to other applicants. This greatly enhanced the mothers' self-esteem. Some organizers were hired by the welfare department, an illustration of how a macrosystem implementation may benefit an individual client system.

Counselor Role

Complementary to the enabling role is the counselor. At the onset of their educations, many social work students voice interest in becoming a counselor with the mistaken notion that social work is a synonymous profession. Of course, social workers are professional social workers and not professional counselors, yet social workers do take on the role of counselor and exercise counseling skills.

Skill: Counseling   In a study of Child Protective Service clients, Magura (1982) found that one of the major factors that impacted on service was counseling. The parents said they liked best the empathy (correct reading of their feelings), genuineness, and unconditional positive regard of the social workers. They disliked unrequested advice and help and the social workers' lack of skills (Magura, 1982, pp. 522–531).

The social work profession recognizes the critical aspects of counseling during the implementation phase, especially with focal systems. Change occurs by gaining insight into why they behave or feel the way they do, by helping them to grow emotionally or socially, and by developing better interpersonal skills (Sheafor, Horejsi, and Horejsi, 1991, p. 37).

To take on an effective counselor role, the social worker must have a good basic understanding of human behavior in the social environment and must translate this into the skill of guiding the focal system through the implementation phase. The counselor role makes the most of the use of the social worker's own abilities and requires practice to refine.

Educator Role

Education is key to developing a new perspective or new skills. The educator role assists in the establishment of conditions under which people can learn, but does not guarantee learning. For example, a teacher cannot ensure that subject matter under discussion is learned. All that the teacher can do is create the best conditions for learning to take place. Students learn from the lectures, exercises, or textbooks by incorporating what they choose into their own minds. The key in effective social work practice is to educate in the context of enabling or supportive conditions. For that reason alone, our view of implementation in the change process demands multiple and simultaneous social work roles.

Positive conditions for learning imply the use of sound teaching principles that can increase the possibilities of learning. We have borrowed Lloyd's (1980) four teaching principles for the social work practitioner to strengthen our discussion of the educator role in the Crystal Model. They include:

a. Begin by assessing what the system already knows and what they wish to learn.

b. Assess the systems capacities and styles of learning.

c. Select exercises based upon your assessments that reinforce systems' strengths.

d. Make learning fun or at least a pleasant experience. (Lloyd, 1980, p. 79)

Each principle emphasizes the importance of early, frequent, and flexible assessments that focus on client strengths and capacities rather than on deficits. The principles recognize the value of creating a positive environment in which growth and learning can happen. The skills of the educator include cultural competence and didactical teaching, modeling, role playing, and coaching (Lloyd, 1980). These are discussed below.

Skill: Cultural Competence   No social work role is more dependent on being clearly understood than the role of educator because its essence is built on the transmission of information from one person to another or to a group of persons. In that light, unrecognized cultural differences play havoc with successful educating. *Cultural competence* is knowing how to obtain information about another culture and successfully work in that culture. A "cultural guide" (someone from a specific culture) can help one learn the rituals, traditions, and forms of information exchange of that culture.

Cultural competence is especially relevant when assessing the style of learning in which client and focal systems engage. For example, the Vietnamese generally value information gained through the written word and, therefore, stay informed through newspapers. Because music is prized in many Hispanic neighborhoods, an effective antidrug campaign message might be put to music so that optimal learning conditions regarding the perils of drug use exist for Hispanic youth. Knowledge of native languages, of common expressions, and of the culture play into the competent employment of teaching skills that social work generalists ordinarily apply in the implementation phase of the change process.

Skill: Didactic Teaching *Didactics* are systematic teaching methods that include lectures, telling stories, and describing and interpreting current experiences or happenings. In employing didactic methods, our speech should be jargon-free and suited to the audience. Using professional, "therapeutic" terms may offend clients. Having a thorough knowledge of the subject matter one is presenting is basic to effective teaching. An educator must admit knowledge deficits rather than disregard them. An atmosphere in which learning can take place is more likely if the person "in charge" freely admits his or her limitations. Generalist social workers are often called upon to describe their programs to community groups and must use their best didactic skills in such efforts. For example, detailed information conveyed regarding drug use and abuse sets the stage for an effective prevention program.

Skill: Modeling Educating through demonstrating (*modeling*) is used in a wide variety of social work situations. A social worker listening to a member of a group speak can model attentiveness and active listening for the rest of the group.

The social worker playing with a child in an age-appropriate way shows the mother how to parent, especially if activities the social worker uses to engage the child are shared with the parent. For example, home visits may include playing with toys that children play with themselves. Engaging a mother as well as a child in a make-believe exercise with dolls helps the mother learn more about her child as well as learn how to have fun, herself, with her own child. Of course, these activities can be a threat to a parent if a good relationship has not previously been established.

In modeling, the social worker should periodically check with the client regarding what the client may have learned from an experience shared with a social worker. For example, a mother who had been in trouble with the law was riding in a car with a social worker who was given a traffic ticket for a minor, questionable, offense. Afterwards, the mother commented on how calm the social worker was during the interaction with the police officer. The social worker asked the officer for important information that she would use in court to challenge the ticket. She explained to the mother that she needed to remain calm to collect the information she needed, such as time of day, distances, where the officer was, and so on. The social worker set a good example for a situation in which she had not received specific training!

If the social worker had reacted personally and had become upset and embarrassed, all understandable reactions, she could have freely admitted her failure to the mother and explained how she wished she had reacted. It is all right not to be perfect as a model and it is helpful to explain where one may have made mistakes.

Skill: Role Playing In your practice class, no doubt you have, or will, role play. You take on the identity and emotions of another person with a perspective probably different from your own. For role playing to be most effective, one needs to take time to prepare by clearly understanding the role—not just our preconceived ideas of the role. This is an effective learning skill with client systems for a variety of purposes (Shaw et al., 1980). Perhaps you are helping a single-parented child prepare for her first job interview, so you, as the social worker, play the boss who interviews the teenage applicant. Afterwards, you debrief and discuss the teenager's strengths, thus building self-confidence and identifying areas that can be improved.

Parents learn about their children's feelings when they role play children in group settings. In a parents' group, a mother was asked to role play a fifteen-year-old girl who was failing in school and who had begun drinking binges on weekends. The mother got so engaged in the role that she recalled her own adolescence with its deep pain and so developed a greater understanding of her own daughter's problem.

Role playing can also be used by the social worker or client to prepare for new experiences. Examples of these could be a court appearance for a teenager or an initial visit to a psychologist for a depressed elderly person.

Skill: Coaching *Coaching,* or cuing, can be an effective teaching skill within the correct context and with client and focal systems open to this type of involvement. Coaching and cuing involve correcting, advising, and making assessments and suggestions as people learn new behaviors.

Coaching is particularly successful with families who are working on nonviolent reactions to each other. A successful series of workshops using coaching techniques was developed in Detroit that taught families to deal with their tempers and unreasonable reactions to everyday situations. Whole families, assigned by the court, attended these workshops to learn positive ways of dealing with stress. Usually the teenager in the family had been in trouble with the law, but the court saw the youth's "acting out" as symptomatic of larger issues within the family. As an alternative to probation or further court involvement, families engaged in nonviolent conflict resolution.

In this series of workshops, those in attendance were divided into groups. One person in a group had a "gripe" with others in the group. The person with the issue was assigned a coach (in the first round—the workshop leader) and the person who the "gripe" was against also was assigned a coach (another workshop leader). In working out the conflict, the person with the issue asked for help from the coach to approach his or her counterpart. The coach gave advice regarding how to state the issue, how to ask questions, and so on. The advice was given so that everyone in the group could hear it. The person who was to respond was also given advice from his or her coach before answering the accusation. Coaches encouraged the group members to state their issues nonviolently and in a nonaccusing manner, using "I" statements. In turn, responders were coached to answer nonpunitively and without accusation. Family members learned entirely new responses to their old ways of engaging in verbal and sometimes physical battle in their families. The coaching techniques offered considerable support for the individuals involved; there was plenty of room for making mistakes and trying again. Follow-up sessions were offered with the families and it was clear to the workshop leaders that families had learned new behaviors through coaching techniques (Hoffman and Charbonneau, 1986).

Successful coaching is built on positive social worker–client relationships. In fact, attempting any provocative implementation technique demands a supportive and encouraging environment in which participants feel unthreatened.

Exercising Influence

Exercising influence is the third component of implementation (Simons and Aigner, 1985). While each of the other strategies, by definition, address influence, the roles most closely associated with exercising influence are power broker and advocate/activist. The power broker is able to control resources, tangible and intangible. Some may not like the term "power broker." Power, however, is not necessarily evil. To exercise influence on behalf of change systems, we must have power. Advocates must influence systems external to the client system in order to assist the client, while activism encompasses change strategies directed toward societal organizations and institutions.

Influence is exerted on change systems and on resource systems. In other words, generalists exercise influence directly and indirectly with clients, focal systems, and action systems. Influence is employed in organizations and in the political area. Influence skills are tailored to the social worker's abilities, personality, and to the activities' professional purposes.

Power-Broker Role

In the power-broker role, generalists use the skills related to the use of authority, leveraging, and information and resource use. Authority must be sanctioned. Authority in public agencies is sanctioned by state and federal laws and regulations. For example, the authority to license a private adoption agency is the responsibility of many state human service agencies.

Skill: Use of Authority   The ability to implement rules, regulation and laws fairly demonstrates the use of authority in generalist social work. Critical to the use of authority is the professional use of self.

Exercising authority in social work is dependent on the personal and professional characteristics of the social worker and his or her acquired abilities (Pincus and Minahan, 1973; Siporin, 1975; Simons and Aigner, 1985; Hoffman and Sallee, 1990; and Shulman, 1991).

The successful exercise of influence through authority is based on strong assertive characteristics, the ability to engage in high-quality professional relationships, and the "knack" for positive teamwork. Persons with likable, charismatic personalities, along with the ability to captivate others' interests and commitments, have the essential characteristics to execute influence through the use of authority.

Skill: Leveraging   If a social worker does not possess power in a situation, then it is incumbent upon the social worker to locate persons who do (Pincus and Minahan, 1973, p. 248). The person who has power and influence is known as a leverage person. This person can access influence not directly available to the social worker. Case Example 10.3 clarifies the concept of leveraging for power to change systems.

CASE EXAMPLE 10.3
Leveraging the State Legislature

The Community Action Agency needs to have access to the house majority leader in a state legislature. The majority leader happens to be from the project manager's home district. The project manager knows that talking with the legislator, informing him or her of the needs of the agency, and describing the needs of the clients served may help free funds for a planned AIDS prevention program.

The project manager peruses the list of board members from the agency and deter-mines one who is well acquainted with the majority leader. The project manager, in turn, contacts the board member, who agrees to introduce the majority leader to the project manager. The project manager was able to have his case heard because the majority leader trusted the board member and/or owed him or her a favor. Funds were released for the program. This is a perfectly legitimate use of leverage to influence the political process.

Skill: Information and Resource Use   The actual control of essential resources, of course, is even more powerful. If an agency director controls a $3 million budget, then he or she can greatly influence the services provided through the day-to-day expenditures.

Control of information as well as the opportunity to be informed of the latest policy developments assists in exercising influence. Through established sources and a careful reading of systems, the social worker can predict major shifts and engage in a systematic information-gathering process. Knowing who is going to be appointed to a key post ahead of time may allow a social worker to promote certain ideas that may be popular with the new person.

Advocate/Activist Role

Advocacy pertains to the method used to lobby for redistribution of power and resources. In advocating for a client system, we facilitate the client's receiving the resource he or she needs and has a right to even if our activities may cause some disruption in the agencies in which we are employed. Clients' rights to fair treatment, including access to resources to which the client is entitled, takes precedence over most other activities.

We advocate not only for individual client rights and resources but also for groups of persons whose resources are limited. Case advocacy (working with one client system) may be the groundwork for cause (many similar types of clients) advocacy. Cause advocacy triggers the social work activist role. For example, advocating for the rights of a mental patient residing in a community group home may develop into advocacy for the cause of all ex-mental patients from this group home.

Sometimes social workers are court or legislative witnesses and testify on behalf of clients or causes. Clearly and firmly stating our position and, it is hoped, in a way such that all sides can claim success is the essence of advocacy. Taking power through political or confrontation action is the essence of *activism* (Galper,

1980). Making major changes in society through activism is a formidable challenge that is as important to client systems of tomorrow as advocacy is for the clients of today. Social workers need to be effective as advocates and activists.

Advocacy and activism usually are applied to the focal system and, less often, with the action system. Case Example 10.4 illustrates an unusual situation involving case advocacy. As you read the case, consider how this case could grow to cause advocacy and perhaps even to activism.

How would the situation described in Case Example 10.4 have been handled if there had been time for all parties to have collaborated as professionals? They could have come together and found commonalities between the adoption systems and how to best facilitate the process by meeting the needs, first of all, of the child and family, and then the legal and agency's needs.

Carrying out the advocate/activist role requires skills that enhance exercising influence. Influence is exerted mainly through the use of two interactional skills: motivation/inducement and persuasion.

Skill: Motivation/Inducement When you are able to offer something people want or need, whether this be a material resource or praise, you may induce change. You have exercised influence. Of course, it is fundamental to the success of this skill that you can deliver the reward. Also fundamental is that the reward is something the client or focal systems wants or needs.

The motivation may come from freeing the system from pain or discomfort or from failure of the focal system to change, which can lead to punishment. With reward, one induces the focal system to do something. Punishment can also induce change. Often federal policy employs this technique to induce states to implement certain programs or meet standards of practice. For example, the Social Security Act under Title IVB requires states to practice permanency planning for children who have been placed out-of-home. If a state passes its Section 427 review, in which case records are examined, then it receives a "bonus" payment from the federal government—a reward. If the records indicate that the state is not practicing permanency planning at an adequate level, the additional funds are withheld—punishment. At the individual social worker level, this means "reasonable efforts" must be documented to keep a child in his or her home or return the child as soon as possible. If the social worker fails to document this, his or her merit pay may be cut.

Social policy makers at the federal level are advocating for permanency planning, already called for in the law, through the use of motivation and inducement. Ethically employed authority can be a powerful tool in motivating the focal system.

Skill: Persuasion By nature, systems attempt to maintain stability. People and groups of people are not inclined to change the way they do things. They strive for constancy (Simmons and Aigner, 1985, p. 127). *Persuasion* is implementing change through the introduction of new information that persuades the system to change behavior, attitudes, and beliefs. How do we make change possible through persuasion? How do we convince systems to do what needs to be done to meet the client's goals?

CASE EXAMPLE 10.4

Parsons' Adoption

A couple in Texas, the Parsons, had been approved for adoption by a private Texas adoption agency. Through a relative, a prospective birth-mother (a woman who was planning to place her child for adoption), Ms. Smith from St. Louis, Missouri, contacted the Parsons, and, after reviewing the completed adoption study and meeting with them, asked them to adopt her child at birth.

A rather complex set of laws and regulations govern cross-state adoptions. The Interstate Compact on Adoptions is administered in almost every state by the Department of Human Services. In this case, Texas had not been involved until contacted by the private adoption agency. The necessary paperwork was exchanged between state capitals, the private agency social worker, and the birth-mother's attorney. The social worker wanted to assure a quick placement in order to comply with the birth-mother's request and to meet the infant's needs for a secure home.

The day finally came, and the Parsons flew to St. Louis to be with Ms. Smith at the birth of the healthy baby boy. Two days later, on a Friday, as the baby was about to be released by the hospital to the Parsons, it was discovered that one paper necessary for the Interstate Compact had not been processed in Jefferson City, the capital city, by the Department of Human Services. The parents called the private adoption agency social worker, who quickly called the Missouri Human Services Department and found that the Interstate Compact on the Placement of Children (ICPC) worker, Mr. Jones, was away from the office briefly. When Mr. Jones called back, he explained he had come in early and was going home at 4:30 p.m. and would not have time to find the form, but he would mail it Monday morning.

In her advocate role, the social worker explained that was not in the best interest of the child (a legal phrasing not lost on Mr. Jones as the ICPC worker), and it was upsetting to Ms. Smith and the Parsons. Mr. Jones said he was going home, that he was not paid enough for this. Again, the adoption worker calmly explained the needs of her clients and then added that this situation had occurred through his oversight, and the clients should not have to assume the additional costs that would be necessary if they had to wait until Monday.

The social worker inquired as to whether or not Mr. Jones' supervisor could complete the paperwork and fax it to the hospital if Mr. Jones had to go home early. This prompted Mr. Jones to complete the work rather than have to explain the situation to his supervisor.

If there had been more time and if the adoption social worker had planned to work with Mr. Jones again, the adoption social worker could have proceeded differently on at least three points. First, she could have acknowledged Mr. Jones' comments about not being paid enough and had he been her client, she would have addressed this. But of course, Mr. Jones is not her client, so this could have diverted their attention when time was critical. Second, she could call back next week to tell Mr. Jones how his "staying late" had facilitated the Parsons being home with a new baby over the weekend and to thank him. And third, she could have found out if Mr. Jones was a member of NASW and, if so, could have reported his behavior through a grievance committee of this professional organization.

The generalist practice literature suggests four methods of exercising influence through persuasion (Pincus and Minahan, 1972; Simmons and Aigner, 1985; and Sheafor, Horejsi, and Horejsi, 1991). They include: inductive questioning, presenting both sides, role reversal, and persistence.

Four Methods Using Persuasion

Inductive Questioning   *Inductive questioning* is a technique that challenges a person's or group's position by asking indirect questions, which causes the person or group to question the accuracy of their original position. This is most useful when the system's position is not founded on fact but rather myths or irrational feelings.

The social worker designs questions that ask what evidence supports the person's or group's belief, in what ways is something true or false, and what makes it so (Simmons and Aigner, 1985, p. 135; and Ellis, 1977). For example, a social worker from a youth agency is meeting with a group of neighbors to persuade them to allow a youth shelter in their neighborhood. She might ask what experience they have with abused children who have run away from home. What has the experience been of other neighborhoods where these homes are located? What do the neighbors fear from the children? Or, the social worker might ask, what options do these children have? Do they have a right to have a place to run to? These questions force the neighbors to confront their feelings with facts and help them understand that young people run away for a number of reasons.

Attorneys often make use of inductive questioning in court, trying to get witnesses or the jury to question their conclusions. In the Parsons' adoption case, the adoption social worker could have asked inductive questions of Mr. Jones, such as "what effect will this delay have on the baby, the birth-mother, and the adoptive parents?"

To give further power to inductive questioning, the social worker should summarize and reflect back what the person or group answers, thus emphasizing the difference between the response and the previous position. Yet, this should be done subtly rather than overtly because overt remarks concerning differences may simply lead to a debate. Allowing the focal system to "discover" contradictions by themselves results in the most significant and long-lasting change (Simmons and Aigner, 1985, p. 136).

Present Both Sides   Billions of dollars must be spent around the world each year to convince people to purchase this product or that service or to join this or that group. Advertising is big business and probably more money and talent goes into how to persuade a father to buy a certain type of car than goes into how to persuade the same father to spend time with his children. Advertising methodology may have some importance for social work practice.

Successful ads present both sides of an argument. Advertisers for car A compare their car to the competition, car B. Both car A and car B have four doors and bucket seats, and car A has a larger eight-cylinder engine and costs less. Perhaps car B has a longer warranty and a bigger trunk, but by presenting both sides, the car A company gains the advantage and car company B will have to rebut the first ad.

When the focal system holds an opposing position, the two-sided argument may be very effective. By presenting both sides, you take the "wind out of the sails" of a defensive system while at the same time letting them know you understand their side. The social worker appears more objective. When the other side hears you making their points, they will listen to you rather than thinking about how they will counter your statement. Of course, after your initial presentation, the opposition may counter and add more points, but, even so, you have set a less defensive and more factual tone.

Role Reversal   Role reversal is a form of role playing. Each person "trades" positions with the other person and takes on the same attitude, emotion, and perspective as the person with whom they traded.

Role reversal has many of the same benefits as inductive questioning; they both encourage a person or group to take on the behaviors and attitudes of the other side. When people take on the role of those they oppose, they must advocate for a new position and, as in inductive questioning, their premises are challenged in an indirect way. Role reversal is an experience that often results in changed attitudes and, thus, behaviors (Simmons and Aigner, 1985, p. 136).

Role reversal can be used with focal systems of different sizes, from a married couple to community groups. In a marriage situation, role reversal may result in the breadwinner realizing the demands and challenges placed on the partner who stays home and "just" does housework, such as lack of contact with other adults. The homemaker may realize the demands of the work place and the pressure of commuting.

In a community, different ethnic groups can be asked to reverse roles. They might begin to learn about stereotypes and how the need for mutual aid plays out in certain behaviors.

The more realistic the role reversal, the more the person will "become" the role and learn. The more learned the greater the change. Effective role playing requires planning and practice so the person can as closely as possible walk in the other's shoes.

Persistence   Even with these skills, a healthy dose of patience and persistence is necessary to persuasion. This may be calmly repeating your position or the client's needs until the other system is "worn down." You may think of persistence as the force required to push the focal system off center, out of the rut in the road. Just as with a car with a tire in a rut, you want to be careful not to oversteer once the tire becomes free. In other ways, we do not want to pressure so much there is a reaction by the system. We want to increase the pressure as needed and persist just enough to induce change, not to irritate or to create an unwanted backlash.

APPLICATION OF ROLES AND SKILLS

Learning implementation through extended case examples challenges us to apply our knowledge to real-life situations that are complex and compelling. In Case Example 10.5, you will find an actual case of a woman who becomes a victim of AIDS. While the social worker is presented with a client microsystem, the social worker needs generalist implementation skills to work with the family, foster family, a group, the action system, and the community.

CASE EXAMPLE 10.5
Lucy Rodriguez

This is the story of Lucy Rodriguez and her daughter, Anna. Anna is a two-and-a-half-year-old Puerto Rican child who is HIV-positive. She is currently in a foster home with foster parents who are in the process of adopting her. Anna's mother, Lucy, used the child welfare system to make a permanent plan for Anna to be implemented upon her (Lucy's) death.

Lucy was three months pregnant when she learned that her husband, Roberto, had AIDS. Lucy and Roberto had been separated for several months when he and his doctor informed her that she was a possible carrier of the virus. They were concerned about the child she was carrying and the possibility the virus could be transmitted to the baby. When Lucy heard this, she panicked; she disappeared for two weeks. She left her son from a previous relationship with Mr. Santos, Jose, age five, with her parents, saying that she would return in a day or two to pick him up. Lucy was prone to excessive drinking when faced with a serious crisis and had left for periods of time in the past, but her parents reported to the child welfare agency that she had never before disappeared for this long a period. This is the situation that Mrs. Martinez, the child welfare agency social worker, was presented as the area of concern.

When Lucy returned, she contacted Mrs. Martinez, as her parents recommended. Mrs. Martinez suggested that Lucy contact the local AIDS testing center. Lucy knew that she had to take the HIV test, but she was not ready to accept the results. Mrs. Martinez suggested to

Ms. Jones, the social worker at the testing center, that she be very supportive of Lucy and gave her a brief summary of the case. At this point, Ms. Jones became part of the action system. Lucy was told by Ms. Jones that she would experience a grieving process if she tested positive, and they discussed her ability to build an informal and societal resource network. When they jointly agreed that she was able to handle the test results—a process that included a screening for assessment of her risk for suicide—the results were given to her. The test was positive, and she knew that in the upcoming months she would have to make many decisions. With Mrs. Martinez' support, she made plans to help in making and carrying out those decisions.

One of the first decisions Lucy faced was the question of continuing the pregnancy. Through Mrs. Martinez, she knew the risk of infecting yet another human being. Like most who face this decision, she had to examine her personal values and cultural and religious beliefs. Mrs. Martinez suggested that Lucy, being Hispanic/Catholic, seek advice from the Catholic priest in her parish. Lucy saw him three times before making the decision to continue the pregnancy. She and the priest discussed the shame and guilt she felt about the possibility of infecting the child. The priest was caring and compassionate. He helped Lucy believe that God was merciful even in situations like this.

Lucy questioned what would happen if she died first. Through Ms. Jones and Mrs. Martinez, she learned that children born of a parent who has HIV do not always get the virus. This rekindled her hope that the baby she was carrying would not become infected with the virus, and she learned that the risk of transmission ranged from 30 to 70 percent. With Mrs. Martinez, Lucy explored her family's feelings about the situation. This was important information gathering.

Lucy's family was upset about her behavior when she returned. After sharing her diagnosis with them, they wept and expressed disbelief, and then became angry and demanded to know how she had gotten the HIV infection. Lucy was ashamed and worried about their reaction, fearing that they would reject and abandon her. She told them about Roberto's diagnosis and said she believed it was most likely due to his intravenous drug use.

The parents blamed Roberto and were much affected in another way by the news: their daughter was the only one of their children on whom they depended for their own care. As elderly parents, they had already been helped through several health crises by Lucy. They were both worried about what would happen to them; the possibility of having their child die first was doubly painful.

Mrs. Martinez learned the family was in crisis. Lucy's two brothers, who were both alcoholics and unmarried, offered no support. The parents were unsure about seeking support from their other relatives as they too feared rejection. Lucy's mother decided to tell her own sisters and brothers, who did become very sympathetic. Lucy's mother said many times that she wished this were happening to her instead of Lucy. Lucy's parents supported her decision to continue the pregnancy but were uncertain about their role in helping her negotiate care for herself and the baby. They worried about who would take care of them, as well as Lucy and the baby, as the disease progressed. They often felt helpless.

During the time of Lucy's pregnancy, she could not afford medical care, but through Mrs. Martinez' help, she had been monitored by the public health department. With the help of the public health department social worker, Mrs. Cunningham, she checked into a hospital emergency room for delivery of her child. The social worker had told the doctor of Lucy's medical condition. The doctor and the staff members were most supportive. The hospital had bilingual personnel, including another medical social worker who spoke Spanish and worked closely with Mrs. Cunningham. This helped, as in times of severe crisis Lucy would speak in her native tongue. The hospital staff members were sensitive to the risks associated with infected blood and took precautions in their own behalf. Through Mrs. Cunningham, they made plans to help Lucy with issues she would face in testing the baby for HIV. The hospital staff did everything they could to help her with the bonding process, including bringing the child to her immediately upon her recovery from anesthesia following the birth. They knew that Lucy's diagnosis and the resulting physical and emotional issues could negatively affect the bonding process.

Baby Anna, like many other children born to HIV-positive parents, tested positive at birth. Because of the mother's condition, Anna would have to be tested at six-month intervals to determine whether she did indeed have HIV. This uncertainty was difficult for Lucy, her parents, and the extended family. Lucy was ready for discharge from the hospital within three days of the delivery; however, due to the condition of newborn jaundice, the baby was not ready and needed more extensive observation. Even with Mrs. Cunningham's encouragement, Lucy had difficulty returning to see Anna during the first few days, and, out of anger and frustration, again fled, leaving Anna in the hospital. Lucy's parents feared that Lucy's shame might put her at risk for suicide.

Lucy's disappearance precipitated another referral to the child welfare agency. When Lucy returned two weeks later, she was told by Mrs. Martinez that she would need to meet with her on a regular basis, as she was no longer a voluntary client. Although Lucy had begun the process as a voluntary client, at this point she became an involuntary client as she stormed out of Mrs. Martinez' office, frightened and angry. She went directly to the hospital, where Mrs. Cunningham found her later. Mrs. Cunningham spoke of the agency's concern for Anna, Lucy, her son Jose, and the entire family. She explained to Lucy that Mrs.

CASE EXAMPLE 10.5 *(Continued)*

Martinez, in the change manager role, would help her obtain the services that she and her children would need in the upcoming months as her disease progressed.

Mrs. Martinez and Lucy discussed the need for a permanent plan for both children in case of Lucy's death. She felt that her family would be more reluctant than she to accept these services. Mrs. Martinez and Lucy discussed the traditional cultural differences for Lucy's family. Her parents believed that help should not come from an agency but rather from family resources. Mrs. Martinez, with Lucy's help, did an assessment of her situation. Additionally, she collected other information establishing that before her diagnosis, Lucy had held a job as a part-time waitress. After being diagnosed, she returned and informed her employers, who were at first supportive, placing her in another position as a hostess. Afraid of losing business, however, they laid her off. There was no labor union available to speak for Lucy. Lucy lost her sole source of income and important relationships with her co-workers.

Lucy was then forced to apply for government assistance to help with her medical expenses and the support of her two children. She had two different experiences with the welfare system. Her first income-maintenance social worker was well trained regarding HIV, and he was especially helpful. The worker, Mr. Perrales, understood the cognitive, physical, and psychological stresses accompanying AIDS, and when Lucy was too exhausted or too ill to make an office appointment, Mr. Perrales would make a home visit. Unfortunately, Mr. Perrales was transferred. The second worker, Ms. Likert, had not had the AIDS training and became angry at Lucy's lack of follow-through on obtaining verifying documents. Ms. Likert had Lucy's financial assistance cut off for one month.

As Lucy's medical condition began to deteriorate, she asked for Mrs. Martinez' help again. At this time, she again became a voluntary client and part of the client system. Mrs. Martinez referred her to a family-based, in-home social worker, Ms. Floyd, who discussed her fear of what would happen to her parents and her children. They also discussed in very practical terms the impact of the losses of body functioning and the control over her life which she was beginning to experience. Meeting with her in her home, the team discussed Lucy's fear of loneliness and how to handle the intensity and variability of her feelings. The team talked to her about her ability to live with as much dignity as possible and about her making decisions as long as she could. Old issues emerged as she discussed her concerns with the team, particularly her family's alcohol abuse. Her parents agreed to join with the team and Lucy to discuss these issues. The social worker helped her talk about the sad ending of her life, including how to discuss her death with her parents and children.

As Lucy's disease progressed, she needed respite care when she was sick and medical follow-up for both herself and Anna. The family-based team provided her with a family support worker (homemaker) to provide respite care in her home and help with the daily housework which Lucy was no longer able to complete. The family support worker and the family-based social worker supported Jose, who often seemed to be overlooked as he faced the impending death of his mother and sister. This attention helped him deal with some of his fears about himself, AIDS, and the future.

Through discussions with Mrs. Martinez and the family-based teams, Lucy decided to place Anna with foster parents who might eventually adopt the child. Lucy feared that as her disease progressed, she would have memory losses and that she would not be able to take care of her children. Jose's father could care for him during these times and at the time of her death, but there were no resources within either Lucy or Roberto's families for child care. Although Lucy's parents and extended family were unhappy about this decision, feeling that something should be done within the family, they acknowledged that they were unable to take care of Anna. Mrs. Martinez and the in-home team worked extensively with them about feeling more comfortable with this decision as this decision was counter to what the community wanted. The fact that Mrs. Martinez was bilingual and Puerto Rican helped a great deal. As the plan was implemented, the foster parents made the commitment to take the baby for short-term care when Lucy's medical needs were overwhelming. If Anna outlived her mother, the foster family was willing to adopt her.

The foster parents, the Garcias, discussed the obstacles to bonding and the baby's needs with Lucy. When Anna received medical treatment and had to be hospitalized, they told her how afraid they felt. Their ability to be open with Lucy and share their feelings was viewed as a strength by Mrs. Martinez. The Garcias saw the baby regress after she was hospitalized and unable to sit up. They also told Lucy of the frustrations of community relations and their own family's criticism for taking a child who might have AIDS. The Garcias' strength and willingness to participate as foster parents were viewed as a strength. Lucy saw that the foster parents had feelings similar to hers. They, too, lived with the uncertainty of this disease. A bonding was beginning to emerge between Lucy and the Garcias, making her feel more comfortable with her decision to place Anna in foster care and the implementation of the plan.

During Lucy's illness, her friends kept in contact with her. Her friends called frequently, asking what they could do to help her. But a number of friends were reluctant to allow their children to play with Jose or Anna. This was disturbing to Lucy, who was surprised to note who stuck by her and who gradually faded away. Anticipating this deterioration of the informal resource system, Mrs. Martinez had arranged for Lucy's children to begin playing in a church day-care center which allowed AIDS children to participate in their activities. As Lucy met some of the other parents, she began to build friendships that replaced, to some degree, those that had fallen away.

Jose, however, did not receive the same friendly reception at his school. The school became a source of contention for Lucy. Wanting to protect him from discrimination, she

asked him to tell no one about her illness. This was a difficult burden for him. He felt lonely and began to have difficulty concentrating in class. Referred to the principal, Jose was disciplined by isolating him from others, which made Lucy more unhappy about Jose's loneliness. In an advocate role, with Lucy's permission, Mrs. Martinez and Mr. Jones, a legal aid attorney, spoke with the principal and helped educate Jose's teacher about his situation and his needs.

Through Mrs. Martinez' suggestion, the Garcias, the foster parents, contacted the school system to enroll Anna in the infant-stimulation program, but the school refused. As an advocate, Mrs. Martinez helped the foster parents and Lucy successfully appeal the school's decision by going to the program's supervisor.

Lucy developed a positive relationship with the local legal aid lawyer, Mr. Jones, and the children's court judge and sought their help, through Mrs. Martinez, with a permanent plan for her children. Together they designed a will that allowed for Anna's adoption after Lucy's death. They also helped her spell out a plan for Lucy's family to visit Anna in the adoptive home. Mrs. Martinez served in the brokering role by contacting each of these key individuals. Lucy felt a great deal of support from these members of the action system, including the attorney's advocacy on the family's behalf with the school system.

Lucy lived in a federal housing project. Her neighbors seemed supportive, but the project director was nervous about her presence. Until the time she could no longer live by herself with in-home support, the director frequently commented on the impact of the disease on the others in the projects. Lucy felt that the message was, "We can't force you to leave, but it would be best if you choose to leave." The month she was without Aid to Families with Dependent Children and was unable to pay the rent, she was harassed for making a late payment and threatened with eviction. Mrs. Martinez stepped in to help influence the housing director, Mr. Martin, to change his mind about an eviction.

Lucy was soon unable to keep her diagnosis

(Continued)

CASE EXAMPLE 10.5   *(Continued)*

a secret. Her neighborhood responded in a variety of ways. Some people tried to raise money to help her with medical bills; others shunned her and her family. Some referred to Lucy's house as "the house of AIDS." Some parents wanted to keep Jose out of school and Anna out of her early-childhood program.

Lucy died a short two years after her diagnosis. Jose went to live with his father, and Anna's foster parents began the adoption process. The plan that Lucy had so lovingly designed with Mrs. Martinez was fully implemented. Anna's grandparents and extended family maintained regular contact with her, enabled by the cooperation of the Garcias.

Case outline contributed by Patricia Sandau-Beckler, 1991.

Cast of Characters

Change System — Child Welfare Agency

Change Agent — Mrs. Martinez

Client Systems

Anna and Jose
Grandparents

Potential client — Lucy

Focal System

Lucy

Roberto

Extended family

Neighbors

Employers

Ms. Likert — Income-maintenance worker

Jose's teacher and principal

Program's supervisor

Mr. Martin — housing director

Action System

Ms. Jones — Testing Center social worker

Priest

Mrs. Cunningham — Public health social worker

Hospital staff

Mr. Perrales — Income support worker

Ms. Floyd — In-home worker

Mr. Santos — Jose's father

Mr. and Mrs. Garcia — Foster parents

Neighbors

Case Analysis

The skills necessary to implement the plan in Case Example 10.5 included nearly all of those discussed in this chapter. Mrs. Martinez used the change management strategy to assist family members in the long, painful process associated with AIDS. Even during the time of Lucy's failing health, Mrs. Martinez implemented the overall plan of the placement of the children and the continued visitation. Mrs. Martinez helped the family become empowered through her enabler and educator roles, and she assisted through the advocate role to exercise influence at key junctures.

As promised in the last two chapters, we will use this case to illustrate a precontract assessment and a contract that includes a generalist plan. Note how the systems principles and models are applied. After the contract and plan, we will review the implementation roles and skills employed by Mrs. Martinez and the action system.

Assessment (Precontract)

Areas of Concern

Client System

1. HIV disease impact on Lucy emotionally, socially, and medically.
2. Arranging permanent plan for children upon death or inability to provide adequate care.
3. Son Jose's discrimination at school.
4. Daughter Anna's HIV-positive medical condition.
5. Lucy's discrimination by both formal and informal systems including income-maintenance, housing, and friends.

Change System

1. Lucy's ongoing issues with death and dying.
2. Lucy and her children's discrimination within societal systems.
3. Lucy's extended family and permanency planning for Jose and Anna.
4. Cultural contexts of providing for care for Lucy.
5. Lack of education and training in social systems.

Focal System

Societal Social Systems:

1. Inadequate knowledge and fears of Lucy and her children.

Family and Friends Informal Systems:

2. Denial and fear of contamination.
3. Family—informal systems—guilt over inability to provide care for Lucy and her children, particularly given cultural context.
4. Family—shame and guilt over drug and alcohol behavior.

Medical Staff:

5. Lack of understanding about cultural healing.

Action System

1. Inadequate staff and resources to care for HIV-positive families and children.
2. Fears of contagion and guilt about expressing fear of AIDS.
3. Lack of knowledge about what to expect or how to engage HIV-positive client systems.
4. Lack of funds for training for prevention.

Service Barriers (Risks)

1. Lack of knowledge of general public.
2. Lack of adequate legislation and policy to protect against discrimination.

3. Income-maintenance workers' lack of training about HIV-positive clients and medical deterioration.

4. School system's lack of resources and knowledge or support for siblings.

5. Lucy's deteriorating condition such as memory loss.

6. Housing director's fear of AIDS clients.

7. Further discrimination.

8. Lack of cultural sensitivity.

Resources

Client System Strengths:

1. Lucy recognizes and admits HIV infection.

2. Lucy's willingness to work with child protection and in-home services.

3. Lucy's willingness to work on death and dying issues.

4. Lucy's interest in a permanent plan for her children, recognizing cultural pressures.

5. Lucy's interest in protecting her children from discrimination and willingness to use systems to advocate on their behalf.

6. Lucy's concern for her parents.

Change System's Strengths:

1. Human Services funding for in-home services.

2. Knowledge about HIV virus and client systems and recognition of what to expect.

3. Home-based team of counselor and respite-care worker willingness to work where Lucy needs support.

4. Knowledge of permanency planning.

5. Knowledge of generalist social work practice skills of problem solving with systems change at all levels.

Focal System's Strengths:

1. School recognizes lack of prevention funding and resources.

2. Lucy's family's willingness to meet with in-home social worker and to provide emotional support to Lucy and her children.

3. Income-maintenance units' willingness to get training for workers.

4. Lucy's willingness to recognize siblings' drug and alcohol dependency and take that into account in making decisions for permanent planning for her children.

5. Old and new friends giving support to Lucy and her family.

Action System Strengths:

1. Church openness and willingness to support networks for AIDS clients.

2. Agency willingness to develop support groups for HIV-positive clients and their families.

3. School's willingness to explore AIDS education for students.

4. Legislative bodies' willingness to entertain legislation mandating education, social services, and protection from discrimination.

Service Opportunities

1. To develop community task force.

2. To develop AIDS curriculum.

3. To develop legal advocacy network.

4. To develop policy and laws to protect HIV-positive individuals from discrimination.

5. To develop training for all human services, school, and medical professionals who deal with HIV-positive client systems.

6. To develop general public awareness for all persons dealing with HIV-positive client systems.

7. To develop culturally sensitive services for HIV-positive clients.

8. To develop adequate funding for HIV-positive client systems.

Contract

Goal: Lucy, her children and groups of people like Lucy will receive adequate, nondiscriminatory systems' response to their HIV-positive status.

Small Systems — Objective #1: To provide Lucy with supervision and support so she can adequately care for her children within the context of her medical condition.

Activity/Client System Task	*Change Systems Task*
Lucy will meet with in-home worker and design a schedule for friends, neighbors, family, and respite-care workers.	In-home worker will coordinate respite-care worker for Lucy's and children's support and supervision. Worker will assess Lucy's capabilities with medical system to provide care.
Time Frame: 1 week	Time Frame: 1 week

Small Systems — Objective #2: To provide Lucy with in-home services to help her deal with psychosocial impact of HIV disease on her ability to provide child care and to develop permanent plan for children.

Activity/Client System Task	*Change Systems Task*
Lucy will meet with in-home worker 2 hours per week.	In-home worker will meet with Lucy to work on death, dying, and loss issues, and to explore permanent plan options.
Time Frame: 8 weeks	Time Frame: 8 weeks

Family Systems—Objective #3: To meet with Lucy's extended family to discuss loss and grief issues.

Activity/Client System Task	*Change Systems Task*
Lucy and her parents will meet with in-home workers for five sessions every other week.	In-home worker will meet with Lucy's extended family to educate them about stages of grieving and loss issues, including Kübler-Ross's stages of death and dying.
Time Frame: 10 weeks	Time Frame: 10 weeks

Family Systems—Objective #4: To provide Lucy's family with information about permanency planning and the child welfare system.

Activity/Client System Task	*Change Systems Task*
To meet with in-home workers and discuss permanency planning biweekly.	To meet with Lucy's family and provide information on child welfare system and legal processes for permanency planning.
Time Frame: 10 weeks	Time Frame: 10 weeks

Group—Objective #5: For Lucy to network and build a "buddy" support system of HIV-positive group members.

Activity/Client System Task	*Change Systems Task*
To meet with group members and find two members with whom to develop a "buddy system."	Group workers and group to network and find "buddies" for Lucy.
Time Frame: 2 weeks	Time Frame: 2 weeks

Group—Objective #6: To provide emotional support for Lucy's loss issues and "roller coaster" emotional reactions to HIV disease.

Activity/Client System Task	*Change Systems Task*
Lucy will meet in group and seek support for loss issues and emotional reactions to HIV disease.	Workers and group will provide Lucy with mutual aid.
Time Frame: weekly	Time Frame: weekly
Ongoing support for 3 months.	Ongoing support for 3 months.

Agency Systems—Objective #7: To provide income-maintenance agency with training about expectations for HIV-positive clients.

Activity/Focal System on Behalf of Client System Task	*Change Systems Task*
Administration will design workshop for income-maintenance workers.	To help network administration with maintenance plans, education, and training project to fund instructor or provide training.
Time Frame: 3 months	Time Frame: 3 months

Agency Systems — Objective #8: To provide housing director with information on contagion of AIDS.

Activity/Focal System on Behalf of Client System Task	*Change Systems Task*
Meet with in-home worker to discuss HIV contagion and address issues for protection of rights of HIV-positive clients.	In-home worker to meet with Mr. Alexander and discuss HIV contagion. Address issues for protection of civil rights of HIV-positive clients.
Time Frame: 2 weeks	Time Frame: 2 weeks

Large Systems — Objective #9: To increase public awareness of HIV disease by 20 percent.

Activity/Focal System on Behalf of Client System Task	*Change Systems Task*
Develop community task force to increase public awareness of HIV disease.	To serve as co-chair of community task force to increase public awareness of HIV disease.
Time Frame: monthly meetings for one year.	Time Frame: monthly meetings for one year.

Large Systems — Objective #10: To increase services and education in the school system.

Activity/Focal System on Behalf of Client System Task	*Change Systems Task*
School administration to work with school board on permission to obtain further grant monies for developing services and training on HIV disease. This is coordinated with in-home workers.	Write start-up grant with school administration for services and training on HIV disease.
Time Frame: 4 months	Time Frame: 4 months

Implementation: Roles and Skills

AIDS cases are made very complex due to the number of systems involved (social, economic, health, and biological, for example), inevitable death, the myths surrounding AIDS, and the fact we have not developed delivery systems for this new area of concern. The context of Lucy's case, a low-income Puerto Rican urban setting, and the human diversity issues of a culturally close neighborhood, demanded generalist roles and skills.

1. *Social Broker.* Mrs. Martinez made extensive use of her brokering role and referral skills when guiding Lucy to various programs and services. With so many services being provided by so many persons, it was critical to monitor, to keep up with all that was happening. Accuracy of information was critical.

2. *Power Broker.* Mrs. Martinez' knowledge, use of authority, and use of members of the action system was important in obtaining Anna and Jose's rights in school. How could a labor union have leveraged for Lucy's right to a job?

3. *Collaborator.* Numerous agencies worked with Lucy, many at the same time. Consistency, forged by Mrs. Martinez, in how the agencies collaborated with Lucy, was critical. What happened when there was a change in income-maintenance workers? Were the various actors in the action system able to agree on goals? It appears when programs were not able to agree with Lucy's goal, those persons became part of the focal system, such as the principal. How could Mrs. Martinez dissolve the myths and stereotypes held by the various disciplines involved? Did the "crisis" nature of Lucy's case help?

4. *Enabler.* Ultimately, by Mrs. Martinez letting Lucy make a plan for her children and by deciding to carry the pregnancy to term, Lucy was empowered. When Lucy fled, Mrs. Martinez exercised her authority to protect the children. Mrs. Martinez allowed Lucy to do as much as she could on her own behalf.

5. *Educator.* Mrs. Martinez and several of the action system members helped educate Lucy on the issue of AIDS and her legal options.

6. *Counselor.* Mrs. Martinez and Ms. Floyd, the in-home worker, counseled Lucy by providing unconditional positive regard and support. At times, Mrs. Martinez had to confront Lucy, while at other times, she expressed empathy and helped her reframe situations.

7. *Conflict Manager.* At times, Mrs. Martinez used her mediating skills with Lucy and her family and neighbors by helping the family tune in to Lucy's and their own needs, come together, and work on the issues.

8. *Advocate.* To implement the plan and manage a large action system, Mrs. Martinez needed to exercise influence in many creative ways. The focal system was often dealing from deep-seated fear of the unknown. In the advocate role, Mrs. Martinez used inductive questioning with the principal and the infant program's supervisor. She presented both sides to Lucy regarding the plan for foster care and adoption. Finally, persistence, driven by the life-and-death reality of an AIDS case, was used by Mrs. Martinez to promote change.

CONCLUSION

Implementation is the "doing" of the change process. This active stage only takes place after the careful groundwork of information gathering, assessment, designing, and planning have been completed. Implementation includes the roles and skills necessary to put the plan into action. The strategies of (1) change management, (2) encouraging empowerment, and (3) exercising influence promote the change process. As we saw in the assessment and plan of Case Example 10.5, not only are small systems involved, but large systems and policies are also part of the case.

Evaluation in social work is completed at the case level as well as the program level. Each component of evaluation is presented in the following chapter. In the next chapter, we will also see how the change process ends for the social worker as the client system moves toward independence.

References

Baer, Betty L., and Federico, Ronald. (1978). *Educating the Baccalaureate Social Worker: Report of the Undergraduate Social Work Curriculum Development Project.* Cambridge, MA: Ballinger.

Bertsche, Anne V., and Horejsi, Charles. (1980). "Coordination of client services." *Social Work, 25,* 94–98.

Briar, S., and Blythe, B. J. (1985). "Agency Support for Evaluating the Outcomes of Social Work Services." *Administration in Social Work, 9*(2), 25–36.

Compton, Beulah, and Galaway, Burt. (1989). *Social Work Process,* 4th ed. Belmont, CA: Wadsworth, pp. 151 and 607.

Ellis, Albert. (1977). "The Basic Clinical Theory of Rational-Emotive Therapy." In A. Ellis and R. Grieger (eds.), *Handbook of Rational Emotive Therapy.* New York: Springer.

Fischer, Joel. (1978). *Effective Casework Practice: An Eclectic Approach.* New York: Mc-Graw-Hill.

Galper, Jeffrey. (1980). *Social Work Practice: A Radical Perspective.* Englewood Cliffs, NJ: Prentice-Hall.

Hoffman, Kay, and Charbonneau, Gerald. (1986). *A Prevention Model for Family Violence.* Paper presented at the 32nd Annual Program Meeting, Council on Social Work Education, Miami, Florida.

Hoffman, Kay, and Sallee, Alvin L. (1990). "Follow-up Study on BSW Social Workers: Implications for Generalist Education and Practice." Paper presented at the 36th Annual Program Meeting, Council on Social Work Education, Reno, Nevada.

Johnson, Louise. (1992). *Social Work Practice: A Generalist Approach,* 4th ed. Boston: Allyn & Bacon.

Kübler-Ross, Elizabeth. (1970). *On Death and Dying.* New York: MacMillan.

LeVine, E., and Sallee, A. (1992). *Listen to Our Children: Clinical Theory and Practice.* Dubuque, IA: Kendall/Hunt.

Lloyd, J. (1980). *Placement Prevention and Family Reunification: A Handbook for the Family Centered Service Practitioner,* Rev. Iowa City, IA: National Resource Center on Family-Based Services, pp. 79 and 144.

Magura, S. (1982). "Clients View Outcomes of Child Protective Services." *Social Casework,*
63, 522–531.

Maples, James J. (1991). "Foresight First." *Sky* (Delta Airlines), pp. 96 and 100.

Pincus, Allen, and Minahan, Anne. (1973). *Social Work Practice: Model & Method.* Itasca,
IL: F. E. Peacock.

Reid, William J. (1983). "Developing Methods through Experimental Designs." In Aaron
Rosenblatt and Diane Waldfogel (eds.), *Handbook of Clinical Social Work.* San Francisco: Jossey-Bass, p. 655.

Saleebey, Dennis. (1992). *The Strengths Perspective in Social Work Practice.* New York:
Longman, pp. 8–9.

Sandau-Beckler, Patricia. (1991). Case outline for Case Example 10.5.

Shaw, Malcolm, et al. (1980). *Role Playing: A Practical Guide for Group Facilitators.* San
Diego, CA: University Associates.

Sheafor, B., Horejsi, C. R., and Horejsi, G. A. (1991). *Techniques and Guidelines for Social Work Practice,* 2nd ed. Boston: Allyn & Bacon, p. 37.

Shulman, L. (1982). *The Skills of Helping Individuals and Groups.* Itasca, IL: F. E. Peacock.

Shulman, L. (1986). *A Casebook of Social Work with Groups: The Mediating Model.* New
York: Council on Social Work Education.

Shulman, Lawrence. (1991). *Interactional Social Work Practice: Toward an Empirical Theory.* Itasca, IL: F. E. Peacock, p. 142.

Simons, Ronald L., and Aigner, Stephen M. (1985). *Practice Principles: A Problem-Solving
Approach to Social Work.* New York: MacMillan, pp. 127 and 135–136.

Siporin, Max. (1975). *Introduction to Social Work Practice.* New York: MacMillan, p. 248.

Chapter 11

Evaluation and Transition

OVERVIEW

This chapter focuses upon the final segment of the Crystal Model—Evaluation and Transition. Although evaluation and transition are found at the end of the change process, their seeds are planted much earlier. The two steps are actualized in the final stages of the social work process, but successful movement through evaluation and termination is predicated on success in earlier stages of the Crystal Model. Evaluation begins during the contract step when goals are discussed, while transition begins when the entire change process, including its ending, is explained to the client system.

Evaluation and Social Research

Evaluation in social work is based upon the central questions of any planned change: Was the change effort successful? Did the client system achieve the agreed-upon aims? Did the client system receive the contracted services? The answers to those questions (1) tell us about our own effectiveness as practitioners, (2) tell us about the effectiveness of programs and services we provide for clients, and (3) lead us toward an improved change effort. Evaluation helps client systems understand the changes in their lives and affords them the opportunity to decide how they will continue once mutual contacts have ended.

Evaluation is one of the uses of social research, but not the whole of research. Research in the social sciences is often divided among the following patterns: basic research, applied research, and evaluation research (Miller, 1991, p. 3). Basic research is aimed toward developing new knowledge, while applied research directs itself toward solving social problems placed before the researcher. Evaluation research assesses the effectiveness of programs and practice. (See Figure 11.1.)

Social workers most likely engage in applied research and evaluation research.

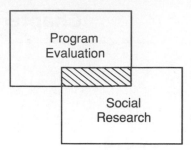

FIGURE 11.1 Evaluation and
Social Research Relationship

Some researchers fail to make a distinction between the two. In order to become adept in applied and evaluative research, basic research theory and methodology must be understood. In fact, there is a reciprocal relationship between the two. Sloppy methodology, ungrounded in basic research, will not help us understand our own practice and programs. Likewise, basic research that neglects the needs of the real world will lose its meaning. Thus, the relationship between applied/evaluative and basic research is clear (Miller, 1991).

Research and Social Work Practice

Social workers have resisted setting evaluation procedures in place because their experiences with social research during their social work education has often been negative. Research classes may seem unrelated to the everyday world of practice and field work (Block, 1978, pp. 55–59). However, renewed interest in applied and evaluative research in agencies, universities, and funding sources is changing the face of social work practice.

Social workers deal with society's most complex social problems—problems that, when left untended, multiply. We strive to find the best solutions to the most difficult questions. Government spends millions on caring for the chronically mentally ill, while comparatively little money is spent on discerning what are the most effective means to assist people whose lives have been shattered by illness. Social work research is directed toward finding ways to enhance practice and program effectiveness so that individuals, families, groups, communities, and organizations will be enhanced.

This chapter does not present an exhaustive study of social work research or evaluation of practice. In fact, our treatment of this segment of the Crystal Model is introductory. Our purpose is only to give you a flavor of evaluation research so that you begin to create the necessary associations between research and practice. We hope students will become "research-practice–aware," and develop a mindset regarding this inextricable link.

Transitions and Endings

Transitions take the client system and the social work generalist to the next phase—a renewed change effort, a different change effort, or an ending. Positive transitions use the knowledge gained from evaluation to move toward a new place.

Social work practice has historically referred to its last phase of work with clients as termination. It was assumed that if the social work process with client systems were successful, contact between the client system and the social agency would be ended. We are beginning to see the last phase of the process in a broader context (Shapiro, 1980).

Recognizing that our work with clients may uncover a variety of areas of concern, clients may be referred to other programs to assist them with additional situations. For example, working with older persons in a time-limited group, Carla Jackson, the social worker, realizes that several members of the group who are widows need additional help in wending their way through the grieving process. Additionally, two group members, both elderly women, were suffering from recurring depression, a condition both had been dealing with for over fifty years. Carla knew that once the group ended, her contacts with several group members would not end, but the foci of her continued contact would be altered.

An even more potent example of a direction away from termination and toward transition involves crisis-intervention contacts that may be singular, the only contact we have (Golan, 1978). A telephone crisis worker discusses an adolescent woman's ordeal involving her boyfriend who left her. Amanda was heartsick, depressed, and even talked of suicide. The crisis worker listened, made a quick assessment, and referred her to ongoing counseling and a group at a nearby health clinic. Amanda sounded positive about the help offered and the follow-up call a week later revealed that, indeed, she had entered counseling. In her case, Amanda certainly did not terminate; rather she participated in a transition to another phase of helping.

As a way of setting the stage before proceeding into the heart of the discussion on evaluation and transition, we begin by reviewing the Crystal Model in relationship to evaluation and transition, followed by mention of the Baer and Federico competency that fits most appropriately with this segment of the change process.

The Crystal Model: Evaluation and Transition

The ending of the change process provides the opportunity to review the Crystal Model, emphasizing the relationships among all the phases in the model. Planned change is not a linear process; in fact, when working with people we can be simultaneously engaged in several steps of the process. Evaluation and transition are clearly illustrative of this concept. When we begin with a client system, identifying an area of concern and engaging the client in the change process, we are also beginning an evaluation.

Consider what may happen if our initial approach with a client system is based on false assumptions. In other words, if we have begun our work with a client system, identifying not the central area of concern to the client and never actually engaging the client in the change process, the results of the faulty evaluation process have been put into place. Perhaps we will not know until the evaluation has ended that our focus was incorrect from the beginning, but the outcomes the client system and the social worker observe will help us know where the change effort lost its way or became sidetracked. A thorough evaluation process permits us to see what went wrong and where (in the change process) the mistakes occurred.

No other step in the Crystal Model affords our seeing the ongoing interrelatedness of a nonlinear conception of planned change. Assessments are the bases for the designing and planning as well as the implementation of those designs and plans. We have emphasized their importance in carrying out change. Again, evaluation points to the relationships among phases in the change effort by giving the social worker and the client system the opportunity to weigh the correctness of assessment as well as the effectiveness of the plan.

The course a client system takes once evaluation and the entire change process ends also illustrates the interrelatedness of the change process. Endings with client systems take a multitude of directions. Some clients continue their contact with the social work community; some have reconnected with networks that offer ongoing support; and some simply leave our purview. The quality of the client system's experience with the change effort, however, is often brought to bear on how the transition is made. An illustration of this is given in the following vignette.

Cindy

Cindy is a third-grader who has been seeing Rita Baker, the school social worker, for over three months. She was referred by her teacher because of her constant disruptions during class. The social worker, burdened by work in three different schools, saw Cindy every week, but was not able to contact the family regularly, nor work with Cindy in relationship to what was going on with Cindy at home. At the end of the school year, Cindy told Rita she was glad she didn't have to see her anymore because she was tired of being singled out in class by being sent to the social worker.

Cindy had made her own personal evaluation of the change effort and began the summer break with negative feelings about Rita. Cindy's transition may have left her with the idea that school social workers really don't help. Rita was also given the opportunity to evaluate and transition with Cindy. Not only did Rita think long and hard about her contacts with Cindy, but evaluated her entire work situation. Many of the children whom she had been seeing may have felt cheated in the process.

Rita's evaluation of the change effort with Cindy gave her the opportunity to look at each of her cases during the school year and develop a better program and plan for the next year, including an ongoing evaluation plan. She presented that plan to her supervisor in special education, and changes were made.

The rest of the chapter is devoted to the evaluation and transition phase of the change effort. You will be introduced to the purposes of evaluation, to tools in evaluation, and to skills the generalist must possess in order to make this segment effective. Likewise, the skills in transitions, special consideration regarding transitions, and expectations all of us hold about endings are presented.

The stage is set for evaluation and transition through a brief discussion of the competencies—that is, what you ought to come away with after you have mastered the final segment of the Crystal Model.

Competencies

Three Baer and Federico competencies (1978) are directly related to evaluation. It is interesting to note that none of the competencies is related to transitions or endings. This is a neglected area in social work education, and we hope our discussion in this chapter will shed some light on the subject. First, we present the competencies.

1. *Evaluate the extent to which the objectives of the intervention plan were achieved.* Evaluating the implementation plan focuses upon the program or service model that the client system and the worker put into place to bring about change. The extent to which it is possible to make such evaluations is based upon our having placed evaluation as a high priority during the change process. For example, if we have collected data relevant to the area of concern and used a valid scale as part of both information gathering and assessment, the evaluation we generate is based on sound data.

Every social work contact cannot begin with the administration of a scale, but we can be sure that our documentation is clear and concise and that the client system shares with the social worker a viewpoint that every component of the change process can be discussed and alterations in the way things are going can always be made. When an open attitude toward evaluation exists, the client system and the social worker can continuously measure the extent to which agreed-upon goals are met. This is most evident when the client system has participated in the mutual development of plans and goals.

2. *Continually evaluate one's own professional growth and development through assessment of practice behaviors and skills.* Our own practice skills and behaviors must be under our own and others' scrutiny if we are to continue to grow as professionals. Evaluating the extent to which service goals with clients are met, whether we are using a single-subject design or a program evaluation, should focus on the focal system's change and the client's goal attainment. Implicit in their change process is the idea that, as change agents, we may have had something to do with effective change. But focusing an evaluation entirely on client change may beg the question regarding our own professional growth.

Evaluating our skills may mean opening our practice to collegial evaluation. We may ask colleagues to view tapes (with client permission), read our documentation (maintaining confidentiality), or listen to our discussion of programs and client system concerns.

Ongoing evaluation also leads us to the use of professional literature and continuing education. Improvement in our own work only comes if we compare what we are doing to what is being done elsewhere in the field, critically analyze our work, and open ourselves to new ideas. Attitudes that allow us to grow are part of the mindset of the evaluation process. We can only evaluate what we are willing to display.

3. *Contribute to the improvement of service delivery by adding to the knowledge base of the profession as appropriate and by supporting and upholding the standards and ethics of the profession.* Adding to the knowledge base of the profession is a formidable expectation, but, in time, most social workers can make contributions that will assist colleagues and students. You may write papers based on your practice; you may give presentations that detail a program that is especially helpful, or you may teach students through field instruction. Adding to the knowledge base on a formal and informal basis must be a goal of all social workers and ought to become part of your repertoire as a professional social worker.

Of course, every evaluation in which you participate is predicated on upholding the standards and ethics of the profession. Data are collected only when clients are informed of the purposes and evaluations take place in the full view of the client system. In fact, we advocate sharing every part of the evaluation process with the client system because the evaluation is based upon client behavior and change. After all, who has more rights to being informed than the person or persons who are being evaluated?

Evaluation, according to the National Association of Social Workers' Code of Ethics, is a critical means for scientifically gaining additional knowledge and developing practice theory and techniques. The code of ethics also states responsible social work practice demands that our endeavors and social programs be monitored and evaluated for effectiveness. Evaluation is the appraisal of an implementation or a program, the measurement of its efficiency and effectiveness in terms of observable effects in their relation to stated objectives (Siporin, 1975). Evaluations and outcome research are done (1) to provide accountability, (2) to audit performance for administrative needs, and (3) to justify a social service program in terms of its cost relative to the benefits it provides (McKay and Baxter, 1980).

In all, evaluation must be guided by our values and principles derived from the code of ethics. Like other steps in the change process, our first consideration must always be the client system's integrity, dignity, and worth and our search for "good" data or knowledge development can never supersede our obligations to the persons we are serving.

EVALUATION IN GENERALIST PRACTICE

Direct Service and Program Evaluation

Evaluation occurs at two levels in generalist practice: the direct service level and the program level. At the direct service level, case evaluation measures the effectiveness of practice in relationship to client goals. A variety of techniques and de-

Evaluation is a critical phase in generalist social work practice.

signs are employed, but the process and ultimate expectations match with program evaluation.

The second level, program evaluation, focuses on the organizational component of our work. How social workers, administrators, as well as policy impacts upon programs are assessed. In both case evaluations and program evaluations, the central aim is the measurement of effectiveness (Miller, 1991, p. 103). We begin our discussion with concepts applicable to both levels of evaluation. Following that, several specific direct service evaluation models accompanied by case examples are presented, including single subject design, goal attainment scaling, ethnographic techniques, and content analysis. Program evaluation models, including an agency example, bring to a close the evaluation segment of the chapter.

Accountability

As individual practitioners, we are accountable to a number of audiences, as is the agency for which we work. In Figure 11.2, we present a form to help you decide to whom you are accountable and for what.

Accountability to a number of audiences drives the evaluation of social work practice (Briar, 1974). Ethical and financial considerations are at the core of accountability. Ethics in social work guarantee client systems' rights to quality ser-

FIGURE 11.2 Accountability Form

To Whom Are You Accountable?	For What?	How Can You Demonstrate Accountability to Each of These Audiences?
1.		
2.		
3.		
4.		
5.		
6.		
7.		
8.		

vice, and the only systematic way to ensure rights is through rigorous evaluation. How do we know if quality service has been delivered if systematic questions that are designed to measure the impact of our work on social problems are not asked?

Social service programs and agencies have lost enormous resources over the years. In fact, since 1981, when methodical dismantling of social welfare programs began, resources have been reduced from the federal to the state to the local levels.

Coupled with the dismantling of social programs has been a reemergence of the "blaming the victim" theme, a concept we have discussed at great length in this book. In an age in which individuals who receive assistance are often "scapegoated" for major social problems, social workers must provide solid information to policy makers regarding programs that are successful and that need continuous support.

Many of the concerns raised from the 1960s War on Poverty involved its supposed failure. In fact, perhaps the "failure" of the War on Poverty was more closely related to a misunderstanding of evaluation research than a failure of results.

Growing out of the necessity to educate students about rigorous, systematic evaluations as well as the important link between research and practice, social work education has included evaluation as a more central component of its mission. Inherent in the growing trend to embrace research is our own word of caution regarding the limits of social work research.

The Limits of Social Work Research

Accountability demands place evaluation as a high priority in many agencies and organizations, but high research costs and methodological problems call to question the kinds of evaluations that are accomplished and the findings these evaluations generate.

Gleaning our understanding of methodology from basic research, evaluation researchers attempted to duplicate the classical experimental design in evaluation research. Only by employing randomization techniques for choosing participants in research studies could we trust the results of evaluations.

In 1966, Campbell and Stanley coined the term "quasi-experiments" and used it to account for evaluation studies completed without randomization (Miller, 1991, p. 89). The limits of quasi-experimental designs are many, but their attempts at rigor and control have brought many useful findings in evaluation research.

Not only does design limit evaluation research, but so do ethical considerations because randomization, the sine qua non of experiments, cannot take place in the real world of case and program evaluations in agencies. For example, if we are testing the effectiveness of an alcohol-prevention program for adolescents that has been proven helpful with other populations, excluding candidates for the program in order to create experimental conditions in which effectiveness can be measured may cause an unsolvable ethical dilemma.

Concommitantly, in a world of scarce resources, when persons are denied even basic needs, allocating funds for research (that may in the long run pay off) puts agency administrators and program specialists in untenable situations. Organized groups of low-income people, specifically welfare rights groups, have great trouble understanding how money can be used for research when their children are denied free lunches at school, medical care, and decent housing. Ethical problems resulting from methodology and cost haunt social work researchers and influence every aspect of our work.

Even with this caveat, we support research—and research-mindedness—in practice. Every research effort may not be perfect, duplicating the expectations of basic research, but evaluation research methodologies and techniques have progressed in the past ten years. Universities see the value of applied and evaluation research, and social work researchers are making ongoing contributions to practice effectiveness. Social work research is a present need and a wave of the future, and students must become "friendlier" to the research endeavor.

Quantitative versus Qualitative Research

Distinctions between quantitative and qualitative research have played a large part in methodologies employed both in practice research and in program evaluation. In general, quantitative research is concerned with counting and finding relationships among events or people. Of course, simple counting is not the end result of quantitative research, but it does depend on numbers (Epstein, 1985). In addition, quantitative research is oriented toward objectivity and the use of valid measurement instruments (Rubin and Babbie, 1989, p. 364).

Qualitative research examines the essence of human experience and relies on participant observation (see Chapter 6) and inductive reasoning rather than on counting phenomena. In fact, Kirk and Miller (1986) characterize qualitative research as "research distinguished by the absence of counting" (p. 9).

Both quantitative and qualitative research methods are used by social workers, but basic disagreements regarding their respective "fit" with social work have developed over the years. Quantitative methods are certainly more clearly founded in basic research. Most research courses taught in social work programs throughout the country teach basic quantitative research as a beginning, fundamental building block for researchers. Qualitative methods are often relegated to elective courses in anthropology.

At the same time, a great many social workers believe that qualitative methods are much more in keeping with the work in which social workers engage, and methods that rely on unobstrusive measures fit social work needs and aims. Our position is that both methodologies are needed in social work research. In fact, given the complex nature of our contacts with client systems, integrating both methodologies seems the only choice (Allen-Meares, 1990, pp. 452–458).

Evaluation Skills

The skills required for evaluation can be grouped as (1) technical, (2) social, and (3) administrative (Kirkhart and Sallee, 1980). Technical skills are those needed to conduct social science research. Knowledge of evaluation research supports these skills. In Chapter 7, we discussed research links to theory and examined some of the technical skills. Specifically, these include data collection, statistical analysis, research design, and report writing. During your social work studies, you will probably take at least one course devoted entirely to learning these skills.

The social skills of evaluation include the interactional skills necessary to gain cooperation and support from other systems in order to conduct the evaluation. Social skills are necessary in either direct service evaluation or program evaluation. Convincing the client system and action system, not to mention the change system, of the necessity for evaluation draws on negotiation and conflict resolution roles. Social skills are also critical in the utilization of evaluation results—either in practice or in formulating new policies.

Administrative skills refer to the management skills necessary to oversee the process, such as tracking information or, in program evaluation, monitoring expenditures and adhering to deadlines. Monitoring even a single-subject design for a one-person client system requires discipline and time-management skills. In a large program evaluation, there may be a number of staff with salaries and operational budgets to administer. Generalist skills such as coordination and managing are employed in administering an evaluation.

Technical skills required for evaluation must be acquired by the generalist.

That does not mean that every B.S.W. or M.S.W. graduate must be a skilled researcher. However, both baccalaureate degree social workers and master's degree social workers must have obtained basic understanding of research skills and, most importantly, they must have the ability to evaluate their own practices and programs, even if that necessitates agency support for such ongoing activities.

Grinnell and Seigel (1988) advocate that all social workers understand the relationship between their everyday activities, in which they solve problems, with the steps in research. They are identical processes, and when social work generalists follow the logical steps of problem solving, they are beginning their work as "practical scientists."

We have emphasized the similar qualities of the Crystal Model with the steps in the scientific approach. The Crystal Model is more adaptable to the everyday lives of social workers and clients because there is a recognition of the constant change that occurs in life as opposed to the unchanging atmosphere of the scientific laboratory. Nonetheless, the similarities are far greater than the differences.

Planning the Evaluation

As with the other steps in the Crystal Model, doing one's homework ahead of time makes evaluation more effective and efficient. Most researchers agree that the planning stage determines the quality of work carried out in the research endeavor. One's first step in planning is to identify the characteristics and the context of what one is evaluating.

A useful checklist for helping us determine the feasibility of evaluation within an agency is known as the A-VICTORY method. A-VICTORY is an acronym for *Ability, Values, Information, Circumstances, Timing, Obligation, Resistances,* and *Yield.* Developed originally for mental health program evaluation, this model has been adapted for planning evaluations (Kirkhart and Sallee, 1980). Each point on the checklist is discussed in relationship to preparation for evaluating direct services and program evaluation.

Ability

Determining one's own abilities to undertake evaluation is the first step in the planning process. Questions regarding knowledge base, appropriateness of knowledge, and skill attainment must be asked. Administrators planning an evaluation must assess these qualities as they relate to the staff who may be participating in the research project. For example, a generalist social worker may wish to do a "pre/post" study of a group he or she has led, and the most appropriate statistical analysis to use turns out to be multiple regression. Few generalist social workers have had the statistics courses necessary to use the multiple regression technique adequately. Such limitations must be accounted for at the beginning of the evaluation.

In addition, it is essential to calculate the resources, both fiscal and supportive, that are available, prior to the research. Are the fiscal and time resources adequate for the study of this type of group? Lacking adequate resources, the chances the evaluation will be used are limited and thus fail its intended purpose. These questions need to be answered to determine if the individuals and the change system agency have the abilities to undertake a specific type of evaluation, whether it be direct service or program.

Values

As with all social work practice, values play a critical role in determining the type of evaluation and the method in which it is carried out. We discussed the ethical considerations that must be met before any research takes place. However, value conflicts may also play a part in determining the feasibility of a research project.

For example, is the evaluation consistent with the social, religious, political, and ethnic values of the client system? Is the evaluation consistent with the philosophies and policies of the change agent system and the funding sources? What about organizational values? Is the director of the organization supportive of this type of evaluation, whether it be in direct service or an overall program evaluation? Finally, are the characteristics of the organization such that the evaluation results will be used to improve practice? These questions help guide our understanding of the values of the social worker performing the evaluation as well as the organizational cultural values.

Information

The information about the evaluation purpose and how it will be carried out needs to be made clear to the client system and any others who may use the evaluation. If the research is to be used for direct service evaluation, is the information about the evaluation relevant to either the program goals or the client system goals?

Research cannot be begun or completed without full disclosure to those involved. Again, we have discussed this aspect of research in relationship to ethical guidelines.

Circumstances

If a program evaluation is to be replicated, questions regarding the circumstances under which the current program is to be evaluated must be ascertained. Are the conditions in this setting similar to those where the evaluation design may have been implemented and found useful? For example, an evaluation of a short-term, basic-need provision program was successfully completed and used. Attempting to implement the evaluation in a program in which service delivery was offered on an ongoing, rather than short-term, basis would not meet the criterion. On the surface, the two programs may seem similar, but the differences in time allocated for service delivery are far too great.

Timing

Finding the right time to complete an evaluation is essential if the evaluation is to be helpful. There may be circumstances in direct service cases in which the evaluation could detract from the implementation of the client's plan. For example, perhaps a family with whom you are working has complained that the change system with which they have dealt over the past two years has done nothing but assess them and make them fill out forms and measure their ability to improve, and now they really want freedom from such intense scrutiny. This is probably not the most appropriate time to talk to them about a single-subject design evaluation!

Timing might be appropriate with an agency that is preparing for an accreditation study. The staff members and administration are willing to look at themselves, and, as part of the accreditation process, an evaluation of the entire program might be put in place.

Obligation

The need for the evaluation exercise needs to be ascertained. Does an agency think it needs to be evaluated, or does it view it as a nuisance and/or a threat? Does the individual who is providing services and with whom you may be working feel he or she needs to be part of an evaluation? The obligation for the evaluation also needs to be compared with the other needs of the client system or, in a program evaluation, the needs of the organization or agency.

Resistances

If resistances to evaluation arise from clients, staff members, or other agency personnel, it is important to consider all the reasons noted for not undertaking an evaluation. They must be considered even if the evaluation will eventually take place. Beginning an evaluation without understanding resistances may result in an abandoned project. A whole new series of problems usually develop when undertakings fall short of expectations.

One resistance that we often confront when evaluating performance is the possible negative side effects of implementing an evaluation and the possible effects of negative results. We need to take these into consideration from a "what is the worst case scenario" perspective.

Perhaps an agency has very good public relations, is well thought of in the community, and has made the right political connections with key policy makers. The funding sources continue to fund the agency with little requirements for accountability. Great resistance to program evaluation might be encountered in this agency. There may be a fear the evaluation will show that there are things the program is not doing effectively, or that perhaps the program is causing client systems more harm than good. We would want to know this before launching an evaluation of this program. Knowing that resistance to the process is high, we will employ social and interpersonal skills before using our technical skills.

Yield

Yield is what each system will gain from investing in the evaluation program. We want a return of useful information from the allocation of time, money, and energy to the evaluation process. For example, what benefits will a social work practitioner receive through evaluating his or her work with a family, group, or community? What is an agency or a program going to get out of investing in an evaluation process? Part of the yield is identifying unexpected outcomes and understanding how these might be examined in the future. You want to evaluate very carefully the benefits of the evaluation and be sure that the investment warrants the possible yield.

The A-VICTORY technique help us take into consideration the questions that need to be answered in any evaluation, whether it be direct service or program. Certainly, at the beginning stages of the evaluation, these questions cannot all be definitively answered, but their consideration will help guide the conduct and timing of the evaluation.

What Is to Be Evaluated?

Specifying exactly what is to be evaluated is essential in both direct service and program evaluation. Asking clear research questions likely results in findings that can be readily applied to one's work. In addition, the research proposal, likely a precursor of a program evaluation, begins with a clear understanding and statement of the problem.

We again remind you of the Crystal Model and the change process. In the beginning, we defined (with our clients) the areas of concern. Defining the concern or problem with clients is exactly what is done in evaluation research.

We must understand just what needs to be evaluated. There are five areas of concern that are generally the bases of evaluation research. They are: (1) effort, (2) performance, (3) adequacy of performance, (4) efficiency, and (5) process (Kirkhart and Sallee, 1980). Each is explained in the following section.

Effort

Effort refers to the expenditure of work, time, and energy. Although we are usually interested in both questions of quality and quantity, our initial focus is on quantity. A child welfare agency may need to know exactly the number of families served in a family preservation program over the past year. Breaking down that information further, the number of social work contacts each family experienced may be important to know. Even more specifically, it may be significant to ascertain face-to-face services as differentiated from social worker travel time, paperwork or telephone contacts. With an individual family, we might ask, how many times did the social worker visit the home and for what lengths of time? The questions we ask concerning effort are best understood by determining the quantity of the service provided.

Performance

Questions we ask regarding performance address the results of the effort expended and the extent to which the program objectives are achieved. In a direct service case, we are interested in the extent to which the client system's goals are attained. Examples include: Have the three hours of intensive crisis-intervention counseling by Ms. Jones met the client system's goal of avoiding placement in a psychiatric hospital? At the program level, how many of the graduates of a career training program are employed within six months after training?

Another example of performance is found in a juvenile justice program for after-school programs. To what extent has the rate of juvenile crime occurring between the hours of 3:30 p.m. and 10:00 p.m. been reduced? This question is asked to measure progress toward the stated goal of an after-school recreation program that opened the schools between the hours of 3:30 and 10:00 p.m. Performance refers to the results of the effort and how many of the client system's goals and the program's goals are achieved.

Adequacy of Performance

While performance refers to actual results, adequacy of performance addresses the quality or effectiveness of the results. Referring to the juvenile delinquency example offered above, adequacy of performance would measure the extent to which the total problem of juvenile delinquency in this community has been overcome as a result of the new after-school recreation program.

As an example of how to apply the adequacy-of-performance concept to an individual, let us look at Mr. Akers, who has an alcohol problem he is working to alleviate. We wish to ascertain how much of his total alcohol consumption has been reduced as the result of the behavior-modification program implemented with the social worker. This is a difficult question to measure, let alone answer, but attempts certainly need to be made.

At a community level, we may seek to measure the impact a telephone crisis line has on the suicide rates in this community. If suicides and suicide attempts have decreased following the implementation of a telephone crisis line, there may be a possibility that the telephone crisis line has contributed to the decreasing rates. Again, conditions such as decrease in unemployment and local regulation of handguns, far apart from instituting a crisis line, may have also affected the suicide rates. These examples address the degree to which effective implementation has been achieved.

Efficiency

Efficiency helps us decide which form of implementation achieved the stated goals with the least amount of effort and cost. Efficiency addresses concerns about the cost of obtaining the client system's or the program's objectives. For example, does in-home intensive counseling with teenagers who are "acting out" and their families achieve the goals of the client system with more efficiency than would in-office, "fifty-minute" hours? While fifty-minute hours may be cheaper, in-office visits may not be as effective, particularly in family assessments. Although the in-home service may cost more, the amount of change achieved per dollar spent may be greater using the in-home approach.

Another question regarding efficiency involves the cost per client served in a specific program. This helps us answer questions such as: In a group, do we work with a number of families at one time or do we work with them individually for shorter periods of time? We may measure, perhaps, working with ten families over a three-hour period as a total group versus working with those ten families, apportioning a part of the three hours to each family. Finally, in terms of program efficiency, given a certain amount of resources, how can we provide the greatest amount and best service to the client systems? Efficiency, then, combines effectiveness with the use of money, time, and the level of staff expertise.

Process

Process questions ask about the degree to which a program offered fits what the program was intended to offer. In other words, was the program fully implemented and did the client system receive the service contracted for? Answering questions about process is certainly difficult and complex, but it also may yield important information we can use to direct our own practice or an agency program.

Focusing on process may uncover ways that the program is managed as well as reveal intended and unintended consequences of programs. We usually rely on agency records in order to determine the manner in which the program is progressing and qualitative research methods are employed.

Measurement

All research attempts to explain and understand events. Evaluation research focuses on the effectiveness of events. In order to determine effectiveness, we must utilize methods that will measure effectiveness. Earlier in the text we discussed differences between qualitative and quantitative research. Although quantitative research is concerned with counting events, while qualitative research examines an event from a subjective format, both research approaches rely upon measurement. Measurement is not limited to counting. In fact, a variety of means outside of counting is available to measure events. The essence of measurement refers to ways of organizing data so that the information we have collected can be understood and applied to our practice settings. In research, we attempt to discern the "presence, absence, amount or type of the concept we are studying" (Rubin and Babbie, 1989, p. 125). Of great importance in making those determinations are the sampling procedures and the reliability and validity of the measurements we are employing.

Sampling

Selecting people to participate in a research project is based on sampling techniques. It is doubtful that an entire population can be studied, and we rely upon parts of the population that are representative. It would be impossible to explain all the categories and nuances of sampling in this text. Entire books are written on sampling procedures alone. The manner in which a sample is obtained from a population and the number of the sample are determinants of how generalizable the results of the research are. In other words, if we survey ten adolescents regarding substance abuse, we cannot make any generalizations about substance abuse among adolescents. We can only say that we know something about substance abuse among the ten adolescents we surveyed.

If the ten adolescents happen to represent a portion of the caseload of a social worker who specializes in work with substance abusers, and, further, the adolescents studied were randomly selected, then we could make some assumptions about that particular social worker's caseload with adolescent substance abusers.

Sampling is divided into probability sampling and nonprobability sampling (Rubin and Babbie, 1989, pp. 228–229). Probability sampling relies on random sampling and uses mathematical procedures to determine how samples are drawn and the number needed for the sample. Social workers often must rely on nonprobability sampling, in which random sampling is not employed, simply because "it is not always feasible to use probability sampling techniques" (Rubin and Babbie, p. 191). There is a logic used in determining the sample, but random sampling is not feasible. The real world of social work practice often limits our uses of random sampling techniques. Nonetheless, there are a growing number of social work researchers engaging in evaluation research who do use random sampling techniques in quasi-experimental studies.

Reliability

Perfectly reliable measures are procedures that result in the same answer regardless of the number of times the measurement is exacted (Kirk and Miller, 1986). For example, a reliable measurement may be a thermometer that records identical temperatures for a given person, regardless of the number of times the temperature is taken. Of course, we do not know whether or not the temperature was accurate in the first place, but we do know that the measurement tool (thermometer) is reliable.

Validity

Valid measurement tools give us accurate answers. In research, a valid measure "reflects the real meaning of the concept under consideration" (Rubin and Babbie, p. 146). Of course, truth regarding any idea, concept, or event can never be fully ascertained. We can only use our best observational skills and logical analysis to work toward truth or understanding. In that sense, no measurement can ever be perfectly valid because we never know the ultimate truth about any phenomenon. However, researchers attempt to use the most valid instruments available.

Time Series

Examining events over time has been used successfully as part of a single-subject design in working with direct service cases. We observe the behavior of a family or another type of client system at given intervals over time, and then introduce the implementation and observe afterwards to see if there was a change in those behaviors. For example, in working with a man who drinks excessively and lost his job, the worker observed over three weeks that he was inebriated fifteen times, including weekdays. This established a baseline. Then through implementing in-

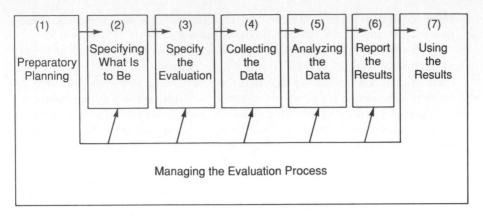

FIGURE 11.3 The Process of Program Evaluation

tensive case management services, including getting him a job, the worker observed he drank excessively three times during the next three weeks, but only on weekends. There had been considerable improvement. Although he was still getting drunk on weekends, it did not seem to affect his work.

Overview of the Evaluation Process

Figure 11.3 gives an overview of a program evaluation in an agency setting. It is also applicable to the direct service evaluation process. We have already discussed the preparatory work, including specifying exactly what is to be evaluated. We now take up the evaluation design. To illustrate direct service evaluation, we have chosen the single-subject design, task achievement scaling, goal attainment scaling, ethnographic techniques, and content analysis. Think of the evaluation process as a sort of "mini" Crystal Model, because each step in the model is duplicated in the evaluation process: data collection, analysis of the data, reporting the results, and using the results.

Direct Service Evaluation: Evaluation of One's Own Practice

Evaluating one's own practice challenges social workers. Although there are a number of designs employed to evaluate practice, we focus on the following.

Single-Subject Design

In *single-subject design,* the subject (case) may be an individual, family, or small group. Centering on observable behaviors as a way of measuring change is the most straightforward way of illustrating this design.

Let us assume you are evaluating the change process in a small group. Once the group has decided its goals, the social worker assists the group members define those goals into specific behaviors they would like to change. The group agrees that in the event that particular behaviors are either extinguished or adopted, the plan has been implemented. We call the behaviors that need to be changed *target behaviors.*

Once the goals have been clarified, you must create a baseline for data collection. The baseline refers to the data collection period before implementation of the planned change effort. At that time behaviors are discussed; duration and frequencies are calculated. Creating a baseline allows us to determine the extent to which the program (the group experience, the change techniques, and so on) affected the goals on which the group had decided. We only know the effectiveness of practice if we understand the situation before we begin the helping process.

If the target behavior is smoking marijuana, and the group agrees on the goal of lessening their marijuana smoking, then frequencies and duration of marijuana smoking is ascertained. In studying frequency at the beginning of the area of concern, the social worker discovers that all of the group members smoke on Friday and Saturday nights and several members also smoke several evenings during the week. In addition, each member of the group admits to getting high in their high school classes two to three times per week. The baseline data collection period gives us the opportunity to focus on some aspect of the group's marijuana smoking behaviors.

Multiple baselines are often created, because in our practice worlds, most areas of concern are complex and involve a variety of behaviors. We may focus on marijuana smoking and school attendance, or even marijuana smoking, school attendance, and grades in several classes.

The last step in the behavioral approach is to assess change in the baseline over time. Sometimes intense work with a client system ends. We may be working with neglectful parents and after a few months the contacts are ended. Focus with the parents had been on learning appropriate disciplining measures. The program in which the parents were participating ends, but follow-up visits are planned for six months and one year after the parenting classes are ended. The social worker returns for the follow-up visits to ascertain the extent to which the parents have adopted more appropriate disciplinary techniques.

If the follow-up worker and the family decide more assistance is needed, in-home treatment may be decided on and a homemaker, able to be present for more extended periods of time with the family, enters the scene. You continue follow-up and monitoring even though the major implementation has ended.

Single-subject evaluation designs can use both qualitative and quantitative research methodologies. We have illustrated the most elementary form of a single-subject design—counting behaviors before intervention and counting behaviors after intervention—to ascertain the extent to which the intervention brought about change. Seldom are statistical analyses completed on a single-subject design, unless numerous practitioners are implementing a single-subject design with similar cases, using identical intervention techniques. Most often, single-subject designs rely on visual representations to determine change. In other words, charting behaviors to ascertain change over a period of time allows the social worker and the client system to monitor the change (Dawson, Klass, Guy, and Edgley, 1991, p. 268).

Task Achievement Scaling

Another way of looking at single-subject designs is through *task achievement scaling*. Task achievement scaling was developed by Reid and Epstein at the University of Chicago as part of Task Centered Counseling (Reid and Epstein, 1972). Its purpose is to determine the degree to which the client and worker agree on the extent to which the agreed-upon task was completed.

Tasks that are measured are usually those that can be completed within a very short period of time—a few days or a week or two at most. Usually, the tasks are very specific and, therefore, easier to measure. A scale of measuring the extent to which these tasks were completed is developed and measured.

Most student field-work tasks are measured on a task achievement scale at the end of each semester. A variety of tasks may be listed in a learning agreement. With the degree of completion, a score indicating the degree of completion for each task is given. Under each task is a number, and the greater the extent of completion of a task, the higher the number. As a student goes through the evaluation with his or her field instructor, the instructor writes down the numbers and, at the end, totals them, divides them by the number of questions, and gets an average score which equals a certain letter grade. The scale measures the degree to which the student has completed a task or learned a specific behavior.

Goal Attainment Scaling

Goal attainment scaling is also a way of measuring change in direct service. The purpose of goal attainment scaling is to measure the degree to which the client system's goals are attained. In order to do goal attainment scaling, the social worker and the client system agree on what the goals to be measured are; and they are usually a little more general than what are used in the task-centered approach. Each goal is given a numerical weight that equals its relative importance to the client system. In Case Example 11.1, we can see how the generalist social worker developed a goal attainment evaluation from the change plan.

Goal attainment scaling can be done with groups and communities. Consider goal attainment scaling for a public relations campaign that is meant to publicize a new aspect of a social service program.

The agency appoints an agency committee to begin the campaign. The committee decides to publicize the new program through developing and disseminating a brochure outlining the new program's goals. The committee decides that the more brochures that are disseminated, the wider the program will be publicized. They score their goal attainment in the following way:

500 brochures distributed—3 points

1,000 brochures distributed—6 points

1,500 brochures distributed—9 points

CASE EXAMPLE 11.1

Amy Ruskin

Amy Ruskin is a thirty-six-year-old mother of a sixteen-month-old infant. Neighbors had called the police because Amy left the child unattended. When Amy returned to the home forty-five minutes after the police arrived, she was intoxicated and in no state to care for the child.

A referral was made to the family preservation social worker, Abby Azar. The social worker found that Amy was in a state of denial with respect to her alcoholism. Additionally, she learned that criminal charges had been filed against Amy.

At the time of the referral, Amy Ruskin was socially isolated, estranged from her family of origin, and at risk of losing her job. Starting where Amy was, the social worker dealt with the mother's two major concerns: the possible loss of her child and her impending court date. With Amy, Abby Azar, the social worker, developed a two-pronged program, beginning with alcoholism counseling and a support group, Alcoholics Anonymous (AA).

While the pending criminal charges were sufficient to influence Amy to at least consider AA, it was the social worker's personal concern, skill, and persistence that effected change in Amy's family, home, and community system, got Amy into alcoholism treatment, and helped maintain her. To do this, the social worker and Amy developed a plan containing clearly stated goals and preferred ways of meeting those goals. The following is a chronology of Abby's work with Amy.

1. Received permission to accompany Amy to her AA meetings until they were sufficiently enforcing her to maintain attendance on her own.

   Goal attainment—The social worker will initially accompany Amy to AA and after three meetings (with Abby along), Amy will attend three out of four meetings by herself for two months.

2. The social worker located and brought into service a natural helper who, as a maternal AA member, was able to provide the nurturance and support Amy had never had in her childhood and youth and still craved.

   Goal attainment—The AA member contacts Amy by phone each day and visits her in person two out of four days. Amy reports she feels nurtured.

3. In her court testimony, the social worker highlighted Amy's strengths, which gave Amy hope, and a change partnership was formed.

   Goal attainment—The social worker highlights at least three strengths. Amy reported to the AA member that she feels good about working with the social worker.

The plan's second part concerned assisting Amy to care successfully for the sixteen-month-old infant. The steps were:

1. The social worker counseled Amy in Amy's home and moved her from wanting her aunt to take the child to deciding that she could and wished to parent her child.

   Goal attainment—Amy states she wants her child, and she achieved specific parenting behaviors necessary to do so, such as learning to play appropriately with the child.

2. The family support specialist (homemaker) provided some transportation to facilitate reconnection with the extended family.

   Goal attainment—Amy visited her family three times in one month and reported it was "OK."

3. Amy focused on her work situation.

   Goal attainment—After two months, Amy had a part-time job.

The results of this intensive intervention, which took two-and-one-half months' time, were Amy's continuing to stay united with her child and her securing employment. At three months, Amy decided she could drink socially.

(Continued)

CASE EXAMPLE 11.1   *(Continued)*

At this point, social services brought the family preservation worker back for several sessions. While criminal prosecution was avoided, the court held the case for some time. At the end of six months, the case was dropped from the court. (Case modified from Sallee, 1992)

Discussion

At the end of each month, Ms. Azar and Amy charted her progress (Figure 11.4). This included the following chart for attendance of AA for the first month of meetings. The chart was posted on Amy's refrigerator.

Amy scored 64 points, well above the 48 which she and Ms. Azar agreed on as the minimum at the beginning of the month. While attending AA meetings probably helped Amy, simply attending meetings or classes does not mean one learns or is able to change behavior. Ms. Azar was measuring how much support Amy needed to help herself. Two events on different days illustrate Amy's continued need for support.

On the 13th, Amy reported she still did not feel comfortable enough to go to an AA meeting alone. The social worker used this information to discuss Amy's fears or concerns regarding the meetings. After attending one more meeting together, Amy did fine until the 21st. Ms. Azar found out that was the day Amy was rudely turned down for a job which shook her confidence in the change process. After one more joint visit to AA, Amy went alone for the rest of the month.

What did Abby Azar learn from this evaluation to help her practice? First, that while it might not be AA's policy to allow her to accompany Amy, it paid off. Second, accompanying a client only three times (at least with Amy) to AA meetings may not be sufficient. Third, there will be setbacks for clients, and reassurance and support works well in helping people get back "on track."

Ms. Azar also used self-reports to chart Amy's drinking, and she knew that self-reports are not always valid. We must always try to corroborate the data from self-reports. For example, we are concerned about providing a safe and nurturing environment for the child. Perhaps the best method of measuring this outcome was not Amy's self-reports, but the fact that no further reports from neighbors or the police were received.

FIGURE 11.4 Amy's AA Attendance Chart

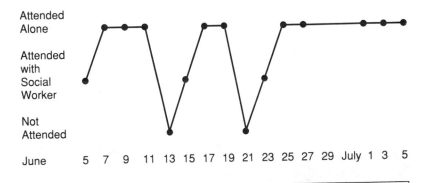

Not Attending	0
With Social Worker	3
Alone	5

Scale	
Total Possible	= 80
Acceptable	= 48
Score for Amy	= 64

The scale is customized according to a measurement on which the committee has agreed. They will have some measure of the extent that publicity regarding the new program was obtained. The committee may decide to add another measurement such as counting the number of articles found in local newspapers featuring the new program. Weighing the two measures will furnish an approximation of goal attainment.

Content Analysis

The purpose of *content analysis* is to understand phenomena and relationships among phenomena through the analysis of communication—both written and oral (Dawson et al., 1991, p. 260). Historically, in social work, the case record has been used as the object of analyses, and in social workers' recordings of client interviews and assessments are found rich data used to understand change.

Content found in the written record must be organized and classified in order for meanings to emerge. For example, analyzing the process of change in a community corrections program for women through a content analysis of 179 case records shed light upon successful outcomes in the program (Hoffman, 1979). A painstaking study of counselor perceptions (ascertained through the detailed recording of each client-counselor meeting) revealed that women whose counselors had positive assessments following each client contact were far more likely to complete the program successfully (finishing their period of incarceration in the program and completing a GED or vocational training) than women whose counselors viewed them negatively. This variable along with other program variables such as type of training or education in which a woman was enrolled, plus certain demographic variables, were related to successful outcome. Gathering the data proved difficult, but a great deal was learned about working with offenders in community programs.

Social workers evaluating their own practices can use written records as a method of critiquing their own work. In fact, the process of recording, a teaching tool we strongly support, is actually a content analysis of the student-client interview and a source of wonderful learning material. Sharing the written record with colleagues in protected settings in which client confidentiality is maintained assists social workers in learning about their own practices.

Communication is at the heart of our work with client and focal systems, and social work practice is based upon its artful and purposeful use. Communication analysis ought to be a component of every social worker's evaluation "packet."

Ethnomethodology

A further explication of communication analysis is found in ethnomethodology or ethnographic interviewing. Its focus is to understand, usually through participant observation, the interactions among persons in families, groups, or organizations. Grinnell (1985) calls it a "theoretical and methodological method aimed at describing how people in everyday interactions construct definitions for their situations and shape their realities . . . to identify ways in which members of society come to make sense of the world" (p. 358).

Its use in social work research is at the beginning stage, but it holds promise if we are to understand, in particular, just how people decide to change their circumstances and alter their worlds.

Home-based services, now used frequently with families and children who are at risk, offers wonderful opportunities for the ethnographic researcher to ascertain the ways in which social workers and focal systems interact that eventually lead to eliminating at-risk behaviors in families.

For example, teaching parenting skills and homemaker skills in families is much more than offering didactic programs to women and men who show an interest in learning how to become more loving and effective parents. Teaching these complex skills involves learning new behaviors in an atmosphere of trust and confidence in the social worker. We learn best in climates in which we feel emotionally safe.

For all that we are sure about the need for a positive climate, our knowledge about how change really happens in such circumstances is based largely on practice knowledge, rather than on systematic study and observation. The ethnographic study in which social worker and participant observer work with families may turn up data most social workers have been waiting for—the understanding of when and under what circumstances people move ahead and take more control over their own lives.

Summary

Evaluating our own practice is essential in improving our practice and in individualizing each client system. While we may not make radical changes in how we practice, based upon one case over a period of time, we may see trends develop from the evaluations which help us refine our skills. Drawing upon several similar cases, we can share our evaluations with our colleagues, enhancing the knowledge of the field. Now let us examine how we evaluate a number of cases together, known as program evaluation.

Program Evaluation

Program evaluations have three general purposes: (1) to determine program outcomes; (2) to describe the processes of program operation in order to determine the extent to which the goals of the agency are explicated through the agency's or program's activities, and (3) to assist in the determination of practice or policy decisions.

Program Outcomes

Determining program outcomes is a major thrust of program evaluations. In fact, the overall question regarding effectiveness of both program and practice guides our evaluation activities. In order to determine outcomes, decisions must be made regarding what constitutes success or effectiveness in a program.

In the previous section, we discussed a community-based program for women offenders. Agency personnel and the board of directors had decided that program success would be measured by the percentage of clients (inmates) who completed the program. If more than half the participants completed the program, it was determined to be successful.

Of course, program completion is only one of the measures of success in programs for offenders. The most important question asked of any corrections program is, what is its effect on recidivism rates? In other words, is the overall recidivism rate of women offenders reduced by community-based programs? How do recidivism rates in community programs compare with recidivism rates of women who have been incarcerated in traditional walled prisons? Answers to these important questions can be determined only by comparing data among programs (prison and community corrections) and then making some judgments regarding effectiveness.

However, we must limit our judgments because we may be comparing unlike pools of subjects (women who are sentenced to prison may have very different criminal backgrounds from those of women sent to community corrections). Most program evaluations designed to determine effectiveness point to possible answers, but are not definitive. In addition, implications drawn from program evaluations in relationship to their success with particular populations must remain limited.

Randomization techniques are usually not employed in program evaluation simply because factors relevant to eligibility are used in determining who are the participants in various programs, and it is rare that people would ever be assigned randomly. Without randomization techniques, broader generalizations about program effectiveness cannot be concluded.

Follow-Up Studies

Program outcomes or effectiveness are often measured through follow-up studies. People who have participated in a program are followed after the program has been completed or after the participants have left the program. Data are gathered from participants to discover the effects of the program.

Families First, a family-preservation, home-based services program in Michigan, follows its clients after Families First services have ended. Families First is designed to strengthen families, thereby reducing the number of children in foster care (Visser, 1991). After six months, home visits are made to determine family functioning, including information about where children are living, continued services that may be offered from other agencies, and clients' views about the impact of the program on their lives and on their families.

Although follow-up studies are expensive because locating people can be time-consuming, their importance in program evaluation is widely recognized. Only when we determine what happens to people after the change plan has been implemented can we determine the effectiveness of programs that are designed to bring about change.

Community-Based Corrections: Follow-Up

In a community corrections program, we interview staff members to ascertain their activities with the focal systems (the women). We find through our interviews that several staff who are responsible for monitoring drug testing of the women had not followed through on their assignments. Several women had not been "clean" for a period of several months and, finally, teachers of the vocational programs they had been attending had noticed their behavior and asked them not to return to the school. Not attending a vocational program meant these women were no longer eligible for the community corrections program and were sent to the regional prison.

Since the program is small, the loss of four women in one month affected the completion rates, and they dipped to below 50 percent. Only after careful analysis of the program's process was the discovery regarding the staff behavior made. Drug monitoring was subsequently taken more seriously by staff members and the reason for the great change in completion rates was finally ascertained. Process description is time-consuming, but once data-gathering procedures are put into place, process descriptions used to determine program effectiveness can become a part of the everyday activities of the agency.

Process Descriptions

Describing the structure and process of programs is essential in determining program effectiveness. We must ascertain exactly what is happening in a program in order to understand what outcomes may mean and the extent to which program goals are realized. For example, we may discover in an outcome study that only 25 percent of participants in a community-based program for women offenders complete the program. We have already decided that 50 percent need to complete it in order for the program to be successful. Finding that only 25 percent do complete it demands that we ascertain what is occurring in the program in order to determine where problems or barriers to program completion exist.

Policy Decisions

Evaluations form part of the backdrop for policy decisions. The continuation of programs often depends upon the results of program evaluations. Alterations in practice within programs are also related to program evaluation findings.

Knowing that a program can rise or fall based upon the results of program evaluations places great pressure on those who are directing the evaluation. Outcome studies can bring negative results and interpretations of studies that impact on policy must be clear and fair. In other words, program evaluators need to take care in making generalizations about their findings; they must be careful to report exactly their findings, with each limitations clearly noted, and they must present their findings in ways that are usable to the audiences to whom they are reporting.

The last point bears further discussion. Even when evaluations are negative, the way in which they are presented must be tailored to specific audiences. Findings can be misunderstood and used in a variety of ways—not all of which are helpful. In addition, even when findings are positive overall, information can be misused. Case Example 11.2 illustrates our points.

CASE EXAMPLE 11.2

Madison Help and Action Center

The population of Madison County is two-thirds urban, residing primarily in Fairview. Just over 50 percent of the population is of Mexican-American heritage, many of whom are recent immigrants from Mexico and/or migrant and seasonal workers. Unfortunately, there is no firm data available on the actual number of migrants or on their economic situation. Forty-five percent of the people in Madison County are Anglo-American, and 1.9 percent are Black, a proportion equal to that of the state as a whole. Madison County is distinguished by the fact that it exceeds the state average of 31.2 percent recent migrants. The Madison Valley provides a north-to-south axis of populated towns and villages in the county.

Unemployment figures, income statistics, and other indicators show that Madison County ranks high statewide as a poverty area. However, in education, infant mortality rates, homicide rates, and other areas, it ranks in a much better position than many counties in the state.

Social services are administered through an office in the county court building staffed by twenty-five workers. The only "mental health" services available (other than from a private physician or a minister of one of Fairview's churches) are those offered by the Madison Help and Action Center.

The Madison Help and Action Center (MHAC) is a storefront, walk-in center located on the main street of Fairview between a doctor's office and a jewelry store. It is open from 10:00 a.m. to 6:00 p.m. Monday to Friday and from 10:00 to 3:00 p.m. Saturday. An emergency "hotline" operates from 6:00 p.m. to midnight daily. Paid staff consists of a full-time director, three counselors (one of whom is part-time), and a receptionist. All staff members are female except for the part-time counselor. The director and two counselors are bilingual. The average age of the staff is thirty-three. The "hotline" is staffed largely by volunteers, both male and female. The board of directors consists of the principal of the high school, the vice-president in charge of

student affairs from the community college, the president of a local women's organization, two ministers, the director of the hospital, and two influential local businessmen. The ethnic breakdown of the board is 28 percent minority and 52 percent women.

MHAC was created as an agency five years ago in response to two well-publicized incidents that drew attention to the lack of mental health facilities: a student from the community college jumped to her death from a railroad trestle and the ex-mayor's wife was arrested for creating a public nuisance and subsequently institutionalized in a state hospital. The stated mandate of the program is broad: "To improve the quality of life and mental well-being of the residents of Madison County." In recent months, the high school principal and local ministers have made public statements to the effect that MHAC should take as its major focus "dealing with moral decay and the use of drugs by young people in the community."

MHAC is funded by the United Way, the county, and private donations. In the face of budget cuts, both United Way and the county have begun to express a general interest in evaluation and a concern with "funding only those programs that can demonstrate how they are helping people."

MHAC offers individual counseling and acts as an information and referral service for persons needing food, clothing, and shelter (the break-down between "mental health" problems and "concrete basic needs" is approximately equal). MHAC is registered as a Travelers' Aid as well, although requests for these services are sparse. Two months ago, MHAC undertook an "Antidrug Campaign" in response to public pressure that consisted of distributing posters and brochures produced by the National Institute of Drug Abuse.

In order to demonstrate "how they are helping people," MHAC has asked Mr. Juan Sosa, B.S.W., a member of their board, to help them begin the evaluation process. First,

CASE EXAMPLE 11.2   *(Continued)*

he met with the staff and the director to gain a sense of the readiness of the organization for the evaluation. He uses the A-VICTORY technique to do this. Then he reviewed the goals of MHAC. Understanding there was a wide audience for the results, including the United Way, the county and private citizens, he gathered representatives together, and he obtained their input by asking them what questions they would ask to evaluate the MHAC programs.

Next, he asked them to record an information source for each question, noting who will collect what information from whom and how. He also assessed whether the information was available or if it had to be collected. Based upon this information, he and the staff developed a design for each program to be evaluated. For example, he proposed a goal attainment design for the new antidrug campaign, realizing the program was too new to have any outcomes evaluated. The best design to document positive results for the campaign was to measure process such as putting posters up in key locations.

Throughout the process, Mr. Sosa used social and technical skills. By inviting represent-

atives of the audiences and carefully listening to their input, he included them in the process. The chances that they were invested in the evaluation were enhanced. The research design and knowing to measure process, not outcome, on the antidrug campaign were technical skills. The statistics professor at the community college consulted with Mr. Sosa and the staff on the analysis of the data.

The final report was presented in draft form first to the director and staff and then to the board. The results are packaged to meet the needs of each audience. Mr. Sosa and the board president held a press conference and presented the evaluation in an abbreviated form so the press and public could understand it. The results are in a different form for a written report to the county; and yet another form, with overheads, was created for an oral presentation to the United Way.

Finally, to ensure the results of the evaluation were used, the board and staff held a retreat and planned how to build on the strengths identified in the report and developed principles and a plan to improve some program components. Each quarter, the board reviewed the staff's progress on the plan.

Review of Program Evaluation Process

Following is a checklist for completing a program evaluation (Kirkhart and Sallee, 1980):

1. Review the linkages between the program's problem statements, goals, objectives, and strategies.

   Checkpoints:

   ✔ Will your selected strategies officially lead to achievement of your objectives?

   ✔ Will achievement of your objectives logically lead to a reduction of your problem?

2. Determine the audiences to whom the change system is accountable for the outcome of your program.

   Checkpoints:

   ✔ Have you considered both persons external to the program and persons internal to the program?

       ✔ Have you considered client/consumers as well as program staff?

3. Determine the information for which the change system is accountable to each audience.

    Checkpoints: Consider:

       ✔ Effort
       ✔ Outcome
       ✔ Efficiency
       ✔ Adequacy
       ✔ Process

4. Plan the evaluation design.

    Checkpoints:

       ✔ What specific questions need to be answered?

       ✔ What measurement strategies will you use to collect the needed information?

       ✔ When will measurements be taken?

       ✔ Have you taken steps to insure the validity and reliability of the data?

5. Plan data collection.

    Checkpoints:

       ✔ Who will collect the information?

       ✔ From what source(s) will information be collected?

       ✔ How (using what procedures/instruments) will information be collected?

       ✔ Have you planned for any necessary training of data collectors?

6. Plan data analysis.

    Checkpoints:

       ✔ How and by whom will data be reduced?

       ✔ How and by whom will data be processed?

       ✔ Who will be responsible for interpretation of data?

7. Plan for reporting results.

    Checkpoints:

       ✔ Did you ask your audiences what would be most useful to them?

       ✔ Have you considered mechanisms for both formal and informal feedback?

       ✔ Have you considered alternatives to written reporting?

       ✔ Have you pretested written reports for readability by intended audiences?

8. Plan for utilization of evaluation results.

Checkpoints:

   ✔ Determine *who* will use the results of the evaluation

- Will each of the audiences to whom you feel accountable actual *use the information?*
- Are there other persons/groups who will use the information?
- Have you identified specific persons as users whenever possible?

How will results be used? (Preliminary)

- Decisions concerning the program?
- Decisions concerning individuals?

When will the results be used?

- What decisions are pending that the results could inform?
- Will the use of the evaluation be formative or summative?
- Have you identified the time constraints involved for each user?

TRANSITION

The Last Phase

Transition, the last piece of the "pie" of the Crystal Model, signifies an end or a change in the professional relationship. Yet, like evaluation, its seeds are planted in the beginning of the Crystal Model. When one engages in a time-limited relationship, the obligation is to inform the client system at the beginning that the time will come when the relationship will end. In fact, it is an ethical responsibility to discuss with the client system the transition at the beginning of the change process.

As an example, if you are in an agency setting which will only fund ten sessions with a client, the client needs to know the time constraints. On the other hand, even when there are no time constraints, all social work has endings of which client systems ought to be aware. When goals have been reached, the professional relationship may end, unless additional goals have been set and agreed upon.

Determining Endings and Transitions

A complicated task for every generalist social worker is knowing when the transition ought to take place. The following criteria are useful in assisting us in making those determinations.

1. Have the goals been reached? If the goals have been reached, then we need to let go, and the client needs to let go.

2. Is the client functioning in such a way that no one is in danger? For example, if you are working with a family in protective services and assisted the

family to a place in which safety is assured, then you know you have completed the permanent plan.

3. Have a reasonable amount of time and resources been expended upon this client but with little or no results? If so, we may not have succeeded, and it may be time to end the change process. We do not succeed all the time. There are clients who are not able to cooperate or ready to begin the change process. However, even in working with "uncooperative" clients, we may have helped persons become ready to work toward change at a later date. Our agendas about change are not always shared with clients or potential clients.

4. Would the client be better served by another agency or worker? If so, you should end the relationship and transfer the case to the other agency or worker.

Transferring and Changing Social Workers

There are usually two reasons for transferring a case and changing social workers: (1) the worker is leaving the agency or being transferred himself or herself to another unit in the agency, or (2) it has become evident that changing workers or agencies will benefit the client system.

Social Workers' Leaving

Changing positions is a frequent occurrence among social work practitioners. Public agencies seem to experience the greatest turnover, but most social workers change jobs a number of times throughout their professional careers.

Clients may cognitively understand that a worker is leaving for a better job or moving to a new location, but feelings regarding being left, losing an important person and having to change are not easy, even in short term change situations (Webb, 1985).

Two illustrations are presented in Case Examples 11.3 and 11.4. The first case involves a social worker who has worked with a senior citizen group for two years and has found a new job in another part of the city. The second illustration focuses on a social worker who has seen a young woman only twice, but finds she has been offered a wonderful job in a new city that she must take immediately. Although the workers' time involvements with the client systems were quite different, it is easy to see that the feelings both social workers and clients had to deal with were powerful.

Both case examples illustrate social workers' transferring or attempting to transfer cases: one was successful, and the other, not. Inherent in both situations were the powerful feelings that are exposed during the ending of the professional relationship. The following section addresses the situation in which the client is transferred to another social worker because the professional relationship has reached the point at which the client system may be better served by another person or agency.

CASE EXAMPLE 11.3

Jackie Smyth

For two years, Jackie Smyth was employed at Thompson Senior Citizens' Center. She had not worked with older persons previously and was not sure she would like the job. However, the pay was good and the hours met her needs because the center closed early, and Jackie could be home by 4:00 p.m. to be with her own school-aged children.

Soon after her employment began, Jackie initiated a group focused on personal growth. Conversations with a number of individuals at the center had led her to believe that a group experience would be needed and well received. The population at the center consisted of retired industrial workers and their spouses, many of whom had been active in the union; neighborhood residents, and people who had left the neighborhood, moving to nearby suburbs, but who had emotional ties to the neighborhood.

They were a diverse group in terms of race and ethnicity, and they were a lively, vital group distinguished by their eagerness to learn. All had high values regarding education and thought they had every right to learn as much as they could, not only about the world around them, but about themselves. The group agreed that learning about themselves would be their focus.

Jackie was as eager as the group members were and spent a great deal of time gathering media for the group's use. Value clarification exercises, topics regarding coping with physical changes brought on by aging, dealing with losses and understanding adult children were all topics the group and Jackie generated.

As a result of discussions regarding adult children, Jackie became very well acquainted with members of the group and they with her. The group discussed ways of remaining independent from children while using them as intermittent support systems. The group also expressed their feelings about continuing dependence of adult children on them and resentments that sometimes festered.

Jackie began examining her own relationship with her parents who lived in another state, and although she did not bring personal experiences into the group, she spent time thinking about her parents, how she related to them and her own feelings about their aging. Jackie was an experienced social worker, and she did not let her personal life interfere with her work, but she realized that she had begun to develop very strong attachments with group members. However, these strong attachments were used positively and the group turned out to be a wonderful growth-enhancing experience.

After the group had been meeting weekly for over a year, Jackie suggested that they might consider broadening their scope and focusing on other issues. The group disagreed with Jackie. They had no intention of leaving the group or changing the group and had begun to use each other in a very positive and supportive way. Friendships that began within the group blossomed outside the group setting. In fact, a man and woman who met in the group were married ten months after the group began. Jackie's suggestion was not well received. The group flourished, and Jackie continued bringing materials, topics, and her own abilities to be both a resource person and facilitator to the group.

Two months before the group was going to celebrate two years together, Jackie and her husband and children made the decision to leave the city and to move closer to their families. They had been considering the possibility, but it became a pressing need when Jackie's mother's health began to fail, and moving back home seemed more important. This was a most difficult decision, but for Jackie the hardest part would be ending with her group at the Thompson Center.

As soon as family plans were finalized, Jackie told the group of her decision. She explained that she and her husband and children had decided to move closer to their own families of origin and that her mother was in ill health. The group was shocked, but supported Jackie and agreed she should be closer to her mother.

Jackie was pleased the group had been so understanding. They continued to meet and Jackie began to feel left out. The group nearly ignored her during one get-together and Jackie wondered if they were beginning their parting so early. She decided that talking with the group about her leaving might be helpful and would fit with their own goals in the group.

At the following meeting, about one month before she left the city, Jackie discussed her own feelings about leaving the group with the members. She talked of her own ambivalence and her warm, positive feelings toward the group. She told each of the members how much she had learned from them.

It was a most surprising event. The group continued to support her decision. Each one let her know how much they appreciated her, but their focus was less on her than on their appreciation to her for bringing the group together. In fact, most of the group meeting time was spent with the group members affirming each other, the contributions members had made to individuals in the group and their decision to carry on with the new social worker who would soon be assigned to the group. They asked Jackie to orient the new social worker to their needs and tell him or her

that they expected a lot of material to discuss and that they were a group interested in growing and learning.

Jackie was surprised because she thought their feelings about her leaving would be as potent as hers were. She realized that her own feelings of loss were stronger than theirs because she had helped them create a support system for themselves that would endure, regardless of the social worker assigned to the group. Her termination with the group was difficult, but the group members were supportive and eager to move forward in their own lives and in the life of the group — with or without Jackie.

Jackie Smyth's experience with the Thompson Center group illustrates that changing social workers can be more upsetting to the social worker than to the client system. In this situation, Jackie's skill with the group paid off. She had assisted them to become an ongoing and important support system to each other. They would endure. Jackie had, in a sense, worked herself out of a job. Of course, the group continued to need the next social worker, especially in relationship to her role as resource person, but the relationships developed among group members outlasted the social workers. This is the sort of ending all social workers wish for but do not always experience.

CASE EXAMPLE 11.4

Selma Livingston

Selma Livingston's husband was arrested and later arraigned on charges of spouse abuse. As part of the services offered by the county prosecutor, Ms. Livingston was offered support to continue prosecuting the case through the Victims' Aid and Support Center. Linda Halstead was the social worker assigned to the case.

Linda interviewed Selma in Selma's home and learned of the details of the spouse abuse.

It seems that Bob, Selma's husband, had beaten Selma for years before Selma finally called the police. According to Selma, he is a brutal and cruel man and prosecuting this case was the hardest thing Selma had ever done. She was grateful to have Linda's support and seemed to connect quickly with Linda.

Linda was not a particularly experienced social worker; in fact, she had just graduated with her B.S.W. degree one year earlier. Al-

(Continued)

CASE EXAMPLE 11.4   *(Continued)*

ready, she had the personal qualities and the perseverance that marked her as an exceptional person.

After the interview, Linda put together a plan she would share at her next visit with Selma. It included projected dates that court appearances might be likely, a list of all people Selma would have to relate to during the court proceedings and a list of ongoing counseling agencies and support systems Selma might consider using after the court proceedings. Linda had made an appointment to share this material with Selma the following week.

Two days before her appointment with Selma, a social work position that Linda thought she would never be offered was, indeed, offered to her. The best part was that it was in a city she had lived in during her college years, and she had several close friends who still lived there. She had daydreamed often of moving back to that part of the country. The agency wanted her to begin as soon as possible, and Linda agreed to begin in two months. That meant she had to transition with all of her clients, finish her work at the agency and pack her personal belongings. The tasks ahead were formidable, but Linda accepted the new position.

Endings with clients and colleagues would have to begin immediately. She told her supervisor and was informed that her position would likely not be filled for at least six months. Budget cuts had been in effect, and the agency would save money in the short run by Linda's departure. Linda was very upset. That meant that her clients might not have the kind of attention they needed because the remaining two social workers in the agency would be handling all the cases between them. She immediately thought of Selma and hoped her leaving would not discourage her from continuing her case against her husband.

At their appointment the next day, Linda shared her plan with Selma. The map of the entire process had been laid out, goals for Selma and Linda were detailed, and Selma thought it looked manageable. Linda talked

to her about the plan and about building a support system to help her through. Selma was not sure she could use the few friends she had and thought she would just rely on Linda. At that point Linda knew she needed to discuss her leaving.

Linda explained the situation. Selma listened closely, and her entire mood seemed to change. She looked at the plan on the kitchen table and methodically folded it into a tiny square. She shoved the plan in her pocket and crossed her arms; her whole body stiffened. Selma glanced briefly at Linda and said, "I can't do it."

Linda's excellent empathic skills came into play at that moment. She sat silently with Selma, knowing that words would not do. Selma had counted on Linda's support, and she felt it was being pulled away from her. A less effective social worker may have tried to talk Selma out of her feelings, pointing out that someone else would be taking over the case. Linda knew that Selma was not ready to hear solutions. She needed time to digest this bad news. Finally, Linda replied that she knew Selma was experiencing a lot of pain, and, perhaps, she felt angry that she was being left when she needed support.

Selma began to cry, and, again, Linda simply sat with her until she seemed ready to talk. Linda explained that she would be working for close to two months, and that though she would most likely not see her through the entire legal process, she would be there as long as possible. Linda hoped that Selma would let her help until then. Linda also explained that another social worker would be assigned to the case, but that it was likely that the new worker would not have the time Linda did because Linda's position was not being filled and Linda's caseload was being divided between the two remaining workers.

They talked for a long time about what Selma might expect to happen in the next two months. The plan Linda had developed would still work, but Linda would not be a part of it after two months. After Selma seemed to have begun accepting Linda's inevitable leaving, Selma took the written plan out of her pocket, and they looked at it again. When Linda left that day, she felt sure Selma would continue to pursue the case against her husband with support from the Victims' Center.

The following week Selma was to have come into the office, but at her appointment time, she did not come. Linda called her home, only to find that the phone had been disconnected. The next day she drove to Selma's apartment, and discovered she had moved. After Linda returned to the office, she wrote a letter to Selma, hoping it would be forwarded with a message saying she hoped Selma would call her and that she would continue her case. Linda did not hear from Selma. The prosecutor's office had also lost track of Selma.

During Linda's remaining time with the agency, she made several attempts to track down Selma but was unable to. Her ending with Selma was not as she had hoped, and her concern for Selma's well-being remained with her.

New Workers and New Programs

Continuous monitoring throughout the change process helps us substantiate the extent to which our work with client systems is effective. Evaluating the process cannot wait until the end of the change effort because alterations in how help is being offered may have to be made before agreed-upon goals are reached.

There are times in our work with clients that changing social workers or agencies, for the good of the client system, is called for. Those situations present themselves for two major reasons: the social worker is not able to deliver the services or a new program has been developed in the agency or collaborative agency that seems most beneficial to the client system.

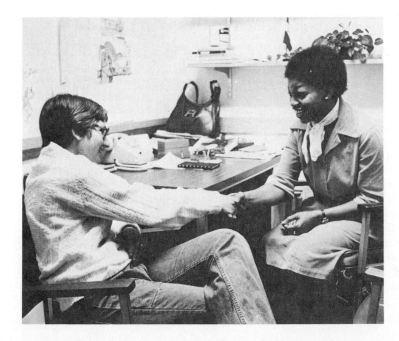

There are times when social work colleagues transfer client systems.

Changing Social Workers

Every social worker is not effective with every client system and every area of concern. Our work with clients demands so much of ourselves that it would be naive to think the professional social worker could transfer all his or her skills and roles to all situations. There are two basic reasons we change workers in midstream during the change process: the social worker requests a change or the client system requests a change.

Social Worker Requests

A social worker, sensitive to client needs and his or her own capacity to deliver services at a given time, takes stock of the work with client systems. All of us, even the most experienced social worker, face situations in our own lives that impact on our work with clients. These situations may be such that work with particular client systems is both too upsetting for us and may turn out to be less helpful to our clients.

When such events occur, the social worker must talk with colleagues and supervisors, attempt to work out whatever is disconcerting and its impact upon the professional work, and take action so that client systems are not adversely affected (Levinson, 1977).

Case Example 11.5 involves a social worker, Tasha Belden, who is in the midst of a divorce and who has been working with an all-male group of Vietnam-era veterans. Tasha had worked with all-male groups before and was quite skilled at

---

CASE EXAMPLE 11.5

Tasha Belden

The group at the Veterans' Hospital had been working with Tasha for three months. Their major goal as a group consisted of improving their relationships with important women in their lives—wives, significant others, sisters, mothers. Much of the work was focused on their behavior change, but talking about their feelings toward women was an important component of the group.

When the group focused on feelings rather than behavior, Tasha found herself reacting sharply to some of the group members, calling them to task about how they felt, particularly the anger some of the men expressed because they felt the women in their lives were always complaining about money and did not realize how the men were feeling harangued.

Tasha's anger toward her husband from whom she was separated also was focused on money, and Tasha felt herself taking sides against her group members. She tried processing her feelings with her colleagues, but she realized that it would be months before she would be through this. In the meantime, she dreaded seeing the veterans' group and felt she was no longer effective.

She asked her supervisor to be relieved of this group. After some discussion, there was agreement and another social worker was assigned to the group. Tasha and June, the new social worker, co-led the group for several weeks, until the group had accepted June. Tasha did not process all of her feelings with the group members, but they seemed to intuitively understand that the change was good for everyone.

helping them present themselves in newer, more appropriate ways with the women in their lives. During the last six months, she had felt insecure about her work with all of her clients, but after the incident shown in the example, she realized the time had come for direct action regarding the Vietnam vets' group.

Client Requests

Changing social workers based upon client requests occurs infrequently. Usually, when a client is unhappy with the social worker, there is a quick termination with the entire change process. Clients who discontinue the change process before goals have been accomplished may be reacting to their own fears about change, but they may also be reacting to dissatisfaction with the social worker. We know very little about this sort of ending because clients are not available to tell us about it. The data we do gather is usually retrospective—that is, experiences clients tell us about social workers they have had and with whom there has been dissatisfaction.

In fact, most of us have heard "horror stories" about clients' experiences with incompetent social workers. All such retrospective data must be used cautiously, simply because it is not verifiable, but common sense tells us that not all social workers are equally helpful to all clients.

Roles and Skills

The last phase of the Crystal Model is tied to every other phase, perhaps even more than previous phases are, and roles and skills relied on in the earlier phases are re-enacted and reused in this phase. The transition phase functions as a review period by both clients and social workers, and what has happened in the change process is examined in this phase. In that sense, roles and skills most used in the entire change process are put into practice during this phase.

Because this phase of the change process is the last and does involve participating in endings, feelings about attachments and loss are often brought to the forefront in this phase. Look back through the text and examine the enabler and counselor role and skills attached to those roles.

Enabler and Empathy

For example, the enabler role with empathy and its associated skills is called upon in the transition phase. We need to be especially tuned to our clients' feelings, simply because endings are inevitably filled with feelings—even if the change effort has not been especially pleasant.

Shulman (1981) discusses seven powerful feelings associated with transition and endings that social workers must not only recognize but assist clients as they work through these feelings. They are: denial, guilt, anger, caring, sadness, relief, and reluctance to face endings (Shulman, 1981).

Involuntary client systems who may have resisted requirements to participate in a change effort appear to welcome a program's ending, but even those endings are fraught with feelings that the social worker must address. In Case Example

11.6, involving a man who had been involved in spouse abuse, all of these feelings are present.

Brokering and Linking

The broker role with associated linkage skills is the other most frequently called upon role/skill compilation in the transition phase. In this phase, we may be assisting clients in finding a suitable resource for ongoing assistance or help that our agency cannot offer.

Crisis intervention and short-term work with client systems calls upon us to offer the entire change process in one time period. Often short-term work for generalists is actually directed toward helping clients get connected with the resources

---

CASE EXAMPLE 11.6

Ned McMeighen

Ned McMeighen had been attending a group for men who had been found guilty by the courts in spouse-abuse cases. He was required to attend a ten-session group with other men who had abused wives or women friends. Ned knew he had been guilty, but blamed his abusive behavior on his alcohol problem. Since he had been dry for close to a year, he had resented his being required to attend the group, seeing it as a further humiliation. He felt that he would not be abusive because he no longer drank. Reminders of his past behavior was very trying for him.

Ned had spent most of the ten weeks feeling anger and resentment toward the social worker, Michael Johnson. Michael never seemed to accept Ned's belief that alcohol was the root of his problem with women. Michael pushed everyone in the group so much that if Ned had had a choice, he would not have returned after the first session. However, he had no choice, and he completed the ten-week group.

This was to be the last night for the group to meet. In Ned's mind, Michael was his usual unbending, confrontational self and Ned was angry, as usual. However, Ned listened closely to some of the other members of the group who expressed regret that the group was ending because they had felt support from one another and because they had appreciated Michael's honesty. Michael never let them hide behind substance abuse, and he forced them to look at their own behaviors.

Michael also never let them forget that they had control over their own lives and that they were worthwhile human beings who, in time, could have good relationships with women. To Ned, on that last evening, Michael seemed to sense his own fears that a woman would never love him or trust him again.

Michael was highly skilled in his ability to really "connect" with people, even those with whom others may have had problems. The truth was Michael believed in change, and he believed people could make great strides when they were ready and open.

Ned left the group that night and, on the way home, began to cry. He had not cried in years. He was surprised at himself. He kept hearing Michael's voice saying he believed in all of them. Ned actually wished the group were not over. He felt genuine sadness. In fact, he considered calling Michael to see if he could see him individually or join another group at the agency. He did not call immediately, but a few months later, still feeling that Michael might help him, decided to place the call.

they need over a longer period of time. Under these circumstances, brokering with linkage skills takes on added importance because the entire change effort is evaluated according to the extent to which client systems are linked with resources.

Making a Smooth Transition

Hepworth and Larsen (1990) give some helpful advice to smooth the transition phase. First, the transition, or the ending of the relationship, should not be a surprise. The expectation that the ending will take place should be built in as client systems progress through the change effort.

When a social worker is leaving, all the parties involved ought to be made aware of it in a timely fashion. People who will serve as back-ups or are permanent replacements for social workers must be identified. For example, a social worker employed in a community organization should let all constituents know that the board of directors will be engaged in finding another social worker and that a successor will be named as soon as possible so that work does not go unheeded. In other words, to the greatest extent possible, endings should not be unexpected.

Second, follow-up provisions must be scheduled. For example, when the change effort is over, follow-up visits ought to be scheduled and kept. Most agencies have built a follow-up contact into their service plan. Evaluators rely on follow-up contacts to gather data from clients regarding the effectiveness of programs.

Third, contacts with client systems might be gradually decreased. For example, if one is seeing a family every week, one may begin seeing them every two weeks, then once per month. Of course, the social worker informs the client system of the purpose for the gradual decrease of contacts. The ending can be a time for practicing behaviors learned in the change process and to try out new roles.

Fourth, the client may want to terminate before the change process is finished or the goals have been reached. In most cases, this is a client's right. Of course, if there is a court order, if a client is imprisoned, is an abusive parent, or on probation or parole, this option is not available. If a client wants to leave the relationship before goals have been reached, the social worker needs to spell out reasons why the relationship should continue.

Fifth, feelings about endings must be recognized. We have spent a great deal of time pointing out the feelings that are inherent in endings and transitions. Workers and clients both experience the loss that inevitably comes when meaningful relationships end or are altered (Fortune, 1987).

The Personal Impact of Ending

The social worker helps the client deal with feelings surrounding loss, and the social worker seeks consultation from colleagues and supervisors. Everyone has a personal story about losses that affect endings, whether we are the client or the social worker. We bring those experiences with us, and they impact upon us (Fortune, 1987).

We began this book stressing the importance of an examination of the reasons why students are entering the field of social work. In fact, the second chapter of the book contains an inventory that assists in this analysis. We are ending the discussion of the Crystal Model with another suggestion about personal examination.

We urge you to think about how you deal with losses and how your experience with endings influences your feelings and your behavior. No segment of the change process is more laden with powerful feelings than endings.

Whether we look forward to change or whether we fear change, all change, especially the change that involves endings and transitions, sets into motion the leaving of old experiences and the beginning of new ones. This means that, at least temporarily, endings upset our balance, and we work to retrieve old or new places in a sea of change.

Conclusion

Evaluation is a key element in the Crystal Process. Plans for evaluation begin in the first steps of change and culminate prior to the transition or ending of the change process. There are two basic types of evaluation social workers are most concerned about: direct service evaluation and program evaluation. Both types are based on methodology used in basic social research. As far as possible, we attempt to use the most rigorous and appropriate means to evaluate our own practices and to evaluate programs. The key to meaningful evaluation is using the correct methodology to suit the problem.

Ethical considerations must always be made when conducting research. Needs of client systems come first — far above our own need to evaluate. Ethical questions guide our own practice and move us toward looking at what we do in the most objective way possible. We owe our clients the very best that is available, and we owe ourselves the opportunity to evaluate our practices openly and fairly.

In one way, transition is a very joyous time, and yet in another way, it is a sad time. It is joyous if you have accomplished the goals and can look back with the client system, feeling pride in all that has been accomplished. However, sadness is a part of change because both parties, client system and social worker, must move on, giving up an experience that was meaningful.

Social workers invest a great deal of themselves in their work. In fact, our relationships with others represent the bridges people use to move forward in life. Letting go is never easy, but is always necessary.

References

Allen-Meares, Paula. (1990). Social Work Practice: Integrating Qualitative and Quantitative Data Collection Techniques. *Social Work, 35*(5), 452–458.

Baer, Betty, and Federico, Ronald. (1978). *Educating the Baccalaureate Social Worker: Report of the Undergraduate Social Work Curriculum Development Project.* Cambridge, MA: Ballinger.

Block, A. M. (1978). Social Work Research: Its Role in the Curriculum. *Arete, 5*(2), 55–59.

Briar, Scott. (1974). Editorial. *Social Work, 19*(1), 2.

Dawson, B. G., Klass, M., Guy, R. F., and Edgley, C. K. (1991). *Understanding Social Work Research.* Boston: Allyn & Bacon, pp. 260 and 268.

Department of Health, Education and Welfare Publication No (HSM) 71-9059. (1971). "Planning for Creative Change in Mental Health Services: A Manual on Research Utilization." Washington, D.C.: Author, p. 30.

Epstein, Irwin. (1985). "Quantitative and Qualitative Methods." In Richard M. Grinnell, Jr. (ed.), *Social Work Research and Evaluation,* 2nd ed. Itasca, IL: F. E. Peacock.

Fortune, A. (1987). "Grief Only? Client and Social Worker Reactions to Termination." *Clinical Social Work Journal, 15*(2), Summer, 1987, 159–171.

Golan, Naomi. (1978). *Treatment in Crisis Situation.* New York: Free Press.

Grinnell, Richard, and Seigel, Deborah. (1988). "The Place of Research in Social Work." In Richard M. Grinnell (ed.), *Social Work Research and Evaluation,* 3rd ed. Itasca, IL: F. E. Peacock, p. 358.

Hepworth, Dean, and Larsen, Jo Ann. (1990). *Direct Social Work Practice,* 3rd ed. Belmont, CA: Wadsworth.

Hoffman, Kay. (1979). "Variables Related to Outcome in a Community Based Program for Women Offenders." Unpublished dissertation. Detroit: Wayne State University.

Kirk, Jerome, and Miller, Marc. (1986). *Reliability and Validity in Qualitative Research.* Newbury Park, CA: Sage Publications, p. 9.

Kirkhart, Karen, and Sallee, A. (1980). "Basic Elements of Program Evaluation" (Workshop materials). Phoenix, AZ: Maricopa County Community Council.

Levinson, H. (1987). "Termination of Psychotherapy: Some Salient Issues." *Social Casework, 58*(8), 480–489.

McKay, A., and Baxter, E. H. (1980). "Title XIX, Title XX, and Catch XXII: Cost Analysis in Social Program Evaluation." *Administration in Social Work, 4*(3), 23–30.

Miller, Delbert C. (1991). *Handbook of Research Design and Social Measurement,* 5th ed. Newbury Park, CA: Sage Publications, pp. 3, 89, and 103.

Reid, W., and Epstein, L. (1972). *Task Centered Casework.* Irvington, NY: Columbia University Press.

Rubin, Allen, and Babbie, Earl. (1989). *Research Methods for Social Work.* Belmont, CA: Wadsworth Press, pp. 125, 228, 229, 146, 191, 364.

Sallee, Alvin L. (1992). "National Trends in Family Preservation: Implications for Region VI" (Working paper). Las Cruces, NM: New Mexico State University Family Preservation Institute.

Shapiro, Connie. (1980). "Termination: A Neglected Concept in the Social Work Curriculum." *Journal of Education for Social Work, 16*(2), 13–19.

Shulman, Lawrence. (1981). *Identifying, Measuring and Teaching Helping Skills.* New York: Council on Social Work Education.

Siporin, Max. (1975). *Introduction to Social Work Practice.* New York: MacMillan.

Vissen, Kenneth. (1991). Testimony of Kenneth Vissen, Director, Family Preservation Services. *Michigan Department of Social Servicse,* before the Subcommittee on Human Resources, Committee on Ways and Means, May 1, 1991.

Webb, N. (1985). "A Crisis Intervention Perspective on the Termination Process." *Clinical Social Work, 13*(4), 329–340.

Chapter 12

Putting It All Together: Integrating Generalist Practice

OVERVIEW

In the previous chapters, we presented the six phases of the Crystal Model: Process of Planned Change. In this chapter, we present a model—the Bridge Model—which places generalist practice in context, incorporating all of the components we have discussed, including the Crystal Model phases, ethics and values, theory, client groups, and their goals. We also present a tool, the Change Process Roles (CPR) Matrix, used by generalists to understand and plan the change with an individual situation.

The chapter concludes with an extended practice illustration, the Community of Dupree. The illustration demonstrates how the Bridge Model components are understood in practice. The Change Process Roles Matrix is then used to understand each role at each point in the Crystal Model in the illustration. We begin with an overview of the concept of bridges and the theme of this book.

The Theme of Bridging

The idea of "bridges to change" captures our notion of social work generalist practice. Social workers are engaged in enterprises that link people together, bridging their differences, and working through their conflicts. Social work generalists connect people to resources they want and need, and they help build new resources for individuals, families, and communities. Encouraging empowerment of persons who do not share equitably in the distribution of goods and services in society and enabling them to build their own bridges to the resources they want and need are two of the most fundamental activities of social work generalist practice.

Our purpose here is to bring together, in a practice model, all of the components of generalist practice we have presented throughout this book. By representing each portion of generalist practice as sections of a bridge, we illustrate the "bridging," or connecting, elements of social work and provide a clear, visual representation of social work that puts all of the segments together.

The Bridge Model

As a whole, the Bridge Model represents generalist practice from client systems whom social workers assist to the change process that clients move through to attain their goals. A suspension bridge is very delicate in appearance. Graceful and long, it can, in fact, carry huge trucks, trains, and cars. Its strength comes from how its parts are assembled. Clearly, a suspension bridge is greater than a sum of its parts, just as generalist practice is far more than a sum of working with different size systems.

In Figure 12.1, the picture of a bridge, notice the three large upright towers. Set by themselves, they will fall, yet the large cable across the top holds them upright. At the same time, the towers hold the large cable which, in fact, supports

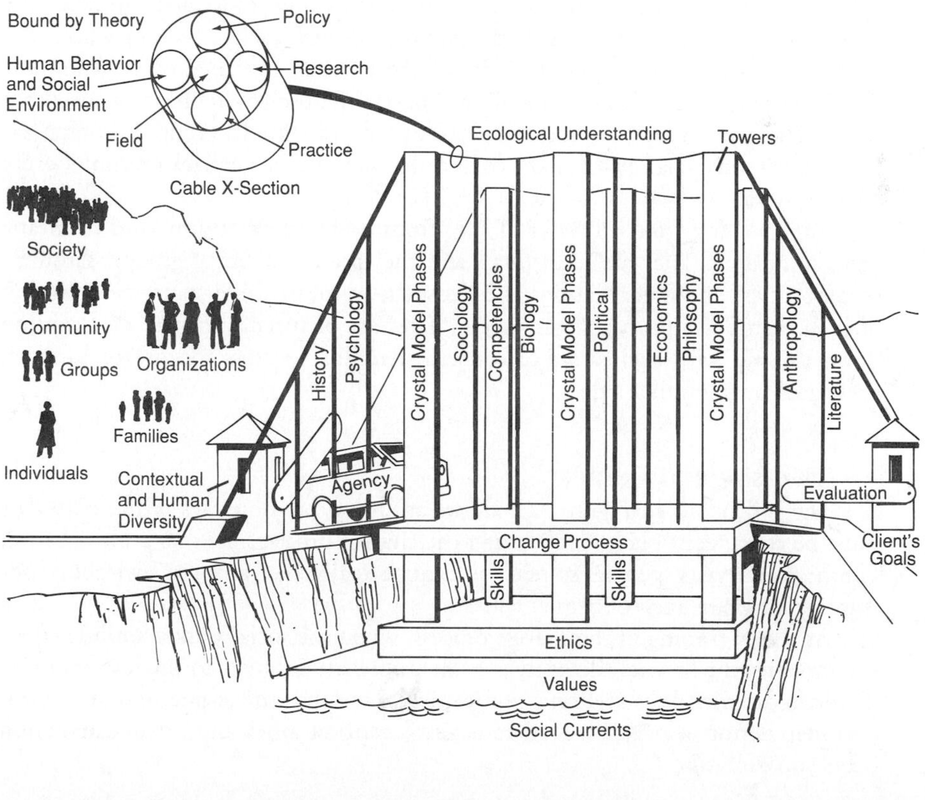

FIGURE 12.1 The Bridge of Generalist Social Work Practice

all of the small cables. These hold the main span. The ends of the large cable are anchored to huge blocks of concrete suspended in deep shafts on each shore line. There is give and take as the cables ride up and down. The cables shift with the load or wind—whatever changes occur (even earthquakes). In generalist social work practice, there must be give and take as systems change.

Bridges, by definition, span rivers, canyons, basins, or any land mass that for one reason or another must be crossed. The bridge in social work practice spans the social currents that affect people's lives. Social work generalists must be aware of current situations, whether they are domestic or international, and they must understand the impact that the changing social scene has upon social work.

Values and Ethics

The bridge in social work practice is built upon a firm foundation of values and ethics. Social work values are the base of our practice. (See Figure 12.1.) Ethics are codified values. Social work values and ethics are built to withstand change and often torrential contemporary social currents. Values are at the very base of the bridge, sometimes indistinguishable to the naked eye because events wash over them, obscuring our view of their importance. In quieter times, they are visible, but social work ethics must guide our work, regardless of social currents.

Client System

Our clients are the consumers of the social work services we offer. Individuals, families, groups, communities, and organizations are the foci of our work, and their goals become the goals of the change process that, together, we work toward. Client systems, however, need not always change themselves in order for their own goals to be met. In fact, the focal systems, or the individuals, groups, or organizations which must change for client goals to be met, are in the background of every client system.

Clients come from all walks of life, from every ethnic group, and from any geographic area. They are individuals and they are members of groups, families, communities, and organizations and, as such, we must understand the meaning of their memberships in a larger system. They are pictured in Figure 12.1 coming down the hill with their areas of concern, needing to cross the bridge to reach their goal on the other side.

Diversity and Context

The toll booth in Figure 12.1 draws attention to the issues of diversity that must be considered before and during the change process. No one avoids the toll booth; social work generalist practice cannot really be "accessed" without confronting diversity and contextual issues.

At the beginning of the change process, when the social worker and the client system enter the "scene," diversity considerations are brought to the forefront. Individuals are members of ethnic groups, racial groups, and socioeconomic groups that help define who they are. In addition, attention to sex and sexual orientation bears consideration.

Not only do we reflect on individual human diversity issues, but we appraise how the diversity that exists in our social and physical environments impacts client systems. The makeup of communities, the geography of locale, and the size of surrounding populations mold contextual diversity issues that further influence people. Service is delivered differently in rural America than it is in Los Angeles or Detroit, and life in the Sunbelt border cities brings a variety of concerns that may not be experienced in the far Northwest. For example, in a Sunbelt border city, one may be working with street children from Mexico who have fled across the border into Texas. Diversity is endless among the billions of people on earth and among the countless places human beings call home. Its effects on how people live out their lives is relevant to social work in North America.

Our society provides definitions of people based on their ethnic, racial, sexual, and physical identities that have far-reaching consequences related to our provision of social work services. Social work generalist practice has as one of its basic tenets the impact of diversity on practice. Adopting social work practice skills requires a diversity perspective.

Agency

Figure 12.1 shows the agency bus beginning its trek across the bridge highway. The agency or organization is the vehicle through which help is given to the client system.

The agency or change system appears in the Bridge Model as the agency bus. The social worker is the change agent. Social workers deliver services in conjunction with others—other social workers, related professionals, and people and groups related to the client system ride on the bus at times, too. We refer to those peripheral groups as the *action system*—that is, the system that must be activated in order for effective change, on behalf of the client system, to occur.

Social services are products of many people and the "agency bus" may even seem crowded. In fact, the agency bus must be roomy enough for the client system, the focal system, the action system, and the change system.

Who is driving the bus? The question points to considerations regarding how the change process proceeds. Is the social worker, "car keys" in hand, in charge of change, or is the client system "driving" the bus? Social work generalists work with people as they struggle toward their goals. Generalists call upon their clients' strengths through the entire process. We may begin as the bus drivers, but throughout the process, the generalist makes every effort to trade seats—to go from driver to navigator.

Change Process

The main span, the Bridge Highway, is the change process. Think of the change process as a highway that takes the client system across the social currents toward goals on the other side.

For some people, the highway of change may be broad with many lanes that represent resources and options. For others, the highway may be a one way street with bumps and pot holes, with few alternatives. In general, involuntary clients operate on a more restrictive basis than voluntary clients.

Change is a complicated process, and the social worker and client must be cognizant of factors that influence the journey. Emergency exits along the highway may be taken; the agency bus may temporarily break down or stall, and "work crews" and barriers may slow the traffic. But the agency bus moves forward, despite inclement weather or potholes. Once change has begun, there is no turning back. If necessary, alternate routes are chosen.

Traveling along the change process brings options that at the beginning of the journey may have been hidden from view, but as the agency bus climbs higher toward the span's apex, the panorama unfolds. Clients open themselves to greater possibilities, and resources become increasingly apparent.

The Towers

Change is buttressed by the three bridge towers (Figure 12.1) that represent the beginning, middle, and end of the Crystal Model. The interactive and analytic skills that are drawn upon during change are represented by each column. The cross-pieces connecting the interactive and analytical skills are the competencies, defining the combination of generalist skills, knowledge, and values. Again, strength is gained from the design. The competencies, cross-pieces, give strength to the bridge as well as generalist social work practice.

The Crystal Model divides the process into six phases: (1) area of concern and engagement, (2) information gathering, (3) assessment, (4) designing and planning, (5) implementation, and (6) evaluation and transition. Each tower combination represents two phases of the Crystal Model, beginning phase (1 and 2), middle phase (3 and 4), and ending phase (5 and 6). Beginning change involves identifying the area of concern and the client system and change systems who are to become engaged in the change effort. The middle stage that is represented by the middle tower in the Bridge Model includes information gathering and assessment, while the third tower, or the ending phase, consists of implementation, evaluation, and transition. Each phase in the process contains significant steps in change that must be considered, regardless of the duration of work with the client system. In other words, we may work very briefly with client systems, sometimes only once. But even that single encounter includes every step of the change process as outlined here.

Skills and Process

The bridge towers' columns represent the skills requisite to bring about change. From the first moment shared with a client system, we use our analytic and interactional skills to understand and to communicate empathetically with client systems. We take into account their stories and their viewpoints of the areas of concern, and we understand them in the context of what we know as professional social workers about human behavior, social policies and programs, and the social environments we inhabit. Our responses to clients are based on our learned ability to communicate professionally, and we respond with care, question appropriately, and confront when necessary.

The competencies associated with each phase in the change process are the integration of the common themes, purposes, skills, knowledge bases and values that come together in a capable social worker. Social work programs across the country have remarkably consistent expectations for their graduates, and these are incorporated in the Baer and Federico (1978) ten Competencies presented in Chapter 1 and in each chapter that outlined the Crystal Model.

The social work skills, the steps in the change process, and the competencies are firmly rooted in a foundation that consists of values and ethics. This continues to hold generalist practice steady, while agency buses cross the span, while the highway is under construction, and while the winds of change move across our environments.

Theory

Holding the bridge together are the cables that represent the knowledge base in social work practice (Figure 12.1). The large cable is really many smaller cables intertwined to give strength. The small cables intertwined represent social welfare policy and services, social research, human behavior, the social environment, and social work practice; and all rely on content that is integrated into the ecological or systems perspective.

Each small strand linking the large cable to the span depicts knowledge from the variety of disciplines. The interdisciplinary knowledge base integrates content from the social, behavioral, and biological sciences and from the humanities. We rely most heavily upon psychology, sociology, economics, political science, anthropology, and biology to inform our social work practice and to influence the foundation curriculum in which each social work student becomes immersed.

This perspective yields a world view that assists the social worker facing client system concerns that range from individual dilemmas to community changes brought on by extraordinary forces in society. Working with a young woman from rural Nebraska and taking into consideration her income, emotional state, family history, community experience, and her unique concerns demands an encompassing knowledge base. Helping an organization survive and change during burdensome economic times also requires a broadly based understanding that only an integrated, interdisciplinary knowledge base can possibly render. Throughout this book, we have described a variety of examples that illustrate social work's reliance on its knowledge base.

No other profession relies so much on the integration of the social, behavioral, and biological sciences. Social work builds its practice on the complexities of interdisciplinary study. Learning to employ this interdisciplinary approach is a formidable task, but doing so helps the social worker, operating in today's complicated and stressful world, become more perceptive and more effective. The challenge for the profession is to articulate organizing principles that will tie together the competing theories in the social and behavioral sciences.

Evaluation/Transition

As the bus exits the bridge, it passes through another toll booth that represents evaluation and transition. Together, the change system, social worker and the client system evaluate the successes and the difficulties of the trip. This knowledge is useful to the social worker for their next trip. On the way back, they may inform colleagues of new routes or "potholes" to avoid, through seminars and journal articles. The social worker makes sure the client system knows how to proceed on this side of the bay. Do they know how to continue their journey?

Goals

Reaching the "other side" of the bridge symbolizes our client systems' goal attainment. Clients choose their own goals, but they are embedded in the four overall purposes of generalist social work practice—building bridges between people, connecting people to resources, building bridges to create resources, and building bridges to empower people. Social workers engage in activities that enhance the well-being of individuals, families, groups, communities, and organizations, and their endeavors are founded in the value base of social work that supports the dignity and worth of every human being.

Summary

The suspension bridge is a complex and intricate structure capable of carrying huge weights over wide, deep, and treacherous waters, linking people with their goals. Generalist social work practice enables us to transport those who ask for our help to their goals through an equally complex, delicate process. Generalist practice not taken as a whole is as weak as a suspension bridge without a large cable or a foundation. When we are able to put all of the pieces of generalist practice together in partnership with the client system, goals are achieved.

Change Process Roles (CPR) Matrix

The Bridge Model provides an overview and explanation of the generalist process. The Crystal Model outlines the phases used in the change process, and the change roles define the participants in the process. Remaining is a way to combine the Crystal Model phases with specific implications for each role during each phase. The Change Process Roles (CPR) Matrix is the framework for accomplishing this.

As can be seen in Figure 12.2, the CPR matrix consists of rows and columns that create cells. The column on the left lists the change roles we have presented: the change system, client system, focal system, and action system. Across the top are the Crystal Model phases, beginning with identifying the area of concern. Under each Crystal Model phase are listed questions that should be answered for each role. For example, in the first phase (area of concern), we answer how each role defines the area of concern. Each cell is completed from that systems perspective. In practice, you may expand each cell to a full page of paper, and, in supervisory sessions, lay the pages out on a desk or put them up on a bulletin board. For example, the focal system will almost always define the area of concern in a way that is different from the client system. We need to have a form for recording that information in an easily retrievable manner. The CPR matrix provides such a form.

FIGURE 12.2 Change Process Roles Matrix (CPR)

Role	Area of Concern: Who is in the system and how does each system define the issues?	Information Gathering: What information do you need? Establish contact and relationship to do data collection.	Assessment/ Analysis: What does the information gathered mean? What are risks plus opportunities?	Design/Plan: Design and plan objectives, goals, tasks, who, what, when, where, how?	Implementation: Skills with each system and resources used.	Evaluation/ Transition: What goals you accomplish and how you phase out?
Change System						
Client System						
Focal System						
Action System						

Developed by Patricia Sandau-Beckler and Alvin L. Sallee, 1990.

After you read the following practice illustration, we will use both the Bridge Model and the CPR Matrix so you can see how these generalist models are applied. The illustration of the Dupree Community is based on a real town with very real areas of concern. The families and the social worker are composites drawn from real people and their achievements.

PRACTICE ILLUSTRATION: THE COMMUNITY OF DUPREE

The Community

The community of Dupree, Missouri is located 90 miles south of St. Louis, in the hill country at the beginning of the Ozarks. Becoming familiar with a small community may begin by locating where the residents generally congregate to ex-

Information is transferred in key locations in a community—here, on a sidewalk bench.

change the news each day. In Dupree, this happens around the courthouse, where in nice weather one can find older men playing checkers on the park bench and talking about the weather, sports, and other things of interest to a small community. Women gather in the laundromat across the street. One must gain credibility and legitimacy to sit in on these conversations. By listening, much can be learned about the workings of a community, including its members' opinions, prejudices, love of the town, and the town's social and economic history.

The Green Shoe Company was the major industrial unit in the community, and when it closed this year, this had a major economic impact on Dupree and its 3,500 residents. The closing evoked a tremendous amount of emotion. The company president and his executives came down from St. Louis for a large meeting in the courthouse to explain the necessity of moving the shoe factory to Mexico. The factory had been open for over a hundred years and had served as the economic base of this community. Wherever one went in the community, one heard of the impact. People were concerned and outraged. One could say that the impact affected almost everyone because every company, service, and store depended on paychecks from the Green Shoe Company being spent in town.

The DuBois Family

One of the families affected by the closing of the Green Shoe Company was a white family, the DuBois family. Tim DuBois and his wife, Linda, have four children: Charles, thirteen; a daughter, Joan, ten; Sean, eight; and Liza, two.

Tim DuBois was employed as a supervisor at the shoe company and not only earned a decent living, but also had the respect of the community as a supervisor in its most important economic system. Shortly after the closing of the shoe company, Tim attempted to find work in the Dupree area and was unable to do so. After twenty-six weeks, his workman's unemployment insurance ran out, and he was soon faced with a very difficult situation.

Additionally, at this time, Linda was hospitalized for a hysterectomy. Complications developed, and Linda was placed in a nursing home for six weeks following her hospital discharge. The health insurance Tim had had at the shoe company had always paid 80 percent of all medical bills up to $2,000 and 100 percent after that. However, after losing his employment, the DuBois family dropped their insurance in order to make the mortgage payments on their home. Linda's bill is nearly $100,000.

The children attend a private Catholic school, which requires tuition payments that Tim and Linda had made regularly, wanting the best education for a better future for their children. Charles, who is thirteen years old, is involved in athletics and plays quarterback for the football team which, for the junior high school level, is well known throughout that region of Missouri. He is an important member of this team.

Joan is active in choir and dance, and is known as a leader among the fifth-grade students. Sean is in the second grade and is a good student and is well thought of by his teachers. Liza attends a half-day child-care program.

The DuBois extended family also consists of Tim's aging parents who are in their early eighties and live in Dupree. They still live in their own home and are able to maintain their independence fairly well, using the Meals-on-Wheels program which brings food from the hospital each day at a very low cost to them.

Tim has one brother, David, who also worked at the Green Shoe Company. David has experienced a somewhat less stressful life after the closing of the plant. As a common worker, he belonged to the United Shoe Makers Union and received unemployment payments from the union after his state unemployment checks stopped. In addition, the union was able to provide health insurance coverage to him for a minimal amount of money. David is supportive of his brother, Tim, and has spent time looking for jobs in the Dupree area with him, also with no success.

Linda's brother, Jeff Smith, serves in the Missouri legislature and is a well-known attorney in the Jefferson City area. Although he is extremely busy with his legislative and legal work, he does make a point of visiting the family at least twice a year and is sensitive to the issues and concerns that the people in Dupree area are experiencing.

Institutions

The Catholic school is an important institution in the DuBois family's life. Tim gained great satisfaction from serving on the board of trustees for the school. He is well respected and in better times had served as the treasurer. Now he is growing concerned, frustrated, and depressed because, as a former member of the board of trustees, he is unable to contribute to the support of the parish beyond the tuition payments. He is sensitive about this issue. Before her hospitalization, Linda had been involved in volunteering at the school and serving as a substitute teacher from time to time.

Another important establishment in the community is the grocery store. The grocery store contributes economically to the community through its advertisements, usually in the Wednesday paper. In fact, whether the newspaper editor supported a political candidate or not was sometimes based upon who the grocery store owner supported.

Linda worked until she became ill and lost her job at the grocery store in downtown Dupree. It was an important job to her, even though she was employed only half-time, because it gave her an opportunity to meet and visit with the town's people and keep up on what was going on, keeping her very involved and active in the community.

The Change Process

Beginning Phase

These are the concerns that faced Tim when he turned to the social worker at Family Services of Missouri. He met with Agnes Scott, an African-American B.S.W. graduate.

Ms. Scott listened to Tim state his concerns. She began to gather information about the situation in which Tim and his family found themselves. Important points are that he had been unemployed and that the skills and training he had received could not be applied within the seventy-mile radius of Dupree. Additionally, Linda DuBois, who serves many important roles and functions in the family, had been ill for six weeks. With her illness, the family accumulated a very large hospital bill. Because of Linda's absence, everyone's life within the family changed dramatically. With Tim out looking for jobs and Linda hospitalized, Charles had to drop out of football in order to care for Liza. Joan's usual enthusiasm and outgoing personality changed. She is now rather sullen and withdrawn. Sean's academic performance has dropped off dramatically and prompted a visit to Tim from the school counselor. The counselor raised a concern about Sean's academic performance and behavior change.

After receiving this initial information, Ms. Scott begins to realize there are many families in Dupree experiencing similar concerns to the DuBois family. She begins to assess those affected in Dupree. Tim and Linda are both depressed and frustrated. The children are caught in the contagion caused by so many losses. Everyone in the family has been profoundly affected.

Ms. Scott understands there are a number of families who are experiencing this area of concern in the community brought on by the economic impact in the community from the loss of the Green Shoe Company plant. She thinks of the increased concern: that there had been more problems with teenagers' acting out behaviors. There is a feeling of depression that has settled over the community as able-bodied males who had always seen themselves as very much a part of the American work ethic become depressed, frustrated, and bitter.

Ms. Scott also understands that before establishing a working relationship with the DuBois family, that she perhaps needs to address the issue of her ethnic identity and Tim's ethnic identity. She spoke openly with Tim about any concerns he might have about her cultural understanding. There is a small population of African Americans in this community.

Tim is very concerned about losing his job and not being able to provide for his family. Linda has doubts about her health. Both worries had greatly affected their marriage and their usual care and love for each other and for their family. The children feel a weakened relationship with each other and their family. With their school activities diminished, they feel less attached to their school and their friends. Tim's parents felt very strongly and positively toward him, yet their failing health means they can contribute very little to actually helping their adult child. The children are very attached to David, their uncle, who, because of his resources, feels more positive, and therefore serves as surrogate father for the children.

Assessment and Planning

The mayor of Dupree, Joe Alshoot, has been mayor for over twenty-five years and thinks there are no serious problems if people just pull themselves up by their bootstraps. He owns a car dealership that routinely attracts people from as far away as St. Louis to buy cars. When people talk about economic development, he states there really is no need to spend county or city money on development. Ms. Scott identified Mr. Alshoot as part of the focal system.

She also begins to assess resources for the DuBois family. She asks Tim if he is aware of Homemakers, Inc. Through a state contract with Title XX, this agency provided homemakers to families where the principal homemaker was disabled or out of the home for an extended period of time. After his Rotary meeting, where he serves as assistant chairperson, Tim stops in to find out more about their services and is pleasantly surprised to learn they can provide homemaker services three days a week.

Linda's brother, Representative Jeff Smith, became concerned not only about his sister's family, but also about the situation in Dupree and the impoverished condition of Washington County. Ms. Scott shares her concerns for the entire community with him. The next month, he brings his subcommittee on prison reform to the Dupree area to study it for the possibility of a minimum-security prison being built in the Dupree. Although he meets with initial reluctance on the part of the community (for example, the men in front of the courthouse), the economic impact and benefits greatly outweigh their concerns. Jeff invites the press to a public hearing in the high school auditorium to discuss the issues.

One of the people at the meeting, Bob Drummond, speaks up in favor of the prison, realizing that as a private contractor, he stands a good chance of putting his business back on its feet. Soon, other business people start speaking in favor of the building in the community, which could employ 200 full-time staff in different capacities, from guards, secretaries, and cooks, to maintenance workers. Based upon the willingness of the community to support the prison and the possibility of land being donated by the county for this effort, the subcommittee gives Jeff's bill a "do pass" vote. Jeff goes back to the legislature and, through his leadership, passes the bill that creates the Dupree Minimum Security Prison.

Implementation and Transition

The building of the Dupree Prison, however, does not resolve all the concerns in this community. It does bring back a stable economic base to Dupree. Two hundred inmates are transferred to Dupree to rehabilitate their lives. The prison social workers work with them, trying to build linkages to their families, to jobs, and other community release programs. These prisoners, however, come in as involuntary clients. There are other concerns of those incarcerated, a high percentage of which are Black males. The prison raises new issues such as the quality of the rehabilitation and the work-release programs. The quality of legal aid afforded to those who were incarcerated during their appeal is questionable.

Citizens still face the task of healing the emotional, psychological, and social scars. Dupree faces a new threat from the north as more and more people move south from St. Louis and begin to increase the property values and drain different services, such as police, fire, and sewage services. The other issues that face many rural areas are still found in Dupree, such as the relative isolation of these communities, making health services hard to come by. Still, there is a quality of life in this community that is a strength. People like to hunt and fish and experience the rural life. They are willing to try to cope with many of these concerns to do so.

Discussion

The story of Dupree illustrates a number of components of the change process. Ms. Scott used the Crystal Model steps with the different-size systems. Diversity issues came up in practice and were dealt with at a policy and direct practice level.

There was an important building of relations, not only between individuals in a family but also between large economic, social, and political systems. In the real world, there are political connections made through family and friends. These may affect an entire community. We see how a community which on the surface does not appear to have many resources, does in fact have resources and support: informal, formal, and societal resources. The focal system includes the mayor, some community persons opposed to the prison, and the legislature. The action system includes Homemakers, Inc., the counseling agency, and Jeff.

Ms. Scott referred the DuBois family to the Family Counseling Agency of Lincoln County for in-home family assessment. The M.S.W. specialist provided Ms. Scott a summary of his assessment after the DuBois family signed a release. The assessment identified the family's strengths and the concerns over the long-term effects the parents' depression might have on the children. Based on the assessment, a plan for short-term counseling was made and implemented. Ms. Scott worked on implementing the social brokering parts of the plan to substitute societal resources for Linda's role, thus allowing the children to resume their activities.

In Figure 12.3, we see part of the Change Process Roles (CPR) Matrix as completed by the social worker, Ms. Scott. This CPR Matrix is for the families with similar areas of concerns as the DuBois family has. The issues and change process addressed in Figure 12.3 are at the "macro," or broad, level.

In Figure 12.3, each phase of the Crystal Model is addressed for each system role, and each cell is completed. For example, in the focal system under area of concern, the mayor does not believe there is a communitywide problem. From his perspective as a car dealer who is dependent on out-of-town customers, he is not concerned. He has been elected for over twenty-five years, and he has become insensitive. By knowing the mayor's view on the area of concern, we get a more comprehensive picture of all systems and their interactions. The CPR Matrix at this broad level helps the social worker keep many variables in order—a major task in this illustration!

Summary

The Bridge Model of social work practice depicts the intricacies and complexities, along with the connections, that are inherent in generalist social work practice. Bridges do bring people and resources together, and so does social work generalist practice.

The Change Process Roles Matrix is a tool that aids us in keeping the total change process in focus by tracking many variables such as roles, systems, and the Crystal Model phases. Each systems perspective and position can be represented.

In the next chapter, we will look to the future, possibly your future as a gener-

FIGURE 12.3 CPR for Dupree

Role	Area of Concern	Information	Assessment	Plan	Implementation	Evaluation/ Transition
CHANGE SYSTEM Ms. Scott, Family Services	Ms. Scott is concerned about the number of out of work families and their risks, such as the DuBois family.	What economic data is available? What have other communities done? Are there strengths?	Family Services cannot do it all—must expand action system opportunities for Family Services to emerge as leader.	Family Services will reduce Ms. Scott's caseload. Board asked to endorse efforts Evaluation Plan developed.	Change managing	Was Family Services mission accepted and supported. Transition from individual families by closing cases.
CLIENT SYSTEM Out of work families in Dupree	Lack income and ability to fully participate in community. Depression	How many families are there? What emergency needs do they have? Begin to establish a relationship through a group.	Risk of poverty or having to leave informal resources to find a job. Opportunity to utilize societal and formal resources. Community depression.	Each family develops a service plan, answering 4 w's and how. Community Action team from St. Louis. Mental Health Center plans anti- depression strategy	Encourage empowerment	Was the economic base expanded and diversified? Long-range Planning Committee formed to continue gains. Were families goals met? New knowledge and value of societal resources and family systems.
FOCAL SYSTEM • Green Shoe Co. President	Shoe company needs more profit for stock- holders.	• What would it take to keep Green Shoe Co. in Du-	Mexican labor costs are much cheaper. Company owes	Candidate to oppose mayor is identified and given back-	Exercise influ- ence Encourage empowerment	Individual sin- gle-subject designs for each family.

System					
• Mayor Alshoot • State Legislators • Families	Mayor wants private business to solve its own problems. Legislature unaware of economic impact. Families want things as they were.	pree? • Mayor aware of extent of problem. • How can legislature become aware? • What do families want, specifically?	nothing to community. Mayor will not change and will take chances with electorate. Legislature will be informed. Families ask for help to change.	ground information and outside funding to raise issue. Plan for retraining developed by union.		Pre-post assessment of community depression. Availability of ongoing counseling as needed.
ACTION SYSTEM Rep. Jeff Smith School Superintendent Union President	Rep. Smith chairs key subcommittee. School superintendent sees impact on children and wants to help. Union President wants jobs.	• What public works jobs are available? • Extent of labor force. • Educational needs. • How can membership be helped?	Prison needed by state in this area. Need diversity in economic base. School counselors and social workers see impact of depression on lower grades and activities. Need new industry.	Subcommittee meeting scheduled. Plan to hire two temporary school social workers. Plan to expand union to include public employees.	Exercise influence.	Was the prison bill passed and signed? Did union membership increase? Did students' academic performance improve? What ongoing informal resources can continue to support students?

alist social worker, and to the future of social work practice. Several themes we have addressed throughout this text are summarized for you, including professional involvement, continuing education, job stress, and the rewards of social work.

References

Baer, Betty, and Federico, Ronald. (1978). *Educating the Baccalaureate Social Worker: Report of the Undergraduate Social Work Curriculum Development Project.* Cambridge, MA: Ballinger.

Sandau-Beckler, Patricia, and Sallee, Alvin L. (1990). Change Process Roles (CPR) Matrix.

Looking to the Future

Using Our Strengths

OVERVIEW

Social work, a profession still in its formative stage, continues to define itself. Emerging from a two-pronged and somewhat contradictory history marked by a profound response to both public and private troubles and by a drive to become an identified, "legitimate" profession, social work is an emerging societal force from a research, practice, and policy position. It is a profession that offers a rewarding career for energetic and forward-looking people (Axinn and Levin, 1982; and Morales and Sheafor, 1992).

Simultaneously, entering the profession at a time when obstacles blocking opportunities to work effectively on behalf of client systems have beset most social workers in most agencies throughout the country, you are met with exceptional challenges (see Figure 13.1). This chapter's purpose is to offer a framework for understanding the position of social work in society today and to assist readers in defining their places in social work's exciting future.

Specifically, we begin with an overview of social work's strengths, followed by a discussion of the challenges we face in our society that are related to our profession, and finally, the chapter contains the "fall out" from societal problems that affect the quality of work experience. Also contained in the chapter are options that speak to means by which new social workers can summon their profession's strengths to impact and affect the grave conditions by which the late twentieth-century United States is defined.

What can you do with a major in

Social Work?

Medical Social Worker • Residential Counselor • School Social Worker • Social Worker for County Welfare Department • Director of Social Services for a Nursing Home • Home Care Social Worker • Employee Assistance Counselor • Community Organizer • Case Manager • Group Home Supervisor • Outreach Worker • Youth Worker • Foster Care Worker • Residential Counselor for Developmentally Disabled • Child Care Worker • Group Home Worker • Information and Referral Resource Coordinator • Home Care Social Worker • Social Service Worker • Sexual Abuse Worker • Occupational Social Worker • Probation Officer • Drug and Alcohol Abuse Counselor • Child Protection Worker •Coordinator of Geriatric Services • Mental Health Worker • Family Court Officer • Domestic Abuse Officer • Program Evaluator for Community Mental Health Center • Child Care Counselor • Senior Case Aide • Intake Worker • Group Leader • Counselor for the Bureau of Vocational Rehabilitation • Instructor for the Mentally Retarded • Adoption Worker • Assistant Director of Social Services • Research Assistant • Social and Casework Supervisor • Patient Advocate • Peace Corps Volunteer • Chemical Health Coordinator

for more information
CALL 646-2143

Box 30001, Department 3SW
New Mexico State University
Las Cruces, New Mexico 88003
Accredited by the Council on Social Work Education

**Department of
Social Work**

Reprinted by permission of the University of St. Thomas, College of St. Catherine, Department of Social Work.

FIGURE 13.1

THE STRENGTHS OF GENERALIST SOCIAL WORK

Social work has long concerned itself with people who experience great threats to their well-being. Persons who are at risk—the economically disenfranchised, ethnic minorities of color, women, gay and lesbian people, the physically and mentally challenged, the elderly, and children—are the center of social work efforts. Of course, not all those who count themselves as members of such large groups are vulnerable, nor are those who are not members of at-risk populations immune from problems, but social work's involvement with these populations and its interest in supporting social policies that affect them especially is well known. Nonetheless, we look around our world and see chaos and pain affecting more and more people; we see institutions that once provided the infrastructure necessary for a humane society crumbling; and we sometimes see government and large corporations turning their backs on those who are most in need.

Social work's voice is too often unheeded and our own energies diffused because society seems unresponsive to changes that will support enhancing the well-being of those in greatest need. The remarkable "flip side" of this bleak coin is social work's perseverance, along with its growing articulation and power as a profession especially concerned with the disenfranchised. Focusing on what social work, and, more specifically, generalist social work, has to offer in the face of the rather ominous signs in our midst seems a fitting way to begin our look to the future.

The Social Work Perspective

The social work perspective—our world view and our framework for understanding—is different from other helping professions and from each of the academic disciplines that support our knowledge base. The difference is in its integration of knowledge gathered from its numerous sources. At once, we use understandings from sociology, psychology, political science, anthropology, biology and economics, coupled with our own experience in working with people. We have yet to articulate organizing principles that can help us use this knowledge. However, in their absence, we do, at least, have a perspective that provides some help: the ecological perspective.

We concern ourselves with individuals' relationships with others, with transactions between and among people, the institutions that provide for them, and with the internal effects that relationships—both negative and positive—leave upon us as individuals. The predominant theme in the ecological perspective is our social nature, both as individuals and as members of families, groups, communities, and organizations. In other words, whatever system we are working with, we understand people in the context of their relationships with others. All of our work, from engagement to evaluation and transition, recognizes this fundamental fact and leads us in our understanding of human behavior.

Social Work and Collaboration

Social work generalist practice is built on a collaborative model that emphasizes mutuality with clients and teamwork with other professionals. Our relationships with clients, although professional in nature, have moved away from the traditional "medical" model of conduct to a model that affirms client strengths and client modes of working through their own dilemmas and problems. Thus, we affirm clients' worth and dignity, and we affirm their abilities to solve their own problems. In fact, the resources we attempt to link them with and the resources we seek to provide ought to be freely chosen, to the greatest extent possible, by our client systems.

The collaborative model that generalist social work supports is a response to the changing needs and conditions of those with whom we work and those whom we serve. Case management has the closest relationship with the collaborative model, and it grew as a response to the deinstitutionalization movement of the 1960s and 1970s (Rose, 1992). In addition, the collaborative model emerged from our understanding of the complexities our clients were facing in their families, communities, schools, and in the country as a whole. There is a recognition that "going it alone" with clients no longer works, especially with the disenfranchised and the economically and socially oppressed populations, and that working together is the only feasible answer (Parsloe, 1981).

Generalist social work took the challenge seriously, and the practice model is based upon an understanding that client systems, social workers, the action system, and the focal system all must be engaged in the work at hand, if effective and meaningful change is to occur. Indeed, working with groups of all kinds, communicating with a whole variety of other professionals and, perhaps, most importantly, tapping into the client's focal system, the place where change must take place if clients' goals are to be actualized, are the components of the collaborative model in generalist social work practice (Holden, 1981). The social work generalist's greatest practice strength lies in his or her ability to be the team leader in the collaborative model.

The generalist is aware of all the intricate relationships that must be attended to in a collaborative working model and the expertise that sets the generalist apart from other professionals is the ability to form teams, to work in teams and to develop solutions to concerns and problems through a team effort.

Social Work and Caring

Underlying all of social work is our emphasis upon caring—caring for others, caring about the conditions in society, caring about our colleagues, and caring about ourselves as individuals and as professionals. From the founding mothers and fathers of social work to present-day practitioners, our clearest motivation has been to offer care to others. Even the values that support social work are based on care and the conduct in which we engage is tested through our concern for others.

Nell Nodding, an educational philosopher from the University of California, describes the ethic of caring as highly practical because it recognizes the relatedness and the reciprocity of caring. Caring is not merely doing for others, but, rather, it is doing for others in light of our own caring for ourselves. She recognizes that reaching out for others is demanding, not "tenderminded," and is instead an ethic that is tough and difficult to sustain because it demands self-understanding and acceptance of all we are (Nodding, 1984, p. 99).

The ethic of caring is particularly suited to social work practice, not only on the basis of our long-standing concern for others, but, further, on our understanding that in order to help others, we must have an understanding of our values, our strengths, and our limitations. Thus, caring is truly reciprocal and in line with our knowledge base that supports interdependence and integration and on our collaborative model of practice that demands enhancing our relationships with others.

Social Work and Diversity

Social work has, as a tenet of its belief system and its practical application, a commitment to valuing diversity, whether it is diversity based on ethnic differences, individual differences, sex differences, sexual-orientation differences or any other differences that define people. Differences are not seen as barriers to be overcome, but as conditions that ought to be made known and celebrated. In a related sense, differences can be seen as a mark of the ordinary, a part of the human condition that does not set people apart, but, in a greater sense, binds us together.

Differences, especially racial, have been used as excuses for the inequities that grow out of our culture and our economic and sociopolitical system; but the differences, themselves, are not the reasons for inequities. In fact, when people understand more about the differences among them, the similarities we share as members of the same species and inhabitants of the same planet and social environment, the differences become less prominent and more a mark of everyday life that we value.

Social Work as Art and Science

Another of social work's present strengths is a heightened tension between art and science. The *art* of social work recognizes the individual style each social worker brings to bear upon the work at hand. Social work as art takes into account the unique moments shared with clients that may make a difference in their lives, and supports the belief that human interaction, knowing another person and listening attentively and unconditionally are the ingredients of effective practice. It is doubtful that any social worker, even today, disputes these practice ingredients.

The *science* of social work underscores the need for a systematic approach to social work practice. In view of the complex problems social workers encounter, determining constructive, identifiable means of helping that can be replicated is the cornerstone of social work as science.

In a profession defined by a caring ethic and a need to replicate effective helping strategies, a tension within social work is inevitable. In our view, the tension is a major strength of social work. Developing practice paradigms that take into account individual ways of working is a challenge that can be addressed only if the profession recognizes its holistic character. Discovering just what the ingredients of effective practice add up to can only happen in social work if students and practitioners, alike, become more systematic in their approaches. There is a tremendous need to find out "what works" and to continue to develop programs with good track records. On the other hand, the heart of social work cannot be left untended. Moral ideals must be the base for our work, and science is always tempered by a critical evaluation of the means used to achieve ends.

Starting with social work's strengths seems fitting in a practice that is charged with working with the great social problems of the day. We must recognize what we have in our profession before we are able to direct our power toward the goals social work has agreed upon and, en route, contend with the barriers and problems in society that place so many people at risk. In the following section, we offer our ideas and concerns presented in such a way that social work students may find their place in a world that needs dedicated, scientifically minded, caring people, capable of working with others and capable of acknowledging differences of all kinds.

SOCIAL WORK'S CHALLENGES

Economic Disparity

Postindustrial society's defining characteristic is an economy striking in its resource disparity between the affluent and the impoverished, all living in one democratic society. To be poor in the United States is "to be a second class citizen in a way that is not found to be acceptable in English or Swedish societies" (Bellah et al., 1991, p. 89). And to be wealthy is to be wealthy enough to buy any resource, any service, and any luxury. Differences among the upper class and the lower class are enormous, and differences even among the great equalizer, "the middle class," are heightening.

Bellah states that our economic system has wrought lives experienced in tender fragility because the reliance on steady work that will bring in the money needed for a decent life in this society now rests on shifting sand. Industrial workers in the Midwest have weathered changes they did not anticipate, and they have seen their own organized power become overshadowed by large corporations' increasing use of third-world countries with low wage scales that make the U.S. industrial worker obsolete. Thus, working class people find themselves hovering on the brink of poverty, unable to provide themselves and their families with health care and decent housing, while at the same time the tax base of their communities that in the past supported adequate schools has eroded.

Increasing numbers of women depend on the welfare system to care for themselves and their children, not only because they are experiencing pregnancies at a younger age, but also because the chance for a real family life where parents can both work and care for their children seems more and more elusive, especially to those who dwell in the large industrial cities of the United States. And the women who live on welfare and the welfare system itself become scapegoats of the market economy.

Meeting the homeless on the street was, until recently, a phenomenon relegated only to a few large cities, but homeless people have changed the face of large cities, small towns, and even suburbs, once the bulwark against any view of poverty on the "other side." We wonder how our children are shaped by this growing picture of people without homes in a society strewn with the electronic marvels — computers, fax machines, telephones with video screens, and high-density televisions that bring lifelike pictures to affluent homes everywhere. Economic disparity that is so evident is a concern for all Americans.

Social work must deal with this enormous challenge that faces our society and our world. Our professional history lends itself to our involvement in meeting the challenge, but the forces in the contemporary life, even experienced within social work, mitigate against effective action.

Many social workers have moved away from working with public sector clients and define social work as psychotherapy that may more appropriately serve those whose external resources are less limited than the people who are receiving AFDC, who are homeless, chronically mentally ill, or abused and neglected children.

The Public Sector

Social work students may need to reexamine their own motivation for social work and consider working, at least for some time, with clients with multiple problems and numerous at-risk conditions. Of course, work environments in the agencies that serve the neediest people are often unfriendly to the professional social worker who expects not only fair remuneration, but also a level of autonomy that work situations in many public agencies do not offer. Nonetheless, avoiding impoverished populations will not solve the problems that people who suffer from the growing distance of a decent quality of life live with each day.

Child welfare agencies experience a high staff turnover rate and high levels of stress among workers (Vinokur-Kaplan, 1991, pp. 81–91). For new workers, job dissatisfaction seems to be associated with poor work conditions in public agencies and for more experienced workers, low salaries in relationship to the responsibilities they assume. Work conditions in agencies that serve low-income people often are crowded, with little space for privacy with clients. In a word, they reflect the overall negative treatment that welfare clients receive in general.

It is quite understandable that social workers may not wish to subject themselves to dubious conditions that do not enhance professionalism, but meeting the challenge of economic disparity in this country does call social work professionals to action and involvement. Recent efforts in professional organizations such as the National Association of Social Workers and the Council on Social Work Education aimed at influencing public sector social work are hopeful signs of changes to come.

Societal Resources

The economic system is not the only institution undergoing strain that affects our profession. Social welfare, education, health care, and criminal justice—all societal resources—are attempting to deal with skyrocketing costs, enormous demands, and inadequate responses to contemporary problems. Institutional responses are largely piecemeal—the "tinkering" approach to problem and solution—and seem to create even more stressful situations for the people they serve.

Illustration: Social Welfare Reform

The Family Support Act of 1988, "welfare reform," has created a whole host of problems that the authors of the legislation likely did not intend. Mandated job training has had little effect on creating new jobs that pay a living wage, and the "workfare" component of the act has not paid off in better lives for recipients (Handler and Hasenfeld, 1991). Many states, experiencing an eroding tax base, are making it even more difficult for people to get the financial help they need, and, thus, homelessness, child neglect and abuse, and a whole host of other social problems are spurred on.

The welfare system itself is blamed for economic woes, and some states are rethinking their transfer payments, tying money to social behavior. The belief that women who are receiving AFDC attempt to increase their monthly payment by giving birth to another child has contributed to controversial policies emanating from many state capitals that cap payments based upon the number of children covered in the original grant.

Concerns over the growing high-school drop-out rate have resulted in an experimental program called "Learnfare." High school youth must stay in school in order for their families to continue receiving their monthly allotments from AFDC. Such policies were developed in a supposedly "pro-family" atmosphere, but the damage that can be sustained on individual families is devastating.

Consider Howard, age 15, alienated and angry with his mother. He threatens to drop out of school and will attend school only if he receives his share of the monthly AFDC payment. Or, consider the situation of Danny, 14, fearful of attending school because of conflict with rival gang members. Carol Croce of the Wisconsin Nutrition Project cites an example in Milwaukee of a teenager who, in his attempt to abide by his mother's wishes to stay out of gangs, skipped school to avoid gang members, and the family was sanctioned three months later by the Department of Human Services (Croce, 1988). Should all of Howard's family be penalized based on adolescent's problems in daily living? Would not humane social work involvement be a more meaningful alternative?

Education

Universal education has not lived up to its potential, and a piecemeal approach to its improvement is the only reaction thus far. Middle school students shooting each other with guns has become a far-too-frequent phenomenon. How do students learn in environments in which they feel threatened? Funding for education is grossly unfair, leaving poor inner cities with a low per-pupil expenditure while wealthy suburbs afford high teacher salaries and programs responding to their children's educational needs. Because education is so fundamental to the ongoing positive growth of a democracy, especially a technologically advanced one, its critical condition is cause for great concern among the social work profession.

Jane Addams acknowledged the importance of education in community life when she began Hull House in the late 1800s. One of Hull House's chief functions was "to offer community education, to make the world of the chaotic American metropolis intelligible to its least favored and most disadvantaged citizens" (Bellah, et al., 1991, p. 152). Having greater control over one's environment so that resources that are unavailable become accessible is fundamental to citizens in a democracy. Addams knew this, and social work's educational role must be asserted in new and creative ways.

Health Care

The health-care crisis touches nearly every person in the United States, and the entire system seems in disarray. Costs in recent years have escalated to the point that unless a family has broad coverage as part of a wage earner's total package, people simply cannot receive adequate medical care. The unfortunate fact is that growing numbers of employees cannot, by themselves, afford health insurance costs and the individual worker and his or her family is left out, expected to fend for themselves. Consequently, public hospitals are overwhelmed with patients who cannot pay and adequate medical care decreases.

The harsh results of reduced medical care are particularly routed to vulnerable populations. Children do not receive immunizations because they are not receiving regular, well-baby and well-child services, and parents often bring their offspring to emergency rooms for every medical need. Adults without extensive education and "high-tech" skills cannot find decent work that includes health care coverage. They do not receive treatment, again, except in the context of emergency rooms that are already overcrowded. When a catastrophic illness touches families, too many are in financial ruin, unable to recover from the enormous burden of medical bills, bills they cannot even hope to pay.

Social work is deeply involved in working toward ending the health care crisis in the United States. Knowing that some sort of universal health-care coverage must come about fuels professional organizations to confront Congress and the executive branch of the federal government, pressuring members to create legislation that will alleviate the crisis. Direct service social workers employed in health-care settings work under severe conditions, attempting to deliver their services to patients and clients. Reorganizing services and focusing on prevention and community-based services are all part of the social work presence in the health-care crisis.

Criminal Justice

Prison construction increased dramatically in the 1980s and nearly every state built prisons at enormous costs and with little impact on the root causes of crime. The criminal justice system includes greater numbers of people, and, for African-American males in the inner cities, going to prison is shockingly commonplace. The belief that "putting people away" will end crime has largely proven false, and we find fear of crime and fear of victimization an overriding concern of many people in this society.

Justice Department Studies (1992) show that criminality tends to cluster in families. In other words, children who are delinquent are likely to come from families in which one or more persons is incarcerated. This is fuel for sociobiological theories regarding causes of criminal behavior, and there may be other explanations for the phenomenon as well. Marc Mauer, the director of Sentencing Alternative in Washington D.C., speculates that children growing up in inner cities have simply lost hope and a prison sentence may be seen as an inevitable consequence of living in poor neighborhoods with high crime.

Whatever the explanation, the findings point to the spiraling effects of widespread crime in the United States. Children growing up in families need a better future and an opportunity to contribute constructively to the building of their own lives and to the building of a better society. In that light, working in the criminal justice system may, once again, become important for the social work profession.

With new emphasis upon community corrections, social work must revisit its relationship to the criminal justice system. Opportunities for impacting policy, for humanizing treatment, and for conducting research regarding what programs work in criminal justice must be part of the new social work agenda.

Isolation in Communities

Community life in the United States is strained. People feel alienated from their government and public opinion polls seem to reflect a growing disenchantment with those who govern. Public life seems more and more distant from the mainstream, enjoyed by groups not associated with the everyday person in everyday life.

Our national worldview, which places the individual above all other considerations, contradicts what viable communities need and the actual interdependence of our lives. Participation in community block clubs, in PTAs, and in local political party organizations seems lackluster. Many people in urban areas do not venture out at night, and the heavy workloads of parents attempting to raise their children and work full time mitigate against involvement. Further, the privatization of leisure activities finds people congregating in private homes with friends rather than in public places. Thus, citizenship becomes a relic of the past, and community life suffers (Bellah, et al., 1991; and Schor, 1992.)

Isolation results in defining troubles in a way that blames the victim for problems that, in reality, find their causes in society. Adolescent women with small babies, isolated from their families and from a viable support network, cannot be expected to give the kind of care to their children that they need. A discouraged worker, whose unemployment has expired and who finds himself on the streets selling and using drugs is more than an individual with a personal weakness. There are countless examples of people who are disenfranchised from community life, not because of their own deficiencies, but because there is little community life on which to lean.

Social work has done some of its finest work in reestablishing community networks, of recognizing the viability of extended family and kinship networks, and by attempting to activate those networks on behalf of their clients. The challenge to continue this work, to make it better known in society at large, and to research the questions that arise from focusing upon community networks remains before us (Lee and Swenson, 1986, pp. 361–380).

Because the profession is engaged in the ongoing lives of people and communities, the list of social problems that we could address is endless. Our purpose is not to develop such a list, but to name what seem to be those areas of greatest concern and those areas on which we, as a profession, might have considerable impact. Understanding how social problems filter into our work situations is the last and remaining section of the book. Our purpose is to help students focus their attention and to prepare them for how these large issues get translated to the everyday job in an agency and interacting with colleagues. Although social work is "other-directed"—that is, directed toward helping others—dealing with ourselves in the context of our work is essential if we are to be the effective helpers we seek to become. In addition, we present this with the added comment that the general application of social work strengths to our work with clients, with other professionals, and with the community is the real key in successful social work practice.

WORKING IN SOCIAL WORK

Facing Agency Issues and Applying Strengths

In the Bridge Model, we saw the social worker and the client riding together over the span of planned change in the agency bus. We have spent much time exploring relationships between the social worker, the client, and the focal and action systems. But what about co-workers in the agency? How do you use regulations to conduct yourself in the agency? In this section, we explore collegial relationships, sexual harassment, and burnout.

Collegial Relationships

Specht (1985) points out that our focus in social work has been largely on our clinical relationships with clients, with much less emphasis upon the quality of relationships within the work place (Specht, 1985, pp. 225–230). Upon examining the complaints regarding violations of ethics, most involve non-client–social worker relationships. In fact, ethical complaints largely deal with actions taken against managers, administrators, and other colleagues (Specht, 1985, p. 225).

Working effectively with colleagues in high-stress jobs where people's lives are at stake is not only demanding, but it involves special know-how and a humane approach to problem solving that can be found in generalist social work, especially in the collaborative model. Using our abilities to resolve conflicts within the ranks and to provide essential support for each other are the keys to positive collegial relationships. Recognizing that similarly to effective practice with client systems, professionals cannot go it alone. We need each other, but we need to know how to conduct relationships with each other that maintain our dignity even in trying situations.

Team leaders, supervisors, and senior staff people ought to meet regularly and include the line workers. Line workers need to know they are understood and appreciated. Affirming the difficult work, making allowances for human frailty and sustaining an environment in which honest disagreement and conflict can be resolved assist social workers of all levels.

Applying the caring ethic we use with clients is equally helpful when working on our collegial relationships. Caring means giving, but in the context of our own dignity and growth. In such an atmosphere, exploitive relationships between supervisors and workers cannot flourish. When such relationships do develop, the caring, ethical supervisor or team leader attempts immediate resolution.

Sexual Harassment

The incidence of sexual harassment, even in social agencies, is a familiar event to most social workers—at least in a second-hand way. *Sexual harassment* is defined as unwanted sexual gestures, overtones, or behaviors that cause the person being harassed to experience exploitation, fear, physical harm, or even to experience discomfort in a work environment that can be related to issues regarding sexuality (MacKinnon, 1979). Most agencies and work places have developed standards that prohibit sexual harassment, but, nonetheless, new workers and people who are at entry-level ranks are especially vulnerable to gestures and innuendos.

Too often, the new worker feels defeated before she can begin and feels as though she has no place to turn. Women and sometimes men who experience it feel powerless in its face. Agencies that inform workers of their own standards, courses of action, and recourse for the accused regarding sexual harassment assure safer work environments for everyone. Figure 13.2 is an example of a sexual harassment policy.

Burnout

Most social workers, employed in surroundings that require their attentiveness, experience some levels of *burnout*. Burnout is associated with high-stress positions such as protective services work, with increasing accountability demands, and with organizational structures that do not allow for professional growth and autonomy (Davis-Sacks, Jayaratne, and Chess, 1985, pp. 240–244). Symptoms of burnout include "feelings of lack of appreciation, illness, tiredness, inability to laugh, dreading to go to work, and sleep disturbances" (Johnson, 1992, p. 361). The social worker no longer enjoys the work and does not feel he or she is making a meaningful contribution. The "ripple" effects of burnout are widespread.

Acknowledging the presence of burnout, connecting it to larger issues present in contemporary society, and using social work's strengths to challenge it are the steps students and professionals need to take to combat the syndrome.

Bringing the issue of burnout to the forefront in an agency usually involves supervisory leadership. Creating an agency climate in which burnout and related stress can be discussed is the first step in confronting it. Supervisory staff must be open and willing to talk with workers in staff meetings and on a one-to-one basis. Naming the feelings and the behaviors that ordinarily accompany burnout helps the line worker accept his or her feelings.

Next, an organizational structure with subsystems that support workers must be constituted. Work units, teams, and support systems can be effective in service delivery and can offer the ongoing sustenance so necessary to survival. Having a place to be oneself, to share experiences, and to become better acquainted reduces the likelihood of burnout (Zastrow, 1992, p. 322).

Applying the strengths perspective to staff relations furthers dealing with and preventing future burnout. In family-preservation teams, working with families in crisis can prove stressful. One child welfare agency has instituted a behavior modi-

Policy Statement Against

Sexual Harassment

It is the policy of New Mexico State University to provide an atmosphere free of sexual harassment for all faculty, staff, and students.

Unwelcome sexual advances, requests for sexual favors and other verbal or physical conduct of a sexual nature constitute sexual harassment when (1) submission to such conduct is made either explicitly or implicitly a term or condition of an individual's employment or grade; (2) submission to or rejection of such conduct by an individual is used as a basis for academic or employment decisions affecting such individual; (3) such conduct has the purpose or effect of substantially interfering with an individual's work performance or creating an intimidating, hostile, or offensive environment; or (4) adversely impacts on students' educational pursuits.

All employees and students should be aware that the university is prepared to take action to prevent and remedy such behavior, and that individuals who engage in such behavior are subject to disciplinary action. Anyone who is violated by offensive sexual behavior is encouraged to pursue the matter by contacting the Equal Employment Opportunity and Employee Relations Director, Elva G. Telles. The office is located in Hadley Hall, room 15, and the telephone number is 646-3635.

James E. Halligan
President

James E. Halligan
November 1, 1991

Reprinted by permission of New Mexico State University.

FIGURE 13.2

fication program for staff called GLOP, an acronym for Generalized Labeling of People. When staff comment upon clients in any sort of derogatory manner that sacrifices the client's dignity, other staff call the "glopper" on it. Reminders are made with care and humor. Staff join in this behavior modification program for themselves because it helps them view their clients as whole persons who can learn and grow, and, further, it seems to create a team, collegial approach to working with people. Affirming clients spills over into affirming each other, and the atmosphere of the agency becomes more positive for everyone.

Burnout is certainly related to working in bureaucratic organizations that seem unresponsive to the individual. Its capacity to touch the lives of many social workers gives pause to us as we attempt to understand our own role in the "big picture." The unresponsive bureaucracy is linked to our notions regarding the crisis in institutions in this society. The infrastructure of all of our basic institutions needs revitalizing, and no profession is more aware of this basic need than social work.

Opening the Agency to the Community

Agencies that operate far from the community's eye, that appear closed to public involvement and concern and turn their backs on colleges and universities that may want to develop relationships with them are doing a disservice not only to their clients, but to the social workers employed there. Burnout, poor collegial relationships, and sexual harassment are more apt to occur in agencies that have closed their doors to the life of the community.

Vital community advisory boards, volunteer opportunities, student internships, and applied research opportunities create healthy environments for agencies, even when the work is difficult and the stress high. Such agencies have adopted the strengths of social work—from our broad-based perspective that supports the notion of the person in the environment to acknowledged tension between the art and science that characterizes social work.

Advisory boards and volunteers bring new viewpoints to agencies and assure community support. Student interns bring the fresh outlook that the eager learner automatically brings to bear upon the agency. And providing research opportunities for students and faculty from schools of social work not only ensures vitality, but assists agencies in some of the most important work that must be accomplished in social work—evaluating service delivery systems, ascertaining who can be best served by what programs, replicating successful programs under slightly different conditions, and developing entirely new practice paradigms are possible when the agency and the university collaborate to further our common goals.

Communities can be sustained only through the attentiveness of the people who live there. Agencies grow out of communities and respond to their needs by providing a wide assortment of services. When interaction between the two is heightened, growth is almost inevitable. Community members may criticize or complain, but when people feel as though they have a stake in policies, in programs, and in how they are delivered, the likelihood of successful work is increased.

Summary

In this chapter, we have provided a framework for what we see as social work's strengths and how those strengths can be applied to the great social problems of the day and to the everyday work worlds of social workers. We have illustrated how the tenets of generalist social work have much to offer individuals, families, groups, communities, and organizations. Bridging the gaps that exist between people, connecting people to the resources they need, and building new bridges to new resources correspond to social work's ultimate goals — enhancing the lives of people and creating just social structures in which people have greater opportunity to live full and meaningful lives.

CONCLUSION

We began this book focusing on the purpose of generalist social work, followed closely by an appeal to students to examine their fit with the profession. We have come full circle and end the book by pointing out the challenges social work faces and by posing an additional plea aimed at each individual reader to pause, becoming momentarily introspective, and ponder his or her interest and commitment to social work.

You will be dealing with the complex and grinding social problems in which individuals, families, organizations, and communities are awash. You will also be inspired by the strengths people garner to cope. Focusing on the strengths energizes social workers to meet the increasing challenges that lie ahead.

How do we focus on strengths while our democracy's responsiveness to disenfranchised and at-risk populations goes wanting? How do we activate our own potency when individual acts seem lost in the maze of unresponsive bureaucracies?

We do so by first recognizing that this profession is built on a solid foundation of values that supports the worth and dignity of each and every person and that promotes a society based on social and economic justice. Such a value system has endured and will continue to endure.

Activating the value base in social work involves our own individual commitment and our joining with people within our profession and others who share the same basic value structure. Realizing that change is largely a collective effort and that striving toward change means joining forces, we must seek first to build our relationships within our profession and our communities.

Social work spreads itself in many directions — mental health, family and children's services, health, corrections, schools, and factories — to name but a few. Social work is found in the public sector as well as the private sector, and in both rural and urban areas. Although diversity can be equated with strength, social work's diversity sometimes contributes to dissension and fragmentation of purpose.

We believe that generalist social work represents a hopeful means to affirm our profession's value base and offers a clear approach to purposeful change in the many arenas in which social work is practiced. Generalist social work brings together the value base, the interdisciplinary and integrated knowledge base, the basic skills, and a systematic approach to change that can be effective in many settings. Generalist social work is the bridge among the divergent parts of social work and learning its tenets as your practice base gives you the tools to continue — to specialize in fields of practice, to link with ancillary professions, or to concentrate on problem areas. Your ongoing demand, as a social work student, is to confront your own values and discover your part in this exciting, challenging profession. We wish you well!

References

Axinn, June, and Levin, Herman. (1982). *Social Welfare: A History of the American Response to Need,* 2nd ed. New York: Harper & Row.

Bellah, Robert, et al. (1991). *The Good Society.* New York: Knopf, pp. 89 and 152.

"Criminality in Families." (1992). *New York Times,* January 31, 1992, pp. 1 and 8A.

Croce, Carol. (1988). *Learnfare Critique.* Madison, WI: Wisconsin Nutrition Project, Inc.

Davis-Sacks, Mary Lou, Jayaratne, Srinika, and Chess, Wayne A. (1985). A Comparison of the Effects of Social Support on the Incidence of Burnout. *Social Work, 30*(3), 240–244.

Handler, Joel, and Hasenfeld, Yeheskel. (1991). *The Moral Construction of Poverty: Welfare Reform in America.* Newbury Park: Sage.

Holder, Dave, and Wardle, Mike. (1981). *Teamwork and the Development of a Unitary Approach.* London, Boston, and Henley: Routledge and Kegan-Paul.

Johnson, Louise. (1992). *Social Work Practice,* 4th ed. Boston: Allyn & Bacon, p. 361.

Lee, Judith, and Swenson, Carol. (1986). The Concept of Mutual Aid. In Alex Gitterman and Lawrence Shulman (eds.), *Mutual Aid Groups and the Life Cycle.* Itasca, IL: F. E. Peacock, pp. 361–380.

MacKinnon, Catherine. (1979). *Sexual Harassment of Working Women: A Case of Sex Discrimination.* New Haven: Yale University Press.

Morales, Armando, and Sheafor, Bradford. (1992). *Social Work: A Profession of Many Faces,* 6th ed. Boston: Allyn & Bacon.

Nodding, Nell. (1984). *Caring, a Feminine Approach to Ethics and Moral Education.* Berkeley: University of California Press, p. 99.

Parsloe, Phyllida. (1981). *Social Service Area Teams.* London: Allen and Unwin.

Rose, Stephen. (1992). *Case Management and Social Work Practice.* New York: Longman Press.

Schor, Juliet B. (1992). *The Overworked American: The Unexpected Decline of Leisure.* New York: Basic Books.

Specht, Harry. (1985). Managing Professional Interpersonal Interactions. *Social Work, 30*(3), 225–230.

Vinokur-Kaplan, Diane. (1991). "Job Satisfaction Among Social Workers in Public and Voluntary Child Welfare Agencies." *Child Welfare, LXX*(1), 81–91.

Zastrow, Charles. (1992). *The Practice of Social Work,* 4th ed. Belmont, CA: Wadsworth Press, p. 322.

Index _____